A TALE OF THREE CITIES

A TALE OF THREE CITIES
The Life and Times of Lord Daer, 1763–1794

Bob Harris

First published in 2015 by
John Donald, an imprint of Birlinn Ltd

West Newington House
10 Newington Road
Edinburgh
EH9 1QS

www.birlinn.co.uk

ISBN: 978 1 906566 94 4

British Library Cataloguing-in-Publication Data
A catalogue record for this book is available on request
from the British Library

Typeset in Adobe Arno by
Koinonia, Manchester
Printed and bound in Britain by
TJ International, Padstow, Cornwall

Contents

Preface   vii

Introduction   1

1 A 'Liberal' Education   13

2 'The Lyceum of Britain'   32

3 Dugald Stewart and the 'Spec'   56

4 Heroic Improver   86

5 The Politics of 'North Britain'   110

6 Witness to Revolution   139

7 Union(s) and Liberty   170

Conclusion   201

Appendix   217

Notes   223
Bibliography   258
Index   273

Preface

This is a rather personal book. I have lived with Lord Daer for over a decade in one way or another. I first came across him when writing about Scottish politics and society in the French revolutionary period. My interest was deepened when working on Scottish urban history in the later Georgian era, which involved frequent visits to the south-west, including the wonderful Ewart Library in Dumfries and the Stewartry Museum in Kirkcudbright. Reading any nineteenth-century history of the Stewartry or of Dumfries and Galloway, you cannot but be struck by the degree to which Daer continued to feature in local and regional memory well into the nineteenth century. No doubt this has something to do with the ways in which he could be conscripted into narratives of progress which recommended themselves to the Victorians. About his politics there was coyness, an unwillingness to say much, except to excuse them as the product of hasty imprudence.

There was, and is, however, a problem. For Daer and his family have left little record because of the destruction of the family library by fire in 1940. A full biography was impossible, or indeed anything approaching a properly biographical study. Nevertheless, there does seem to me to be more to say about him than you will find in the existing literature and more to say about him and the world(s) that shaped his personality, activities and unusual political outlook, unusual that is for a member of the Scottish aristocracy. Above all, he offers a fascinating vehicle for exploring a series of themes that we sometimes think we already know too well, but bear renewed scrutiny. Daer's political trajectory also cannot be understood independently of thinking about the Union and its impact on Scottish politics and ideas in the later eighteenth century. The later eighteenth century is sometimes seen as the highpoint of assimilationist impulses within Scottish society and politics, a moment of uncritical contemplation, at least among the elites, of the superiority of English liberties and English culture. This is, however, a very crude caricature. More to the point, Daer's view of the 1707 Union was wholly negative; and his ambition was to replace it with an altogether different union, one which would have bound together the Scots and English people in true liberty. Why he came to believe this is a story that merits telling, especially as today we try to think constructively about the condition and future of the British Union-state.

There are a good number of debts that have accrued in the research and writing of this book. I would like to thank staff for their help and assistance in the following archives and libraries: the Ewart Library; the Stewartry Museum, Kirkcudbright; the National Records of Scotland; the National Library of Scotland; the Edinburgh Central Library; the Edinburgh City Archives; the University of Edinburgh Special Collections; the Bodleian Library; the National Archives, Kew; and the British Library. The following have made suggestions and offered help and inspiration along the way: Mark Philp; Jon Mee; Harry Dickinson; Michael Brown; Andrew Noble; Andrew Mackillop. I am very grateful to Professor Chris Whatley for reading this work in draft and commenting on it. Critical and constructive readers can be hard to find in the academic world as currently constituted, and I am very fortunate to have benefited from this support and help over a good many years. I am grateful to the University of Oxford and Worcester College for giving me the Sabbatical leave which enabled this book to be completed.

Thanks are also due to Hugh Andrew for showing enthusiasm for this project when I explained it to him one day late in 2014. His continuing commitment to publishing books on Scottish history and culture is something for which historians of Scotland have reason to be enormously grateful.

This book is dedicated to Matthew. Believe the best of people, and always look for reasons to do things.

Oxford, May 2015

Introduction

This book is *not* a conventional biography, although it does have a principal protagonist – Basil William Douglas, Lord Daer, eldest surviving child of the fourth earl of Selkirk and his wife, Helen. Born in 1763, Daer died at the relatively young age of 31 in 1794. His cruelly curtailed life – he was a victim of pulmonary consumption, a prolific eighteenth-century killer – was full of incident, interest and, especially in its final decade, achievement. This was a product of a restless, driven personality, a notably progressive education, relentless curiosity, but also a staunch and fierce commitment to a very particular conception of the 'public good'. It was the result, too, of opportunity, for Daer lived in an age of youthful rebellion – the era of the American and French revolutions. It was a moment that produced several aristocratic radicals, although extremely few were Scottish or became, as Daer almost certainly did, republicans. Daer was in Paris to witness the opening of the Estates General, the formation of the National Assembly, and the fall of the Bastille, the latter of which signalled the victory of liberty in France and was heralded by many as presaging the spread of liberty and peace across the globe. He was there again in the summer of 1791 as a significant, but as yet small group of France's revolutionaries began openly to promote a republican future for their country. Whilst in France in 1791, Daer met and befriended Thomas Paine, scourge of the British establishment, republican and, according to conservatives and loyalists, malign inspirer of radicalism in Britain in the 1790s. One of the aims of this book is to seek to explain how it was that a man like Daer, from a privileged, landed background, became a friend of Paine's and an advocate of advanced political reform in Britain.

Historians have not ignored Daer entirely, although he has remained very largely in the background. One might say this is for good reason, since nobody could claim that he was, in David Cannadine's phrase, 'a man who mattered in his day' – which is to say, someone who compelled the broad attention of his contemporaries.[1] To the extent that he did 'matter', it was mainly within small circles of advanced political radicals, and primarily in respect of building relationships between them, especially between Scotland and England; and within south-west Scotland, where the family estates were located. Nor has he left much by way of a personal record – no diaries, no journals, no sustained run of letters and no family and estate papers.[2] Daer will always, therefore, be a somewhat spectral presence; and he has to be approached through the stray comments made about him by others, but also, and much more importantly, from the record of what he did. The Daer we encounter in the archives is the public individual. It seems, nevertheless, very likely that his public persona grew pretty seamlessly from the private one, or more accurately that the latter was to a significant degree subsumed by the former, and that this reflected the nature of his education in and pursuit of a very specific conception of public duty and virtue.

Why, given the looming gaps in the evidence and the fact that his influence was strictly limited, do Daer and his life merit a book-length study? By any measure, he was, as we will see, a fairly remarkable individual, and a compelling, if somewhat elusive, one. But he was also in several respects unusual; and this very unrepresentativeness poses an enticing challenge in respect of explanation. Of course, one could put this down to eccentricity, although this would be merely to duck the challenge. By focusing on the atypical, moreover, we can often learn things that we would otherwise overlook. In my view, this proposition is one that holds good for Daer.

Secondly, this is a book as much about Scotland and Britain in the later eighteenth century as it is about Daer. Indeed, we will range back and forth, at some moments placing him very squarely at the centre of our vision, whilst at others leaving him at its edge. By seeking, however, to bring into sharper focus Daer's life and actions, and the various contexts that helped to shape them, fresh perspectives offer themselves on what was a very important moment in the Scottish and British past(s), and, perhaps more saliently, the ways in which these were intertwined. By striving, in short, to get close to Daer and his worlds, there is the potential to perceive afresh several larger histories in which his life was enfolded. These histories – concerning the nature of political life, the interactions between intellectual developments and political commitments, the ways in which British political cultures and national identities operated in the later eighteenth century, the nature of and attitudes towards the Union and Union state – are ones which we tend to think we know very well, but may in fact do less so than we imagine.

Thirdly, admittedly sizeable gaps in the historical record do not pose as much of an obstacle to reconstructing Daer's story as one might suppose, although I do not want at the same time to understate the difficulty. In what follows, I try to reconstruct as much of his life as is possible from indirect testimonies, to search for clues to his developing political commitments in the contexts and experiences that helped to form and influence his personality as well as the possibilities and choices that confronted him. Perhaps some of the conjectures made will reach out to touch only the plausible and the probable rather than the demonstrable, but I am confident that the shape of the truth about Daer and his unusual political trajectory is discernible. I cannot guarantee that everything can be explained, but we can get very close to the truth.

Insofar as Daer has attracted the notice of historians, it has usually either been because of his role in radical politics in Scotland in the early 1790s or because he has appeared to some people to be that rarest of animals in the later eighteenth century, a Scottish nationalist. To portray him as a nationalist, however, in anything like the modern sense, is to misrepresent the essential character of his politics. He was a proud Scot, and he had, as we will see, some very interesting things to say about the Union and the fate of his country under that arrangement. Yet his political imaginary never rested on the idea of 'nation'. More to the point, he was a unionist, albeit of a relatively unusual kind in this period. He is, in fact, best described as a 'unionist radical', as someone committed to seeking genuine and more complete union between England and Scotland. This, however, would be a union of 'peoples', in contradistinction to the 'corrupt' union of states that, so Daer was convinced, had been imposed on an unwilling Scotland in 1707. Daer would have agreed with Robert Burns that a previous generation had 'bought and sold' their country and its political independence for 'English gold'. The early 1790s, with their fleeting promise of fundamental social and political transformation, presented an opportunity to remedy and redeem that deep national shame. Daer's political imagination, fired by the convulsions and transformations under way in France and a deep-rooted cosmopolitanism, was fixed not on the good of the nation but on that of the 'people' and 'humanity' more broadly, and on seeing Scotland and Britain swept up in that epic of transformation. A leading figure in the Scottish Friends of the People, the main Scottish radical society founded in 1792, he was also a member of several London-based popular radical societies, including the most notable of all of them, the London Corresponding Society (LCS); the body that was famously but also somewhat curiously identified by Edward Thompson as a key actor in the making of the *English* working class, curious because the London Corresponding Society was a consciously *British* body and key to its foundation were several London Scots, including its first secretary, Thomas Hardy, a native of Stirling.[3] Daer's was a politics that connected Edinburgh, Paris and London, and which connected him as an aristocrat to a new world of artisan radicalism in the early 1790s. These facts on their own might warrant closer exploration of his life and politics.

If Daer acted, therefore, to link together several different political worlds in his pursuit of a *British* politics of radical transformation, there is something further that recommends him as a subject for close investigation. This is the relationship between his character and political journey and what we know today as the 'Scottish Enlightenment'. His education was steeped in the Enlightenment, first as a pupil at a Dissenting academy (i.e. school) run by Anna Letitia Barbauld and her husband, the Rev. Rochemont Barbauld, at Palgrave in Suffolk and then as a student at the University of Edinburgh, the leading university of the European Enlightenment in the later eighteenth century. On the face of it, however, this, or the latter element at least, presents us with a bit of a puzzle. Enlightenment Edinburgh was certainly not a milieu conducive to the development of a radical political commitment. Edinburgh in the eighteenth century may have been the home of much creative and epistemologically innovative thinking and writing – that 'intellectual city', as the LCS ideologue and later teacher of elocution, John Thelwall, would put it in the early nineteenth century – but it was also a place in the steely grip of a powerful political and social establishment. In the early Hanoverian period, it formed a key element in the political empire of the Argyll interest, which ran Scotland for Sir Robert Walpole and his Old Whig ministerial successors. Briefly in the 1770s, life was breathed into Edinburgh political culture by the rivalry between Sir Lawrence Dundas, nabob of the north, and a young (unrelated) Henry Dundas, then launching out on a political career that would take him to the apex of power as a leading minister in London and close confidant of William Pitt the Younger.[4] By the start of the 1790s Henry Dundas, by then Home Secretary, had the city and its interests under his firm and eagle-eyed control as he sat in his Wimbledon villa imbibing with his close political cronies. Conservative reaction would exert an ever-tighter hold on Edinburgh society in the 1790s, squeezing the life out of political dissent through the pressures of a stifling conformism, later vividly recalled by Henry Cockburn, Tory by descent but Whig by conviction. A small knot of opposition Whigs, led by Henry Erskine, and reformers stood out against the main current, but with strictly limited effect.[5]

Consistent with this picture, the politics of the Edinburgh Enlightenment were for the most part cautiously conservative. It is tempting to explain this in terms of success and of the rewards reaped by its luminaries – William Robertson, Adam Smith, David Hume, Adam Ferguson, Hugh Blair, Henry Home, Lord Kames and a host of other more minor figures – in an age of burgeoning print capitalism. To its stars, writing furnished a heady mix of financial reward and literary celebrity.[6] Their books were read throughout the British Isles, and indeed much of Europe, a process aided by the explosive growth of booksellers and libraries of different types. Theirs was an age of reading in which Scots played a notably creative and important role – as writers, publishers, salesmen and as avid, voracious readers.[7] There emerged a fringe of much less successful writers, and one or two of these, such as the remarkable James 'Balloon' Tytler, embraced the radical cause after 1789. Much harder to detect, however, is anything comparable to the French 'literary underground' of disaffected scribblers of the later eighteenth century whose travails and often picaresque-like existences have been brilliantly and painstakingly retrieved from the French police archives by the American historian Robert Darnton.[8] Edinburgh's literary world was both open and intimate and consensual, albeit regularly disturbed by personal feuds; but this was feuding born of claustrophobic interaction and rumour-mongering. It was a world of tight-knit clubs and tavern meetings, and one where intellectuals and booksellers rubbed shoulders on the capital's High Street. Indeed, it was this culture of propinquity which in a very real sense allowed the flourishing of what George Dempster of Dunnichen once termed the 'rational & honest kind of society' that defined a good deal (but not all by any means) of the distinctive forms of sociability practised by Edinburgh's male elites.[9]

It was a world, nevertheless, firmly yoked to the establishment. The ruling elites were the gatekeepers of advancement and success, controlling appointments to positions in the universities or as tutors to the sons of landed families, or in Hume's case, a diplomatic posting. Edinburgh drew intellectuals and governors together in the same social circles. As one eminent historian of the Scottish Enlightenment, Roger Emerson, has observed: 'London and Paris had their cliques, clubs and coteries, but until about 1780, enlightened Edinburgh to all intents and purposes formed a single society of which all the kingdom's cultural leaders and governors were prominent members.'[10] Scottish Enlightenment thinkers were hardly likely to dream of displacing a system that treated them so comfortably.

The conservatism of the Enlightenment in Scotland can be exaggerated, of course; and it possessed a sharp critical edge. In the hands of Adam Smith, for example, it produced a profound questioning of the status quo, a side to Smith's thinking that is sometimes forgotten in the desire to reinvent

Smith as the father of modern economic thought, and even on occasion of modern free market capitalism (as if this were something unitary). It is worth recalling, however, that it was Smith who declared starkly, 'the earth and the fullness of it belongs to every generation' – one of the sternest of tests, surely, of the fitness of any set of economic and social arrangements. If the market was sovereign in Smith's eyes, it was only because it and not government could potentially deliver on the promise of plenitude *for all*. Smith, it cannot be over-emphasised, was a moral theorist who thought first and foremost in terms of the realisation of moral goals. One of his main interlocutors was Jean-Jacques Rousseau, who in 1749 awoke from a dream (so he later said) to launch an assault of such vehemence and hostility on modern, commercial society that historians have not quite known how best to characterise him – man of the Enlightenment or rather perhaps of the counter- or even anti-Enlightenment.[11] Smith may ultimately have reached very different conclusions from Rousseau about the character and potential of commercial society, but, given the continuing anxieties felt among Scots about the moral and broader social effects of commercial and economic change, he needed to answer him; and in so doing he conceded to him significant ground. Smith's solution to Rousseau's challenge was education paid for almost entirely by the state; parents should pay something to ensure that they were committed to the process. Nor was it the most basic education that should be provided; rather instruction was to include reading, arithmetic and the basic principles of geometry and mechanics. According to Smith, justice also demanded that taxes fall on the wealthy and on luxuries and not necessities.

Smith and his fellow Enlightenment thinkers were not slow either to lambaste the idleness and parasitism of the rich. A central preoccupation of the Scottish Enlightenment was with the progress of society; duties and obligations were viewed in relation to this. Lord Kames is often today remembered for his attacks on the idea of compulsory poor relief, but the true targets of his hostility were the 'idle and the indolent', who might be rich as well as poor; and actually they were more likely to be rich. What mattered was the good of society. 'Because so many vices that poison a nation, arise from inequality of fortune,' Kames wrote, ' I propose it as a [. . .] rule to remedy that inequality as much as possible, by relieving the poor [of taxes] and burdening the rich.'[12] Probably it took someone from the landed classes to make the point quite this bluntly. Landowners had, to be sure, a vital role to play in society, but a very particular one in which the public or national interest was defined in terms of a commercial present and future. Smith, whose social position was more ambiguous than Kames's – he was the son of a lawyer who, like him, was at one time Comptroller of Customs at Kirkcaldy, while his mother was from a landed background – went a stage further. According to Smith, if one really wanted land to be properly and best exploited as an economic resource then it should be turned over to men of 'scheme and project', those, in other words, with the capital, will and ability to carry out its improvement. Smith's view of noble dominance, as expressed in his *Theory of Moral Sentiments*, was hardly flattering to the noble order. Lack of incentive to develop real skills meant that they were rendered unfit for public office or indeed any position that required continuous application, thought and tenacity.[13]

None of this was necessarily or directly antagonistic to the notion that hierarchy was a natural and, indeed, inevitable feature of a modern, commercial society. Nevertheless, hereditary authority was (if sometimes only implicitly) under question. Institutions and social structures had no eternal legitimacy; rather, like political systems, their claims should be subject to the test of utility, and indeed justice. Patriotism on this account meant commitment to the public good and to the values that promoted this. The Scottish Enlightenment may have been basically conservative politically, but it was the product and view of those who T. C. Smout once called the 'culturally creative Lowland middle class', the swarms of lawyers, medics and clerics who sought fortune and advancement in the Scots capital and indeed further afield.[14] Landownership and landowners were to be made subordinate to their values. If it took Thomas Paine and the French Revolution to attack the landed classes openly – to define, in short, the political, social and cultural hegemony of the landed elites as 'the' problem – the charge against them was being laid in the preceding decades in the works of notable Scottish Enlightenment writers.

If most Scottish Enlightenment thinkers were, therefore, certainly not articulating a message of complacent optimism, another of their key themes was that of limits – the limits to reason and politics. To understand human nature and the development of society was to grasp this fundamental condition. David Hume's was the most ambitious, sophisticated, sustained and subtle examination of this theme. Justice and the rules of property, on which society was founded, emerged, he argued, slowly and without design or indeed conscious intention. The consequences of such a view for attitudes towards the existing system of justice were profound. As has been pointed out, what it implied was that the sole task of the justice system was defending the existing order of things, even if this offended people's sense of benevolence and fairness.[15] Historians have long argued about whether

Hume was a Whig or a Tory; that his deepest political instincts were politically profoundly conservative is incontrovertible. The natural mood of the
Humean and Smithian Enlightenment was ironic, perhaps partly to deflect
attention from its religious heterodoxy or scepticism. There was no place
for heroes (other than one feels sometimes themselves, their books and the
figure of the public philosopher). Explanations for things usually sat below
the surface of events; therein lay the poignancy, even tragedy of the past;
individual actors were revealed as prisoners or victims of circumstances they
could never have hoped to comprehend. If a (perhaps the) key political skill
in any politician concerns historical intuition, knowing or sensing what is
possible given the circumstances and conditions of the time, for Hume and
his ilk, this kind of insight was actually beyond the grasp of individuals. The
emphasis was consistently laid on the accidental and unintended, but also
on the long term, on what historians could discern from the distance of time
that contemporaries could not. This was a new type of historical narrative in
which politics and statesmanship were displaced from their hitherto central
positions; in their place arrived manners, customs, taste and culture and such
like. The goal was impartiality, a view of the past espied from a distance.

More generally, the liberty that Scottish Enlightenment thinkers were thus natural gradualists. They
may not have shared Edmund Burke's reverent attitude towards the past –
summoned powerfully in his warning on the menace posed by an uncontrolled revolutionary spirit in his *Reflections on the Revolution in France*
(1790). In fact, their view of it was notably unsentimental, although they were
capable of writing in different emotional registers depending on whether the
focus was on the individual or society and the general causes of change. On
the principle of reform, however, there was precious little between them and
Burke. All societies needed to reform to endure and progress, but reform
should be pragmatic, considered and informed above all by concern for
political stability.

More generally, the liberty that Scottish Enlightenment writers valued
most highly was civil liberty, by which they meant primarily the rule of law
and the security of property. To this extent, actual political arrangements
were a matter of indifference; or rather these should be judged in terms of
what they produced and whether they protected civil liberty. The British
constitution might well be the best in the world; but people should not
be mistaken about how this had arisen. It was the result of good fortune;
and British exceptionalism was both less precious and as precious as it
would seem in the nineteenth century under its Whig celebrants, including
Macaulay, for being accidental. The British constitution was also the best

because it had produced growing prosperity, stability and security, and not because it included any element of public participation. This was 'modern liberty' as opposed to the liberty of the ancients where male citizens were all involved in the disposal of power and legislative authority.

Daer's education, as will become clear, was profoundly coloured by the role and writings of thinkers such as Hume and Smith, but as mediated by men of a younger generation – above all Dugald Stewart. Daer came under Stewart's influence and tutelage in Edinburgh in the early 1780s. Stewart was then just setting out on what would develop into a remarkably influential career as a teacher of moral philosophy, becoming the key figure in the handing on of the torch of the Scottish Enlightenment to a new generation of progressive Whigs who, in the early to mid nineteenth century, would go on to transform Britain and its politics. Daer lodged with Stewart for several years as a student, also visiting Paris with him in 1789. Stewart's influence on Daer forms a vital part, therefore, of our story. Stewart is an intriguing and important individual who has attracted increasing attention from historians in recent years, but as yet no definitive study.[16] He is also politically elusive, perhaps necessarily so as he strove to cover his political tracks in the dark and repressive moods of the 1790s. When Daer knew him he had much less reason to be guarded, and what later became clothed in an evasive prolixity may well have been articulated much more clearly. This is speculation since we have, sadly, no record of their conversations. What is not, however, is Stewart's abundant enthusiasm for the French Revolution up until 1793 and, secondly, his unshakeable and deep-rooted conviction that mankind was on the path of continual betterment. Daer very likely shared fully in this conviction.

If the influence of Stewart and his teaching requires attention so more broadly does the influence on him of Edinburgh and the Edinburgh intellectual world of the 1780s. It was a world that stood on the cusp of important change. This new phase might be labelled the 'late Enlightenment' or even perhaps 'the end of the Enlightenment'. The sharp change in political mood after 1791–2 – towards repression and rigid, anxious conservatism – was one important influence, but so too was a dynamic of specialisation and growing fragmentation internal to the world of learning. The older relationships that had held the different elements of the Enlightenment in delicate balance were breaking down. Moral philosophy that had stood at the heart of this world was finding its place under challenge as other focal points of creativity become more influential, while academic life was beginning to define itself in new ways.

All of this was incipient or embryonic in the 1780s. It is, however, significant perhaps that Daer described himself on one occasion not as Stewart's pupil, but Joseph Black's, the famous chemist.[17] Foreign influences had always been crucial to the Enlightenment – in Scotland, as elsewhere; however, this was more than usually true in the spheres of medicine and botany, or indeed the rapidly developing sciences of geology and chemistry. The ethos and praxis of science in this period was profoundly cosmopolitan.[18] As the American Benjamin Rush declared to the Welsh Dissenting minister, Richard Price: 'In science of every kind, men should consider themselves as citizens of the world.'[19] Science looked beyond political, religious and national divisions; its practitioners formed a community of mutual effort and exploration, although the practice might a bit fall short of the theory at times. Scientific societies, founded throughout Europe and the colonies, such as Edinburgh's Philosophical Society and the Royal Society of Edinburgh into which the former developed in the early 1780s, institutionalised these transnational ambitions. The ideal natural philosopher was a cosmopolite, someone who looked beyond nation to the interests of human knowledge and common benefit of humanity. The centrality of science to the Enlightenment, and the Scottish Enlightenment in particular, is a matter of controversy.[20] Yet, whatever its contributions, it forms a further crucial context for understanding Daer and his world.

If Daer's world was closely shaped, therefore, by Edinburgh and rooted in the excitement of scientific learning and discovery at the end of the eighteenth century, it had an eminently practical dimension, and, related to this, a strong regional focus. In this, it was largely typical of men of Daer's background and time – at least typical in certain respects. Daer left Edinburgh and its university at some point in 1786, and in the same year his father handed over to him management of the family estates in Galloway and the Stewartry of Kirkcudbright. In a very short time, Daer gained a reputation as a heroic agricultural improver. Coincidentally, he stood at the forefront of a revolution in road transport in the south-west of Scotland. Nor did his formidable energies rest there. In 1790 he became the provost of the small burgh of Kirkcudbright, initiating a programme of change to the town that would, over the next twenty years or so, transform it into the form that remains readily recognisable to visitors today. What links these various activities is 'improvement', both as an ideal and set of practices. The 1780s marked the high point in eighteenth-century confidence in the scope and benign consequences of improvement, whilst in the subsequent decade new, increasingly sharply pessimistic notes were sounded about change and its limits.

Death came much too soon for Daer to witness the real impact of his improving activities, which, in any case, was only realised in the years that followed. In many ways his younger brother, Thomas, later fifth earl of Selkirk, found himself performing the role of executor of his brother's plans. Thomas would go on to find fame and notoriety as a coloniser of Canada and supporter of emigration from the Highlands. Thomas differed from Daer in several ways, not least in his political trajectory, which was from an early, but evidently not deep-rooted, radicalism to an increasing conservatism by the early nineteenth century. Yet as his modern biographer, J. M. Bumsted, notes, his was a life lived in the luminescent memory of his older brother, with whom he also shared certain characteristics, not least his unceasing, restless endeavour, his commitment to the 'public good', and his independent spirit.[21] While it may remain frustratingly just outside the range of our clear vision, the family inheritance forms another important part of the story of Daer's embrace of radicalism in the early 1790s; and we will need to give attention to it in what follows.

This, then, is a book that takes one man's life and politics as its starting point and an apt and powerful focus for a series of enquiries about the nature of Scottish and British culture, society and politics at the end of the eighteenth century. We catch only glimpses of Daer in the historical record – there, but not there, so to speak. We only know that he was in Paris in 1789 because he met the future American president, Thomas Jefferson, then American ambassador in the city. The sole record of his trip to the same city in 1791 comes in the form of a journal written by one of his companions on that occasion, Sir James Hall of Dunglass. He was a committed supporter of abolition of the slave trade, but almost nothing survives to allow us to reconstruct his participation in this very important campaign in the later eighteenth century. His role in radical politics in the early 1790s emerges indistinctly, but occasionally vividly, from minute books and the odd letter between radicals. Yet the fragments, when put together, combine to produce a picture in which Daer the student and radical politician starts to emerge much more clearly, and much more clearly than I had appreciated when I began this journey in pursuit of him some years ago.

Robert Burns met Lord Daer in 1786 at Dugald Stewart's house at Catrine in Ayrshire, a meeting he later very memorably memorialised in his 'Lines on Meeting with Lord Daer'.[22] Stewart would later recall: 'The first time I saw Robert Burns was on the 23rd of April, 1786, when he dined at my house in Ayrshire. My excellent and much-lamented friend the late Basil, Lord Daer, son of the Earl of Selkirk, happened to arrive on the same day, and by the kindness and frankness of his manners left an indelible impression on the mind of the Poet which was never effaced."[23] In an age when stark social differences were very much the accustomed order of things, and when men such as Burns were forced to suffer the many and on occasion severe indignities of supplication, Daer stood forth unencumbered by his rank. Daer's egalitarian spirit, it seems, was about more than the impact of the French Revolution, although, as we will see, it was this event that gave it clear political direction and shape.

Daer was, in sum, a notably unusual individual who lived in dramatic times. If we can never know him fully, we can, nevertheless, reconstruct a good many of his interests and activities; equally we can use his life to explore afresh the contexts that shaped his personality, outlook and commitments. Organised in roughly chronological fashion, the chapters that follow examine in turn these contexts and various episodes from what was a remarkable life, and one that may well have more relevance to us in the early twenty-first century than may, at first sight, be apparent. Circumstances are today compelling us to think hard about the Union, what it is for and whose interests it serves; these were issues that Daer was confronting at a moment when the total transformation of British politics and society seemed (albeit very briefly) to be tantalisingly within reach.

CHAPTER ONE

A 'Liberal' Education

People in Britain today are often deeply sceptical about the notion of public duty as a major force in political life. Such views seem to be cyclical, or a common feature perhaps of periods of apparent political stasis and ideological convergence. Whatever the case, it was true also of many people in eighteenth-century Britain. According to David Steuart Erskine, the eleventh earl of Buchan, it would have required a moral revolution to produce meaningful political reform in later eighteenth-century Britain, a fairly common view among political reformers of the period, although some side-stepped the challenge this appeared to present, arguing that political reform would automatically bring in its wake moral renewal.[1] Daer's pursuit of the 'public good' was, however, unswerving, and by most people considered to be patently sincere, albeit many saw his political judgments as being hopelessly misguided. His 'heart', the Liverpool historian and art patron William Roscoe, who met him on a visit of his to the city, declared in 1793, 'I am sure, is right'.[2]

Whence derived this disposition and outlook? An obvious place to begin to search for clues is in his family background. His father, Dunbar Douglas, the fourth earl of Selkirk, was born Dunbar Hamilton in 1722, only assuming the name 'Douglas' when he inherited the Selkirk title from a grand-uncle in 1744. Our knowledge of him is rather sketchy, although, as we shall see in a later chapter, his political commitments and path in the 1780s can be reconstructed in a fair degree of detail. He was educated at the University of Glasgow, matriculating in 1739, where he fell under the spell of Francis Hutcheson. Hutcheson was appointed to the chair in moral philosophy at Glasgow University in 1729, although he only took up the post in the following year, and he continued to teach there up until his death from a fever in 1746. His lectures – delivered in extempore style and in English – covered natural religion, morals, jurisprudence, government and the Greek and Latin moralists. He also gave regular Sunday lectures on the excellence of Christianity.[3]

Hutcheson's teaching always contained a substantial element of politics, and in several ways was politically more radical than that of most Scottish Enlightenment thinkers, something which one historian at least has attributed to the fact that his intellectual maturation took place within an Irish Presbyterian context.[4] Today, he is probably best remembered for his insistence on the existence of a 'moral sense' in man, which made moral conduct natural rather than a product of selfish motivations as was argued notoriously by Thomas Hobbes in the mid seventeenth century and more latterly and very controversially by Bernard Mandeville. He also emphasised, however, the importance of pursuing the 'good of all', the supreme value of political and civil liberty, including freedom of opinion and near total freedom of religion, and of equality, all of which has led to him being portrayed as a major figure within the 'Commonwealth' or 'True Whig' ideological tradition. There are several clear parallels between Hutcheson's political views and those of Dugald Stewart, which will be explored in chapter 3, although Hutcheson envisaged a more interventionist role than Stewart for government, and did not share Stewart's unshakeable conviction in the inevitability of progress. Hutcheson was a strong advocate of the rights of less powerful members of society, including women, servants and more surprisingly, perhaps, animals. For Hutcheson authority was always limited by its purposes – to promote the general happiness of society – and its nature, a trust, which also dictated that it was revocable. This was the source of his well-known defence of the right of rebellion, a right that, as we shall see in chapter 3, Stewart also admitted, and which has made Hutcheson an important figure in the history of the ideological origins of the American Revolution.

Hutcheson was probably the major influence on Selkirk's staunch Whiggism. The third earl of Selkirk supported the Stuart cause in the 1715 rising. His successor, however, was fiercely loyal to the Hanoverian regime during the second of the major Jacobite risings, helping to raise volunteers to fight the Jacobite army. After leaving Glasgow, Selkirk travelled on the continent for several years. In 1758, back in Scotland, he married Helen Hamilton, the fifth daughter of the second son of the earl of Haddington. This was decidedly not a marriage contracted for financial reasons, since Helen brought little money with her by way of a dowry. It was, however, a fruitful one. Together the couple had thirteen children, ten of whom survived infancy. As the oldest surviving boy, Daer became his father's heir presumptive in whom, as we shall see more fully later in this book, he invested his hopes for the stewardship and continued improvement of the family estates, and with whom he nurtured shared political goals and ambitions. Daer's early death came as a very severe blow to him in this context, and one that cast a long shadow over the rest of the family, especially Thomas, later the fifth earl.

Through their father, Daer and the rest of his brothers were inducted into a politics of virtuous independence. Where the fourth earl of Selkirk stood out among the contemporary Scottish landed elite was in his conscious distancing of himself and his family from that singular preoccupation with connection and familial and factional advantage that characterised most eighteenth-century Scottish politics. His was a politics of deliberate renunciation. As he declared on one occasion: 'except having the disadvantage of a useless Scottish title, I am in all respects as much a Private Country Gentleman as any one can be, having a retired life in the country and engaging in no factions whatever.'[5] Independence was a badge, therefore, of pride, and a source of personal identity. In a letter written in 1784 to Lord Camden, he referred to having thrown away his electoral interest; 'obscurity and insignificance' were to be preferred to dependence on ministers.[6] This also suggests a deep alienation from power, which was identified with servility and subordination. He seems to have devoted much of his time in the 1760s and '70s to the management of his estates, where he compiled a record as a notable agricultural improver, although it is hard to tell which initiatives should be attributed primarily to Selkirk's influence and which to Daer's, who took over the management of the family estates in 1786.[7] He was also a participant in the famous Douglas case, caused when Archibald, duke of Douglas, died without issue in 1761, spending a considerable sum pursuing his claims against the estate, but without success. With the untimely death of Daer in 1794, and three more sons between 1794 and 1797 – Alexander, Dunbar and John – on his death in 1799 the title and the family estates passed to Thomas.

Thomas was in some respects a very private individual, who initially found burdensome the assumption of responsibility and prominence which he would not have anticipated for most of his previous life. This, together with his consciousness that he had been thoroughly overshadowed in his father's eyes by Daer, seems to have driven him in search of personal achievement. This he found in the early nineteenth century as the promoter of the colonisation of Canada, starting with the foundation of a settlement on St Edward's Island in the Gulf of St Lawrence in 1803, followed by the Baldoon settlement and somewhat later (beginning in 1812) another one on the Red River, both in Ontario. It was a project – although this term perhaps suggests more coherence than was actually the case – that he began to conceive in *c.* 1801 as patriotic and humanitarian, but also scientific.

How this obsession with colonising initiatives came about is quite a complex story and one that has been told in very full detail elsewhere by J. M. Bumsted.[8] Here we can confine ourselves to the broad outlines. His earliest plans for colonisation envisaged the resettlement of Irish Catholics in Louisiana. The ostensible purpose was both to help stabilise Ireland and Irish society after the convulsions of the bloody Irish rebellion of 1798, and also contain the expansionist ambitions of the young United States. Ministers' responses to his initial plans, however, were unenthusiastic, and it was this, and hints thrown out by Lord Pelham, the then Home Secretary, which prompted him instead to look to the Highlands as a source of colonists, starting with the Catholic clans of the north-west Highlands.

Whatever the reasons for the shift in focus, once Thomas Douglas's attention had settled on the Highlands, he came to view the cause of emigration from the region as something of a personal crusade. He also developed a series of arguments in support of emigration that were, in several of their emphases, quite novel. At the core of his case was a view of traditional Highland society as being doomed to extinction. This was not itself that unusual – Henry Dundas had raised the same prospect in a memorandum he had submitted to William Eden in 1775 during an earlier scare about Highland emigration. But the conclusions that Selkirk drew from this conviction, and his estimate of the prospects of the region, were both stark and starkly pessimistic. For what he rejected completely were the visions of a new fecundity and industry for the Highlands that had exercised the minds of many among the Scottish elites, and those who advised them, from at least the mid eighteenth century.[9] Much touted projects designed to improve communications and to stimulate industry and commerce in the region – of which the latest iteration were Thomas Telford's roads and bridges and the Caledonian canal, completed only in 1822 at the eye-watering sum of £912,000 – offered at best a temporary respite. They were, he declared, but 'temporary relief'.[10] That he said so in print in 1805, just a few years after these schemes had been launched, with parliamentary support, as pathways out of poverty and depopulation for the region was hardly calculated to make him or his message popular with their influential promoters. The victims of 'progress', he argued, were the Highlanders below the level of the clan elites, clinging to a way of life that harked back to an earlier, essentially feudal phase in the history of the region. The hardy, loyal and martial Highlander, then rising to a new height of fame as bastion of the fight against Napoleon, was the product of a social system that was undergoing its death throes. The only reasonable (and humane) answer was to transplant them into an environment where aspects of their traditional clan-based culture could be sustained in a way that, at the same time, would serve to reinforce the power and influence of the British empire. Only this way could the Highlander remain the loyal and heroic soldier of empire, which so many opponents of emigration from the region proclaimed was their goal. It was a project that, as Dugald Stewart firmly and accurately predicted, earned him the fierce enmity of the Highland landowning class, who, for a variety of reasons, including naked self-interest, opposed the emigration of the Highland rank-and-file. The Highland landowners were trapped in the contradiction, as Selkirk saw it, of promoting 'Highlandism' – the notion of the Highlands as constituting a special culture of tradition, loyalty and hardy virtue – whilst at the same time aggressively pursuing profit on their estates, which in some cases entailed clearing these very same paragons off the land, and relocating them to crofting settlements, to create space for the new living machines of regional wealth – the blackfaced and Cheviot sheep. Seen clearly, progress – or what later economists would term comparative advantage – destined the Highlands for sheep, and the West Riding of Yorkshire for woollen mills.

There are several elements of this tale of patriotic colonisation that are worth underlining in the present context. One is the remarkable commitment and tenacity that Thomas showed in pursuit of his colonising projects and their goals. This was true in terms of investment of personal effort and energy, but also willingness to bear heavy financial burdens. Already by around 1805 he had laid out around £30,000 of his own money on building settlements in Canada. Despite many difficulties and repeated resistance on the part of ministers and officials in Canada, he did not give up. Indeed, it was only this persistence that served in the end to break down some of the resistance shown by ministers to making him grants of land in British North America. The second is how these projects were informed by a fertility of imagination, a combination of practical and scientific expertise and a capacity for thinking on a bold, often visionary scale. He was someone who bombarded ministers and officials with plans and schemes of different kinds, who dreamt on paper as well as schemed on the ground. And underpinning it all was, firstly, a profound patriotism – perhaps not that surprising given the background of war and Napoleonic threat – and, secondly, a formidable curiosity and appetite for knowledge. Many of these were traits and disposi-tions that he shared with his older brother.

To point to shared family traits may well serve to bring them into sharper relief, but hardly furnishes a proper explanation for the deep sense of commit-ment to the public good, or the patriotic promptings and sheer stubbornness that enabled both Daer and Thomas Douglas to stick to their purposes in the face of discouragements and hostility that would have deterred many lesser people. To begin to do this, we must look elsewhere, to the first stages of their formal education. It is to this subject that we turn in the rest of this chapter.

Unusually for members of the Scottish landed elites, this phase in their lives connects them directly to the culture of English rational Dissent. A Dissenting education was one that was progressive or, as the rational Dissenter, polymath and onetime tutor at the Warrington Dissenting academy, Joseph Priestley put it, 'liberal' – by which he meant useful, but also designed to form individuals who would be motivated to discern and promote the increasing happiness of 'the people'; to form, in short, 'the intel-ligent and useful citizen'.[11] For rational Dissenters, education was, amongst other things, the inculcation of a particular idea of patriotism.

The earliest steps of Daer and his brothers in learning were no doubt within the family, and may well have involved the encouragement and direc-tion of their mother. When they were still fairly young, they would have had a tutor appointed to teach them to read and write, and also to start them on learning Latin. In 1774, however, when Daer was aged eleven, the decision was taken to send him to Palgrave, Suffolk, to a school founded in that year by the Rev. Rochemont Barbauld and his wife, the writer and poet, Anna Letitia Barbauld. Both were Dissenters – Protestant nonconformists – Anna Letitia by descent and family background, Rochemont by conversion from the Church of England. If Daer did indeed join the school in 1774 – there is some doubt as to the exact date – he spent eight years under their instruc-tion, being joined there by his brothers, John, Alexander and Thomas, before leaving to complete his education, as would Thomas and John after him, at the University of Edinburgh.

The choice of Palgrave is, on the face of things, rather strange. Located near Diss in Norfolk, although Palgrave sits just over the county boundary in Suffolk, and with relatively easy access to Norwich and Ipswich – both are about twenty miles distant – and to the busy market town of Bury St Edmunds, the school was intended to attract pupils from the ranks of East

Anglia's Dissenting communities. While it did draw pupils from further afield, including the West Indies, most came from the regional gentry and commercial classes. Two of Daer's fellow pupils, William Taylor and Frank Sayers, both of whom went on to notable careers as writers – William as a translator of the new German literature of Goethe, Lessing and Wieland, and Sayers as the author of a series of verse dramas that made up his *Dramatic Sketches of the Ancient Northern Mythology* – were sons of, respectively, a prosperous cloth merchant from Norwich and an insurance broker from Yarmouth. Secondly, while Scots attended Dissenting academies in England, they were the institutions that existed as alternatives to university, notably the famous Warrington Academy, which was fairly unusual in attracting a relatively high number of lay students. Palgrave was a school where pupils were taught from a very young age up to around nineteen years old. Eleven when he arrived there, Daer was the same age as Taylor, while Sayers was several years younger. Based on biographical data relating to fifty-nine known pupils at the school, entry at this sort of age was fairly common. Richard Enfield, son of William Enfield, a tutor at the Warrington Academy between 1770 and 1783 and then minister of the famous Octagon Dissenting congregation at Norwich, was probably twelve; John, Daer's brother, probably thirteen; and Thomas perhaps rather younger at seven.[12] Anna Letitia increasingly devoted her attentions to her infant pupils, who might be anywhere between two and four years old, and who included her nephew, Charles, who was adopted by her and her husband, and Thomas Denman, who as Attorney General in 1830 would help to draft the famous Reform Bill of 1832. It was a focus that would elicit her *Lessons for Children* (4 vols, 1778–9) and *Hymns in Prose for Children* (1781), which went on to become her most influential publications in the Victorian era.

The explanation for the Douglas boys being sent to Palgrave may in fact be rather simple: Anna Letitia, or Anna Letitia Aikin as she was before her marriage, came from a family with Kirkcudbright roots. Not only had her Aikin ancestors lived in the town, but her brother John was between 1761 and 1764 apprenticed to Dr Maxwell Garthshore, who was a native of Kirkcudbright. That the school was founded in 1774, and Daer may well have been one of initially only eight pupils certainly supports this idea. Yet, even if local connections were quite possibly the main factor, by itself this furnishes at best a partial explanation since there was a choice involved here – forms and types of schooling were being rejected, as well as one being embraced.

We can only speculate about this in the absence of evidence to lead us any further. Daer and his brothers became what were known as 'parlour-boarders' at Palgrave; in other words, for payment of a higher fee than normal, they essentially lived as part of the Barbauld household. This was quite an expensive option – 40 guineas a year – although considerably less so than had they gone to, say, Eton, Winchester, Rugby, or any of the other major English public schools.[13] On the other hand, had they done that, they would have been largely drilled in the classics. Notes left by a master at Eton between 1766 and 1771 indicate that of the order of twenty-one hours a week were devoted to learning Latin and Greek.[14] This is what the English public schools existed to teach; it was the basis of an English gentlemanly education. As Anthony Fletcher has written: 'The most striking development of the period from 1660 to 1800 was the insistence of the upper gentry [in England], while the grammar schools diversified their curriculum, on sticking to schools which preserved the classical regime, with its associated values of restraint on boyhood vigour and harsh discipline through corporal punishment.'[15] To learn Latin was to learn the 'male elite's secret language', but it also formed the essential training for those who, it was assumed, would go on to be the future rulers of society.[16] The public schools were there to teach self-control, endurance and conformity through competition and emulation. Schools like Eton and Winchester had a reputation for allowing immoral behaviour among the pupils, for general unruliness – they did very little to organise and control the lives of their pupils – and, although this might seem contradictory, but in fact was not, the brutal forms of discipline that often seem to have prevailed. It was an education in a combative form of masculinity that appealed to a very high proportion of the propertied elites, especially among the nobility, and it undoubtedly offered the opportunity for the sons of the English and increasingly British ruling elites, and those who aspired to ape them, to forge relationships between themselves that were one of the keys to the perpetuation of their rule.[17] These things evidently counted for little, however, with the fourth earl of Selkirk.

Other things that Palgrave did *not* offer – which the public schools did – were instruction in fencing, dancing and drawing, although it is probable that Daer would have been given instruction in dancing elsewhere, perhaps by a dancing master who visited St Mary's Isle.[18] His classmate, William Taylor, had lessons in polite comportment from a dancing master before arriving at Palgrave, evidence of the extent to which politeness as a form of manners was ubiquitous in propertied society in Britain by this period.[19]

Another option would have been to send Daer and his brothers to a Scottish grammar or burgh school, in Dumfries perhaps, then emerging as a service centre for the south-western gentry, or in the capital, Edinburgh, where Selkirk had a residence. This was still the norm for Scottish gentry families, and in the early eighteenth century for many families at the apex of landed society.[20] Lord George Murray, for example, the military commander of the Jacobite army during the '45 Jacobite rising, and the sixth son of the first duke of Atholl, attended the Perth grammar school. The type of education would have depended on which school and where. As in England, where many grammar schools departed from an exclusively or even mainly classical curriculum in the course of the eighteenth century, there was among the Scots burgh schools a long-term trend, beginning in the later seventeenth century but deepening and broadening in the second half of the eighteenth, towards the modernisation of their curricula. A key phase and further stimulus in this process was the rise of the academies after 1761 – the date of the foundation of the first of these, the Perth Academy – which were established to offer an economical alternative to university for those wishing a more practical education suited to the commercial middling sort. Burgh schools took concerted steps to update their curricula, presumably driven by the demand for such instruction for which the academies and multiplying private tutors and schools were seeking to cater. Not all burgh schools followed this course. The curriculum at Edinburgh High School, for example, remained steadfastly focused on classical learning, as did that of the Montrose Grammar School.[21]

Another way, however, to look at the choice is to consider what Palgrave would have appeared to offer. This included a diverse curriculum – one that embraced geography, history, languages and science – but did not ignore the classics. It may well have been the wider vision of education nurtured in the school that was the larger appeal. Given that it was new, it would have been the connections and background of the Barbaulds that mattered in this context; and these were to a tradition of Dissenting education that reached back into the early eighteenth century, but which, as far as the education of lay people was concerned, achieved its greatest success with the establishment of the Warrington Academy in 1757.

Through both her mother and father, Anna Letitia was intimately connected to, and had been formed by, this tradition. Her mother was the daughter of John Jennings, a notable Dissenting schoolmaster, while her father, John Aikin, was educated at Philip Doddridge's academy in Northampton, one of the outstanding Dissenting academies of the first half of the eighteenth century. Doddridge was a former student of Jennings. Doddridge's Northampton academy was notable for the breadth of its curriculum – which included science, geography and modern languages, as well as divinity and the classics – and the quality of its teaching. The form of instruction was also quite unusual. Students were expected to consider the arguments on both sides of issues, and were left to make their own judgments about the strongest after reading the various authorities.

Instruction, on this model, was thus a search for truth, and not a matter, as with the teaching of Latin at the public schools, of imbibing a particular body of knowledge. For Doddridge, this was designed in part to promote tolerance of different religious views, and reflected more broadly the politically eirenic disposition of Presbyterian Dissent under the first two Georges, a stance that was, in turn, shaped by the carefully balanced religious policies of Sir Robert Walpole and the Whig ministries of the period and, equally, the Dissenters' acute consciousness of the continuing threat which the Jacobites posed to the Hanoverian and Protestant Succession. To apply the critical test of reason became, however, the very essence of rational Dissent as it developed in the very different political and cultural conditions of the years after 1760.[22] At the same time, there was growing confidence about the positive possibilities and probable consequences of such free enquiry. This was a reflection in part of the growing prosperity, confidence and cohesion of rational Dissent as an extended, but closely interconnected series of communities. Rational Dissenters emerged as leading players in several rapidly growing English provincial towns and cities, such as Manchester, Liverpool, Sheffield and Norwich, creating around them, or helping to do so, new cultural institutions which, in turn, were an expression of an increasingly independent provincial civic identity. The 1770s brought an influx of new blood to the ranks from individuals who, frustrated by the failure of the campaign against subscription to the thirty-nine Articles for clergy in the Church of England, finally left the church. Theophilus Lindsey, who had led the petitioning campaign against subscription in 1772, opened a new Unitarian church in London in 1774, which gave rational Dissent a prominent and well-supported base in the British capital, also providing it, through the chapel's patrons, with important establishment connections. The new outlook and mood among the rational Dissenters also, however, drew on important intellectual and theological shifts, notably the growing incorporation of sensationalist ideas and the idea of association, as well as the development of more heterodox religious opinions. Adherence to the principle of freedom of thought became a badge of identity for rational Dissent, but was also intimately related to a wider corpus of developing ideas about progress, providence and the duty of the individual to strive for the general happiness. The exercise of free thought and better understanding were the route to progress – in science, politics and religion. This was a matter of disposition, as well as capacity. As Priestley declared in 1791:

> Only inspire the minds of youth with the love of truth, and a sense of virtue and public spirit, and they will be ready for every good work. But if, on the contrary, their minds be cramped by systems, and thereby habituated to servitude, and disinclined to think for themselves, in their early years, they will be prepared to oppose, instead of savouring any great and noble efforts.[23]

Methods and goal were as one – to inspire a conviction of the duty *and* capacity of the individual to pursue the 'public good'. This may have been an education designed for patriotic purpose, but of a questioning, critical kind, and one focused squarely on the prospect, indeed inevitability, of human betterment.

After studying divinity at Aberdeen, John Aikin returned briefly to Northampton as Doddridge's assistant, before in 1741 establishing his own school at Kibworth in Leicestershire. In 1758 he was invited to become tutor in languages and *belles lettres* at the newly established Warrington Academy. It was at Warrington that Anna Letitia met her future husband. It was also where, as her niece later recalled, she was most happy as part of a social circle formed from the Warrington tutors, such as Joseph Priestley, William Enfield, initially employed as tutor of literature before becoming tutor of mathematics and natural philosophy, her brother, John, who returned to Warrington to establish a surgical practice in the town and lecture on chemistry at the academy, and students and members of the liberal intelligentsia based in the region.[24]

The Warrington Academy may not have been typical of the Dissenting academies; nor may it have had quite the importance for rational Dissent that an earlier generation of historians supposed.[25] The quality, however, of its instruction across a range of modern subjects was unmatched, enabling it to attract pupils from across the British Isles, including (as referred to above) from Scotland. It fostered a vision of education as instruction in a particular conception of citizenship, as a commitment to the 'public good' understood in a broad, inclusive sense, and where that good was identified with the condition and happiness of 'the people'. It was whilst a tutor at Warrington that Priestley devised his course in 'civil history and civil policy', which culminated in a series of disquisitions on issues of general public policy, such as national debts, commerce, policies towards promotion of agriculture and so on.

The choice, therefore, of the Palgrave school was a clear rejection of an education based on classical learning; but it was also a repudiation of an education that equated fitness to rule with control of self in order to control others. More positively, it was a choice in favour of an inclusive conception of the 'public good', one that looked to the future rather than the past. It was also a declaration of support for the values of a particular variant of the Enlightenment.

The Palgrave academy has been the subject of some very careful research by the literary scholar William McCarthy, the modern biographer of Anna Letitia, and we do not need to repeat here everything that he has been able to discover.[26] There are, nevertheless, several features of the school that require discussion since these have a direct bearing on the conditioning of Daer's personality and political outlook.

The first of these is the subjects that Daer was taught. The advertisement for the school declared instruction to be available in the 'Classics, French, Mathematics, &c'. Rochemont and Anna Letitia were responsible for all the teaching in the first year, although in 1775 they were joined by two assistants, one of them a French usher. It seems that the curriculum broadly followed the 'Plan of Liberal Education' described in 1760 by Priestley, which, in turn, reflected that which had been offered at Doddridge's Northampton academy and several other Dissenting schools since the early eighteenth century. This involved instruction in Latin and Greek. As the nineteenth century biographer of William Taylor described in relation to his subject's time at Palgrave: 'Here dead languages became the objects of his study [. . .] he acquired the knowledge of as much Greek and Latin as he appears ever to have found needful or available in the extensive and varied course which he afterwards pursued.'[27] Yet, as is also apparent from these comments, classics did not dominate. This reflected the goals of education on offer in Dissenting schools, but also the assumptions that informed them about the current state of society and learning. Education in the classics may have fitted a world in which knowledge was limited to the few and which the proper 'ends' of society were little understood; but the economy of learning and learned communication had been transformed. As Priestley wrote: 'At present, almost all valuable knowledge is to be found in modern languages, and if a man communicates his thoughts to the public, it is in the same channel.'[28] Print had spread knowledge much more widely, and made learned subjects fit for 'sensible conversation'. '[The] Politeness of the times has brought the learned and the unlearned into more familiar intercourse.'[29] Citizenship, learning and sociability were, in this conception of society, mutually complicit. For the rational Dissenters, the polite, the useful and the religious blended into one another. One historian has recently talked of the rational Dissenters being part of the 'mainstream' of society, although perhaps a better characterisation might be that they sought the transformation of this society in their own image.[30] 'Mere politeness' was after all no substitute for 'real sense' and virtue; or, as Priestley disparagingly put it: 'A first rate musician can never be anything else, and an incomparable dancer can make nothing but a dancing master or a coxcomb.'[31]

Rochemont, whose grandfather was a French Huguenot, and had spent time in Geneva, taught French, and Daer in later life was a fluent French speaker. To this would have been added 'useful branches of practical mathematics', as well as algebra and geometry. There is some evidence that instruction in science was offered, and a hint that this included chemistry, which Daer went on to study with Joseph Black at Edinburgh.[32] Natural philosophy played a very important role in the educational practice of Dissenters, and in their public intellectual life, although how much of a role specialist science learning played in their schools rather than the academies is unclear.[33]

Anna Letitia was responsible for instruction in history and geography, and also English composition and natural science. Her method of teaching English composition was quite unusual, and was later described by William Taylor:

> On Wednesdays and Saturdays the boys were called in separate classes to her apartment: she read a fable, a short story, or a moral essay, to them aloud, and then sent them back into the schoolroom to write it out on the slates in their own words. Each exercise was separately overlooked by her: the faults of grammar were obliterated, the vulgarisms chastised, the idle epithets were cancelled, and a distinct reason was always assigned for every correction: so that the arts of editing and criticizing were in some degree learnt together.[34]

As McCarthy has noted, the appeal was to the 'child's intelligence in giving reasons'.[35] Her pedagogy, like that employed by Doddridge at Northampton (as we saw above) and Aikin at Kibworth, aimed to instill an attitude of intellectual independence, but also to show pupils important truths rather than teaching by precept.

This was also true, insofar as we can tell, of her instruction in history and geography. History was viewed by the rational Dissenters, as indeed by the historians of the Scottish Enlightenment, as an invaluable form of public instruction, engaging the imagination, but also teaching lessons of public utility. In the case of the rational Dissenters, this also probably reflected the important role played by collective memory in the culture of Dissent.[36] As has been noted elsewhere, it was an attitude of mind which elicited a good number of biographical writings from Dissenting authors, including, for example, the multi-volume *General Biography, or Lives, Critical and Historical, of the Most Eminent Persons of all Ages, Countries, Conditions, and Professions* (1799), compiled by John Aikin jnr and William Enfield.[37] Yet History was an exercise too in intellectual humility in the face of conflicting and inadequate sources. As Anna Letitia later wrote: '[It] is always good to know the real measure of our knowledge.'[38] This approach to history, emphasising the role of different types of sources, and the role of other building blocks, such as chronologies, was very similar to that employed by Priestley at Warrington, on which it may well have been directly modelled. For those such as Priestley, who held Unitarian beliefs, history had a deeper importance as a tool to expose the corruptions of religion as it had developed in its institutional guises, and this encouraged something of a growing division between history viewed as a set of critical methods and as a form of public instruction.[39] In respect of geography, McCarthy argues that Anna Letitia's emphasis was on appreciation of 'natural and cultural variety'.[40] Maps and literary sources were frequently used in the teaching of both history and geography. For rational Dissenters, as for most people who accepted Enlightenment values and principles, there was no contradiction whatsoever between patriotism and cosmopolitanism; indeed, in a very real sense, they fed one another.

The final aspect of the curriculum that merits comment is the emphasis that was placed on elocution and public speaking. This was partly driven by the same basic purpose that underpinned all the teaching at the school – to form pupils for a role in public life. The end of each school year saw the staging of plays; and reciting from works of English literature formed part of the annual examinations held in December. McCarthy stresses the ethical dimension to this activity, and the extent to which it grew from a specifically 'Dissenting ideal of the "citizen orator"'.[41] This may be true, although he produces no evidence to support this proposition; and rhetorical proficiency was one of the basic aims of learning the classics. Contemporary preoccupation with elocution was also much wider than this implies, and had various roots, which were more broadly cultural as well as political, and can be related to the growing power of metropolitan norms, shifting reading practices and the degree to which polite society prized conversation as the recommended model of social interaction.[42] Debating societies proliferated in the 1770s and 1780, before many of them were squeezed out of existence in the repressive atmosphere and conditions of the subsequent decade, while reading essays and debating questions was standard practice in Enlightenment clubs and societies. Lecturers on and teachers of elocution, and readings, were widely available by the later eighteenth century in towns and cities across Britain. The Dissenters increasingly found themselves a part of polite society, although the forms of sociability they nurtured had, as indicated earlier, distinctive emphases, and politeness, like beauty, was at least partly in the eye of the beholder; what was polite to one person or group was not necessarily polite to another.

Schools communicate a specific ethos to pupils, more or less overtly, depending on their purposes and leadership, and at Palgrave, as far as we can tell, it was one of responsible citizenship, which entailed the ability to judge for, and, to a degree, to instruct, oneself. The school was constituted as a community, one governed by rules and duties, but the pupils had rights as well as obligations. We know from an undated document in Anna Letitia's hand that at some date was instituted the position of school captain, voted for by the pupils who were to cast their votes 'unbiassed by any motives but a serious and deliberate regard to the merits of the candidates'.[43] The expectations of the captain were rather weighty. They were to pledge themselves to behave 'in such a manner as may best promote the reputation, order, happiness and improvement of the society' to which they belonged. They were also to protect younger boys from 'oppression'. Should they fail to meet these expectations, or do things directly contrary to them, they were to be immediately 'degraded from [their] [. . .] dignity'. Whether this system was in operation when Daer was at Palgrave, or instituted perhaps during his period there, is unknown. But it reflects, surely, how the Barbaulds saw the school as a model for the social and political roles that they envisaged their pupils as assuming in adulthood – as useful, responsible citizens concerned always to promote the 'public good' or, as it was more commonly denoted in the language of rational Dissenters in this period, the 'happiness and improvement' of society.

Anna Letitia was close to many of her pupils, unsurprisingly, given the size of the school. The higher paying parlour-boarders were very much part of the household, and some of them were very young when they arrived in her and her husband's care. It is obviously impossible to say what influence she and her husband had by virtue of the conversations and interactions that took place beyond the classroom. That Daer was a favourite of Anna Letitia's is abundantly clear, nevertheless: 'He was,' she wrote, 'before the finest boy; he is now the finest young man I know,' also writing in 1782 to William Taylor, 'Your friend Mr Douglas is grown a very fine youth & is in every sense one of the first if not the first among his fellow students.'[44]

In the 1790s, a good number of Daer's fellow pupils became, like him, political radicals, although quite what this owed to their education as opposed to their being part of a culturally sophisticated and accomplished rational Dissenting community in Norwich is moot, insofar of course as these can be separated. It was almost certainly the combination of factors that mattered. Norwich in the later eighteenth century saw a remarkable cultural efflorescence, a process led by individuals, quite a few of whom had been pupils at Palgrave or who were otherwise linked to the school, such as William Enfield, who had known the Barbaulds at Warrington, where he was a tutor before taking charge of the Octagon congregation in the Norfolk capital.[45] As Harriet Guest has recently commented, 'the level of political engagement and free thought among dissenters in the city was exceptional'.[46] Several former pupils – William Taylor, Charles Marsh, Richard Enfield, to cite only a few of them – played notable roles in radical politics in Norwich in the 1790s, which proved to be more resilient than elsewhere in provincial England, probably because it, or a good part of it, arose from such a well-established and culturally self-confident community; the war against revolutionary France, which had disastrous economic consequences for the city's manufacturing economy, may have also helped to sustain the alliances between artisan and more respectable forms of radicalism. Several of the Palgrave former pupils were avowed republicans. William Taylor, together with his father, also called William, played a key role in the Norwich Revolution Society, joining several local debating societies. Like Daer, he visited France, although in his case in 1790; and his reaction to the Revolution was one of fervent enthusiasm. 'For this country,' he declared from Paris

> it was reserved to prove, that science as she plumes her wings extends her power; till at last they shall overshadow the earth, and winnow from its surface every scattered chaff of corruption. For this land it was reserved to offer the finest spectacle which the mind of Deity can contemplate, that of a nation of heroes obeying by choice a senate of sages.[47]

In recent years, historians have tended to stress the limits to Dissenting radicalism, and how far it was outflanked by a more genuinely popular radicalism associated with the popular radical societies, such as the London Corresponding Society.[48] Political opinions among the rational Dissenters were far from uniform, however, and, as already emphasised, we can find a good number of republicans emerging from their ranks in the 1790s, such as, in a Scottish context, Thomas Christie of Montrose. We shall meet several others in later chapters.

Anna Letitia wrote several political pamphlets in the early 1790s, in protest against Pitt's failure to support the Dissenting campaigns to repeal the Test and Corporation Acts and in opposition to the war against revolutionary France. It is, however, what she would write about her husband shortly after his death in 1808 that may well be more relevant in the present context. At the same time as emphasising his liberal, benevolent outlook, and his desire to see opinions tested rather than simply endorsed – '[he] gave the most liberal latitude to free enquiry' – she declared:

> Of the moral perfection of the Deity he had the purest and most exalted ideas; on this was chiefly founded his system of religion, and these together with his own benevolent nature led him to embrace so warmly his favourite doctrine of the final salvation of all of the human race, and indeed, the gradual rise and perfectibility of all created existence.[49]

This notion of a providential order and purpose for the world unfolding gradually through the agency of reason and search for truth appears to have been very similar to that espoused by Priestley or indeed many other rational Dissenters, which led them to exult in the outbreak of the French Revolution as a sign of global salvation or the onwards march of reason – or indeed both. Priestley consistently insisted on the duty of active patriotism, but this was underpinned by an utter conviction in history following a providential path, one that could and would necessarily be discerned ever more clearly by the exercise of a human intellect that was itself subject to improvement. How much of this outlook Daer imbibed at Palgrave we can never of course know for certain, although it seems highly likely that it left a profound impression; it is also worth noting that an unshakeable confidence in progress, and in a providential order in history, was shared by Dugald Stewart who took charge of the next stage of Daer's education in Edinburgh.

There is one further consequence of Daer's period at Palgrave that is worth dwelling on briefly here. There are scattered bits of evidence from later in his life that suggest that he was well connected to leading English rational Dissenters, for example, the Roscoe circle in Liverpool. It is very likely that some of these connections were made at the University of Edinburgh. Many of those educated at the Warrington Academy who went on to pursue medical careers gained their medical training and education at Edinburgh. John Aikin, Anna Letitia's brother, spent two years there studying medicine, although his medical degree would be awarded some years later from the University of Leiden. Another who studied medicine at Edinburgh was Daer's old school friend, Frank Sayers, whom William Taylor would recall being frequently in the company of Martin Davy, who would go to become master of Caius College, Cambridge, Joseph Cappe, one of the sons of the York Dissenting minister, the Rev. Newman Cappe, James Mackintosh, the opposition Whig political writer, who whilst at Edinburgh was president of the famous student society, the Speculative Society, and Daer.[50] Other connections may have emerged through shared commitments and interests in, for example, chemistry, or abolition of the slave trade. Another of the pupils at Palgrave was Joseph Priestley's son. I have found no evidence that Daer ever met Priestley, or that they corresponded, although that does not mean that this did not happen; and that he was connected to Priestley and his circle in the Midlands seems very likely. He was certainly known to the Wedgwoods, as a letter from 1791 from the Rev. Theophilus Houlbrooke to Thomas Wedgwood reveals:

> A Mr Douglas, Br.[other] to L[or]d. Dare enquired after you & Dr. Darwin [Erasmus Darwin] and desired his compliments to you and your Br.[other] he said Mr Wedgwood and I did not ask him which. he is a very sensible young man a great Naturalist and a friend to Liberty – as you may suppose when I inform you he is gone to France with Sr. James Hall to see free Men.[51]

(As we will see in a later chapter, Daer was on this trip.) Houlbrooke was a clergyman in Shropshire, before resigning his ministry and becoming a Unitarian. In the early nineteenth century, he went on to play a leading role in the intellectual and cultural life of Liverpool, and he was almost certainly another of Daer's contacts in that city.[52] Daer's brothers also made their own friendships whilst at Palgrave; Thomas, for example, became a close friend of Arthur Aikin, Anna Letitia's eldest nephew. Rational Dissenters, as several commentators have recently emphasised, were highly sociable and also excellent networkers.[53] It is at least very plausible that through the connections he and his family formed, partly through attendance at the Palgrave school, Daer would have known, known of and been known by, many of the leading English rational Dissenters in London and the English provinces.

The London Dissenting minister, Andrew Kippis, argued in a sermon that he preached at the opening of the Hackney Dissenting academy in 1786, where he was appointed a tutor: 'We are creatures of instruction, association, and habit; and according to the principles we imbibe, and the tincture we receive, will be the ordinary tenor of our behaviour.'[54] This is precisely the sort of thing that educationalists will say, although this was the very crux of the 'idea of association' that had become central to the ideology of rational Dissent. Eighteenth-century rational Dissenters were extremely confident of the benefits of a 'liberal' education, not just to the individual but to wider society and the nation. As well as answering to the imperative of utility and to advancement in a world driven by commerce, this education underlined the role of truth and virtue as motors of social, political and religious change, and the responsibility of the individual as a 'citizen' of his country. Daer's profound sense of public duty owed a good deal to Palgrave and this view of education and the notion of patriotic citizenship which took shape within it. How it would develop and express itself would, as the different paths followed by him and his brothers, especially Thomas, underline, depend a great deal on the circumstances and opportunities that faced him as a young adult; and it is to these that we turn in the following chapters.

CHAPTER TWO

'The Lyceum of Britain'

This book can be seen as a tale of three great cities: Edinburgh, London and Paris. It is the first of these, however, that really lies at its heart.[1] Between 1782 and 1785 Daer was in Edinburgh as a student at the university, lodging with Dugald Stewart, then Professor of Mathematics, but who in 1785, with the full support of Principal William Robertson, succeeded Adam Ferguson as the Professor of Moral Philosophy.[2] We know that Daer returned to the city on several occasions in the next few years as a winter visitor. Where he stayed is unknown. The earl of Selkirk's dwelling in the Scottish capital – which stood in St John's Street (that ran off the south side of the Canongate) – was either sold or let in 1784, although this was very probably done to facilitate a move to the New Town.[3]

We know little in detail of Daer's sojourns, or precisely how his time in Edinburgh may have moulded or reinforced his developing personality and views. Some of this and the following chapter is thus rather speculative in nature, and the main protagonists are, firstly, the Scottish capital itself and, secondly, Dugald Stewart and several other members of the University; and not Daer himself.

Daer was, nevertheless, resident in the Scots capital during a moment of surging optimism about 'improvement' as a benign and creative force for transforming society and the economy, as well as of renewed momentum in the project of re-creating Edinburgh as a modern town, a project which had commenced three decades earlier with the building of John Adam's Merchants' Exchange on the High Street (now the council offices) and the formulation of plans for the first new town on lands across the North Loch –

or, as it was usually known at the time, the 'Nor' Loch'. The heady, expectant mood reflected unexampled economic buoyancy as the Scottish economy recovered strongly from the downturns of the previous decade, a process led by linen manufacturing – in the vanguard of this first, early phase of Scottish industrialisation – which grew spectacularly in these years. A very visible symptom in the capital of the recovery was the resumption of large-scale building. John Grieve, a key member of the burgh council and several-times Provost, noted in early March 1784 that the town had feued over 800 feet for building on George and Princes streets, which had 'exceeded by much any former year'.[4] In the following year, a visitor reported that 'the buildings carried on in this city, employ 1500 workmen, and the expences are estimated not less than 60,000l. sterling *per annum*'.[5] This new phase of the building cycle would last until 1793, when a sharp downturn caused by a credit squeeze triggered by the outbreak of war with revolutionary France brought it to a sharp halt. The downturn would derail for a good few years the construction of the new college on the street leading from the South Bridge, which was itself built from 1785 as the town council, under the leadership of James Hunter Blair, looked to extend the route over North Bridge from Register House southwards over the Cowgate and onwards.

In retrospect, the 1780s may well also have represented the last years of the University's pre-eminence as *the* university of the Enlightenment. Led by William Robertson, shaped by his leadership and direction of patronage, and with moral philosophy at the heart of the curriculum, the University boasted a truly international reputation. 'You'll agree,' one young French nobleman wrote to his father in 1786, 'that there is not a university in Europe that merits such celebrity'.[6] What held the University's curriculum in balance – in truth, a somewhat precarious one – was the dynamic tension between the range of topics taught and their integration within a wider education. It was, moreover, an education, which in the arts faculty at least had a strongly ethical and theological dimension. Dugald Stewart's pedagogy, as we shall see in the next chapter, possessed a clear moral ingredient; it was also directed to people in public life and the duties that they owed the public. In this sense, it was infused with a clear political message.

While Stewart was a considerable influence on Daer so too were Joseph Black, the Professor of Chemistry, and (although harder to document) John Walker, the Professor of Natural History. Their influence can perhaps be seen as indicative of how the focus of intellectual life in Edinburgh was beginning to shift away from moral philosophy and towards the natural sciences; or alternatively, the relationship between integration and specialisation (and a more directly vocational education) was beginning to alter in favour of the latter, a development which would take a much stronger hold in the University during the course of the first half of the nineteenth century. The 1780s saw a revolution in the discipline of chemistry led by Antoine Laurent Lavoisier in France, in the dissemination of which in Scotland Black's students played a critical role. Another of Black's students in the early 1780s was Thomas Beddoes, whose experiments in the therapeutic uses of different gases would lead him to attempt (sadly unsuccessfully) to cure Daer of consumption in 1794. The mid-1780s were also the years of aerostatic experiment in Europe: '[T]he whole world,' James Watt wrote rather crabbily in September 1783, 'is full of these flying balls at present.'[7] The Italian Vincenzo Lunardi visited Edinburgh and Scotland in 1785, while the city's home-grown balloonist, James Tytler, had been air-born twice in the preceding year, although he had crashed to the ground on the second occasion in the city's short-lived and rather sorry pleasure gardens – the beautifully defiantly named Comely Gardens. (It was the climate that in the end did for this extension of polite parade and entertainment in the city.) Having been taught by William Cullen, from 1773 the Professor of Practical Medicine at the University, but earlier the Professor of Chemistry, Tytler had a life-long interest in experimental chemistry. One of several people forced to flee Scotland in the early 1790s because of his radical political views, he finished up in the United States, refuge to a sizeable group of British radicals in this decade, arriving there via Belfast, an altogether more radical city than the Dundas's Edinburgh.

The focus of the present chapter is on the nature and development of Edinburgh and its social and cultural life in the 1780s, while the next one explores the influence on Daer of Stewart, but also Black and Walker, together with Daer's experiences as a student. This is, in one sense, an entirely arbitrary division, because the University was very much at the centre of the town's cultural life; University and town were bound together, as the former's proper name implies – the 'toun's college'. The burgh council was the patron of the University, a role it only relinquished in 1858. It is the close relationships between town and gown that help to explain much about the distinctive concerns and form of the Enlightenment in Edinburgh. Unlike Glasgow, there was no special accommodation within the college for its professors – with the exception of the Principal – although they tended to live quite close to the college buildings in their Kirk O' Fields' site (the college's current location). Nor were the students provided with lodgings, except for a brief, abortive experiment at the beginning of the eighteenth century with a boarding house, which may have been a response to heightened anxieties

after 1689 about student disorder and 'immoral' behaviour. In the later eighteenth century, however, such concerns seem to have been less frequently
aired. One contemporary guide to studying at the University boldly declared:
'Gentlemen, who attend the college of Edinburgh, enjoy advantages which
are denied them in other universities, they are allowed to reside where they
please, are not distinguished for the other inhabitants by any peculiarity of
dress, and are confined to no particular routine of study.' The conclusion from
this may well have been a touch optimistic, and was certainly not impartial:
'genius is not [thereby] cramped, and gentlemen have not an opportunity
of loitering away their time in licenced idleness', which was of course what
happened elsewhere.[8] The accommodation arrangements, however, served
to reinforce stark social differences among the student body. Wealthy, well-
connected students, such as Daer and indeed his younger brothers, John and
Thomas, lodged with the professors and received private supervision from
them. Daer was one of the first to stay with Stewart. More broadly, relationships between professors and students were notably close, and were often
maintained well after the latter left Edinburgh, one of the principal ways in
which their influence extended well beyond the teaching room.

Stewart and his colleagues were also very active participants in the
distinctive patterns of sociability that prevailed in Edinburgh's Enlightenment world. This was a place of clubs and societies – the proliferation and
diversification of which were such marked features of life in the capital in
the eighteenth century. Frequently linking 'toun' and gown, these generally
met in the taverns huddled off the High Street in the old town. The old town
and its taverns remained key sites of male sociability in the Scottish capital.
James Boswell and his cronies spent a good deal of time gambling, chasing
whores and simply drinking large quantities of claret in Edinburgh's taverns
in the third quarter of the eighteenth century. In the first half of the eighteenth century, most legal consultations took place in taverns, although this
practice was dying out by Daer's time. By the 1780s, however, in a development that was to deepen and broaden thereafter, gatherings were increasingly taking place in the multiplying public assembly halls but also the
drawing rooms of the private residences of the professors. Unlike taverns,
these were, by design and their modes of operation, thoroughly hetero-social
spaces where women could gain new cultural visibility and influence – as,
for example, hostesses or directresses of the assemblies – and could also,
as a new type of coterie culture took shape, participate in the debates and
ideas that defined the Enlightenment. Stewart's wife, Helen D'Arcy Stewart,
was a formidable personality in her own right, and theirs was very much a

partnership when it came to supervising their young charges. These social worlds stretched more broadly still, to encompass Stewart's Ayrshire home at Catrine, where Daer met the poet Robert Burns in 1786, and the family home of the Douglas's, St Mary's Isle in the Stewartry of Kirkcudbright, to which Stewart was a fairly frequent visitor. Another connection here, one cemented through the marriage of his sister, was between Daer, Stewart and Sir James Hall of Dunglass, with whom Daer visited France in 1791. We shall meet Hall again later in this book. Here it suffices to stress the inseparability of intellectual and social worlds, ones that in Daer's case were characterised by their progressive Whig politics and outlook, and also their commitment to practical knowledge.

The strong appeal of Georgian Edinburgh to the historian is the ease with which it can be incorporated into an overarching narrative that connects buildings, topography and change to society. This was very much how it was presented at the time, not least in the famous *Proposals for Carrying on Certain Public Works in the City of Edinburgh* (1752), which inaugurated its mid-eighteenth-century revival, or which appeared rather to do so. Part exercise in town planning – albeit of a very rudimentary kind – the *Proposals* were first and foremost a 'cultural manifesto' on behalf of that generation of Edinburgh thinkers and doers who, in the ensuing decades, would help to guide and adorn its Georgian flourishing as the capital of 'North Britain'.[9] At the heart of the *Proposals* was a vision of a society divided by rank, in which the new civil society dreamt of by the enlightened would map seamlessly onto new divisions inscribed with bold clarity into the built environment. The old Scottish tradition of tenement dwelling, whereby different ranks lived hugger-mugger by one another, in which status was reflected by the floor on which one's dwelling sat within the tenement, would be replaced by living in the 'English style', with families inhabiting separate dwellings and in which genteel accommodation and business would be kept strictly separate. The old urban order was to be cast over for something entirely different.

Architectural historians have, therefore, written about the emergence of new types of segregating living space in the city, beginning in the later seventeenth century, and emerging in a fully-fledged form with the development of the first new town, peremptorily dismissed by one writer when it existed only as a paper plan as that 'pompous Extension of the City'.[10] If earlier developments should probably *not* be seen as marking a fundamental break with the inherited townscape, in the case of the new town the disjuncture was complete. Edinburgh was here pictured in terms of the dramatic contrast between old and new, as they sat facing each other across the expanse of the drained Nor' Loch. It was a trope that would be endlessly repeated from the later eighteenth century, being encapsulated visually for the first time in one of the engraved illustrations to Hugo Arnot's *History of Edinburgh* (1779).[11] Social historians, meanwhile, have tended to organise their discussions around the rise of new, more sharply delineated horizontal social and cultural divisions, albeit there is little agreement on exactly when these came to exert a controlling influence in society, perhaps because the upsurge of anxieties about the conduct and habits of the lower orders was as much cyclical as linear.[12] Class, like the middle classes, is always rising in modern urban history.

Such emphases are symptomatic, moreover, of how in the second half of the eighteenth century Edinburgh reinvented itself as a place of high-class living, not least as a site of winter sojourning for the Scottish landed elites (albeit below the level of the magnates or higher aristocracy who spent much of their time in London). By the 1780s, this development was in full swing. As one contemporary rather breathily reported: 'The Good Town is uncommonly crowded & splendid at present', something which they attributed to the example being set by the notorious hostess and socialite the duchess of Gordon who was, they noted, 'never absent from a public place & the later the hour so much the better [. . .] Dancing, cards, and company occupy her whole time.'[13] The new fashionable status of the Scots capital would be further underlined by the impact of the French Revolution and Napoleonic Wars, which effectively cut off the Scottish landed classes from the continent for almost a quarter of a century, albeit with a very short hiatus between 1802 and 1803. This was the era that the opposition Whig lawyer Henry Cockburn would recall fondly from the mid nineteenth century as the capital's 'age of brilliancy', although he most decidedly was referring to social rather than political life.[14]

While home to manufacturing of several kinds, and Leith was a very important port – regionally and nationally – later eighteenth-century Edinburgh was in essence then the principal service centre for a resurgent Scottish landed elite, politically reconciled, and buoyed economically by rising rents and the influx of capital from overseas (India, the Caribbean and North America) and, frequently, service to the British state. It was the place where they networked, conducted politics and, not the least important, transacted their copious legal business. It was thus only natural that it was where the 'landed interest' met in defence of its interests – for example, meanly to combat proposals to raise the salaries of impoverished parochial schoolmasters, or, more frequently, to deliberate on the various proposals from 1773 to amend the corn laws on which their rents were seen as depending. In 1782, there even emerged, during a further round of debates about the corn laws, a body that aimed to be a representative body of the entire national landed interest in the form of a quasi-parliament – there were supposed to be four representatives from each of the counties – although the model may have been the Convention of Royal Burghs, which met annually in Edinburgh as a delegated body.[15]

The capital, however, was also where – together with other wealthy residents and visitors – the prosperous landowners purchased their luxury goods and services, with high status shops clustering around Parliament Square and the Exchange and later on the North and South bridges, as well as, increasingly, in the new town, especially Princes Street.[16] New styles of living, involving much greater emphasis on display within the home, developed first and furthest in Scotland in the capital. Unsurprisingly, the city stood out by the 1780s in terms of the number of carriages present on its streets – far larger than in Glasgow, although the Glaswegian merchant class may have deliberately eschewed such showy ostentation[17] – and the number of male servants employed – both highly visible indicators of the genteel pretensions of its wealthier residents.[18] Typically higher values of insurance policies – usually covering buildings, but also, very often, contents – and the absolute and relative amounts of house tax levied on higher value properties indicate the unusual concentration of genteel inhabitants, and the degree to which they developed new styles of comfortable living.[19] Just as London was the crucible of social and cultural innovation south of the border, so in the north was Edinburgh. Part of the explanation for this was its strong connections to the British capital, not least through that frequently under-estimated vehicle of cultural change, the rapidly developing postal services, but also, in conjunction with the former, a burgeoning, diversifying print culture.

However, if such emphases are entirely justifiable, they can serve to occlude some quite subtle changes within society and to the townscape, but, more importantly, the extent to which the old town remained its cultural heart. What they can also tend to underplay is the degree to which Edinburgh society is, in some ways, best characterised by the depth of its contradictions. These, to be sure, derived in part from the sheer scope and extent of the cultural transitions under way, a pattern mirrored in more recent times in places which have seen similarly profound transformations, as, to take just one example, in the Dutch city of Amsterdam in the 1960s and '70s. There was a generational aspect to this, but this does not, as we shall see below, furnish a full explanation.

To understand properly Edinburgh in this period, we need to begin by exploring the changing nature of the townscape and the attitudes of inhabitants towards this. The new town, with its stiffly rectilinear layout, and carefully differentiated dwellings on different streets, was undeniably an important development, as were the rise of George Square and its flanking streets on the south side. In 1782, however, when Daer arrived in the city, the building of the first new town had not proceeded very far. The 1780s, indeed, marked a crucial phase in its advance, as construction, which had largely halted in the mid-1770s, resumed, and as, directly reflecting this drive, the Mound, formed from the earth and rubbish dug out to create the foundations of new buildings, was created to join Princes Street and the Lawnmarket. Hanover Street was first feued in 1784 and Frederick Street two years later; St Andrew's Square and Street were completed in this decade, as was St David's Street, while there was much building on Princes, George, Queen's and Rose streets.[20] 1784 also saw the initial feuing of St James Square divided from the new town proper by Register House; and, thus, to a degree, sheltered from the chill winds that periodically battered the inhabitants of the new town and to which the planners had appeared gloriously and, frankly, bone-headedly indifferent.

The new town was, in any case, very much viewed as the subordinate partner to the old; although, with hindsight, the 1780s may well mark a turning point here as more and more wealthy citizens took the decision to relocate from the old to the new town. Nevertheless, significant in this context was the decision to locate Register House at the end of North Bridge. Begun, inopportunely as it turned out, in 1774, the building was still not fully completed at the beginning of the following decade. As Dorothy Bell has noted, by placing such a symbolically important building on this site, North Bridge was being viewed as a 'wynd with the Register House' at its foot; so, from this perspective the new town was 'merely a gargantuan backland'.[21]

Stewart's Edinburgh home in the early 1780s is unclear, although he is known to have later been resident in Drumsheugh and Argyle Square, before moving to Lothian House at the bottom of the Canongate in the later 1790s.[22] Built around 1750, Lothian House was redeveloped by 1773. This was part of a wider process of rebuilding, both on the Canongate, and more broadly through the old town, in the second half of the eighteenth century. New frontages on the High Street were, for example, being built from the late 1780s. The Edinburgh to which Daer came to live and study was, in short, a town that had seen significant change throughout the previous century, and which was now entering a new phase of accelerated transformation.

The roots of Edinburgh's eighteenth-century improvement and modernisation go back at least into the latter part of the previous century. This
included steps to reduce (if not totally eliminate) fire risk – still in this
period a very considerable threat to towns with their abundance of wooden
galleries, projections and booths (the first two being made illegal in
Edinburgh in 1674), thatched roofs, where these survived (they had been
banned on new buildings as early as 1621, a regulation repeated in 1677, when
new timbered and thatched houses were prohibited, and on *all* buildings in
1681), and with the presence of manufacturing and craft processes, including
baking, boiling (such as in candle-making), or other uses of fire such as one
wright (i.e. carpenter) who used it to dry the timber he used to make chairs.
Other prominent goals included controlling the scale and nature of building
(something which occurred from 1674); enhancing the cleanliness of the
streets and circulation through them (to which end, timber shops or booths
built below stairs or entries on the High Street were ordered to be removed
in 1674); improving the supply of water through laying of pipes carrying
water from a cistern fed by a spring (implemented in 1675 and extended in
the following year); relegating noisome processes such as slaughtering of
cattle to sites away from the main streets (flesh markets were removed from
the head of the Canongate in 1671): deterring and removing the beggars
who, as one council minute put it, 'swermes in the streits'; and improving
the efficiency of the town guard and watch. The city's rulers had pursued
each and all of these ambitions from at least the Restoration onwards.[23]

The duke of York's brief sojourns at Holyrood Palace in 1680–1, designed
to spirit him out of London and England during the so-called Exclusion crisis,
where his presence might have further fanned the flames of Whig militancy,
was a spur to further significant changes at the end of the seventeenth century.
A more longer-lasting impetus, however, was the growth of the population
– within the royalty (i.e. inner city) this rose by around a third between the
middle and end of the seventeenth century. From 1688 public lamps were
furnished to illuminate the winter nights – although regulations regarding the
hanging of lamps on the lower storeys of tenements on the High Street and
open vennels were issued from the sixteenth century onwards; while in 1684
the council even funded two new public privies![24] In 1682, following several
years of trying different ways to improve the cleaning of streets, the whole
business of street cleaning and waste disposal was delegated to a 'constant
comittie', which oversaw a team of thirty muckmen. By 1684, this committee
was headed by a 'General Scavenger' with two overseers working under
him.[25] Unpublished research by Lorna Skelton has shown that street cleaning

became a major preoccupation of the city fathers in the later seventeenth century, and that as many as a third of all discussions in council about the subject between 1560 and 1700 took place in the final part of the seventeenth century with a particular spike in the 1680s.[26] From 1687, streets and closes were raked and cleaned three times a week, a practice funded by imposition of a local tax. In 1692, muckmen were given the additional responsibility of patrolling the streets between 9pm and midnight every Saturday to report on people pouring waste from their windows.[27] Baillie Drummond even gifted four swans in 1677 to paddle on the Nor' Loch in an effort to beautify the scene, although since rubbish was deposited on its sides, this was where the slaughter houses were located, and run-off from the channels on north side of the High Street drained into the loch, one might well doubt that it made all that much of a difference. Tellingly perhaps, the council found it necessary to seek to protect the swans by declaring that anyone found to have killed, shot or otherwise disturbed or frightened the birds would be liable to a fine of a hundred pounds and possible imprisonment and placement in the stocks.[28]

Aspiration and achievement as a rule rarely coincided in the improvement of early modern European towns, and action typically occurred in fits and starts. It was a case of a few steps forwards and very often several back. Above all, altering the habits of urban dwellers took time. Edinburgh's reputation for stench and dirt – hence the soubriquet 'Old Reekie' – lingered, and probably long after reasonably effective measures had been taken to remedy the shortcomings. This negative reputation was, to be sure, significantly owing to ingrained English prejudice; English visitors expected to find dirt and other tokens of barbarism north of the border, and their frequent jaundiced comments on this can readily be found throughout the period 1500–1800. As one such traveller declared in the early nineteenth century, dirt was something 'which an Englishman is taught to believe [is] [. . .] inseparable from the constitution of a Scottish town'.[29] The city's odiferous reputation also, however, reflected its strikingly dense urbanism, the narrow wynds and closes and the soaring, closely packed tenements; again things alien to English experience, although common in many parts of northern Europe. Throwing dirty water and rubbish from windows was banned as early as 1701, although the habit seems only to have been truly broken in the 1760s, and even as late as 1808 the police records contain references to continued throwing of rubbish from windows.[30]

Significant progress was, nevertheless, made, albeit rarely of a smooth kind or ubiquitous, and voices can be fairly readily found complaining of dirt and stench. That such voices were often those calling for further reforms may, nevertheless, be the best indicator of their nature, although they may also reflect the sheer difficulty of sustaining for any length of time the impetus behind improvements.[31] These voices, heard at their loudest in the early eighteenth century, may well also reflect the dismal effects of economic stagnation, as Edinburgh struggled to recover from the hammer blows of famine and dislocated trade in the 1690s and the adverse impact of the Union, conditions which led to widespread support for the dissolution of the Union in the capital on the very eve of the 1715 Jacobite rising.[32] The record, however, of the council minutes indicates at the very least a continuity of action and aspiration during these difficult years, and, indeed, several new initiatives.[33] Further improvements to the water supply took place in 1722 and 'fairly regularly thereafter'.[34] An inventory of goods in the tolbooth in 1747 suggests the existence of 107 lamps in the city streets by that date, and a further note suggests at least 140 by the following decade.[35] And, by the 1750s at least, by which time economic conditions in the city had brightened very significantly, street lighting had spread to the city's suburbs. Under the direction of six-times Provost George Drummond, steps were taken in the same decade to remove forestairs and booths from the High Street; streets were paved; and side pavements of dressed stone created.[36] Before 1800, only one other Scots town followed in this last aspect – Perth, where in 1771, the council, following advice from the Edinburgh authorities, began to experiment with paving with dressed stones (as opposed to the customary whin stones, which were round), and proceeded systematically to repave the heart of the burgh from 1785.[37] Significant impediments to the circulation of people and goods around the capital were removed – the Mercat Cross in the High Street (1756) and the Netherbow Port (1764), which stood at the head of the Canongate, marking the boundary between the royalty and Canongate, and which possessed its own jurisdiction as a burgh of barony.[38]

The 1770s, moreover, saw further important initiatives to render the town more efficient and amenable, especially in respect of the cleanliness and lighting during winter nights of the streets. Nor were these measures limited to the city proper, extending to the suburbs of Canongate, South Leith, the southern districts and the extended royalty created in 1767 to encompass the new town.[39] In Canongate important new regulations were issued for keeping the streets clean in 1770, almost certainly in direct response to a recent initiative of a similar kind in the city. The crucial aspect of the latter was to reduce the existing number of scavengers from thirty-five to twenty, but to employ them to maintain the condition of the streets throughout the day (not just in the mornings), and to seek to use them as a quasi-police force to report on transgressions against the rules on rubbish disposal and street cleanliness.[40] A few years later, alterations to this new system were already being proposed, indicative of the formidable challenge of street cleaning, but also the sharply increasing intolerance of dirt among Edinburgh's inhabitants.[41]

Why the pace of urban reform and transformation picked up quite so markedly in the 1780s is hard to say definitively, although important were the very positive economic conditions. What was happening was part of a much wider pattern of deepening and quickening of urban change manifest in this decade in quite a few Scots burghs. Thus could one Englishman claim in 1787 that the improvements then under way in Edinburgh, Glasgow and Perth were turning them into the finest towns in Britain; while our young Frenchman, quoted from earlier, declared, in terms which reflect the new taste for the irregular which started to come to the fore in the later eighteenth century, 'In a few years, Edinburgh will be a town quite as agreeable and a good deal more picturesque than any other town in Europe.'[42]

Progress was cumulative; it built on important initiatives taken in the previous decade and earlier than that; expectation, will and capacity in this context grew together. It also, however, depended to a significant degree, as indeed it had done earlier, on the quality of civic leadership. While certainly not working alone, the person who above all seems to have given the lead in this context in the 1780s was a man who was mentioned briefly above, James Hunter Blair.

Hunter Blair, who had first served on the town council between 1763 and 1768, and been re-elected in 1677, succeeded Lawrence Dundas as the city's MP in 1781 (Edinburgh was the only town in Scotland to have separate parliamentary representation), and he became Provost in 1784. Like his predecessor as MP – the origins of whose vast fortune derived from his role as a military contractor to the British state during the '45 and even more so the Seven Years War (1756–63) – he is a good example of the kind of social mobility achievable in Scots society in this period; that is below the level of the grand magnates. The son of a merchant, he was a successful banker who married a niece of the earl of Cassilis and through her inherited an Ayrshire estate (Dunskey), at which point he changed his name from Hunter to Hunter Blair. His correspondence conveys the impression of an individual entirely at home in the peculiarly tight-knit, frequently claustrophobic world of eighteenth-century Scottish politics, a world to a large degree defined by connection and oiled by patronage. His banking background, and the connections forged thereby with many among the landed elites, was no doubt useful training here. Hunter Blair's rise to the top of the Edinburgh political tree was also, however, a function of his role in helping to resolve the divisions and rivalries that afflicted the capital in the previous decade as the two Dundases, Lawrence and Henry, the latter backed by the duke of Buccleuch, contended for political dominance. One-time ally of Lawrence, Hunter Blair assumed his new position with the backing of Buccleuch and more importantly Henry Dundas.[43] The significance of this in the present context may be considerable, insofar as Dundas was, in alliance with another such individual, William Pitt the Younger, very much the coming man in British politics. Several of Hunter Blair's schemes for improvement in Edinburgh required Westminster legislation, and this can only have been eased by his proximity to persons of power in London and Scotland.

From another perspective, Hunter Blair looks like a fairly typical example of a member of the Scottish ruling class at this time, a committed improver on his estates, but also in other spheres, notably in respect of the Wigtownshire port-town of Portpatrick. The main importance of the latter in the eighteenth century was in terms of communications with Ireland, since packet boats carried the post and passengers between Portpatrick and Donaghadhee on the Antrim coast. In the 1760s a military road had been built linking Portpatrick and Dumfries. Hunter Blair, whose estates of Dunskey lay on the edge of the town, played a key role in expediting the development of the harbour and town, which, together with its important role in communications with Ireland, lay behind its later Georgian growth and prosperity, until that is the town found itself eclipsed by the growth of Stranraer and the rise of steam travel. It is perhaps ironic, therefore, that today it is Stranraer that sits in the doldrums economically, staring moodily across Loch Ryan at the new harbour facility sited at Cairnryan – a modern version of the tale of silting and raw economics that has undermined many a port in the past.

The Edinburgh development with which Hunter Blair is closely identified is the South Bridge scheme, the most controversial element of which was its financial implications for those living in the southern districts. In the event of it going ahead, they would become liable for city taxes to offset the benefits accruing from the new route. This project was only one of a raft of initiatives which took shape in the early 1780s, including the revival of Robertson's ambitions for the construction of new college buildings – which led, in turn, to Robert Adam's grandiose designs and the commencement of construction in 1789; plans for a bridewell (i.e. prison) (eventually built on Calton Hill from 1791 and opening in 1796); initiatives to render more efficient and effective poor relief and to eliminate vagrancy; a scheme to remove the Luckenbooths from the High Street and the butchers' slaughter houses from their position on the side of the Nor' Loch close to North Bridge, which itself had only been completed in 1771.

While not necessarily new – Robertson had been talking about the need for new college buildings from the later 1760s, while removing the slaughter houses from the town had been periodically discussed in the seventeenth century – they were bold initiatives. Not surprisingly, as such they ran into plenty of opposition (mainly on financial grounds), and several were unsuccessful.[44] The Luckenbooths, which squeezed the flow of traffic and people from the High Street into the Lawnmarket, were only eventually demolished in 1817, although the Guard House, which stood in the middle of the street below the Luckenbooths, was immediately removed. Cost was almost certainly the principal obstacle in the case of the Luckenbooths, since the owners would need to be paid compensation before the plan could proceed, and the council was already spending large sums on other schemes, several of which required parliamentary legislation, a step which was financially burdensome. Nor did the plan to remove the slaughter houses and fleshmarket from their current site next to the North Bridge come to fruition, even though acts of parliament and of the council to bring this about were passed in 1782.[45] The problem was partly compensation for the fleshers (i.e. butchers) who were to be dispatched beyond the boundaries of the royalty. The proposal was to create a new fleshmarket at Paul's Work at the bottom of Leith Wynd. And, while the feuars of the extended royalty were enthusiastic, those resident in the Canongate and South Leith were predictably much less so. The parliamentary bill to enable the project to proceed was vigorously opposed by the butchers and their supporters. As Lord Galloway reported from the Lords: 'Never was so much pains taken to prevent a Bill passing.'[46] When a subscription was begun to raise the money to compensate the fleshers – a measure required by the act of parliament – despite the claims that the present location was 'justly considered as the greatest and most offensive nuisance that ever disgraced the capital of a kingdom', as well as causing a 'disgustful stench' in the summer months – there was plenty of opposition. 'Why,' one writer complained, 'should the public at large contribute to pay a premium of several thousand pounds, to gratify the New Town feuars?'[47] Evidently many agreed because the money was not forthcoming. So, in the event, and without this, a new fleshmarket with twenty-feet high walls was constructed in 1788, which at least represented some improvement on the old one.[48]

There were a series of other, rather more limited initiatives undertaken by the council in the 1780s. These included, most notably, steps to reduce the gradient on the High Street and widen it at the south end, which were associated with the development of South Bridge. While the need to do this was widely acknowledged, this was not plain sailing either, for the affected property owners insisted on compensation, taking their case to the Court of Session, although a deal was eventually brokered.[49] The upshot was again the burden of additional costs to the council. Gaps were filled in between the balustrades on the very exposed North Bridge. In 1787, the entry to Bridge Street from the High Street was widened by the removal of property in Miln's Square, and a series of new markets were constructed on the north side of the Nor' Loch, including a new green market as part of a renewed drive to remove hawkers and temporary sales pitches from the streets.[50] In April 1787, the council agreed to erect a stand on Leith Sands for the accommodation of ladies during race week. Dorothy Bell, moreover, suggests that the council spent around £12,000 between 1786 and 1795 on the communication between the Lawnmarket and Princes Street.[51] Together all of these measures and schemes were indicative of a strongly activist magistracy, supported by the mood of reform and change that took a hold in the Scottish capital in this decade.

There were other, less well-known successes – for example, the Police Act of 1785. Historically speaking, this has been somewhat overshadowed by its 1805 successor, usually deemed to be the more effective, and sometimes the origins of a modern police system in the capital. Nevertheless, under the terms of this earlier act, separate commissions were created to take over the responsibility for lighting, respectively, in the city and the extended royalty.[52] One of the first steps these commissions undertook was a detailed survey of the state of existing lamps and where new ones were needed. In the city proper, there were 321 of the first kind by 1785, and it was proposed to add to these a further 189.[53] The effect of the commission was, therefore, not simply to create more financial resources for lighting, but also to furnish a mechanism for ensuring further progress in enhancing the supply of light on winter nights, which might mean more lamps, their regular inspection, but also changes to their design to improve their efficacy. By 1787 the streets and closes within the ancient royalty were lit on winter nights by 594 lamps, although this total is only for public lamps and does not include privately funded ones, of which there were probably a very significant number. This, to be sure, was insufficient to satisfy all; and at the beginning of the nineteenth century the rather testy travel writer John Carr would complain about the city's lighting being limited to winter nights and, as he put it, 'parsimonious.'[54] What was his comparator is unclear, for under the stewardship

of the new commissions, the number of illuminated nights increased significantly from the 1780s onwards. Indeed, as elsewhere, the flourishing urbane
culture of the later eighteenth century simply demanded the conquest of the
night by lighting, although, as we shall see below, there were other compelling reasons for conquering the dark.

Edinburgh in the 1780s, therefore, presents a picture of quickening
movement and progress, a process that was focused as much on the old town
as the new. There was much confidence abroad about the capacity further to
enhance the amenity of the city, to make it more efficiently managed, and
better able to support the aspirations of its inhabitants, or some of these at
least, to lives of 'civility'.

There was, at the same time, significant cultural innovation and vitality, as
the Scots capital finally, and with few lingering inhibitions, fully embraced
the basically secular urban and urbane leisure culture that had developed in
many British towns in the course of the eighteenth century. Earlier battles,
which had waxed between the 1720s and 1750s, with an intolerant, rigidly
orthodox clergy over the presence of the theatre and dancing assemblies had
been well and truly won. The place of theatre may have been embattled in the
Scots capital before the 1760s, but by the 1780s English and Irish actors, such
as the great Sarah Siddons, boasted triumphant Edinburgh seasons – one
newspaper contributor even suggested the need to hold a lottery for tickets
to Siddons's performances in 1785, such was the huge demand[55] – while
the Edinburgh press from this period spent much ink following in minute
detail the fortunes of theatre in London and Edinburgh. The 1780s saw not a
continued battle for assemblies, but a battle *of* the assemblies, with separate
assembly rooms operating on the south side in George Square, off the High
Street and being built in Leith, and, pre-eminently, on George Street. One
enterprising tavern keeper, William Scott, fitted up a ballroom adjacent to
his tavern in the Advocate's Close on the north side of the Luckenbooths in
1782.[56] Constructed between 1783 and 1786 at a cost of around £6,000, and
opening in January 1787, the George Street assembly rooms were the largest
in Britain, apart from those in Bath, that cynosure of eighteenth-century
polite society. They were, one paper boasted, 'the most elegant of any in
Britain.'[57] The scheme had its origins in a proposal in 1781 to purchase land
in the new town for a new assembly rooms, but the need for such a building
had evidently been felt for a number of years by then.[58] By 1785, the George
Square assembly season ran from January to June, with weekly dancing and
card assemblies.[59] The following year saw the first ever masquerade ball in
Edinburgh, organised by William Dunn, who had been staging subscription

assemblies in his ballroom since the winter of 1781–2. Boswell attended two of these in 1785, one with his wife.[60] Dunn it was who gave his establishment in the new town the title of 'hotel' – so new was the term in Edinburgh that in Williamson's 1780–1 trades directory it appears as 'hotell', although this might just be a printer's error[61] – the first to do so, signalling the new pretensions that fuelled the city's leisure economy and which provided much of the subject matter for the somewhat crabby pen of William Creech, in a series of letters to the Edinburgh press, later published collectively as his *Fugitive Pieces*.[62]

The increased visibility and multiplication of public entertainments were themselves part of a wider freeing up and even, to some degree, democratisation, of cultural and social life in the capital. This process became strongly visible in the previous decade, with, for example, the founding of a small number of public debating societies, the most notable of which was the Pantheon Society, formed in 1773, and which attracted paying audiences of between 100 and 300, and from 1775 admitted women to its debates.[63] Beyond this, there was a growing array of other commercial entertainments and exhibitions, which tended to flock to the city during the annual race week, that held out the prospect of a large potential audience – a pattern common to the whole of urban Britain – and beyond that the many clubs and societies, some of which were very closely identified with the University, which were such a feature of Georgian Edinburgh. Even further behind, or rather intertwined with it all, was an increasingly ebullient commercialism in cultural life, in which publicity became a vital tool in pursuit of audiences and, therefore, profit.

This trend was typified (albeit in extreme fashion) by the visit of Dr James Graham in 1783. Graham's 'hymeneal' lectures were opposed by the city authorities, leading to his imprisonment, but they went ahead, nonetheless, and in a blur of publicity.[64] One might well see Graham as bringing to Edinburgh, like so many others, a culture that was essentially forged in London; except that Graham was, in fact, a native of the city and would die there in 1794. The combination, however, of entrepreneurialism, showmanship, publicity and an appeal to scientific curiosity could be more authentically home-grown, as it was in the form of James Tytler's balloon experiments in 1784, precariously funded by subscription and thus heavily dependent on the publicity they secured in the press. Tytler can be seen as an exponent and conductor of popular enlightenment, both as a writer and experimenter, a variant of the Scottish Enlightenment about which currently little is known.[65] For present purposes, striking is how science, publicity and culture came together in the early 1780s in creative synthesis, albeit this was part of a transnational phenomenon, as contemporaries were well aware and as was fully reflected in the coverage the Edinburgh press devoted to the phenomenon of aerostatic experiment. Sadly for the accident-prone Tytler, whose failures more than matched his achievements in his experiments with flight, he was much less the beneficiary of this than Vincenzo Lunardi, whose stay in Edinburgh in 1785 was a sparkling success, a process aided by his winning the right kind of patrons, his attentiveness to the female component of his audiences, and the enthusiasm of the press for him and his exploits.[66]

Meanwhile, standards and expectations of private comfort were growing sharply – especially (although not exclusively) among the wealthy. Symptomatic was the remodelling of old town apartments to include dining and even drawing rooms, while much of the accommodation, whether separate houses or apartments, built especially in the extended royalty and south side was specifically designed for so-called 'genteel' living. No. 5 St Andrew's Square, for example, had, in addition to stabling for six horses and a separate coach house, a large lobby, dining room and parlour on the second floor, drawing room one floor above, as well as sundry other rooms, including two that were described as 'genteel'.[67] Notices of houses for sale in George Square, meanwhile, regularly noted the 'remarkable elegance' and large sizes of the drawing rooms.[68] This was the period in which William Trotter began his rise as purveyor of fine furniture to Edinburgh's elite residents, a career that would end with his purchase of the Ballindean estate on the Carse of Gowrie.[69] It was to his firm of Young and Trotter that Gilbert Innes of Stow turned in 1780 when setting up a new home at 24 St Andrew's Square.[70] Edinburgh could not match London ostentation; as Innes, who had been commissioned by his sister, Jane, to buy some diamonds in the British capital, reported to her, in half mocking fashion in 1791: 'It is quite a new and a wonderful scene in everything you can conceive elegant and beautiful, but the sums that are lavished on diamonds, paintings, and shew of every kind are perfectly unknown at Edinburgh and incredible to sober sensible folks.'[71] But London was unique, including in its concentration of the super-wealthy in its west end squares, whose houses were designed in large part for lavish displays of hospitality. Innes of Stow, reporting back again to his sister in 1791, self-mockingly boasted: 'I pass my time here in constant Dinners and Dissipation and have drank as much in the last week as I do in Edinburgh in a month, yet I am never somehow drunk or sick.'[72] Edinburgh society remained, as wonderfully captured in the journals of James Boswell, less formal than that of the British capital and more '*hamely*', as Bozzy would put it, in part no doubt because of its much smaller size, and the absence of the very top stratum of society.[73] Yet it also reflected how far the distinctive social spaces of the old town continued to structure and shape social and cultural interaction, and the habits and manners of its inhabitants. Even in the early 1800s, certainly in the summer months, the new town could still appear dull in comparison with the old. As one English visitor declared in 1813: 'The old town pleases me more than the new, because it is less regular, *full of shops, more busy, more populous, & therefore more amusing*' (my emphasis).[74]

The mood of Edinburgh in the 1780s was, insofar as it is possible to talk in such terms, a confident one; standards of comfort and amenity were increasing quite sharply, certainly for those towards the top of society; and there was a much more visible emphasis on entertainment and leisure. Female influence over cultural life and habits was becoming much more evident at the same time; and much more important, as the directors of the Musical Society recognised at the beginning of the 1780s when they sought means to revive the popularity of its concerts by instituting lady patronesses for each concert. As William Tytler enthused to fellow director of the society, Gilbert Innes of Stow: 'This new institution of 12 Patronesses who are in their turn to attend & preside every fortnight with a splendid suite of ladies, will certainly bring us into fashion, which is the very thing we want.'[75] But the consequences of these changes were contradictory – in two principal ways. Firstly, old and new sat very closely alongside one another. One might think of this in terms of layers, with the new only rather superficially covering or disguising old habits and types of conduct. Boswell, with his acutely self-conscious switching between different social personae, captures much of this, as do the sharp differences between the types of club which flourished in later Georgian Edinburgh, a good number of which were little more than male drinking and gambling clubs. Politeness was an identity one could assume in certain contexts, but throw off with little inhibition in others; and patterns of sociability were notably diverse. This was, of course, true elsewhere, but the juxtapositions seem particularly overt in the Scots capital, probably because they had more than purely social significance. They were a product of a society that had been compelled to come to terms with its transformed condition under the Union, as both *national and provincial*.

Language became, as several historians have stressed, a very sensitive marker of this process of political and cultural reorientation. To adopt a metropolitan norm in speech or not – the choice facing Scots in this context was simply different in its meaning from that which faced their counterparts elsewhere in the British Isles. Boswell's irritation at his son's and his friends speaking in thick Scots accents may be intimately tied up with his own sense of self – most things were in his case – but it reflects a deeper-lying tension strongly present in Edinburgh society in this period. One might ponder here the personal style of Robert McQueen, Lord Braxfield, who became Lord Justice Clerk in 1788, head of the criminal justiciary. Braxfield, a famous drinker and committed card player, spoke, as Henry Cockburn described, in 'exaggerated Scotch' delivered in a 'low, growling voice'. As Michael Fry has observed, however, he was not lacking in finer tastes, being an important figure in the city's musical society. His home in the city was also in George Square, which emerged as an elite enclave from the 1760s.[76] Braxfield was politically fiercely conservative, and affected a very blunt demeanour, but similar kinds of contradictions and tensions were played out on a much wider scale across the capital.

Secondly, for all the emphasis on improvement, one does not have to look very far for dark shadows cutting across the bright optimism. In many ways, these were two sides to the same coin: the aspiration to improvement brought into ever closer focus that which endangered progress or stood at odds with it. To cleave to civility was by necessity to disparage, or fear, that which remained outside this charmed life.

The inflammability of the Edinburgh lower orders, their propensity to protest and riot, are the subject of some argument among historians. Food rioting, it is true, largely died out in the Scots capital in the second half of the eighteenth century, although there were attacks on several distilleries in June 1784 during a period of high food prices – the distillers were accused of using grain of all types and thus inflating prices – and there were sporadic food disturbances again in the extreme conditions of the winter of 1801, when the price of oatmeal, the staple of the lower-class diet, spiralled by around 300%, and the economy contracted sharply.[77] If unrest was infrequent, however, this owed a great deal to the pre-emptive actions and canny pragmatism of the magistracy, and the energies and will of the wealthy to defuse potential social tensions through provision of relief.[78] Grain was frequently stock-piled to ensure that the bakers were kept supplied, and bread at affordable prices found its way to Edinburgh's residents.[79] Markets themselves seem to have been very carefully policed, especially in periods of alarm about rising prices and social strain, with magistrates keeping an anxious eye not just on the supply of affordable bread, but also fuel, which in this case meant coal. Suspected forestallers (i.e. those seeking to buy up grain with the aim of commanding supply and thereby prices) were arrested, as were others infringing, or suspected of so doing, the sizeable web of regulations that governed the operation of the markets.[80] The year 1779 had seen a nasty outburst of anti-Catholic rioting, triggered by rumours of a plan to extend the 1778 Catholic Relief Act to Scotland. One of the properties attacked had been that of Principal Robertson, and it has been argued that this marks in some ways the end of untroubled Moderate ascendancy in the capital.

At the same time, moreover, there was heightened concern about disorder and a consequent desire to reinforce the mechanisms to keep this in check. Tensions between rich and poor, or between order and licence, had long been a feature of life in the capital; but they widened again in this period. Provision of lighting may have enabled or facilitated the extension of leisure into the night, but more immediately it meant security for people and their property. Thus did the inhabitants of St David's Lane petition the town council in 1783 for lamps to light their neighbourhood because, or so they claimed, it 'has become more subject to Riots and disorderly behaviour than almost anywhere in the City in so much that the Petitioners are apprehensive of danger when obliged to Go out under cloud of night'. Another petition in the same year complained of the entire absence of lamps during the winter and the difficulty this presented to inhabitants finding their houses 'besides their being under the utmost terror of being robbed'.[81]

Vagrancy was a perennial problem, as it was for many other towns, particularly in periods of depression and economic distress. The 1780s saw, nevertheless, efforts to control this ratchet up yet another notch. Many of the concerns about public disorder and the nuisance and threat this created were distilled into the plans for the new Edinburgh bridewell, first mooted in 1782.[82] The inspiration behind this derived, however, from more than local circumstances, being part of a wider upsurge of debate about prison reform in British society at the end of the War of American Independence, in which John Howard's writings played a key role. In Montrose, for example, in early 1784 a subscription was started to defray the costs of a series of improvements to the local prison directly influenced by Howard and his writings.[83] There were clear parallels between the Edinburgh bridewell scheme and near contemporaneous proposals for poor law reform in England by Thomas Gilbert in 1781, which produced Gilbert's permissive Workhouse Act of 1782.[84] Nonetheless, the rhetoric of the proposal was stark, being focused particularly on the problem of disorderly youth. In 1784, the council issued a new proclamation against beggars, declaring their intent to see the laws against begging and vagrancy rigorously implemented, to which end they had provided a 'house of correction' in one of the vaults below the North Bridge. Anyone seen begging or 'strolling' within the city or its liberties after a certain date, was to be confined to hard labour and fed only on bread and water. Anyone who sought to obstruct the town guard apprehending such individuals would also be subject to punishment of the 'outmost [sic] rigour'.[85] Whether this was more effective than earlier measures is doubtful, but it captures very well the anxieties that lay very close to the surface in the capital in the later eighteenth century, and which both reflected and reinforced a hardening of attitudes, and to some degree, redefinition of the problem of the 'poor' that informed a new wave of philanthropic and policing initiatives which gathered even further pace in the subsequent decade. Even the relatively minor disturbances of 1784 had led to calls among some for changes to the system of policing, while in 1786 an abortive piece of parliamentary legislation had proposed a new system for managing the poor, which would have involved an officer conducting an annual survey of the inhabitants of the city's ten parishes with the aim of preventing fraudulent claims for relief.[86] Collection of information was a disciplinary tool, as well as a means to greater efficiency and economy, and was symptomatic of changing poor relief policies throughout urban Britain in this period. In Scotland, Glasgow may well have led the way in this respect, as befitting its status as Scotland's first industrial city.[87]

What Daer took from his experience of living in the capital in the first half of the 1780s is, sadly, hidden from us. It is very likely, nevertheless, that he attended assemblies – Stewart's later students certainly did so – although by the early nineteenth century Edinburgh social life had changed in several ways, as its centre of gravity, for the elites at least, moved further towards the new towns (first and second) and into the grandly decorated and furnished rooms of their houses. His friend Sir James Hall of Dunglass, who came to Edinburgh in the year before Daer, was a very keen dancer, and his correspondence frequently alludes to the many 'balls' being staged in what another resident called on one occasion 'our gay town'. Daer may well have seen Siddons at the Theatre Royal in the winter of 1783–4. Apart from the Speculative Society, of which more in the following chapter, the only club we know he was a member of was the Oyster Club, which met in a tavern in Old Fishmarket Close (in the old town). This was essentially an informal dining club, membership of which comprised Dugald Stewart and his university cronies – Hutton, Smith, Walker and so on – with the emphasis being on conviviality rather than serious discussion, insofar as these were ever separate. As John Hope, the Professor of Botany, reported of one meeting of the club in the spring of 1784: 'We had *as usual* a great deal of pleasantry' (my emphasis).[88] The great Enlightenment clubs that had defined much of Edinburgh's intellectual life in earlier decades were extinct by the 1780s, although there was a brief attempt to revive the Poker Club associated with renewed plans for a Scottish militia at the end of the American war. There is no evidence that Daer was a member of this.[89] For students, in any case, more relevant were the proliferating societies associated with the University and its Faculty, such as the newly formed Natural History Society (1782) or the Chemistry Society (1785). Daer does not appear to have been a member of either. Increasingly, the main forum for wider intellectual debate was the Royal Society of Edinburgh, chartered in 1783, and comprising two sections, the 'Literary' and the 'Physical' or scientific. Both Daer and his father, the fourth earl, were elected on the same day – 24 January 1785. Daer's proposers were Dugald Stewart, James Gregory and John Walker, while his father's were Stewart again, James Hutton and Adam Smith.[90]

How people respond to place depends ultimately of course on disposition and interest, and probably the stage of their life; and there is a risk of circularity in any proposition here. Nonetheless, it seems very plausible that Daer, with his Dissenting education and its focus on progress and serving the 'common good', would have been buoyed by the debates about and even more perhaps by the spirit of improvement that prevailed in the Scots capital in the first half of the 1780s. It was this spirit that infused the Canongate minister, John M'Farlan's confident restatement of the Scottish Enlightenment case for large towns as the crucibles of progress in 1786, a case that owed much to Robertson and behind him, David Hume and Adam Smith.[91] M'Farlan's optimism is all the more notable since he was not part of the charmed circle of Moderates who presided over the city and its kirks for much of the eighteenth century, but came from the Popular, evangelical wing of the Kirk. He was also an important participant in the debates about combating poverty in the capital in the 1780s.[92]

As we will see in a later chapter, Daer may well also have been caught up in tentative steps towards and discussions on political reform which occurred at this time, a development that in the national context began in Edinburgh, but which, as with so much else in this period, was intimately related to developments taking place elsewhere, in England and Ireland especially. To a degree that is often downplayed, the reform movements of the end of the War of American Independence had an important Scottish and Edinburgh dimension. It being Scotland, however, a good deal of the energy behind this fed into a renewed campaign in 1783–4 against the role of patronage in the selection of ministers in the Church of Scotland. This upsurge of interest in reform formed an important part of the context in which Daer's father took up an older reform cause, that of Scottish peerage elections, a campaign which was extended to include the voting rights in Scottish parliamentary elections of the eldest sons of Scots peers, in which Daer would play an important part and which marked his formal entry to the politics of 'British liberty'.

CHAPTER THREE

———◆———

Dugald Stewart and the 'Spec'

Daer's major reason for being in Edinburgh was to continue his education; and to this end, his father placed him under the tutelage of Dugald
Stewart, then Professor of Mathematics, with whom he lodged, probably
from the spring of 1782 until at least 1784. How the connection was made
is, as with so much else about his life, unknown, although Stewart and the
earl of Selkirk quickly became close friends, and Stewart would be a fairly
regular visitor in later years to St Mary's Isle.[1] Daer's younger brothers, John
and Thomas, would in their turn lodge with Stewart during their times at
the University. In 1782 Stewart was at the beginning of his teaching career,
and it was only in 1785 that he was appointed to the post, the chair of Moral
Philosophy, from which he would go on to achieve quite extraordinary influence over a generation of British Whig politicians, including three future
prime ministers – Russell, Melbourne and Palmerston. Stewart's politics are
elusive, and he has been portrayed as both a deeply cautious, albeit progressive Whig *and* a covert radical. Whichever was the case, he had a profound
effect on Daer's developing views and on his marked sense of public duty, as
he did on those of many others who came under his charge. Stewart's ideas
and teaching thus form one of this chapter's principal themes.

We need, however, to glean what we can about Daer's other experiences
as a student. In March 1782 he enrolled in a class in natural history taken by
John Walker, the Professor of Natural History, and in 1783–4 he matricu-
lated as a medical student. It was almost certainly in the latter capacity that
he became a pupil of Joseph Black's, the Professor of Chemistry, although
it is possible that he attended Black's lectures in both sessions, apparently

quite a common practice among students.[2] In February 1783, he was elected to membership of the Speculative Society. Founded in 1764 by a group of six students, one of whom was the intensely clubbable William Creech – who went on to become one of Edinburgh's most influential booksellers, the publisher of Burns and finally, in old age, Lord Provost – it became the most successful and enduring of the numerous student societies that emerged during the eighteenth century. The 'Spec' was where a very select group of students honed their ideas and debating skills on the issues of the day – political, intellectual, ethical and literary.

One modern authority has portrayed the Spec of the 1780s as guided by a spirit of radical whiggery.[3] This, as we shall see later, is not quite true, although it undoubtedly contained individuals prepared to adopt some very bold views. James Mackintosh, also a member in the 1780s, albeit a bit after Daer, would later recall a mood of youthful disdain for authority from his time at the University:

> Youth, the season of humble diligence, was often wasted in vast and fruitless projects. Speculators could not remain humble learners. Those who will learn, must for a time trust their teachers, and believe in this superiority. But they who too early think for themselves, must sometimes think themselves wiser than their master, from whom they can no longer gain anything valuable. Docility is thus often extinguished, when education is scarcely begun. It is vain to deny the reality of these inconveniences, and of other more serious dangers to the individual and to the community, from a speculative tendency (above all) too early impressed on the minds of youth.[4]

Mackintosh was perhaps here repenting of, and offering a justification of sorts for, his own youthful revolt, which led him to write, in response to Burke, a defence of the French Revolution – the *Vindicae Gallicae* (1791) – an act and work which may well have been considerably influenced by Stewart and his teaching. We can, however, readily credit the basic truth of his recollection if we consider the collection of strikingly confident, strong personalities who came together in the 'Spec' in the 1780s. It was a group who included, together with Daer, the French future novelist, man of letters and politician Benjamin Constant, the leading Irish radical Thomas Addis Emmet, and Malcolm Laing, Robertson's successor as Edinburgh's leading historian and a fierce liberal.

In 1799 the Spec attracted criticism as a 'den of Jacobinism.'[5] Students appear, moreover, in alliance with several of Edinburgh's leading radicals, to have been behind a series of concerted political demonstrations in Edinburgh's Theatre

Royal in April 1794. These took place over several consecutive nights at performances of the *Tragedy of King Charles I*, involving amongst other things the repeated failure to respect the singing of 'God Save the King', which, along with other calculated provocations, led to a series of brawls with incensed loyalists.[6] Despite such incidents, however, members of the Spec from the 1780s would find themselves drawn up on opposite sides of the new political battle lines formed under the impact of the French Revolution. So, to take a prominent example, the Irishman Thomas Addis Emmet, in Edinburgh in the early 1780s to study medicine, would end the decade a prisoner of the British government in Fort George for his leading role in the Society of the United Irishmen that were behind the Irish rebellion of 1798. By contrast, John Wilde, who went on to become joint Professor of Civil Law at the University in 1792, would in 1794 write a lengthy, in truth rather exhausting, loyalist history of the present times.[7] The son of an Edinburgh tobacco merchant, Wilde had been a dominant figure in the Spec during much of the 1780s, and would be granted honorary membership in 1793. In him a somewhat bohemian lifestyle combined with an anxious political conservatism. Another member in this period was Charles Hope, who went on to become the country's leading legal official in 1801, the Lord Advocate, and MP for Edinburgh, and thus a vital cog in the conservative political machine that ran Scottish politics under the direction and vice-like grip of Henry Dundas. Hope was one of Daer's sponsors for membership of the Society.

Facts such as these are an important reminder of the sharply polarising effects of the French Revolution and of the potential dangers of reading back the politics of the 1790s into the previous decade. It is a warning that we need to bear closely in mind as we continue to pursue the sources of Daer's radical politics.

The university that Daer joined in 1782 was flourishing and highly influential. Edinburgh University in the later eighteenth century was *the* university of the Enlightenment, inheriting the distinction from another civic institution, the University of Leiden. Leiden's faculty in the early eighteenth century boasted such academic luminaries as Herman Boerhaave (1668–1738) – or 'le célèbre Boerhaave', as Voltaire called him – the most famous medical teacher in the Europe of his day, and Willem Jacob van 's Gravesande, who became Professor of Physics in 1717 and whose teaching drew hundreds of foreign students to Leiden to study the new Newtonian science, which he played a key role in popularising in Europe. The golden age of the Dutch universities was all but over, however, by the 1740s, and numbers of Scots studying in them had fallen away markedly from the 1720s by which time

reforms to the Scottish universities, which drew heavily on Dutch experience and models, had become well established.[8] The foundation in the 1720s
of the Edinburgh faculties of medicine and law were capstones of a process
of reform that began three decades earlier. These, crucially, had included
in 1708, as part of a wider package of measures, the abolition of regenting,
whereby a single tutor took a group of students for all their subjects during
their time at university. This removed a major obstacle to further modernisation of the curriculum and the refinement of specialist skills and knowledge. Scots who in the later seventeenth and early eighteenth centuries
might well have gone to Holland and Leiden for the best available medical
and legal educations, in the second half of the eighteenth century almost
invariably stayed at their home institutions, although a few, such as James
Boswell, continued to spend time at Leiden into the 1760s. Yet, as Boswell
noted in 1764, the 'universities here [i.e. in the United Provinces, the modern
day Netherlands] are much fallen', the number of foreigners at Leiden being
then fewer than half those who had been attracted there even in the second
quarter of the century.[9] The Edinburgh professoriate in the later eighteenth
century included a veritable cluster of international academic stars, such
as Black, Hugh Blair, Adam Ferguson, John Hope, James Gregory, Dugald
Stewart and Robertson himself, under whose patronage and direction most
of the others had been appointed.

The student body at Edinburgh at the end of the eighteenth century was
around 1,000 strong, while in the mid-1760s it had numbered around 600. In
the academic session of 1789–90, the total climbed to 1,090, comprising 130
in the divinity school, 100 in law, 440 in medicine and 420 being enrolled
in general classes.[10] As Nicholas Phillipson has noted, we know surprisingly
little in detail about the composition of this group, although they were fairly
heterogeneous.[11] Recruited from across Europe, North America and the
Caribbean, as well as throughout Scotland and the rest of the British Isles,
they were also socially fairly mixed, encompassing aristocrats like Daer and
a good number of the sons of merchants, professionals and even artisans, as
well as country boys from poor rural backgrounds.[12] Some of the professors,
such as Walker, reduced their class fees for those less well off so that they
could attend, while others, including Black, appear on occasion to have given
out free tickets to those who they deemed to be specially deserving.[13]

While some students, notably those relatively few seeking a vocational
training, followed a set curriculum, many did not. As a result they could
enrol for any course they chose. Most of the professors' incomes came from
class fees from enrolled students, and numbers tended to follow successful

lecturers, although, then as now, celebrity bred its own success. The academic year lasted from November until the beginning of May, with professors giving up to five lectures a week over those months, including in some cases on Saturdays. Some also gave a summer course of lectures, lasting from May to August, although for many of them this was occasional. In 1801, for example, only the Professor of Botany, Daniel Rutherford, appears to have been giving such a course, while in 1792 seven did so.[14]

The rising number of students created intensifying pressures on already cramped teaching accommodation; Robertson had identified the need for new buildings as early as 1767, although a scheme to remedy this had run into the ground owing to a failure to secure funds to defray the costs. Black was provided with a new classroom and laboratory in 1781, but the wider problem only worsened. In early November 1783, one Edinburgh newspaper reported: 'The medical classes in the University of Edinburgh, are so crouded this season, that the usual places where the lectures are delivered, have been found too small to contain the number of students.' 'There cannot be,' the same writer boasted, 'more substantial proof of the flourishing state of the university.'[15] This was one way of presenting a rather awkward fact, but not everyone was quite so positive. Another writer, noting that William Cullen, Professor of the Practice of Physic, had been forced to lecture in the Episcopal Chapel in Skinner's Close, pointedly contrasted the money recently spent on new assembly rooms with the absence of efforts to remedy the problem.[16] This was the context for the revival of plans for new college buildings in 1785, Robert Adam's designs for which included a museum for natural curiosities; an anatomical theatre; a chemical laboratory; and a large room for the instruments and experiments of the professors of mathematics, and natural philosophy and agriculture. The desire for such facilities underlines the contemporary importance of demonstration and a degree of showmanship as aspects of courses of scientific lectures – one way in which the academics mirrored the shrewdly judged exhibitionism of the many scientific lecturers who pursued their fortunes by touring towns across the British Isles. John Walker showed his students specimens from the natural history museum and may well have performed chemical experiments on some of these. Black's lectures may have been notable for their clarity and audibility, but Henry Brougham later recalled Black's 'perfect philosophical calmness' as he poured liquid from vessel to vessel without spilling a drop.[17] This dexterity was the result, apparently, of sedulous preparation, although John Robison was less complimentary in comments made in a letter to James Watt in 1800: 'Dr Black seems to have turned his whole attention to rendering his lectures as popular and profitable as possible, by a neat exhibition of Experiments [. . .]"[18]

It would be easy to suppose that wealthy, privileged students such as Daer did not work very hard whilst at university. There is plenty of evidence that some of them played hard; but this was not necessarily, or normally even, at the expense of diligent attendance at lectures or cultivating meaningful, even profound intellectual interests. James Hall of Dunglass, whose time at university overlapped with Daer's, and who was later a close friend and from 1786 his brother-in-law, reported to his uncle, William Hall of Whitehall, at the beginning of December 1781:

> We came to Edinburgh the next day – ever since that we have been hard at work with two lectures every day but Saturday – Natural Philosophy and Chemistry – the first takes a great deal of work out of school as Mr Robison goes very deep – and brings in the hardest propositions of Newton that I have read for the first time. The chemistry is very entertaining and Dr Black delivers his lectures in the best manner so that not a word is lost.

In March of the following year he was reporting, 'Our serious business agrees much better with the balls than I should have thought. I have mist very few balls and not a lecture, I am still as keen as ever about chemistry'; while several months later (in November), the news was still of diligent application, 'The balls have not yet begun but the lectures with a vengeance – I go to five different classes though upon the whole I believe I have less work than last year as it is enough to listen at the time without any study afterwards.'[19] Hall, who we shall meet again more properly in a later chapter, may have been quite unusual in the range and, indeed, depth of his intellectual interests and curiosity. A busy schedule of attendance at lectures and classes was not untypical, however.

We can get a better sense of what a normal week during term-time might have looked like from several letters written by a young Henry Temple, later Lord Palmerston, who studied at Edinburgh under Stewart's guidance between 1800 and 1803. The second Viscount Palmerston dispatched his son northwards to Stewart in pursuit of the improvement of his manners and morals, as well as to 'enlarge his understanding'. This was in preference to keeping him in the upper class of an English public school, such as at Eton or Harrow, where he would have been limited, as was emphasised in chapter 1, to further instruction in the classics; and his son's companions would, or so his father was convinced, been of a kind hardly suited to improving his conduct and disposition.[20]

At the beginning of the 1803–4 academic session Temple composed for one of his sisters a timetable of the different classes that he had begun to attend. Most of his days – excluding of course Sunday, but including Saturday – were fully occupied from 8am until 3pm, while every evening for a couple of hours he went over his day's lecture notes writing them out in a fair copy, although he also observed that he had, for lack of time, let these 'run in arrears'.[21] As well as attending lectures by John Playfair (mathematics), John Robison (natural philosophy), T. C. Hope (chemistry) and Stewart (moral philosophy), he was taking instruction in bookkeeping, drawing, dancing, fencing and riding.[22]

Aristocratic parents thus expected from professors to whose care they had consigned their child careful oversight of their studies, but also a broader, more encompassing guardianship. As far as we can tell, Stewart's lodgers were treated as full members of the household. By the early 1800s, he was taking charge of no more than two or three students at a time, which was probably his practice earlier; co-resident with Daer in the early 1780s was almost certainly Lord Ancram. When Temple was under his charge, the only other student then present in the household was Lord Ashburnham, although Stewart's own son, Matthew, was then of a like age and also pursuing a similar course of study at the University. Not only did Stewart correspond fairly regularly with the second Viscount Palmerston, so did his wife with the Viscountess. Thus, in October 1800, she reported of their young charge: 'Mr S is delighted with his talents, his attention to his studies, & his visible wish to excel, & says that his progress in Mathematics &c exceeds his most sanguine hopes – but it is his good sense & good temper than makes him such a favourite with us all.'[23] That 'Harry', as the Stewarts called him, and the young Matthew Stewart evidently got on well helpfully aided this process. He and Ashburnham joined the Stewarts on their summer expeditions; in 1800 both were invited to St Mary's Isle by the fifth earl of Selkirk, while they also accompanied the Stewarts on a recuperative jaunt to the seaside in 1801. Daer, as we saw in the last chapter, joined Stewart for the weekly meetings of the Oyster Club, while he was also present at several dinners given for Edmund Burke in April 1784, then in Scotland for his installation as Rector of the University of Glasgow. Boswell, who was no opposition Whig, but was a friend of Burke's, intruded himself on one of these occasions, recording: 'Lord Daer, Professor Dalzel [the Professor of Greek at Edinburgh], Professor Dugald Stewart, Professor Millar [John Millar, Professor of Civil Law at the University of Glasgow], and Dr Adam Smith were all of the party.'[24]

In the winter of 1800, the Viscountess visited Harry and the Stewarts in Edinburgh, attending several of their evening dinners, including on one occasion a 'very agreeable party of scientific people', among whom was T. C. Hope, the Professor of Chemistry; whilst on another occasion the gathering included John Playfair, the Professor of Mathematics, Henry Mackenzie, the sentimental novelist and impresario of the Edinburgh literary world and George Cranstoun, the opposition Whig lawyer.[25] Stewart's conviviality is well documented, and in the early 1800s he and his wife regularly hosted intellectual gatherings at his house, of which those lodging with him would naturally form a part.[26] In 1803, one visitor was the novelist Maria Edgeworth, who Harry reckoned a 'very entertaining conversationalist'.[27] Edgeworth's brothers had boarded with Stewart and attended his lectures, including the new course, introduced in 1800–1, on political economy. Stewart's evening parties were, Maria Edgeworth later reported, 'the most happy mixture of men of letters, men of science, and of people of the world, that we had ever seen'.[28] No wonder then, that the second Viscountess Palmerston had earlier concluded: 'The more I see of Mr and Mrs Stewart the more charmed I am with them & more fully convinced of the wisdom of the plan of placing Harry under such Protection *in the midst of so much real learning*' (my emphasis).[29]

Whether Daer heard Stewart give his lectures on moral philosophy is unclear; and it is most likely that he did not. Stewart had substituted for Adam Ferguson in 1778–9, when Ferguson was in America as part of a peace delegation on behalf of the North ministry. It is certainly possible, although not certain, that he undertook Ferguson's teaching in the session of 1781–2. His next set of lectures may have been given in 1784–5.[30] Daer was present during 1782–3 and 1783–4, so if he attended lectures on moral philosophy in either session they would have been given by Ferguson. It is just possible that Daer attended some of the lectures in 1784–5, but was only intermittently present in Edinburgh during that winter.[31] Daer would, however, have discussed ideas about moral philosophy in private discussions with Stewart and his visitors. It was Stewart's practice to give his young charges topics to discuss in the evenings.[32] That their relationship continued throughout the 1780s – Daer, for example, visited Stewart on returning from France in 1786, and they visited France together in the spring and summer of 1789 – reflects the kind of close relationship Stewart cultivated with many of his charges, and the family connections which existed between Stewart and the earl of Selkirk; but it also speaks to a genuine intellectual and political affinity.

If one account of Stewart's personality and wider influence is to be believed, however, the affinity was far from complete. For Stewart has been portrayed as at bottom a cautious, even rather cowardly individual, one who quickly and all too readily bent with the biting winds of political reaction in Scotland from 1794.[33] Unlike, say, his friend John Millar, there is no evidence of him taking a public stand in support of political reform in the 1780s and '90s, while in 1797 we find him joining one of several loyalist volunteer companies formed in the town.[34] Stewart's particular brand of 'common sense' moral philosophy, which held that the ordinary responses of humans to social circumstances provided the empirical evidence required for constructing the 'science of man', has been said, moreover, to represent a retreat from the intellectual experimentalism of the Enlightenment of Smith and Hume.[35] In this sense, his influence is closely bound up with the story of the end of the Scottish Enlightenment, or so it has been represented. Stewart's growing influence within the University thus signals a moment of closure, or the dilution of the Scottish Enlightenment in a manner that befitted an increasingly conservative and anxious age. This might be more positively construed, as an act of defensive recuperation of a set of ideas for a new context. It came, nevertheless, at the expense of eliminating any of the unsettling or overtly political elements so as to deflect unwelcome hostility from the serried ranks of conservative loyalists primed to espy and denounce anything that smacked of, what to them appeared to be, dangerous speculative licence.

These are not easy issues on which to adjudicate. There are several reasons for this. Firstly, our sole guide to Stewart's thinking before the 1790s comes in the form of several sets of notes on his lectures taken down by students. Stewart's lecturing style, as perhaps befitted the relationships that existed between the university and wider society, and the continuing role of aristocratic patronage, was quite open and discursive.[36] Stewart, however, also, more basically, saw his role – quite properly, one might well say, and not unlike the rational Dissenting schoolmasters we met in chapter 1 – as being to equip his students to form their own conclusions based on what he believed were the most important, relevant authorities. '[G]uard you against a bigoted attachment to any opinion,' they were counselled.[37] In line with his own injunction, he cultivated a self-consciously humble, but also notably eclectic intellectual style. This did not produce or, indeed, provide warrant for outright scepticism – as we shall see later, he was adamantly opposed to such a position – but the purpose of enquiry was not the generation of grand theories but rather 'to register particular facts'. The corollary was that his personal views tended to remain implicit. 'My business,' he informed his students in 1803, 'is to combine the scattered lights which have been thrown out; to present the arguments to you with impartiality, & to limit the conclusions when too unqualified, is all that I propose in these lectures. Without advancing any conjectures of my own, I only attempt to sketch out a path of inquiry to excite the industry & facilitate the labours of others.'[38] To be sure, there was a hint here of that habit of bogus humility that one meets all-too-commonly in *academe*, which on occasion acts as a screen for the most astonishing intellectual certitude. Yet in Stewart's case, the commitment to a non-dogmatic posture and rhetorical presentation was entirely genuine. His lectures were, moreover, undeniably very different in style from his written works or his correspondence, being closely shaped by their pedagogic intent and context.

Secondly, much seems to hinge on how we construe certain isolated remarks, and indeed on how we read silences; what he did not say becomes potentially as important as what he did. A dangerous enterprise for the historian, there is an ever-present risk of reading comments, or their absence, in the light of the thesis one is seeking to prove. This is a temptation that bedevils a certain kind of intellectual history, especially for periods of repression and stark political division, such as existed in the 1790s; which is not to say that reading between the lines is not an entirely legitimate technique, but it requires great care.

Thirdly, related to the above issues, how we view Stewart will depend ultimately on how we judge the reasonableness of political prudence and self-censorship in the 1790s; or perhaps what kinds of acts of resistance we deem possible given the circumstances. From late 1792, Edinburgh was the site of a series of formidable waves of political reaction, a process catalysed by what, to many, appeared a menacing combination of the rapid rise of a domestic reform movement, in which Daer played a leading role: the declaration in August of the French republic; and the startling political violence – most obviously the 'September massacres', when hundreds of prisoners in Paris gaols were killed in an uncontrolled rampage – which accompanied the radicalisation of the French Revolution reeling under the twin pressures of domestic political polarisation and foreign invasion by European powers dedicated to its extirpation. This reaction was almost certainly starker than elsewhere in the British Isles for being relatively late in emerging, but also dividing more clearly the elites from the lower orders. In July 1794 Stewart's close colleague, Andrew Dalzel, would report to the opposition Whig political fixer, William Adam:

such an infatuation prevails here among most of those whom one used to look upon as sensible people, that every thing coming from a member of opposition in parliament though abounding in the most forcible arguments, is reprobated with a degree of keenness that amounts to absolute frenzy. I believe the delusion and absurdity of the higher ranks of society here has proceeded much farther than it has done in England.[39]

The University, as Dalzel's comments amply witness, was not isolated from these currents given its intricate and close relationships to the town and local structures of authority. In 1792, the University's governing body, the Senate, promised to work diligently to instil in students 'just sentiments with respect to the nature of Society'.[40] No doubt an eminently sensible thing to advertise, but most of the professoriate were in any case robust supporters of the status quo – in some cases, such as the Professor of Natural Philosophy, John Robison, notably fierce ones. The Scottish bench, under the senior judge, the Lord Justice Clerk, Lord Braxfield, was tenaciously and overtly hostile in its pursuit of radicals and the suppression of political dissent. Braxfield made no effort to hide his political partiality, berating those radicals who appeared before him with his bludgeoning tongue, and the judges were in an unusually powerful position to guide the deliberations of the court: it is not an accident that no trial for sedition against a radical failed to secure a prosecution in Scotland in this period. Nor is it coincidence that it was from one of Braxfield's colleagues that Stewart came under scrutiny in 1794 for a relatively innocuous quotation from the French philosopher and revolutionary Condorcet in his *Elements of Moral Philosophy* (1792). That Stewart thereafter kept his head down politically and seemingly took the path of discretion might seem to be cowardice to some, but to others it might equally appear to be an entirely sensible response to his unwanted predicament. Henry Cockburn later recalled: 'Stewart, in particular, thought too spotless and too retired to be openly denounced, was an object of great secret alarm,' also noting that when Stewart commenced in 1800–1 his famous lectures on political economy, 'not a few hoped to catch Stewart in dangerous propositions'.[41]

Stewart was peculiarly vulnerable, therefore, and had his friendships, connections and sympathies been better known would have been only more so. His caution can, nonetheless, be exaggerated, for in 1805 he became embroiled in a dispute over the appointment of a new professor of mathematics – the so-called Leslie affair.[42] What makes this episode all the more significant is that John Leslie, whose candidacy was in dispute, was under suspicion and opposed by a strong faction within the University and Edinburgh ruling circles because he espoused a Humean scepticism about the necessary connection between cause and effect. This served to undermine the argument from design – the idea that the order revealed in nature required an architect and thus provided evidence for the existence of God – the validity of which Stewart was, as we shall see below, deeply persuaded. '[It] was,' one modern scholar has noted, 'the only occasion on which [. . .] [Stewart] decided to indulge in overt political action and ideological commitment.'[43] Admittedly, as one historian has recently argued, the context had shifted from the 1790s, and by 1805 the spectre of Napoleonic invasion was lifting.[44] But Stewart's actions were in pursuit of the goal of maintaining a careful separation between the University and the Kirk, and to uphold a certain idea of both the free spirit of enquiry as fundamental to academic life, and the crucial role of moral philosophy in the education of the young – to defend, in short, the idea of the university that had prospered under Robertson and which had produced its eighteenth-century efflorescence. We might also take notice of his friend, Andrew Dalzel's judgment in 1798 that Stewart was 'one of the few learned men who in these extraordinary times have not allowed their minds to swerve from the true principles of science, and to be overwhelmed with prejudice, intolerance, and, I may say, insanity.'[45]

However, a further challenge in characterising Stewart's thinking and political outlook is that it was, in various important ways, contradictory. The labels of 'radical' and 'conservative' only get us so far in comprehending his outlook – precisely because his ideas displayed elements of both. Or, to put it a bit differently, it depends on what is meant by these terms, which are, it needs to be emphasised, merely a form of shorthand. In Stewart's case, as in a good many others, their usefulness is strictly limited.

Prior to 1794, Stewart made a series of utterances that demonstrated marked enthusiasm for political liberty. His closing words, as reported by a student, to his lecture series in 1778–9 exhibited, for example, a striking optimism:

> Philosophy will gradually diffuse itself thro' the world, and when her 'beams' have pierc'd the gloom of superstitions & ignorance, they will never fail to kindle the flame of Liberty – Fate therefore may have yet in store, scenes of Political happiness, more perfect than have ever been exhibited in the Theatre of the World.[46]

We can only speculate how this paean to the 'march of the mind' was received in the context of the War of American Independence, then reaching a critical and parlous stage for the British, as first the French (in 1778) and then the Spanish (in 1779) entered the war, and as the initial expectations of quick victory over the colonists vanished, to be replaced by the reality of war for the survival of the first British empire and even, it seemed, the future of Britain as a great power. In these same series of lectures, Stewart provided his students with a defence of revolt (or armed resistance) as an entirely legitimate means to combat tyranny, at the same time linking this with the struggles in the Britain of the previous century against Stuart absolutism. Like Hume and most other Scottish Enlightenment thinkers, Stewart firmly rejected the notion of an original compact as the origin of government, or indeed any notion of virtual consent, seeing authority rather as a product of custom and utility – as rooted in man's nature and society, in other words. But the relationship – which resembled, in Stewart's view, that of a tutor over his or her pupil – was emphatically one that placed responsibility on the ruler; it existed for the good of the ruled. 'When we have a persuasion,' he told his students, 'that the present state of Government is inconsistent with the natural liberty of men, & that society would be better by being thrown into anarchy, it is not only lawful, but it is incumbent on us to resist the reigning power.' The right to resist was not absolute, therefore, but balanced against the imperative of preserving stability. On the other hand, students should be clear that Britain's freedom was the product of resistance, and it was 'the Revolution [of 1689] from which we may date the era of our freedom.'[47]

Did Stewart approve, then, of the actions of the American colonists in defying Lord North and the British redcoats and their German mercenary auxiliaries? At one point he noted: 'Perhaps the rebellion of our own American colonies is the only instance where people have taken arms merely on speculative grounds.' Were speculative grounds a sufficient cause? The term 'merely' here is capable of being read in very different ways. And yet, at another point he declared: 'There is very little danger that men should err on the side of rebellion without a just cause.'[48] The logic here was both psychological and historical: men were naturally prone, Stewart believed, to favour royal authority. What the attentive student made of this is very hard to say. For Stewart also made it abundantly clear that he saw conditions in Britain as uniquely favourable to liberty; and he specifically refuted many of the key ideas of the Welsh Dissenting radical Richard Price, including, crucially, the notion that freedom meant 'every person can be his own legislator.'[49]

This was the period also in which Stewart met William Drennan, the Irish Presbyterian reformer and later key early figure within the Society of the United Irishmen, then in Edinburgh to study medicine. Drennan, appropriately given his political sympathies, was granted membership of the Speculative Society in 1776, the year of the American Declaration of Independence. Stewart and Drennan struck up a close, harmonious friendship, one rooted, apparently, in shared principles and sympathies.[50] It was a friendship, moreover, which endured well into their later lives, and after Drennan had fallen foul of Dublin Castle and the Irish courts in 1794 for his authorship of what was deemed a seditious address issued by the United Irishmen.[51]

With respect to Stewart's response to events in France from 1789, the evidence is again fragmentary, but similarly suggestive. Like quite a few of his students – Ancram, Hall and of course Daer – Stewart seems to have been a regular visitor to France during the 1780s; we know he was there in 1788 and again during the summer and autumn of 1789, where he was witness to the fall of the Bastille and the October days, when Louis XVI was brought back to Paris from Versailles at the head of a Paris mob. Daer was with him during some at least of this visit, when Stewart spent much time in the company of Thomas Jefferson, then American ambassador to Paris. Stewart carried a remarkable letter to Jefferson from Richard Price, in which Price laid out the views that he would express later in the year, and much more influentially, in his famous 4 November address to the Revolution Society in London, the 'political and patriotic powder keg' that would compel an agitated Burke to respond with his *Reflections on the Revolution in France,* and thus ignite one of the most famous debates in British political life.[52] Daer carried back Jefferson's reply, which was dated 17 July.[53] Stewart kept journals during his trips, but frustratingly these, and other correspondence relating to his French connections, were burnt on his death by Colonel Matthew Stewart, his son and the one-time companion of the young Palmerston.[54] Was this because they contained politically incautious commentary? We can't say, although it is entirely plausible; and we do have several letters that Stewart wrote in 1789, 1791, 1792 and the last in January 1793 to Archibald Alison, author of the influential *Essays on the Nature of and Principles of Taste* (1790).[55] These reveal that Stewart was strongly sympathetic to the Revolution in its early phases, and utterly convinced of the need to show patience and understanding in face of the scope and significance of the political changes then under way. In November 1791, he wrote: 'The little political disorders which may now and then occur in a country, *where things in general are in so good a train, are of very inconsiderable importance*' (my emphasis). Even in late October 1792, he could declare: 'France goes on well', also expressing optimism that the National Convention, which had first met on 20 September, would be the equal of its revolutionary predecessors. On this latter occasion, his views appear to have been based in part on a letter that he had received from Paris from Daer's younger brother, Thomas. By the 1800s, Thomas was a ministerial supporter, and basically a conservative; but in the early 1790s he seems to have shared

much (although not all) of his older brother's radical political instincts, as
suggested by his barely concealed delight, expressed in a letter to their father,
on witnessing an effigy of Henry Dundas being burnt by a Dundonian mob
in the early summer of 1792. 'The people seem to have a dash of the French
qui vivre,' he breezily commented.[56]

In order, however, fully to grasp what Stewart's comments might be
suggesting, we need to set them in their proper context. Scottish reactions to
the French Revolution were, as elsewhere in Britain, initially overwhelmingly
positive. One Edinburgh burgess simply recorded in his journal on 31 July
1789: '[D]uring this month the National Assembly met in Paris – the Bastile
pulled down and the remarkable Era of Liberty to France commenced.'[57]
Between the summer of 1789 and end of 1790 the Edinburgh and other
Scottish newspapers were full of reports celebrating the victory of liberty
and public spirit in France. 'Go on, generous nation', intoned one newspaper
correspondent at the end of March 1790,

> set the world an example of virtues as you have of talents. Be our model, as
> we have been yours. May the spirit of wisdom and the spirit of moderation,
> the spirit of firmness, guide and bless your counsels. Overcome your wayward
> perverseness by your steadiness and temper. Silence the scoff of your enemies,
> and the misgiving fears of your timorous well wishers. Go on to destroy
> the empire of prejudices, (that empire of gigantic shadows) which are only
> formidable while they are attacked. Cause to succeed to the mad ambition
> of conquest, the peaceful industry of commerce, and simple, useful toils of
> agriculture.[58]

In the previous month, attendees at the Edinburgh debating club, the
Pantheon, strongly endorsed the motion that the revolutions on the Continent would, 'if established, promote the interests of Europe'.[59] In early June,
the Dundee Whig club sent a congratulatory address to the French National
Assembly, and when its members met again in late August they appeared
sporting the French national cockade. Present on that occasion was the Rev.
Robert Small, a noted local scholar who would come under strong suspicion
as a 'democrat' in 1792, but also the Angus landowner and son of Dundee
cornfactor, George Dempster of Dunnichen, who by 1792 would become
a staunch anti-radical.[60] Henry Mackenzie, writing under the pseudonym
'Brutus' in the *Edinburgh Herald* in late 1790, and who later became a leading
figure within the Edinburgh loyalist community, depicted Burke's warnings
in his *Reflections*, which appeared in November, as mostly wrong-headed.
Seduced by his imaginative capacities, Burke had lost sight of the real truths

of the revolution: 'The distresses of the lower orders of the people, the want of food, of cloathing, of fuel, are not calculated to figure in painting and sculpture, to melt in poetry, or to rouse in eloquence.' But Mackenzie continued: 'These orders [. . .] are what political and philosophical truth must own to be the nation.'[61] Paine could not have put it better. In 1790, the student members of the Speculative Society, who then included Daer's brother, Thomas, were overwhelmingly supportive of the revolution in France.[62] Opinions, however, began to shift quite sharply in the summer of 1791, coinciding with the French king and royal family's unsuccessful attempt to flee France – the so-called flight to Varennes. From this point onwards, negative views, warnings and anxieties were much more frequently heard in press and public discussion, beginning steadily to grow in volume until by late 1792 they obscured any continuing positive commentary in a thick red mist of alarmism.[63] As we shall see in more detail in a later chapter, Daer was present in Paris in the summer of 1791, in company with his brother-in-law, James Hall of Dunglass, and his brothers, Thomas and John. Intriguingly, Hall wrote two letters on politics to Stewart from Paris, although again these have failed to survive. Writing to his uncle, William, from Paris, Hall seems to hint at a politically sensitive content: 'I refer you for politics to two letters I have written to Mr Prof[esso] r Stewart and that I desired Helen to take copies of – you may consider them sort of addressed to you – I thought it best to keep that subject within one channel.'[64] To a growing number of people, Stewart's dismissal of the unfolding political violence in France in late 1791 as 'little' disorders would have appeared as at best naïve and at worst positively reckless; while his continuing hopes for a successful outcome in France in the winter of 1792–3 would have given rise, had they been widely known, to the gravest suspicion.

Thomas Reid, who had taught Stewart at Glasgow and on whose ideas Stewart drew heavily, was another Scottish moral philosopher who was initially politically very sympathetic to the principles of the French Revolution, and who also entertained a vision of the possibilities of future moral and political perfection.[65] Unlike Reid, however, Stewart's enthusiasm for the French Revolution survived the alarming turn of events during 1791–2. In January 1793, he wrote to Alison that he had recently received 'a very handsome box, with the *Rights of Man* inscribed upon the lid'. This he intended, he told Alison, to give to the latter's new son in his capacity as his godfather. It is one of those nice ironies of history that this baby, also named Archibald, would go on to become a leading Scottish Tory politician, political writer and enemy of political and industrial radicalism in the middle decades of the nineteenth century. In December 1792, however, Paine's trial for his authorship of the *Rights of Man* had opened in London, which would lead to his being found guilty of sedition and outlawed in absentia. Was Stewart here signalling his political sympathy or at least an opposition or indifference to the fears and anxieties of an insurgent loyalism? His opposition to the war fever that was sweeping Scotland and Britain at the same time, shared by Hall and Daer, would seem strongly to support the latter proposition.[66]

Such is the rather slim evidence for Stewart's political opinions and sympathies prior to 1794. Yet, if there was a truly radical, as opposed to opposition Whig, strain in Stewart's makeup, it may well have been of a rather different kind from how it is sometimes portrayed. It was also combined with a much more conservative side, which is why his politics is very tricky to pin down. To begin to see how this was the case, we need to consider some of his ideas, especially those that were at the core of his convictions.

Stewart, following in the footsteps of Adam Smith and before him Francis Hutcheson, believed that happiness was the correct measure of the condition of society. Again like Smith, and also David Hume, he saw modern societies as fundamentally different in nature from ancient ones. It was a point emphatically made by Hume at the beginning of the 1750s in a series of very influential essays;[67] and it was similarly fundamental to Stewart's thinking. Where, however, Stewart differed from Hume, and indeed Smith, was in his confidence in the capacity of humanity and society for improvement. For Stewart, notions of progress and modernity were inextricably interlinked. 'The race,' he declared, 'was stationary to all appearance in ancient times, and at this period it is impossible to estimate the rate, or fix the limits of its improvement and progress.'[68] Citing the French *philosophe*, the abbé Raynal, in his support, he went on to explain why this was so: with the rise of global maritime trade and the 'discovery' of the new world the prospects of society had been fundamentally altered:

> A total revolution in commerce, in power, in manners, in industry and government – the establishment of new connections with different nations – the accession of new wants and desires – with the means of their gratification – the introductions of the nations of north to those of the south – & of the east to the west. An intercourse of opinions, languages, customs and virtues and vices – of diseases and cures – such have been the mighty effects – the universal changes – that have taken place and they have paved the way – laid the train for new and more important changes still.[69]

The conditions of modern society, including the effects of trade, created the expanding possibilities for knowledge, and the sharing of knowledge, which, in turn, were the motors of moral and social progress.

Thus, if utopian thinkers such as William Godwin spent their lives enwrapped in a 'fantasy of reason', as one his modern biographers has put it, so in his own way did Stewart, although in his case this might better be described as a fantasy of history. Stewart's preoccupation was not, however, *pace* Godwin, with a vision of a future in which man realised his full moral and intellectual potential under the agency of a disembodied reason. Instead, it was with the duty to the present, and in particular to securing the 'happiness of the millions'. Moral philosophy for Stewart had an eminently practical purpose; this alone provided the justification for its central place in the curriculum.

Behind Stewart's conviction about progress was, therefore, a specific historical narrative. This shared a great deal with the kinds of historical narrative that were central to Scottish Enlightenment social thought. These essentially sought, in tracing the main trajectory and patterns of social and political change, to describe and distinguish modern commercial society within a primarily European but also global framework.[70] One of the most famous versions was William Robertson's 'View of the Progress of Europe', which formed the preface to his much-read history of the reign of Charles V, the Habsburg Holy Roman Emperor. Stewart's narrative, however, had distinctive emphases and played a rather different role in his thinking, which makes it singular. For his history – if we can really call it that – was concerned above all with the role of ideas and their circulation, together with the growing connectedness of the globe in an era of maritime trade and commercial expansion. In one way, it had a thoroughly democratic dimension in its depiction of knowledge in the modern world as the product of the union of many minds. As he explained in 1793 in his account of the life of Adam Smith:

> In those departments of literature and of science, where genius finds within itself the materials of its labours; in poetry, in pure geometry, and in some branches of moral philosophy; the ancients have not only laid the foundations on which we are to build, but have left great and unfinished models for our imitation. But in physics, where our progress depends on an immense collection of facts, and on the combination of accidental lights daily struck out in the innumerable walks of observation and experiment; and in politics, where the materials of our theories are equally scattered, and are collected and arranged with still greater difficulty, the means of communication afforded by the press have, in the course of two centuries, accelerated the progress of the human mind, far beyond what the most sanguine hopes of our predecessors could have imagined.[71]

Through print and the myriad interconnections forged through trade, knowledge had, since the Reformation and discovery of the new world, grown markedly and would necessarily continue to accumulate, to transform understanding, and to unshackle the potential of societies throughout the world to develop in peaceful, harmonious co-operation. As historian Edward Gibbon had argued, unlike in the case of ancient Rome, modern 'civilization' was secure because through print, knowledge would not be lost, and societies would continue to develop rather than inevitably decline. If the ancient world was trapped in a cyclical history, modern history was basically linear. It was not reason so much that would engender progress, but understanding as captured, stored and circulated in print. 'Among all the circumstances,' Stewart declared in a later work, 'which distinguish the present state of mankind from that of ancient nations, the invention of printing is by far the most important; and, indeed, this single event, independently of every other, is sufficient to change the whole course of human affairs.' Printing deserved to be seen no less than as 'a step in the natural history of man' – in other words, the history of mankind.[72] Interconnection, of people and ideas, would necessarily bring about further knowledge and enhanced understanding.

If there was thus a fantasy about the future implicit in this, Stewart's vision, it was one of a prosperous, peaceful global society created through the twin forces of trade and the improved understanding of all and not just the ruling elite. In this at least, he and Thomas Paine – who also drew heavily (although unacknowledged) on Smith's *The Wealth of Nations* in Part II of his *Rights of Man* – were as one. Where Paine, however, saw global peace and prosperity as goals that were realisable in the present and, equally importantly, through the destruction of a parasitic, corrupt old order, for Stewart it remained in the future and the product of *evolutionary* not *revolutionary* change. For Stewart the notion of 'perfectibility' – an idea for which he seems to have been considerably indebted to French thought and for which there was no ready English translation, hence Stewart's preferred term of 'improvability' – was utopian in one sense, but in another not. It was an idea of continual progress; it was not so much a destination as a matter of unshakeable confidence in a direction of travel.

So, when Stewart protested that his quotation from Condorcet in his *Elements* in no way committed him to condone the latter's actions in the French Revolution or to endorse the entire body of his thought, and in any case, on any reasonable reading, 'breathes a spirit of moderation', we do not necessarily need to read him as masking or distorting the truth.[73] In the relevant section of the *Elements*, Stewart had emphasised the necessarily gradual nature of change, and he did so in a manner that can reasonably be characterised as owing a good deal to Hume and his notions of political science. Another of the features of modern society, Hume had insisted, as did Stewart, was the importance of 'public opinion'; the modern art of politics was in part recognising and adapting to this reality. Politics was the art of the possible, one conditioned by the knowledge that cause and effect were rarely straightforward, and that if the goal was improvement it was *also* stability. Gradualism in politics was unavoidable since politics was both a theoretical *and* practical art. As Stewart declared in 1792, in words which perfectly capture his janus-faced politics: '[T]he perfection of political wisdom does not consist in an indiscriminate zeal against reformers, but in a gradual and prudent accommodation of established institutions to the varying opinions, manners, and circumstances of mankind.'[74] The political utopianism of Paine and his sort was rejected, as was radicals' habit of explaining abuses in terms of the failures of individual politicians or even particular political systems, or investing their hopes in immediate plans for the reform of humankind. '[N]o greater errors have marked the history of man,' Stewart insisted, than to 'mistake the means for the end – frequently to the loss of both'.[75]

What, then, of the spirit of liberty that he had celebrated in fulsome manner in 1778–9? At bottom, for Stewart, as for most other Scottish Enlightenment thinkers (as stressed in the introduction to this book), the crucial liberties were civil rather than political. What mattered were the rule of law, freedom of the press and, perhaps topping them all, security of property. Property, contended Stewart, was in the end the source of all human improvement and of the law that secured liberty. 'The commencement of landed property,' he insisted, 'fixes the most important of all epochs in the history of civil society & in the progress of moral & intellectual improvement.'[76] It followed that social inequality was equally natural and, indeed, necessary to prosperity. Political institutions and political participation mattered, meanwhile, only so far as they were accompanied by a proper understanding of the true source of prosperity and progress. Happiness and prosperity came not from politics but from proper understanding, and beyond that from society, from the individual pursuing his or her own interests free of interference from government. It was thus protection of individual rights that counted, not the amount and nature of political participation. '[W]ith good laws a people may be happy – tho' deprived of all share in government – and if the laws are bad – the possession of power by the multitude so far from being any compensation – only an aggravation of the evil.'[77] This was not quite the full story, for as Stewart also acknowledged it was 'the possession of constitutional privileges by numbers' that was 'the surest bulwark against the tyranny of one or a few'.[78] The French Revolution, in its early phases, could certainly be assimilated readily to these ideas; and it may well be that we should read Stewart's responses between 1789 and 1792 in exactly this way.

Stewart's comments, meanwhile, about the English/British constitution were always fairly cursory, and one can perhaps read a bit too much into his decision to relegate and truncate his discussion of political forms in 1800–1, when he divided and reorganised his lectures to enable the development of a separate course on 'political economy'.[79] One can, to be sure, interpret this as a form of tactical retreat, but one can equally well see it as fully consistent with his broader, longer-term patterns of thought. Drawing on such authorities as Hume, the English jurist Sir William Blackstone and the Swiss political scientist Jean-Louis de Lolme, he presented the British constitution as securing a balance between liberty and order. That this was a product of happy accident might be worthy of note, but in the end was unimportant. Under the British constitution, a productive balance was achieved through mutual influence and interdependence, not, as Montesquieu had suggested influentially, through a strict separation of powers. Through representation in the Commons, the 'people' gained an 'effective voice', but so too, through the deployment of patronage and influence, could the executive operate with expedition and efficacy. Republican democracy was dismissed as appropriate only for small countries without trade or manufacturing – as was conventional in the eighteenth century – but also as intrinsically violent and anarchic: '[W]e may,' he told his students in 1793,

> upon the whole conclude, the Democratical form of Government is a very improper one. The laws are enacted amidst tumult and violence; generally according to the pleasures of unprincipled and worthless men; who being all desirous of power, and equally regardless of the welfare of their country, tear the state and harass the people by their intrigues, violence and ambition. The executive power is still in a worse situation. It has generally very little effect, and when it has any, its authority is little less than supreme [i.e. dictatorial].[80]

Not even the most die-hard loyalist could find anything to object to in these words, and they can only have brought the dramatic, turbulent events in France to the minds of his audience. Stewart also in 1793 firmly rebuffed the notion that the British lacked a constitution, an idea then identified clearly with Thomas Paine and Part I of his *Rights of Man*, published in 1791. Britain, *contra* Paine, did have a constitution, not a written one it is true, but an evolving, constantly improving one. Its genius was that change was its essence. In a rather different way, Burke made the same point in his *Reflections on the Revolution in France*.

How one assesses Stewart, therefore, hinges in the end on what aspect of his thinking one wishes to emphasise, and from what kind of chronological standpoint. After 1805, an increasing focus of his lectures became an anxiety to defend the naturalness of marriage, a defence catalysed by William Godwin's writings.[81] Godwin it was who described marriage as 'a system of fraud'; but for Stewart Godwin's 'licentious doctrines are equally absurd in a political as in a moral view'.[82] What is striking is the ferocity of his reaction to Godwin and his views on marriage, as Stewart himself appears to have recognised.[83] Stewart was always a decided opponent of Humean scepticism, adopting and adapting the 'common sense' principles advocated by Reid, and stressing the providential ordering of society and the world. For Stewart, the careful ordering of the world could only be of divine origin. 'I shall further observe,' he declared to his students in 1793,

> that ideas of skepticism have in general arisen, when the mind is distressed by anxiety, care, or disgust; and the least adapted to the proper apprehension of truth; and that it is when we are happy, joyous, and contented, and when nature & fortune smile around us, that we are disposed to a belief and trust in Religion.[84]

Why this furnished a powerful argument in favour of religion was not explained. It was nature, Stewart believed, and thus divine intention – in the form of the helplessness of infants, the passion between the sexes, and the delicacy and modesty of women – that decreed marriage as one of the pillars of society. The moral sense was not, as Smith contended, the product of esteem (or sympathy) or, as Hume believed, utility, but divinely implanted to conduce towards the happiness and virtue of individuals and society. It was, he intoned, 'sufficiently clear that there is in man an universal, similar and essential power of discerning right and wrong: and that all the seeming varieties of it cannot, *in the smallest degree*, tend to weaken the certainty of its actual existence' (my emphasis).[85]

Stewart was here turning his back very clearly on one aspect of the Enlightenment of Hume and Smith; although so had many others, and well before the 1790s. What he never turned his back on was the message of perfectibility or improvement and the duty to pursue this; and he steadfastly maintained this in face of the toxic conservative reaction of the French revolutionary era. Those who ascribed everything in life and society to the operations of chance were dismissed. 'The obvious tendency of these principles,' he insisted in

1816, 'is to damp every generous and patriotic exertion, and to unite the timid and the illiberal in an interested league against the progressive emancipation of the human mind.'[86] It was also to deny the providential ordering of society, and the benevolence of God, propositions that were absolutely fundamental to Stewart, as they were to his early teacher, Thomas Reid.

Thus, in some ways, the differences between him and Thomas Malthus, who also very influentially rejected the idea of a 'perfect government' in his *An Essay on the Principle of Population*, first published in 1798 and reissued in a substantially revised edition in 1803, were ones of emphasis. Malthus, unlike Stewart, was very happy to speak unguardedly of the French Revolution since his was an explicitly anti-revolutionary tract through the pages of which stalked the spectre of a fearsome, destructive revolutionary mob. But it was not in any simple sense a dully conservative work. Indeed, as with Stewart's teaching, it grew from the seedbed of profound immersion in Enlightenment ideas, albeit, as mediated through the Dissenting Academy at Warrington and University of Cambridge, and of an English rather than Scottish variety; it can also be seen very much as an attempt to rescue a moderate Whig outlook from the oppressive paralysis of political reaction. To combat the tyranny of the executive in current conditions – the traditional role in the Whig imagination of the landed gentry – one had first to destroy the 'mob', both as a reality and an imaginary threat. Malthus believed that his ideas provided the best instrument for achieving this.

Malthus and Stewart had a good deal in common in their views. Both saw poverty and the best means of preventing it in similar ways; and Stewart was very firmly opposed to the extension of the English system of poor laws to Scotland. Both believed public education to be the key to increasing the happiness of the majority, and were dismissive of conservative anxieties that it might have dangerous consequences for social and political order; rather the consequences were much more likely to be the opposite. Malthus's mature message, as expressed in the revised 1803 edition of his *Essay*, was a carefully qualified one, admitting the possibility of gradual improvement in the condition of society, but only if the passions of the sexes were kept in check by 'prudential restraint' – in other words, chastity and delayed marriage. (Malthus definitely did not approve of contraception as an answer to his population predicament.) For Malthus *and* Stewart, proper understanding of the sources of prosperity constituted the true means of improvement. Where, however, Malthus tended to see shadows – the limits on improvement, the niggardliness of nature, the inevitability of poverty and struggle – Stewart saw light – the capacity for improvement, the potential for greater prosperity, the inventiveness that could create its own demand and sustain higher levels of population. While Stewart recognised that there were limits on growth, and the ability of the land to sustain higher levels of population, these were, he contended, so far in the future as to have no immediate relevance. Malthus's anxieties were, in short, not Stewart's.

Stewart's teaching was designed above all to equip his students to understand the modern world and prospects for its betterment, as well as their duty to expedite these. Malthus may have thought that he was saying something rather similar; but his readers were more likely to recall his message about the pressing limits to improvement and about suffering and misery as a natural and unavoidable aspect of the human condition. Malthus could never shake off the belief that his was a heartless or soulless philosophy, however much he might protest otherwise.[87]

Stewart's philosophy and its social function were, therefore, as one. Implicitly, they were a rejoinder to those who might have been tempted to follow Burke and other alarmist voices in seeing speculative ideas, including those of Smith and other political economists, as the source of the descent into revolutionary violence in France, and the threat thereby created to wider European civilisation. As Stewart told his students in 1803–4: 'An illiberal and uncandid cry has been raised against philosophy, and accusations have been laid against it for crimes which it has no part.'[88] Did he here have in mind his colleague John Robison, whose *Proofs of a Conspiracy against all Religions and Governments of Europe* (1798) contained shrill warnings to this effect, and who had repeated them in his contributions to the *Supplement to the Third Edition of the Encyclopedia Britannica*? Stewart's was a call to arms to a new generation of post-revolutionary politicians not to abrogate their duty to seek the progress of their own society and humanity in general. In the end, this perhaps was the essential lesson that Daer imbibed from Stewart, albeit it took him towards radical politics, as well as programmes of practical improvement.

Stewart has been dealt with at length here because of the peculiar proximity between him and Daer, and because his influence on the young Daer was almost certainly very significant. What Daer absorbed from attending the lectures of Black and Walker is even harder to say definitively; although several things suggest themselves. It is very likely, in the first place, that Daer was swept up in the excitement of the new chemical discoveries associated with Lavoisier in France. Black, whose work on latent heat laid much of the basis for pneumatic chemistry, was initially resistant to Lavoisier's discoveries, and he only ever accommodated them piecemeal in his lectures; it was left to his students, including Hall (and probably Daer), to embrace the new chemistry in Edinburgh and popularise it.[89] No doubt there was a generational element to this, an aspect of the young embracing new ideas more readily and swiftly than their teachers; though this is far from the whole story since Lavoisier was challenging the very basis on which Black and others had constructed chemistry as a reputable science at Edinburgh and elsewhere, and, moreover, phlogistic theories received further significant experimental support in Britain in the 1770s.[90] James Hutton, who was very close to Black, never, for example, accepted the new chemistry. Hall visited Lavoisier in France in 1786 and two years later gave two papers on the same topic to the Royal Society of Edinburgh, where he also engaged in a debate with Hutton about Lavoisier's experiments.[91] It was through Daer, who also visited him in 1786, that Lavoisier in 1789 sent Thomas Charles Hope a copy of his famous *Traité Elémentaire de Chimie*, translated the following year in Edinburgh as the *Elements of Chemistry* by another of Black's students, Robert Kerr. Shortly after receiving it, Hope wrote to Black, in terms that suggest that Daer and Black remained quite close, or were perceived to be so:

> I have just received from France by the hands of Lord Daer from Mr Lavoisier a copy of his traité Elementaire, the treatise I spoke to you of when in Edinb: According to my promise I should have transmitted it to you for perusal instantly, did I not conceive by the Channel thro which it has come that in every probability you have got a copy of it.[92]

Walker's lectures contained a large element of chemistry, and Black in turn was an important patron of the Natural History Society (or to give it its proper title, 'The Society for Investigating Natural History'), which was formed in 1782. As one scholar has observed, over half the papers given at this society in its first two decades employed chemistry to examine some aspect of the mineral, vegetable or animal kingdom.[93] The popularity of natural history has, meanwhile, been seen as instrumental in the founding of the Royal Society of Edinburgh in 1783, to which Walker was appointed secretary of the physical section; although it also had origins in complex personal and institutional rivalries within Edinburgh's intellectual culture.[94]

Science was always an important part of the Scottish Enlightenment, but the 1780s were a decade of particular scientific excitement and ferment, and not just in the field of chemistry. The unveiling at the Royal Society of James Hutton's theory of the earth in 1785 represented a profound breakthrough in the understanding of the history of the earth and indeed time, expanding sharply and transforming the mental framework within which geological investigation proceeded. John Playfair's *Illustrations of the Huttonian Theory of the Earth* (1802) would expound and develop Hutton's theories in a way that served to protect and enable the future independence of geological enquiry, playing down, whilst at the same time reaffirming, Hutton's arguments that they did not challenge, but rather supported, natural theology.

Black and Walker – as indeed did others in the Edinburgh intellectual firmament, such as Robison, who had made his reputation in applied mathematics – emphasised the practical applications of science. In this, Black was following his teacher (at the University of Glasgow) and predecessor in the chair of Chemistry at Edinburgh, William Cullen. Partly through his relationship with his principal patrons, Lord Kames and the third duke of Argyll, the latter of whom had pronounced scientific interests – and his own laboratory at his Twickenham villa of Whitton – Cullen was much involved in agricultural and industrial topics, notably the application of science to bleaching.[95] In this, he set a pattern that was followed by a good number of Edinburgh academics, but which more broadly reflected the nature of the developing audience for science in Edinburgh and how it acted to structure the careers and outlook of men such as Cullen and his successors.[96] In 1796, Black told his students, in words that were later echoed in almost the exact same terms by James Hutton:

> I call every man a Philosopher who invents anything new or improves any business in which he is employed – even the Farmer who considers the nature of different soils or makes improvements on the ploughs he uses, I must call a Philosopher, though perhaps you can call him a Rustic one.
>
> Nor am I inclined to give much credit to those men who shut up their Closets in study and retirement have obtained the appellation of Learned Philosophers they in general puzzle more than they illustrate, they are wrapt in a veil of Systems and of Theories and seldom make improvements or discoveries of Use to Mankind.[97]

And shut himself up in a closet is not what Black did; for he was consulted very widely indeed on industrial processes, and like Cullen before him, took a particular interest in the manufacture of new improved and cheaper bleaching agents, acting as advisor on this matter to the Board of Trustees for the Improvement of Manufactures and Fisheries, the Edinburgh Linen Board and the Irish Linen Board. Black, together with Robison, was also in the 1780s consulted on several occasions by the Leith police commissioners about the purity of proposed water sources for supplying the burgh with piped water.[98] Walker, meanwhile, was a key figure in the further development of another thread which connects back to Cullen: a formal educational concern for agriculture. Cullen had given a private, extra-mural series of lectures on agriculture in 1768; Walker played a crucial role in the establishment in 1790 of a chair of agriculture at Edinburgh, endowed by Sir William Pulteney.[99] Daer may have played some role in the appointment of Walker to the chair of natural philosophy, although there is no direct evidence for this. What we do know is that he donated specimens to the collection of natural history specimens that Walker was building in 1781–2, and which formed the basis of the Museum of Natural History, which was an essential aid to his teaching.[100]

The links between the Edinburgh professoriate and the wider world were thus very close ones, in a way that no doubt ministers for higher education today would heartily approve. The emphasis on the practical applications of learning is often viewed, meanwhile, as another hallmark of the Scottish Enlightenment. So, indeed, it was; but, through its academics and the close relationships that existed between them and their many pupils, the University of Edinburgh also took its place firmly in what has recently been called a 'knowledge economy', one that was British as much as Scottish in scope and nature, and which also had strong international dimensions.[101] Recently, there has been renewed attention on this nexus of knowledge and experimental and industrial practice as a major cause of the inventiveness that lay at the heart of the 'industrial revolution' – that decisive acceleration in economic activity which impelled the British economy's escape from those constraints on growth and productivity that haunted Malthus and most of his fellow political economists, truly the 'dismal science'. Common goals and interests linked scientists, inventors and industrialists in a loosely structured community of learning, one in which habits of sharing and secrecy were, rather paradoxically, equally strongly present. Black, for example, never published his experimental findings, for reasons that remain a bit mysterious, but may be partly explained by his preoccupation with teaching. In a sense perhaps, this multifaceted economy of knowledge *was* the contemporary referent of Stewart's vision of the motor of social and moral change, although he may well have seen it more in the form of the contemporary proliferation of intellectual and reading societies and libraries across Scotland and Britain. The concern with practical improvement, meanwhile, was something that, as we shall see in more detail elsewhere in this book, men such as Hall and Daer displayed in many aspects of their lives.

There is one other place, however, where we catch a sight of Daer as a student – as a member of the 'Spec'; and it is to this that we now turn very briefly in the final part of this chapter.

Daer's petition for membership of the Society was submitted on 5 February 1783, and he was admitted, following the customary ballot, at the next meeting (11 February). Minutes of the Society do not record how individual members voted on questions; they tell us who spoke on each occasion, although not on which side of a question. Daer's first spoken intervention came on 25 March, when he talked to the issue of whether capital punishment was 'just & expedient'. A narrow majority – twelve to ten – voted in favour of the proposition. He spoke fairly regularly thereafter, including on the question of whether Britain should have any control over Irish trade. On this occasion, fourteen voted in the negative and only eight in support, the majority influenced perhaps by Smith's advocacy of 'free trade'. On 22 April, the Society voted without a division in support of the notion that the liberty of the press had been 'upon the whole beneficial to Great Britain', the only occasion during this period when no division took place. Perhaps the wording of the motion explains this unanimity, but it also reflects how far freedom of the press had become accepted by this time as a distinctive and crucial plank of British liberties; it is notable that even in the anxious times of the 1790s no-one, or almost no-one, suggested reintroducing pre-publication censorship, and 1792 saw the passage of Fox's Libel Act, which represented a further expansion of press freedom, conferring as it did on the jury (and not the judge) the right to decide what constituted a libel. In early January 1784, we find Daer proposing that part of the Society's annual income be devoted to creating a library for its members, a proposal that was duly accepted; and Daer was later voted a curator of the library. Curiously, in light of his later expressed views on the subject, he did not speak on the question debated on 17 February 1784, which was whether the Union had been positive for Scotland; and we do not know whether he was one of the five who dissented from this proposition. That there were these five, however, is notable given the strength of the pro-Union consensus in Enlightenment Edinburgh; and it is certainly possible that Daer was one of these, given his later expressed views. Other questions debated during his membership concerned the current political crisis at Westminster, as George III battled to keep Pitt the Younger in power against a majority in the House of Commons and on issues of current foreign policy. On 30 March 1784 Daer delivered a speech on 'the ground and tendency of the benevolent system of philosophy', an act of homage perhaps to Stewart. More significantly in light of his later political commitments, he was one of a number who protested at the defeat of a motion to identify each person's vote in the minutes, a motion that had it passed would have been of great utility to future historians. Among fellow signatories to the dissenting protest was Benjamin Constant, but also John Wilde, again demonstrating the difficulty of inferring over-much about political views from the opaque hints afforded by the Society's minutes.

Opinion among the society's members was clearly divided on most issues, and it is, in fact, hard to pin down its centre of political gravity in this period. Daer did not speak on the issue of whether a 'learned education' for women would benefit society. Only five present voted in its support, compared to twelve against, so on some issues conservative views prevailed fairly easily. On the question of whether the execution of Charles I had been justified, the vote split ten to eight against, while on the very topical issue of whether George III's use of 'secret influence' to direct the Lords to defeat the Fox–North ministry's India bill and thus ease them from office was justified it was evenly divided. On the other hand, perhaps influenced by the presence of the Irishman Emmet, ten voted in the affirmative on the motion that the independence of Ireland or Great Britain might be of 'material advantage to either country'. Very few people were openly advocating or indeed thinking about full political independence in 1785, and the context for this debate was almost certainly Pitt's efforts to place the relationship between Britain and Ireland on a new, clearer footing after the grant of parliamentary independence to Ireland in 1782 with his commercial propositions. These sought essentially to parlay free trade for limited, but decisive metropolitan control of external trade and foreign and military affairs and an Irish financial contribution to the costs of imperial defence. Daer's last spoken contribution to the Society was on the question of whether an aristocracy in Britain would be preferable to an absolute monarchy. Daer was on this occasion the teller for the ayes, who were outvoted eight to five. Perhaps the notion of a virtuous aristocracy was one that Daer found compelling at this stage, or what he had in mind was a true aristocracy, one of merit rather than birth. In the 1790s, under the impact of the French Revolution, the landed elite would come under unexampled critical scrutiny, and Daer would at moments seek to deny his aristocratic status, or rather its relevance to a true politics of equality. Apart, however, from his gesture in support of transparency and accountability, and his enthusiasm for forming a library, we can infer only a limited amount from his participation in the Society.

Daer ended his studies in Edinburgh in 1784, but he did attend a few further meetings of the Speculative Society. Between March 1785 and

February 1786 he was absent, presumably from Edinburgh as well as the meetings, and was only very intermittently present between mid-February and mid-April 1786, after which he again left the city. He returned briefly in February of the following year, but was present at just one meeting and had left by 6 March. One of the main reasons for this absence was that in 1786 his father handed over to him the responsibility for running the family estates in the Stewartry of Kirkcudbright and Wigtownshire. Daer's world now lay firmly beyond the walls of university and out in the 'great theatre of the world', which, as Stewart once reflected, would necessarily 'enrich' the mind with many new ideas, as well as correct many 'misapprehensions of life and manners'.[102] It also turned, as we shall see in the next two chapters, to what Boswell, typically self-consciously, styled on occasion as 'active and rational' measures.[103]

CHAPTER FOUR

———◆———

Heroic Improver

'Improvement' was the pre-eminent patriotic endeavour in eighteenth-century Scotland.[1] Landowners were in the vanguard of this – or rather they were the ones with the financial resources and raw legal and political power to make the most visible and obvious strides in this sphere.[2] It is easy to be cynical about why they were such keen improvers, or at least to see this primarily in terms of economic advantage; for improvement usually meant higher returns on their lands, mainly in the form of increased rents. There is no doubt that many of them paid very close attention to the likely financial benefits of improvement. That making money was a patriotic duty may well have been agreeable and very flattering to landowners, but profit not patriotism drove them – or so several notable historians have argued.[3]

Whether this is a debate that can ever be fully resolved is doubtful; and perhaps ultimately it depends on one's view of human motivation. On the other hand, what exclusive focus on financial advantage cannot explain is the sheer intensity of the commitment to improvement from landowners, the amount of energy they invested in it, and its centrality to their sense of identity in the later eighteenth century. Take the example of George Dempster of Dunnichen, admittedly very much at one end of the spectrum of improvers: the soubriquet 'honest George' derived primarily from his staunch political independence in an era when this quality was seemingly in sparse supply north of the border.[4] Prior to 1790 Dempster's considerable skills as a political operator were focused on Westminster, where he was the MP for Perth Burghs, and the dangerous but very lucrative shoals of East India House in Leadenhall Street. At Westminster, he fought hard for the 'Scottish interest' as he saw it, and carved out a very notable role as a defender of the Scottish linen industry, a role that earned him a good deal of popularity in the country's rapidly growing linen manufacturing burghs and areas. He was one of a veritable clutch of Scots who achieved great influence in the highest reaches of the East India Company in London in the eighteenth century, a position which allowed them to dispose of considerable patronage to their kin and countrymen; in Dempster's case this included his brother, John.[5] In 1786 he bought the Skibo estate in Sutherland, and from 1790 his main pre-occupations became the improvement of this estate and the nearby estate owned by his brother, Pulrossie, and of Dunnichen, his Angus property.[6] Dempster, one of the architects of the British Fisheries Society (or to give it its proper title, 'The British Society for Extending the Fisheries and Improving the Sea Coasts of Great Britain'), a vehicle for bringing prosperity to the Highlands as well as shoring up British naval power after the end of the War of American Independence, was in complete thrall to the practice and ideology of improvement. When Daer's brother, Thomas Douglas, fifth earl of Selkirk, published an influential pamphlet in 1805 attacking Highland landlords for seeking to prevent emigration from the area, Dempster was perplexed and angered.[7] Selkirk turned the tools of an Enlightenment education – the same education from which Daer had benefited – on those who might have thought that it only supported their case. The humanitarian motivations behind the Passenger Act of 1803, which imposed conditions on shipmasters carrying people across the Atlantic, were, suggested Selkirk, a sham; the real purpose of the legislation was to keep a surplus, exploitable population in the Highlands for the narrow, economic benefit of the Highland landowners. For Dempster, Selkirk's assault was a betrayal of all he stood for and his patriotic vision.

We know now, of course, that Selkirk was in many ways on the right side of the argument; that the law of comparative advantage did probably doom the Highlands to economic marginalisation; and that underpinning schemes of improvement in the region was often a bland, uncritical optimism.[8] Yet to Dempster, with his inexpungeable faith in improvement, the message was pernicious. Surely, he demanded in a piece that he penned for publication in a newspaper, improvement had the capacity to regenerate the Highlands and provide prosperity and employment for its population. 'I was,' he declared, 'startled at the novelty & coldness of the Doctrine For History & my own observation concurred in convincing me that freedom and good & encouraging Tenures had converted the wild Alps, the Mountains of Wales and even the Rocks of Norway into Gardens, and filled those regions with a race of highly industrious & brave People.'[9] Surely it was downright daft to be talking about investing in colonies overseas – as many did – when that money could be spent on realising new prosperity in an important part of the British Isles. That the Highlander was brave, patriotic and industrious made Selkirk's betrayal only more blameworthy.

Dempster may have gone further in his faith in improvement than many, but he was far from alone in his enthusiasm. In the Dempster correspondence (now kept in the library of the University of Toronto) is a wonderful letter penned to him by the former Edinburgh banker but by now agricultural improver, William Forbes of Pitsligo, a letter that openly betrays the psychological satisfactions that such activity offered.[10] Forbes had read the statistical account for the parish of Criech in Sutherland, which included a description by Dempster of his improvements on the Skibo estate and the estate owned by his brother, solicited from him by Sir John Sinclair, a native of Sutherland and the national cheerleader of improvement. In this, Dempster had expostulated:

> Shall we state none of the advantages, but those of a *pecuniary* nature? Is nothing to be set down, for the PLEASURE OF BEHOLDING THE PROGRESS OF THE PROSPERITY OF A COUNTRY? IS THE JOY OF SEEING TOWNS AND HOUSES ARISING AROUND YOU OF NO VALUE? NOR THE ULTIMATE BENEFIT DERIVED TO YOUR COUNTRY, BY ADDING TO IT, INDUSTRIOUS INHABITANTS AND CULTIVATED LAND; THRIVING TOWNS AND FLOURISHING MANUFACTURES?[11]

And there was much more of the same. Inspired by these injunctions, Forbes described for Dempster his own efforts on his estate in Buchan. Forbes was full of regard for his own achievement and of the promise of his new settlement. 'I could not,' he boasted, 'but feel an honest pride, last autumn when I dined with upwards of an hundred of my people, who all seem'd to be extremely happy with their situation.' The phrase 'my people' sticks out like a sore thumb. He was seeing what he wanted to see; but then such was the happy condition of the landowner. A later paragraph describes the premiums he was offering tradesmen and inhabitants for such things as weaving and bleaching the first web of linen cloth of not less than thirty yards. In full paternalistic flow, he remarked:

> With regard to the premiums, although they seem to amount to a considerable sum [there were twenty five of them of values varying between one and three guineas], my chief fear is, that it will be a long time before several of them be claimed. Five of them, however, have been already gained.

It is, however, what he then went on to say which illuminates so tellingly how landowners often could not or would not see beyond their own sense of virtue. The silver medals handed to the winners bore on one side the inscription 'The Reward of Industry at New Pitsligo' and on the other the winner's name. Forbes seems to have expected the grateful recipients to wear their medals proudly on Sundays and holidays, presumably pinned to their best suit of clothes 'like an order of merit'. 'Even that circumstance,' he informed Dempster, 'trifling as it is, I am not without hopes, will have its effect.'

The meanings of improvement were various, therefore. It was a means of legitimating the power and influence of an elite which since 1707 ruled over a stateless nation; or more subtly perhaps was a demonstration that the landed classes had heeded the Enlightenment's call to prove their utility; and it was about demonstrating a paternalistic face, albeit one with a hard edge.[12] And, it was frequently nakedly a form of social engineering, an attempt to produce an industrious and contented populace certainly, but a pliant and compliant one. To improve was to eliminate a landscape of disorder and in its place bring into being one characterised by order, regularity and industry.[13] Lord Gardenstone's message to the population of his planned village of Laurencekirk in Buchan was blunt, if dressed up in a typical rhetoric of benevolence, and characteristically gendered at the same time:

> The sum of my admonitions is this, That the three great blessings of this life are, HEALTH, PEACE, and COMPETENCE. – The first you may enjoy to old age, by a life of piety, virtue, and temperance. – The second every well tempered man among you will possess, with the leave of your wives, who I know are generally very good women. – The third will be a certain and gracious reward of your frugality and honest industry.[14]

In the end, improvement was about rather more than making money, although it was certainly about that as well.

When Daer was handed the reins by his father of the family estates in 1786, the role of improver was thus for him a very natural one into which to step. That the fourth earl was an improver made this more likely; and his decision to hand Daer management of the estates was almost certainly intended to facilitate the introduction of new techniques and new approaches in their direction. The fourth earl was giving control of the family estates to a young man with the energy, vision and tenacity of purpose to, as one modern historian has put it, 'revolutionalize' their management.[15]

The timing is also significant in another way. For the 1780s were, as we have already seen in chapter 2, a moment of great optimism about the transforming potential of improvement; the shadows which from the 1790s would begin to be cast over the social and political impact of economic change were distant ones. James Anderson, the radical Whig writer on agricultural and economic improvement, mused in 1790 on a future when the impossible would be possible; progression was, according to Anderson, inevitable 'among a free people' such as the British.[16] The return of the forfeited Highland estates to private ownership in 1784, and the formation of the Edinburgh Highland Society in February of the same year, signalled renewed optimism about the possibilities of economic renewal in that region.[17] Anderson visited the Highlands and Islands in 1784 together with Dempster; and what they saw, or believed they saw, was a people who were poor amidst 'a superabundance of the means of obtaining wealth'. Poverty in the Highlands was attributable to 'a system of injudicious laws', and all that was required to bring prosperity was to free the Highlander 'from their present thraldom'.[18] Nearly everywhere the Scots looked in the later 1780s they seemed to see abundant evidence of change and growth, or prospects for this.

Nor was this climate of opinion based merely on hope. For underpinning it was unprecedentedly rapid economic growth and development. Rural and manufacturing economies surged ahead in tandem in the 1780s. Towns and industrial villages were expanding fast, or being created from nothing. In Daer's region of Dumfries and Galloway, according to one authority, the 'peak period' for formation of industrial villages was between 1780 and 1810; no fewer than forty-seven came into existence in these years.[19] Close to his family home, James Murray of Broughton laid out Gatehouse of Fleet from 1777. In 1790, such was the settlement's evident success that hack writer, Robert Heron enthused: 'The enlightened and public spirited proprietor had soon the pleasure of seeing a fine village rise near his principal seat; more orderly in its arrangement, more uniformly handsome in its buildings, happier in its situation, than perhaps any other village in Galloway.'[20] The third duke of Buccleuch's settlement of New Langholm was laid out from 1777, growing to three streets lined with houses a decade later.[21] Agricultural societies, devoted to spreading the gospel of agricultural improvement, sprang up in many places. The Society for the Encouragement of Agriculture within the Counties of Dumfries, Wigtown and Kirkcudbright held its first meeting in Dumfries in 1776; Daer's father was one of several aristocratic subscribers. A further purpose of these societies was to encourage or rather perhaps drag tenant farmers from their old ways, to induce them to adopt the new ones approved by the gospel of improvement. Provision of premiums, such as Forbes of Pitsligo used in New Pitsligo, was a favoured means. Dempster of Dunnichen would be appointed perpetual praeses (chairman) of the Lunan and Vinney Water Farmers' Society, founded in 1803. At the opening meeting Dempster, it was reported, 'expatiated on the importance of maintaining superior breeds of cattle and horses, on the duty of extirpating weeds, on the necessity of stern resistance to smuggling, and on the desirableness of upholding the constitution.'[22] (Dempster may have been progressive in a good many things, but not his politics.)

Further symptomatic of this new economic dynamism, and crucial to sustaining it, was the drive to improve existing roads and to extend road networks. Ayrshire led the way in the 1760s and 1770s;[23] but other Lowland counties were not far behind. The first steps were usually the product of actions by local Commissioners of Supply brokering agreements between landowners about the development of new roads and providing some financial support.[24] Or individual landowners would take the initiative as an aspect of wider programmes of estate improvement, as in the case of the third duke of Buccleuch.[25] A further key stage at county level was then to secure an act of parliament commuting statute labour – the means by which roads had hitherto been maintained, usually very inadequately – into a money payment. Dumfries and Galloway had accepted the necessity of such an act in 1771, although it was initially agreed to do this by voluntary agreement, after a model followed in the neighbouring county of Roxburghshire, and in light of the fact that the government was considering a public commutation act.[26] A similar path was taken in the Stewartry of Kirkcudbright, where the inadequacies and unfairnesses of the statute labour system had been fully acknowledged in 1759, and a plan accepted and put into operation which allowed commutation.[27] Voluntarism proving ineffective, however, a general road act for Dumfries and Galloway was duly secured in 1777, while a similar one for the Stewartry of Kirkcudbright was passed in 1780.[28] Turnpike acts became increasingly common, which established Commissions with powers of borrowing, as well as to manage the funds raised by the erection of tolls on the roads; or, as with the Dumfries and Galloway act of 1777 they could be combined with clauses providing for commutation of statute labour. New general road acts for Dumfries and Galloway were passed in 1788 and 1809, while the commissioning of a general county map in 1804 was intimately linked to the drive to improve communications regionally, but also to a wider improvement agenda; included with the map was a mineralogical survey.[29] The politicking behind these measures was frequently hard fought, for what was at stake was access to markets and thus the incomes that might be earned from the land, but also who should bear the financial burden of road improvements and building new roads. Different groups and factions wrestled for advantage; and these measures also frequently brought town and country into opposition, since towns feared (perfectly reasonably) threats to their prosperity through raised transport costs and taxes, and town councils resented any loss of their powers within their boundaries.[30] This was in many ways the real matter of politics in later Georgian Scotland, at least insofar as many local communities were concerned. Overall, the results were relatively rapid progress in transforming road networks, and very substantial increases in amounts of money spent on this in most Lowland areas.

Driving all these developments were landed elites that were achieving renewed cohesion and indeed confidence after the disruptions of the first half of the century, and influxes of new money and personnel returning from winning fortunes in the service of empire and Britain overseas or, indeed, from the proceeds of trade and the plantation economies of the Caribbean. During this period, they were being drawn closer together by the shared interest in the business of improvement, but also new forms of and opportunities for sociability, such as multiplying hunts (led by the Caledonian Hunt, founded in 1777) and race meetings. The Dumfries and Galloway Hunt, for example, started meeting in the late 1780s, usually, like the other hunts, holding annual meetings lasting anything between a week and a fortnight. Proliferating clubs were part symptom and part further cause of this increasing cohesion at county level, bodies such as the Bowmen of the Border, of which Sir James Hall of Dunglass was a member,[31] or the Jedforesters or Peebles Shooting Club. The Angus gentry met at Forfar at regular intervals in the summer for assemblies organised by the Angus Beef-Steak Club. The growth of more assertive county government from the 1770s or thereabouts, and the growing importance of Westminster and parliamentary legislation in local governance in Scotland, further reinforced this development.[32] More county business entailed increasingly frequent county meetings, which, in turn, led to the development of halls for them to meet in, such as the new County and Town Halls in Kirkcudbright (1787) or Forfar (1785). Even before the completion of the new Kirkcudbright County and Town Hall, the old tolbooth had had to be enlarged in 1775 to accommodate the County Commissioners. The new buildings were designed explicitly to house the *records* of county government, indicative of its taking on a much clearer, more continuous institutional form. Daer and his father played leading roles in several Kirkcudbrightshire county meetings in the 1780s.[33] More frequent, better-attended county meetings were the spur also to the enlargement and redevelopment of quite a number of inns in county towns across the country.

To reconstruct in great detail Daer's programme of estate improvement is impossible in the absence of extant estate records. Our best sources are two surveys of the agriculture of Galloway conducted under the aegis of Sir John Sinclair's Board of Agriculture, the first published in 1794 and the second in 1813. What these tell us is that this programme was systematic, far-reaching, innovative and, within the south-west, trendsetting. Samuel Smith, author of the second of these surveys described the period Daer managed his father's estates as 'a most important epoch, in the history of the rural oeconomy of Galloway'.[34] For Smith, Daer was nothing less than a paragon of improving energy and vision.

In his late-nineteenth-century history of the burgh of Kirkcudbright, the Rev. George Ogilvy Elder tells us that above thirty farms in the parish of Kirkcudbright 'shared in the improvements introduced by Lord Daer', the names of many of which can still be found on a map today.[35] Quite what this entailed is unclear, but reorganisation of land use and substantial investment were certainly crucial elements. Improvement often involved very substantial capital investment, and landowners were the source of much of this.[36] Smith tells us that Daer had the farm buildings rebuilt, with the implication that, unlike in some cases in this period, he (or rather his father) was the source of funds for this. In a move that heralded the growing economic and social importance of the tenant farmer in Scotland, the later Georgian era saw rural landscapes transformed by the construction of new stone and lime built farmhouses and associated farm buildings, usually in simple classical designs. Many of these remain prominent features of Scotland's rural landscape today. As Alexander Fenton and Bruce Walker have noted, the picture was in this context one of uneven, but clear progress before 1800. In the south-west, Ayrshire and more especially Dumfriesshire led the way. In Galloway, the earl of Galloway's tenants built their own farmhouses from around 1790 on farms let on twenty-one year leases.[37] As was the case in other regions, Daer's farmhouses were differentiated by size according to the importance and presumably acreage of the farm. They were also of the two-storey variety, the approved type in the burgeoning literature of agricultural improvement. They almost certainly had five or six rooms, including a dining room. (Detailed inventories of the personal estates of tenant farmers from this period show how far the 'luxuries' associated with urban living – mahogany furniture, china and glass ware, carpets and window curtains – were creeping into use in the countryside at this social level.) Each farm had its own barns, stables, cow houses and sheds. They were also provided with threshing machines.

Daer was a leading supporter and exponent of turnip husbandry, a means of increasing nitrogen levels in the soil by allowing those 'dung-producing machines' – cattle and sheep – to be kept through the winter. T. C. Smout tells us that turnip cultivation had not proceeded very far beyond Fife, Angus and East Lothian in the eighteenth century.[38] According to James Webster, this was certainly true in Galloway, although there was some change apparent by 1794. Leading the way, inevitably, was Daer, who together with another landowner, 'may', Webster tells us, 'be considered to raise nearly as much of this useful root, as all the rest of Galloway put together.'[39]

That Daer's measures had a substantial impact seems equally evident. In 1793 he sold the barony of Baldoon to the earl of Galloway for a sum based on a rental of £5,000. Significantly, however, Daer retained the lease of the estate for ten years at a rent of £7,000 per annum, and on its expiral, after independent valuation, the earl was to pay twenty-five years' purchase of the surplus valued rent above £5,000. In the event, Galloway was forced to pay £125,000 on the expiry of the lease. In other words, Daer's improvements had doubled the rent within a decade. We can only surmise that Daer had from the outset been supremely confident in the potential of his programme to realise much higher yields and profits from the family estates.

Another of his initiatives was an extensive programme of tree planting. Tree planting around landowners' policies was commonplace in the previous century; what was new in the eighteenth was large-scale planting away from the surroundings of the great houses. As with so much improving activity, it had an aesthetic, as well as utilitarian rationale. It was about creating a new type of landscape – but equally it was about realising the best return from all available land. Trees were a mark of prestige as well as a well-managed estate. As Smout notes, some of the great magnates – for example, the fourth duke of Atholl on his Blair estate – planted on a heroic scale.[40] In the south-west, one obstacle to renewing wood cover was sea spray, which might in stormy weather be carried far inland. The earl of Galloway apparently experimented on his estates with pinaster – a Mediterranean pine – that seemed to flourish despite this condition.

The lie of the land may well have sheltered plantations on the Selkirk estates – some said it did this on the Galloway estates – and sea spray does not appear to have caused any problems for Daer and his programme of planting. A visitor to the south-west in 1800 noted the presence of a 'very large nursery' about a mile from Kirkcudbright where, 'trees of all descriptions' were being raised. Large seems in this context to have meant almost fifteen acres, and the nursery contained, according to one contemporary, more than a million plants.[41] The later eighteenth century saw the development of nurseries in many parts of the country, often located close to towns. They reflected the drive to create tree plantations, which had an aesthetic as well as practical function, and tree hedges marking the boundaries of fields in some areas, but also the development of gardening as a major preoccupation among a much broader cross-section of society, including among the urban classes.[42] The same visitor quoted from above also observed: 'From the top of the Hill before you descend into Kirkcudbright, you have a fine view of the town and the surrounding hills beautifully variegated and enriched by numerous and extensive plantations, belonging to Lord Selkirk [. . .]'[43] Almost a century later, Ogilvy Elder declared, as only a man of the Word could: 'In a literal sense it is true of Lord Daer, that the wilderness and the solitary place were glad for him – the desert rejoiced and blossomed as the rose.'[44]

The varieties of tree planted included oak, beech, ash, elm, birch, chestnut, sycamore, hornbeam, rowan, larch, as well as different kinds of pine – Scots, American spruce, black (Pinus negra), Weymouth (Pinus strobus), silver and balm of Gilead. The introduction of North American species, such as Weymouth and balm of Gilead, was another feature of this period, reflecting the close ties which many Scots had to the colonies in North America, whether as traders, sojourners, military and administrative personnel, or as emigrants. Daer, or possibly his father, also created six hot-houses at St Mary's Isle, for bringing on fruits and exotics. The aim was, it appears, to establish a small orchard of fruit trees at every farmhouse on the family estates.[45]

The other main plank in Daer's improvement programme from 1786 was the development of roads. He first appears in the minutes of the Wigtown road trustees in September 1786, when he was immediately made praeses (chairman) of the trustees.[46] One can sense reading these minutes, which are now in the Ewart Library, Dumfries, a man driven by his commitment and enthusiasm for the cause. In 1788 he proposed that it was 'highly proper' that the roads already contracted by the trustees were kept in state of 'constant repair'. This was to be done by 'irrevocably' appropriating money from trust funds for the purpose and conducting a regular parish-by-parish survey of the roads. He sat on various committees of the trustees. In proposing the alteration in 1790 of the route of one road which ran through Selkirk land near Baldoon, he offered in his father's name 'to allow the public to make free of the Damages' – in other words, not to claim compensation for use of the family land – provided that the trustees funded the construction and repaid the money which the Douglases had already spent on the project. In August 1792 he advanced to the trustees the costs of improving the road from Bridge of Bladnoch towards Kirkinner. Very often the development of roads in this period depended on such loans of capital, either from landowners or, on occasion, from town councils. (This was why the matter of the securities under which money was lent to commissioners of roads had been such a hotly debated topic when considering the Dumfries and Galloway road bill in the mid-1770s.)[47] The final occasion on which he appears in the minutes is in the entry for 27 November 1792, when he was again praeses of the meeting.

Roads, as already alluded to, consumed the attention of many a landed gentlemen in the later eighteenth century. As our visitor to the south-west noted in 1800: 'The Gentlemen in Scotland, almost universally, very much to their credit, and the improvement of the country, spend much time and pains in altering and amending, or in laying out entirely new roads.'[48] Dempster was a leading promoter of road development in Angus, which dragged him into a good number of fraught battles with other landowners and with the local burgh councils. Again one could, as was done at the time, argue that this was because it was in their interests, in terms of bringing grain and other goods from their estates and farms to the rapidly expanding urban markets. As the magistrates of Paisley, which from no more than a village at the beginning of the century grew at an astonishing rate to become a major industrial town by its end, argued in 1757, with much justification: 'the Landed Gentlemen have a very great Benefit arising to their estates, by supplying vivers and other necessaries to a populous Burgh, and are primarily interested in making the Roads to their Market easy and convenient for their Carriages'.[49] No doubt Daer fully recognised the importance of better communications to greater efficiency and productivity in the rural economy. Nevertheless, it is the fierce intelligence and energy that he brought to bear on the issue which stand out, the wish to do things much better than in the past, to break with that past, and the willingness to follow the latest methods to enhance road transport.

It is Samuel Smith who is again one of our best sources for this; however, his observations were fully supported by evidence given before a parliamentary committee in 1808 by Sir Alexander Gordon of Culvennan.[50] Gordon had been Sheriff of Wigtown and later Steward Depute of Kirkcudbright and, in these capacities, responsible for road development in the region, a role that had led to his working very closely with Daer, and seeking to implement Daer's plans after his death. What can be gleaned from Smith and Gordon are several things. Firstly, in this sphere as in others Daer was a force for change and innovation; he set examples that other local landowners were to follow as they became convinced of their merits. One example of this, which again tells us a great deal about Daer as a man of practical enlightenment, was his determination, following a model established by the Midlothian landlord, George Clerk of Penicuik, to alter routes of roads so as to reduce their gradients. This entailed careful surveying using chain and level. Daer did this himself, aided by a land surveyor, perhaps John Gilone, who surveyed lands for quite a few of the local landowners in this period, as well as the properties of the town of Kirkcudbright. One pictures Daer pacing the region, searching for the best routes, literally getting his knees muddy in pursuit of better roads. Gordon told the parliamentary committee that he had had many conversations with Daer

> on the best principles of directing and making of Roads, which are chiefly these, that the Roads be made in the shortest direction, level, hard, smooth and dry, and of solidity and width, sufficient for the trade that may be expected upon them. *It is indispensably necessary, that very exact and carefully taken levels, plans and estimates, be made by intelligent Surveyors, previous to the work being commenced* (my emphasis).

Faced with resistance among his fellow landowners and road trustees, for his schemes often involved damage to existing enclosures and taking out of use good agricultural land, and entailed, therefore, considerable initial capital outlay, it seems that Daer embarked on a trial of the new method on his father's estate. This may well have been the road referred to in the minutes of the Wigtown road trustees for 1790. The Baldoon estate came to the Douglas family through Dunbar Douglas, the fourth earl's marriage to Helen Hamilton, fifth daughter of the earl of Haddington.

Secondly, Daer's fertile brain could not be content with ad hoc adjustments; rather he produced a plan for a completely new and expanded regional road network. If his fellow landowners did not initially share his vision and conviction regarding the benefits, he set them, so to speak, on the right road. Smith suggests that part of what helped to transform opinion was the increasing use of liming to enrich the soil, and reduce its acidity, that 'excited a very eager desire for the improvement of roads'. Lime was imported by sea from Carlisle, and was then carried by cart from the port at Kirkcudbright inland. But better transport required more funds, and Daer set out to realise these by promoting a new bill in 1792 to double the rate of assessment for the conversion of statute labour, to establish tolls on the main thoroughfare roads, and to introduce a new method of road making.[51] In the event, this became law only in 1796 – Gordon had been chairman of the

committee appointed to secure this act – probably because it took this time
for a consensus to build around it within the county. (Such consensus was an
essential pre-requisite of the passage of local legislation such as this through
parliament.)[52] Under the new act, the road commissioners set about making
a road from the river Dee (crossing it at Tongland bridge) to Castle Douglas
and thence to Dumfries, all but the final two miles of it on a route laid out
by a land surveyor who had been previously instructed by Daer. It was this
road that finally persuaded the doubters of the superiority of Daer's methods
of road construction. 'Many of the roads in both counties long since recommended by Lord Daer, and neglected as chimerical,' Smith relates, 'have now
been executed upon his plans with universal approbation.'[53]

Daer's record as an improver is striking, therefore, although there were,
to be sure, many other notable landed improvers in this period; each area of
Scotland tended indeed to have its own heroes of improvement, those whose
measures were characterised by their boldness and scale. Daer's friend and
brother-in-law, James Hall of Dunglass, was a deeply committed improver
on his Berwickshire estates, as we shall see in a later chapter, as was his tutor,
Sir John, before him; but they were part of an extended network, albeit a
very loosely structured one, of experimental farmers that extended across
the British Isles by this period, one that was made increasingly visible in the
burgeoning literature of agricultural improvement and husbandry, to which
Sir John Sinclair's new Board of Agriculture, founded in 1793, gave a very
powerful new stimulus. Where, however, Daer was much more unusual was
in his involvement in the burgh of Kirkcudbright in the early 1790s; and it is
to this that we now turn.

Eighteenth-century Kirkcudbright has barely been noticed by other than
local historians; but there is no real reason for this, other than the limited
interest shown until relatively recently in Scottish urbanisation beyond
the big three or four – Glasgow, Edinburgh, Aberdeen and Dundee.[54] For
the town presents a fascinating and instructive example of a much wider
phenomenon – the transformation of many Scottish towns and townscapes
in this period, a development fuelled by the growing prosperity and ambition
among urban elites and the broader middling ranks, and an urban version of
the wider cult of improvement.[55] It is difficult to think of a town of comparable size in Scotland and perhaps the British Isles in this period that saw
so much intervention designed to enhance the amenity and appearance of
its townscape. And, within the south-west it stood out, at least among the
existing burghs, although Dumfries may have acted as some kind of local
exemplar. Wigtown, by contrast, despite the close involvement of the earl of

Galloway, saw very limited change, certainly before the 1810s, and its record of improvement overall in no way matched that of Kirkcudbright.

For almost the entire eighteenth century, the layout of Kirkcudbright remained pretty much unchanged from its early modern footprint, a single L-shaped street set on a low gravel ridge beside the river Dee. Running off the street were wynds (i.e. alleys) and closes, where the bulk of the population lived in cellars, rooms and other dwellings. The population grew modestly, although the rate of growth picked up markedly from around 1770. In 1792, its population stood at a little over 1,600; by 1821 it was 2,400.[56] It was a town closely integrated with the local and regional rural economy, a fact that was the key to its Georgian regeneration, with the town servicing the demands of its hinterland for such commodities as coal and lime, for example, and facilitating the transhipment of agricultural produce.

Quite a few of the town's mercantile elite seem to have retained a foothold in farming, underlining the close connections with its rural environs. When merchant Andrew Muir, for example, died in 1804, his estate included a substantial sum for stock and farming utensils.[57] We shall meet Muir briefly again below. The town's main trading links were southwards to Whitehaven and Liverpool, northwards to the Clyde estuary, but also westwards, to Ireland and across the Atlantic.[58]

The connections across the Atlantic were significant at both a personal and collective level. Most famously, the Lenox family sent several of its sons across the pond to lives of prosperity and substantial achievement in New York and Philadelphia. William, who remained behind, was provost in the 1770s. This pattern of seeking fortunes across the Atlantic was repeated many times over. The second son of a later provost, James Dalyell, was a merchant in New York. Baker Thomas Reid's son was a physician in Jamaica. The repatriation of fortunes garnered abroad (by fair means or foul) was a crucial contributor to capital formation and the acceleration of improvement in Scotland in the later eighteenth century to a degree that historians have until recently probably seriously underestimated.[59] The Rev. Robert Muter, whose sons all sought their fortunes in the West Indies, was struck by the 'constant emigration of young people' from the town. 'No town in Scotland,' he wrote, 'sends perhaps, for its size, so many of its children abroad to foreign countries.'[60] The reason was probably lack of opportunity at home, but also the links, through family and region, to people overseas. Kirkcudbright boasted some manufacturing by the end of the eighteenth century, including cotton weaving, but it was small scale; there was also a brewery, tan yard and a growing amount of shipbuilding.

Kirkcudbright was a town of small tradesmen and shopkeepers, sailors, weavers and other traditional crafts people, labourers and servants (female and male) with an upper rank consisting of merchants and a small number of professionals (mostly writers [lawyers], but also several surgeons).[61] It was, however, an upper rank that seems to have imprinted its image and aspirations on the town with unusual effect. In the early 1790s, the hack writer Robert Heron observed:

> the gentry and the well-educated part of the community bear a greater proportion in numbers to the poor, the labouring, and the illiterate, than in most other places. Consequently, their spirit and manners are predominant. A degree of liberal intelligence may be observed amongst the lower classes, such as the same classes do not display in many other places. The richer burghers, too, seem rather to take their manners from the neighbouring country gentlemen.[62]

Heron may have been influenced in these judgments by the fact that Kirkcudbright had a subscription library from as early as 1777. Only a few towns in the borders (Hawick, Selkirk, Jedburgh and Kelso), Ayr (1762) and Stranraer (1771) had founded libraries of this type at an earlier date than this. Many larger towns, moreover, were significantly later – Montrose, Dundee, or Perth. Perth, for example, sometimes viewed as a provincial stronghold of the Enlightenment, only had a library of this kind from 1786.[63]

The subscription libraries of the later eighteenth century generally had relatively few members; Kirkcudbright's had forty-four founding members, whose number included the fourth earl of Selkirk. Not all were from the town, but of those that were most were professionals (including the minister, Robert Muter) and merchants. Muir, who we met above, was a founding subscriber. So too was James Murray, the local bookseller, although his membership could well have been self-interested since he was hoping to supply books to the library. Beacons of the provincial Enlightenment, their holdings usually comprised most major works of the Scottish, British and often European enlightenments. Religious and vocational literature was deliberately excluded, as usually was popular literature. Muter declared in his account of the town for the *Statistical Account*: 'Their [the inhabitants'] reading is extensive; and being furnished with an excellent subscription library of the best modern books, they have access to all the improvements in literature and politics.' (Interestingly, in light of Daer's political opinions he also noted that they were all 'loyal to the government, and no less attached to the British Constitution'.)

On the matter of what was being read, as opposed to what was available, we will have to take Muter's word for it.[64] Borrowing records for libraries in this period are singularly rare, although the Hornel Library in Broughton House in Kirkcudbright holds those for one library, but sadly not Kirkcudbright's.[65] This is the Wigtown Subscription Library, founded nearly a couple of decades later, in September 1795.[66] A prominent member was William Mure, who would become provost of Kirkcudbright in the early nineteenth century, and who was factor on the Selkirk estates. Like so many of the local elite, he had a house on the High Street. He was also involved in several different important spheres of activity in the burgh in the early 1800s, including as president of the management committee of the Kirkcudbright Shipping Company established in 1811, and chairman of the Old Building Society, under whose auspices new houses were built at the north end of Castle Street and Castle Gardens in Kirkcudbright. Other members of the Wigtown library included leading local landowners, the earl of Galloway and Sir William Maxwell of Monreith and his wife. There was just one other female subscriber, a Mrs Jean McKie. She, like several other Wigtown residents, was evidently an avid user of the library, unlike the landowners such as Galloway. (He appears never to have borrowed a single book, but then perhaps he didn't need to.) These libraries may have been patronised by the landed elites, but fundamentally they were an expression of the appetite for reading and wider cultural aspirations of an increasingly dynamic, self-confident urban middle class.

If Heron may have thus been impressed by the existence of such an institution in a burgh like Kirkcudbright, his comments on the relationship between the town elite and neighbouring gentry were similarly based on reality. Most famously, James Murray of Broughton and Cally lived in one of the High Street's finest eighteenth-century houses – Broughton House, now owned by the National Trust – becoming provost in 1750. Murray bought the house from a merchant and erstwhile provost, Thomas Mirrie, who seems to have altered or rebuilt an earlier dwelling on the site in the later 1730s. This story of evolution and modernisation in buildings, as we shall see later, was replicated along the High Street in this period.

However, in the later eighteenth and early nineteenth centuries, the key landed influence in, and on, Kirkcudbright were the earls of Selkirk, whose family seat, St Mary's Isle, lay just outside the town on a peninsula poking out southwards into Kirkcudbright Bay. The Douglases owned around five-sixths of the land in the local parish by value. One explanation for the record of improvement in the three decades leading up to 1820 was the constructive alliance forged between the Douglases and the town council from 1790; and one of the keys to this was Daer.

However, while Daer deserves much of the credit, it is certainly not all of his to claim. The roots of improvement in Kirkcudbright were deep ones, going back well into the early-Hanoverian period. The early activity focused on 'ruinous properties', presumably on the High Street, which the council began to take systematic action to remove and have replaced from the early 1720s, and better stewardship of one of its two main assets – the town lands.[67] (The other main source of income was rental from fisheries on the Dee.) As early as 1730, the council enclosed and divided the Meadows and the Borelands, imposing long, improving leases on tenants.[68] This care and effort to extract increasing benefit from its property was a near continuous theme in the Georgian history of the burgh. In 1787, the town's revenue was £333. By the 1810s, the burgh's rental income had climbed to around £1,000, although presumably this increase partly simply reflected the buoyancy of the rural economy during the Napoleonic wars.[69] Unlike in many other Scottish burghs, Kirkcudbright's governors were generally very reluctant to borrow to finance improvements; they also imposed no assessments on the towns-people. Rather, they relied, to a degree that was quite unusual, on raising funds by voluntary subscription. Debt increased in the early nineteenth century, but modestly; Kirkcudbright was a town, in short, which lived carefully within its means.

If signs of improvement are present, therefore, well before the accession of George III (1760), it was from the early 1760s that the local town council displayed a fairly continuous concern with enhancing the amenity, salubri-ousness and, on occasion, appearance of the town.[70] In the early 1760s, spring water was brought into the centre through a system of pipes. Another aspect of the water scheme was the construction of a forestair to the tolbooth that enclosed a lead water cistern, at the top of which was placed the Cross, which was removed from its previous position on the main street. At around the same time that the water scheme was conceived, it was decided to take action against butchers slaughtering cattle before their doors on the High Street, the ultimate aim being to construct a flesh market away from the street. An opportunity arose to expedite this aim in 1762 when several ruinous tenements behind the High Street were put up for sale. Construction only began, however, in 1769, being completed in the following year; a separate slaughterhouse followed a few years later, located at the south end of the flesh market. In 1770, ten street lamps were erected, a number which was doubled seventeen years later; Wigtown got its first public lamps in 1833, pretty late, therefore; Dumfries had got its first public lamps exactly a century earlier (1733). The condition of the streets, meanwhile, was enhanced by the covering of open drains and sewers, measures taken to ensure water ran off cleanly and easily away from the High Street, and in 1789 the widening and repaving of part of the High Street; house-owners in the east of the town were also to provide side pavements between their dwellings and the street, which might indicate that side pavements were already present to the west.

Similar steps to these were being taken in a growing number of other Scottish towns from the central decades of the eighteenth century.[71] Usually, however, these were towns that were larger and economically more dynamic than Kirkcudbright; places such as Dumfries, Perth, Stirling, Inverness, Dundee and Montrose. Montrose was in the vanguard, engaging in a major programme to modernise and 'beautify' its main streets from the mid-1730s. In the south-west, as already alluded to, Dumfries had been a centre of considerable activity at a relatively early stage, focused, as in Kirkcudbright, on the removal of ruinous properties from the main streets and the widening of several streets and entries. An initial impulse was the disastrous impact on the urban environment of several decades of economic decline and stagnation between the 1690s and 1720s, which is amply attested to by many petitions to the Convention of Royal Burghs, including from Kirkcudbright.[72] From, however, the mid eighteenth century the need for enhanced circulation around and through towns, created by the rise of wheeled transport and much greater movement of goods between and to and from towns, and between town and country, was a further powerful, ever strengthening incentive to change. At the same time, new expectations were taking hold regarding amenity and salubriousness, and there was growing intolerance of noisome activities that had previously occupied central spaces in the towns. A new flesh market was constructed behind the main streets in Dumfries at the end of the 1760s. Ayr got a new flesh market in the early 1750s, and street lamps several years before that. And so on. Kirkcudbright was thus unusual not in respect so much of what took place, but that it occurred in a burgh of very modest size and remote from areas of rapid manufacturing and urban growth. In most similar burghs and towns across Britain this kind of improvement had to wait until at least the early decades of the nineteenth century.

At the same time that concerted steps were being taken to enhance the amenity and efficiency of the Kirkcudbright townscape, there was appreciable modernisation of buildings in the High Street, as already referred to in the case of Broughton House. This entailed partial regularisation of the building line, some rebuilding and some new construction. How much and exactly when is hard to say. There is very little evidence to help us with this, although we do have a wonderful map drawn by local land-surveyor John Gilone in the 1790s, and of course the evidence of our own eyes. But buildings themselves can deceive as much as illuminate, given they have their own complex history of adaptation and evolution. Much of what we see today appears to date from the late eighteenth and early nineteenth centuries. Sasine records reveal some activity in the early nineteenth century, and closer inspection of these might show more. In 1813, for example, Alexander Melville purchased a ruinous tenement from the earl of Selkirk on the west side of the High Street, and built a new tenement there. Writer Robert Gordon did likewise in 1814, Blair House being built on this site in 1817, while Thomas Reid, a Baxter (ie baker) rebuilt a tenement on the east side of the street, also in 1813.[73] But if there was significant building and rebuilding in the opening years of the nineteenth century, this certainly does not preclude significant activity earlier. The Gilone map indicates regularity intermittently achieved in terms of building lines, a product very much of the way in which this must have occurred, building by building, or perhaps several at a time. What this also meant was that some parts were left unmodernised, such as the two houses on the southern side of the eastern limb of the High Street just above the town hall with their gables proudly, and in old fashioned style, facing the street, which were only removed in the 1890s. Robert Heron noted in the early 1790s that the houses in the town had slate roofs, which may indicate an earlier important phase of activity.[74] Slate roofs were one of a number of markers of a modern townscape – side pavements and street lighting, both referred to above, were others; another was the absence of middens from the front of houses, something which clung on in quite a few Scottish towns into the early nineteenth century, such as Adam Smith's home town of Kirkcaldy, together with the ages old and distinctively Scottish tradition of throwing rubbish and soiled water from the windows. Use of slates had a practical as well as aesthetic rationale; it reduced the fire risk that continued to haunt urban authorities in this period.

There is one further indicator of rebuilding or perhaps new building before the end of the eighteenth century. In 1770 the decision was taken by the council to remove the Meikle Yett, a gate which stood across the eastern end of the High Street, and which had been repaired at considerable cost as recently as 1739.[75] The ostensible reasons were to improve access along the street; the fact that it 'neither adds ornament or strength' to the town; but more importantly, in the present context, the encouragement this might give

to people to build 'decent houses' to the east of it. The catalyst was the intention of an individual to build a 'genteel house' on its north side, provided the
gate was removed.[76]

Modernisation of the exteriors of buildings was often matched, moreover,
with modernisation inside. What this meant, amongst other things, was the
emergence of dining and other reception rooms as distinctive spaces for
display and new forms of sociability within the home. Almost no detailed
inventories survive to offer us a glimpse inside the homes of the town's elite
on the High Street; but we do have one. This is for William McClure, draper
and merchant.[77] When this inventory was taken (in 1817) McClure was over
£6,000 in debt. His stock comprised drapery, ironmongery, jewellery and
perfumery goods of bewildering variety – umbrellas, shawls, scarves, caps
and bonnets, pins, powder puffs, spectacles, locks and so on – a further illus-
tration of how new, fashionable items were finding their way into the town
and its environs by this period. His house, which was almost certainly on the
eastern leg of the High Street, probably had eight main rooms, including a
parlour and drawing room. The latter was equipped with sofa, mahogany tea
tables, laburnum chairs, window curtains, backgammon table, mirrors, five
pictures, carpet and hearth rug. The parlour, which seems to have functioned
as the dining room, housed a two-ended mahogany dining table, smaller
mahogany table, sideboard, two arm and six rush-bottomed chairs. This
was evidently an amply furnished house – although obviously we can't say
anything about the quality of the furniture and fittings, or about when and
where they were bought – and one which was designed to enable frequent
displays of hospitality. In the storeroom was a good range of silver, two sets
of gilt and china cups and saucers, decanters, wine glasses and plated candle-
sticks. The evidence, such as it is, appears thus to bear out Heron's impression that Kirkcudbright's urban notables lived in a style and manner which
was quite similar to local landowners. In terms of their horizons and lifestyle
there was probably very little to separate these groups. More importantly the
urban elite were more than capable of protecting and directing their own
fortunes and those of their town.

Prior to 1790 improvement was very largely confined, as we have seen,
to enhancing the amenity and appearance of the existing public street, and
several smaller passages leading off it.[78] It was a process that was the collective achievement of what was a prospering, culturally quite sophisticated,
outward looking urban elite. It was prudently managed, so as not to load
a large and difficult burden of debt on to the council. Consistent with this,
the only new public building, apart from the flesh market, was a county and

town hall, first mooted in 1774, but finally agreed between town council and commissioners of supply in 1787. This was built on the north side of the High Street to the east of the Cross. Daer's first involvement with the town may well have been as one of the commissioners of supply who reached agreement with the council on the new building; certainly it's the first which has left a record.

The early 1790s, however, marked the beginnings of a new phase in the history of improvement in Kirkcudbright; and the inspiration behind this, at least initially, seems to have been Daer. Admitted a burgess in March 1789, he was elected as councillor and then provost in October of the following year. A year later he was again elected provost. He continued to sit on the council in 1792, although no longer as provost, and in 1794, just before his death, he was elected as a baillie.

Just how or why he came to be on the council is not entirely clear, although it was related to fractious divisions among the councillors, which came to a head in the general election of 1790 and which led to legal action being taken in the Court of Session.[79] It may also have been related to Selkirk's electoral activities within the region, as he sought to reactivate his electoral interests (a move discussed elsewhere in this book). However he came to be there, Daer's popularity within the town was striking. When he was provost, the General Trades, in return for the 'attention' he had shown the incorporated trades, resolved to present a letter or address to Daer expressing their gratitude. What that attention was the relevant minute does not say. On news of his death, in 1794, his successor as provost, James Dalyell, another merchant with a house on the High Street, immediately had the magistrates' seats, the pulpit and precentor's desk in the Kirk covered in black cloth as a mark of the community's respect for Daer. At its next meeting, the council formally expressed their 'great grief' at the news and the 'great loss' which the burgh had sustained by Daer's death. They also officially recorded in the council minutes the 'sincere respect they and all the community justly have for his lordship's memory'.

Dinners and the like to mark the birthdays or coming of age of major local landowners were quite frequent in urban Scotland in this period. On occasion, portraits might even be commissioned of the local big-wig to hang in the council chamber; Dumfries, for example, had a portrait done in 1769 of Charles, third duke of Queensberry, which when finished was hung with portraits of William and Mary in the town house. At such a distance from the events, it is hard to know what they really tell us. At other moments, councils might well be fighting in the Court of Session to protect their rights

and privileges from encroachment by the same individual.[80] Buttering up
the local landowner might of course have a strategic motivation; you did it
because you needed his goodwill, patronage and support. However, in the
case of Daer and Kirkcudbright the emotion seems genuine and without
ulterior motive. Daer long remained very fondly remembered in the town.[81]

So why? The simple answer is that he brought to his role as provost and
member of the council his characteristic improving vision and indefatigable
energy. Already before his election as provost, he was promoting new attention to development of Kirkcudbright's harbour, which involved a successful
appeal to the Convention of Royal Burghs for financial support. In the event
the project stalled, for a variety of reasons, including being connected with
the issue of building a bridge over the Dee. Thomas Telford would survey the
harbour in 1801, while work only eventually went ahead from 1817; but this
was hardly Daer's fault.[82] At the same time, he came up with plans for a major
reconfiguration of the town through the construction of several new streets,
starting with Castle Street. This emerged as an alternative to previous plans
by the council for building on the route to St Mary's Isle, opposed by the earl
of Selkirk and Daer. It was a typically bold and indeed felicitous scheme.[83] It
may just also have involved a bit more than was eventually developed, in that
a later entry in the town council minutes (from 1814) seems to suggest there
had been a plan for a square at one end of the new street, which was, in the
event, not proceeded with. (This is very plausible since squares were important features of many a new town plan in this period.) He sought to alter
and straighten the line of several roads, compensating the town for loss of
property involved through exchanges from his father's lands, or purchasing
property to enable new roads to follow the optimum lines expecting only
moderate compensation from the council for his costs. He also appears to
have planned various other exchanges of property with the council. The goal
here was rationalisation and straightening of boundaries between Selkirk
and town-owned land. This was again a relatively common enterprise in this
period, as consultation of the minute books of any number of other towns
might show. In Selkirk in the borders, for example, there was a good deal of
this kind of activity at around this time, while in Irvine in Ayrshire the town
council and earl of Eglintoun, the dominant local landowner, engaged in a
round of exchanges of property to achieve exactly this end.

As far as Kirkcudbright is concerned, however, all this activity inaugurated a twenty-year period of intensified and sustained improvement to the
town. This included the creation of Castle and Union streets, St Cuthbert's
and St Mary's Street, the last following the new route to Tongland; construc-

tion of an embankment along the river Dee; a major programme of repaving and levelling of the burgh's streets; and concerted measures to improve their cleanliness. Daer's younger brothers, John and Thomas, later the fifth earl, followed him onto the council in 1795, and Thomas, as earl, would donate the land for new seminaries in 1815, as well as being the key influence behind the construction of a new gaol and court house in the town in 1815–16. A few years before that Thomas would also give land free of charge for the creation of Union Street.

This is not the place to describe in great detail the development of Kirkcudbright in the years that followed Daer's death. Daer's legacy was a very positive one, and was built on with care. Some aspects of this have been referred to above. Perhaps the most striking and important, however, were the further development of Castle Street, the laying out of Union Street from 1808 and the construction of housing along St Mary's and St Cuthbert's Streets. The arresting elements of this were, firstly, the careful control over building that was exerted by the council and the earl of Selkirk, who had bought up property to enable the laying out of the new streets. One means, as elsewhere in urban Scotland in this period (such as in Dumfries's new town in the early 1790s), were the terms under which ground was feued for building. In 1810, for example, when it came to building along the east side of St Mary's Street, the houses were to be built in a straight line; the front houses were all to have sash windows; to be 'well roofed and covered with slate; to be of two storeys of similar height; lintels were to be of freestone or dressed granite; there were to be no forestairs to the front, and no dunghills or other nuisances to remain 'on any account'; the feuars were also to make a pavement of ten feet on the front of their plot, and keep this clean. In 1814, when development had turned to the west side of St Mary's Street and the west side of St Cuthbert's Street, the conditions were almost the same. None of the houses in front, the council decreed, 'should be used as Barns, Byres, Smithys, Tanneries, Soap and Candle Houses, Breweries, or other hazardous manufacturing Houses, or other creating a Nuisance but that all the said Houses should be used as Dwelling Houses, Shops, or warehouses.' When the earl of Selkirk disposed to John McClellan property in 1793 to build the first house on the south-east corner of Castle Street, the conditions were again very similar. The goal was a townscape of modest appearance, but one of regularity and free of the kinds of disamenities common to many other towns in Scotland and the rest of Britain in this period.

Secondly, and perhaps as notable, most of the new building was done under the management of two co-operative building societies, the so-called

Old Building Society, referred to earlier, founded in 1807 and the Kirkcud-bright New Building Society formed three years after that.[84] This is the only example in Scotland of such societies in this period that I have come across, although they were more common south of the border. Partly, this may be explicable in terms of size and local culture, the fact that this was occurring in a small town; but it was also a town that appears to have had the happy capacity to organise very effectively around collective goals, as demonstrated by its record of improvement in the Georgian period. As the Rev. Mackenzie would declare at the beginning of the 1840s: 'Kirkcudbright [. . .] has always shown a laudable anxiety to be the foremost in the career of improvement.'[85] The existence of the two building societies was symptomatic of this.

Towards the end of the 1810s, one commentator observed:

> Kirkcudbright has been vastly improved during the last 30 years. The streets, which are well paved and lighted, intersect each other at right angles. The houses are generally two stories high; and although those in the new streets, built by the societies, have a somewhat monotonous appearance, they are all neat, clean and comfortable. There is no alternation of stately edifices and miserable hovels; but the general aspect of the whole town bespeaks at once the good taste and easy circumstances of the greater proportion of its inhabit-ants.[86]

So it did – something that can still be seen today. It also reflected, neverthe-less, as do many roads and groups of trees in the region, the influence of Lord Daer and (in fairness it should be acknowledged) that of his younger brother, Thomas, who, following the early deaths of Daer and his other older brothers was left to implement many of Daer's far-reaching plans.

CHAPTER FIVE

The Politics of 'North Britain'

Bruce Lenman describes eighteenth-century Scotland as 'a machine politician's paradise', with good reason.[1] The 'formal' Scottish political nation, by which we mean essentially that part of it which was able to vote at elections, was tiny. At the 1774 general election, the electorate may have numbered no more than 478 people, 428 county and just fifty burgh electors. Fourteen years later (in 1788), the county electorate numbered 2,662, ranging from a mere twelve in Bute to, at the other end of the range, 205 in Ayr, politically the most independent of the Scottish counties. By contrast, the largest county 'voterate' in England was Yorkshire with its 20,000 voters, while even the smaller English counties boasted around 3,000 voters at any given election. Even allowing for the fact that many English county voters did not get to vote – because elections could be vastly costly and thus increasingly went uncontested in the eighteenth century – the disparity was stark. By the early part of the following century, moreover, approaching half of all Scottish county electors were so-called 'fictitious' or 'nominal' voters – those in other words who did not possess the real property on which the vote was based – whose increase, particularly during the 1774 and in subsequent elections, was symptomatic of rampant electoral manipulation. 'A mere mockery upon the name or idea,' was one prominent English parliamentary reformer's curt verdict on the Scottish 'system of representation.'[2]

Most constituencies were, moreover, dominated by a small group of families or a single magnate; and Henry Dundas's political empire in the later eighteenth century was built in part on creating alliances and reconciling differences between the great Scottish magnate interests.[3] What bound the system together was pursuit of factional and personal advantage, which is why, with notably few exceptions, Scots MPs supported whoever was in power; MPs were expected to promote the interests of their constituents, usually in the form of jobs and similar kinds of advancement, and this required ministerial support. John Shaw has even written about the 'trivializing' of Scottish politics in this period, in reference to its narrow preoccupation with issues of personal and factional interest.[4] He attributes this to Scotland's politically subordinate condition after 1707 and the crucial importance of patronage and connection in the construction of political interests and influence. Even those who prospered in this world could on occasion express distaste for it, although mostly this was pure rhetorical camouflage.

Some would say that this, however, is entirely to miss the point – or rather that these features *were* the point. For this was a system that reflected and perpetuated the overwhelming social and political dominance and prestige of the great landowners; that was the reason for its existence and why it persisted.[5] Another of its features is also sometimes overlooked; namely, despite its susceptibility to control, it could confer considerable leverage on people such as the small mercantile oligarchies that ran the burgh councils or county electors. These individuals had a keen sense of their price and they could bargain hard.[6] Nor were 'great folk' always afforded much respect, as the third duke of Queensberry discovered on an electioneering visit to the tiny burgh of Lochmaben in Dumfriesshire in 1789. As Sir William Maxwell reported to the third duke of Buccleuch:

> The Duke [of Queensberry] I am told has been indefatigable in his canvas for the Boroughs, and yet, as I am informed, he is by no means certain of success – He was insulted by the Mob at Lochmaben when he dined there on the 7th of this month – Several stones were thrown into his carriage on his leaving the Town, and he was <hissed &c> and abused in a most shameful manner.[7]

Landed dominance of the political system did not mean the interests and views of urban elites and wider county communities could simply be taken for granted, which is what gave it much of its resilience and flexibility. What is perhaps more debatable is how often these interests were about much more than personal or local advantage.

If dynastic and personal ambition, pursuit of patronage and landed supremacy were, therefore, prominent features of the contemporary political landscape, there were, nevertheless, some important shifts occurring in Scottish political life in the later eighteenth century. Many of these involved, in different ways, growing assimilation with English politics and political divisions. This was partly the product of the slow, continuous operation of broad factors – the impact of a relatively free and increasingly politically mature and powerful press, and the widening importance of Westminster and British parliamentary legislation for different parts of and groups within Scottish society. But it was also being driven by Scots themselves pursuing fuller integration into British political life or what they understood to be 'English' liberties. The 1780s were an important decade in this context, one in which these patterns became much more clearly visible. Daer and his father were, as we will see later, drawn increasingly into this process, and this was another key moment in Daer's political journey.

Convergence, however, did not mean the eradication of difference. This reflected, in turn, distinctive national social and cultural features – the facts that Scotland in *c.* 1780 remained considerably less urbanised than England and Wales (although its towns and cities were beginning to grow at unexampled rates in a European context) and that its social hierarchies and order were differently constituted in urban and in rural society, both in the Lowlands and Highlands. Such differences could be an obstacle, amongst other things, to a common British fiscal policy, as the likely burden of proposed new taxes in the later eighteenth century might fall differently north of the border, and Scots MPs of the time were forced to spend increasing amounts of time seeking to explain these facts to ministers and their fellow MPs in London.

Another key source of difference was religion, and this was probably the one that consistently struck most contemporaries, although there were many others. The enthusiasm, especially in and around Glasgow and Paisley, but spreading much more widely, including to Edinburgh, for Lord George Gordon had few parallels elsewhere in the British Isles. Briefly between 1779 and 1781, Gordon became the hero of the anti-popery cause as he led the campaign, first, to prevent the extension of the Catholic Relief Act of 1778 to Scotland, and, then, to secure its repeal at Westminster in 1780. The sheer intensity of Gordon's popularity north of the border – the 'abundance of Enthusiast zeal & fury' – was distinctive, and profoundly unsettling to the Scottish elites. Thomas Miller, the Lord Justice Clerk, diagnosed a crisis of order and control in 1779 created by the upsurge of anti-Catholic sentiment and the limits of the coercive power at the disposal of the authorities, a fear that he returned to in 1781 during renewed concerns about the state of popular opinion during Gordon's trial in London.[8] Gordon's politics and that of his supporters can, nevertheless, be viewed as Scotto-British in at least two senses. Firstly, there were important links between the Protestant societies of the west of Scotland and leading anti-Catholic politicians in

London, such as the City of London Alderman, Frederick Bull.[9] Secondly, Gordon's supporters appealed to a 'British' Protestant identity that was first and foremost anti-popish, and sought (unsuccessfully) to have this reaffirmed as the official position of the British state.[10] There was more than an echo here of earlier Scots Presbyterian *British* ambitions; the idea that it was the duty of the Presbyterian Scot, inherited from the mid seventeenth century and the Solemn League and Covenant of 1643 – the agreement of Scottish Presbyterians with the then Long Parliament at Westminster to extend Presbyterian church government to the whole of the British Isles – to spread the true reformation throughout Britain. Opposition to patronage in the Church of Scotland – the system whereby landed patrons, the crown, or sometimes town councils controlled the selection of ministers – was also, as a contemporary memorial to government frankly acknowledged, 'The point on which the common People [. . .] are maddest'.[11] The early 1780s saw the rise of a popular campaign to repeal the Patronage Act of 1712, which restored patronage in the Church of Scotland after its abolition in 1690, that came to a head in 1784, when the General Assembly of the Church of Scotland, prompted by an anxious William Robertson as moderator, narrowly rejected a motion to petition parliament for repeal. The anti-patronage campaign persisted, nevertheless, although much of its energy and leadership was drawn into the cause of burgh reform after 1783. At a local level opposition to the imposition of ministers remained a very common source of tension and protest, and within very different sorts of communities.

Nor is it a straightforward matter to judge how significant was the convergence with politics and political culture south of the border. There were moments earlier in the eighteenth century when Scottish political divisions and rivalries became temporarily aligned with party divisions at Westminster – as happened in the mid-1730s or at the end of Sir Robert Walpole's ministry. From certain perspectives, moreover, what convergence did occur can appear to be fairly superficial. The deeper structures of political life remained those of personal and factional rivalry or a narrowly custodial form of politics identified pre-eminently with Henry Dundas – 'Harry the Ninth' as James Boswell dubbed him in 1785[12] – and resistance to this. The pattern could be repeated at the local level, where old rivalries rumbled on, for example, between the duke of Atholl and earl of Breadalbane in Perthshire. From a longer-term perspective, nevertheless, the 1780s mark an important moment of change, and one that has considerable significance not just for our understanding of what led Daer and his father into involvement in national political life, but for the shape and contours of modern British political history.

The first part, therefore, of the rest of this chapter explores this theme of assimilation and difference in greater depth so as to put in its proper context the growing engagement of Daer and his father in the politics of 'British liberty' at the end of the 1780s. In the second part, we pick up again the trail of Selkirk and Daer as they took up the cause of 'British liberty' in the form of a campaign that began by promoting reform of the elections of the sixteen Scottish representative peers.

The existence in British political life in the later eighteenth century of persistent national divergences, but also creeping areas of convergence, emerges very clearly when we consider the impact on Scotland and the rest of the British Isles of the War of American Independence (1775–1783). In England and Ireland, this war – the only major one in which Britain was defeated in the eighteenth century – was not only politically very divisive, but acted as a major force deepening the politicisation of wider public opinion in the later eighteenth century. This was first evident in a series of widespread campaigns of petitions and addresses in 1775, either in support of war or calling for conciliation with the colonists. In England, British failures and vulnerabilities in the war, together with the rising financial costs and economic impact of the conflict, catalysed the emergence in late 1779 of the Association Movement, which first took shape among the spikily conservative, but also notably independent Yorkshire gentry.[13] You may recall that Yorkshire boasted the largest number of electors of any English county in this period; and its contests were regularly seen as bellwethers for the national mood. Beginning as a protest against supposed government malfeasance and inefficiency, to which failure in the war and accompanying economic strains were attributed, the campaign broadened from pursuit of so-called 'economical reform' – measures to reduce corruption and increase efficiency and economy in government – to encompass parliamentary reform. Very quickly reaching the peak of its influence in terms of wider, national support, the movement fairly rapidly lost momentum over the next few years as the task of holding together its disparate elements proved insurmountable, and as the confidence of public opinion in the country's political institutions, leadership and prospects revived. The latter was a process aided by Admiral Rodney's victory at the Battle of the Saintes in April 1782, the failure of the French and Spanish to take Gibraltar – the siege was finally lifted in February 1783 – and, even more so, the emergence of the youthful, untried and thus untainted William Pitt as the figurehead for a politics of national revival. The Association Movement had been born, as the Rev. Christopher Wyvill expressed it in retrospect, 'in times of national distress and alarm'; but the sense of national anxiety dissipated fairly fast, and, despite the loss of America, many English people were able to persuade themselves that the war had not been so much a *military* as a *political* defeat, and that the Americans would, in any case, quickly come to regret their independence and novel republican form of government.[14] In Ireland, meanwhile, in addition to being divisive, the war presented new political opportunities that were keenly grasped by Patriot politicians and their supporters, particularly in Ulster and Leinster.[15] The Patriots sought the elimination or at least drastic lessening of English influence and what they saw as 'corruption' over Irish politics, and the removal of Ireland's politically subordinate status. The rise of the volunteers from 1778 – a civilian defence force necessitated by the removal of regular troops to fight in North America – provided the raw political muscle for a series of Patriot-inspired campaigns, at the same time serving to deepen and widen the politicisation of Irish society.[16] In 1779, the Patriots achieved their first goal, that of so-called 'free trade' – really nothing of the sort, but instead equal access to British imperial markets and imperial trade – while in 1782 the fall of the North ministry created the opportunity for Henry Grattan, the Patriots' leader, to secure parliamentary independence from the new ministry in London, now lacking the capacity to resist. With this latter goal attained, the focus of many of the Irish Patriots turned, almost inevitably, to parliamentary reform in 1783–4, although this served simply to expose the underlying tensions that existed within their ranks, and the new campaign also stumbled in face of the issue that increasingly overshadowed Irish politics in the later eighteenth century – the Catholic question, and whether the vote should be extended to the majority population, and if so, what part of it.[17]

While these movements in England and Ireland remained distinct, there were inter-connections between them, both rhetorically and ideologically.[18] They also began to look to one another for guidance and support. On the English side, key figures in this development were Wyvill, the leader of the Yorkshire Association Movement and master strategist behind the wider national English reform movement in the early 1780s, and the rational dissenter and advanced metropolitan radical, John Jebb. Wyvill and Jebb were among six English and Welsh radicals – the others were John Cartwright, Lord Effingham, Richard Price and Thomas Northcote – written to by the Belfast Committee of Correspondence on behalf of Ulster's volunteers for their responses to a series of queries about the desirable scope and nature of reform of the Dublin parliament.[19] Jebb especially, who had family ties in Ireland, had several Irish correspondents in the early 1780s, notably Francis Dobbs, John Forbes and the Belfast radical, Henry Joy.[20] In early 1781, Jebb moved a motion at the Westminster Committee – the key radical body in Westminster – in support of Irish free trade and parliamentary independence, although this was defeated by the influence of the Rockingham Whigs, the party of which Burke was an important member and ideologue.[21] Jebb seems to have come to believe by the mid-1780s that the causes of reform in Ireland and Britain were interdependent; defeat for the cause of liberty in Ireland would mean the eventual extinction of liberty in England.[22]

Wyvill, who was born in Edinburgh, also took steps from late 1782 to develop links with Scottish county and burgh reformers, as part of the same broad impulse towards communication with reformers elsewhere in the British Isles. Already in the spring of 1781 the Yorkshire reformers had made contact with the earl of Buchan, presumably because of his very public advocacy of freedom of election in the Scottish peerage elections (of which, more later).[23] It was to Buchan, and to Gilbert Stuart, the testy, rather intemperate opposition Whig writer, journalist and historian, that Wyvill wrote in late November 1782 declaring that the Yorkshire committee wished very much to make contact with the Edinburgh committee on the matter of 'parliamentary abuses' as part of their preparation for a full meeting in December to frame a general proposal for reform, which would include reform of Scottish county elections.[24] John Campbell from Stirling began corresponding with Wyvill at about this time, while from Edinburgh Thomas McGrugar did likewise from the following year.[25] The Kirkcudbright burgh reformers made contact with Wyvill and the Yorkshire reformers early in 1783.[26] A further likely point of contact was Thomas Dundas, the MP for Stirlingshire, who had family links with the marquis of Rockingham and Yorkshire, and was emerging as something of a figurehead for a developing opposition Whig interest in Scotland. He was also very active in Scottish reform circles and in defending Scottish interests at Westminster.

McGrugar and the Edinburgh burgh reformers remained in touch with Wyvill at least until the end of 1784. McGrugar was clearly persuaded of the advantages of this connection. As he declared to the earl of Buchan in June 1783: '*It is to the English we look chiefly for support*, who (as your L[ords[hip has observed) will certainly esteem a people who begin to sympathise w[i]t[h] them in the assertion of their liberties.'[27] Wyvill's plans for moderate parliamentary reform in the 1790s would always include a Scottish component, but much more significant in the present context is that McGrugar was probably the first to articulate the notion of a *British* – rather than purely English or Scottish – reform convention – and it is likely that his commitment to a convention as a key vehicle for pursuing Scottish burgh reform was partly inspired by Wyvill's Association movement, although a more immediate model was provided by the Scottish county reformers.[28] Conventions, composed of delegates from reform associations, and which might boast more or less impressive credentials as embodiments of 'public opinion' or the 'political nation', were, alongside petitioning, the chosen vehicle for expediting political reform in the later Georgian era.

The Anglo-Scottish reforming connections referred to above might appear to be mainly opportunistic, and so they were to a degree. McGrugar, the author of the famous 'Zeno letters' in the Edinburgh press which inaugurated the burgh reform campaign nationally, as well as being in communication with Wyvill, wrote to Richard Price, the Welsh Dissenting radical, in 1784 informing him of the activities of the Edinburgh reformers. Price's response, which was published in the *Edinburgh Advertiser* and several other periodicals, more than anything betrays how remote Scotland was from the thinking and horizons of many (probably most) metropolitan radicals.[29] While welcoming news of the Scots reformers, Price showed no real understanding of their condition or the conditions of Scottish politics; but rather responded with some characteristically high-flown rhetoric about the cause of liberty:

> God grant that this spirit [or resistance to tyranny] may increase till it has abolished all despotic government, and exterminated that slavery which debases mankind. The spirit first rose in America. – It has soon reached Ireland. – It has diffused itself into some foreign countries; and your letter informs me, that it is now animating Scotland.

It was Price's very indifference to the particularities of Scottish politics that stands out. His letter offered in truth nothing other than a succession of generalities. He even seems to have been surprised about the facts related to him by McGrugar about the political circumstances of the burghs: 'From the accounts you have sent me, I learn, that, in *Scotland*, the state of the representation is *worse* than in *England*; and that the body of the people, particularly in the *Royal Burghs*, do not enjoy the *shadow of liberty*.' Advanced English reformers and radicals quite frequently combined profound English patriotism and an equally strong commitment to cosmopolitanism; this was, for example, true of Jebb. While this did not necessarily lead them to anti-Scottish views, anti-Scottish prejudices often lurked within the minds of English radicals and opposition Whigs. The earl of Shelburne, of whose Bowood Circle Price was a member, informed him on one occasion that Scotland was 'composed of such a sad set of innate, cold hearted, impudent rogues that I sometimes think it a comfort when you and I shall be able to walk together in the next world [...] we cannot possibly then have any of them sticking to our skirts.'[30] The view of the grasping Scot as a ready tool for corrupt government was one that was deeply entrenched south of the border.

Within English radical circles, ignorance about Scottish political conditions and anti-Scottish prejudice began to be tackled by the Society for Constitutional Information [SCI], the metropolitan radical society founded in April 1780 by Major John Cartwright and other advanced metropolitan radicals, including Jebb and Price. This had the aim of diffusing knowledge of the 'lost rights' of the public at large, including 'even [...] into the humble dwelling of the cottager', as a preliminary to restoring the 'Freedom and Independence' of the Commons.[31] It was the indomitable Jebb who may well have been responsible for the new focus on Scotland in some SCI propaganda by the mid-1780s. He it was who inserted an extract from *An Historical Account of the Ancient Rights of the Parliament of Scotland* (1703) in the Society's collection of tracts, declaring, 'It has been, too much, the custom to represent the inhabitants of a neighbouring kingdom [Scotland], as friendly to despotism, as insensible to the genuine feelings of patriotism [...] The following quotation and authorities [...] speak the sense of free parliaments and a gallant people.'[32] Elsewhere, he claimed that Scotland had been the 'scourge of tyrannical power in many a former generation'. By the summer of 1784, he was hoping that the 'Celtic regions' might take the lead on reform. On 20 July 1784, he wrote 'A Letter to the Secretary of the Society for Constitutional Information', which urged Englishmen to arm themselves and agitate for parliamentary reform, and pointed to patriotic support for 'free parliaments' among the 'gallant people' of Scotland. The society's third address was, perhaps significantly, entitled 'to the People of Great Britain and Ireland', and included the rallying call: 'At what former period of our exertions were the people of England so strongly supported by the voice of their brethren in Scotland and Ireland.'[33] This new emphasis on Scotland and Ireland was, however, symptomatic of the increasingly obvious weaknesses of the English reform cause by 1783–4. It is also fair to say that it remained a fairly minor element of the English radical platform.

Nor is it at all clear that Scots reformers saw themselves principally as part of a wider British reform cause; or, if they did it was only ambiguously so. On the one hand, there were clearly those who, however momentarily, viewed the cause of liberty as an interconnected one. Scottish newspapers contained plenty of information on and reportage of the reform movements in the rest of the British Isles. This was true for Ireland, the politics of which was closely followed by most Scots newspapers in the 1780s. There was, for example, plenty of coverage of the famous Irish Volunteer conventions at Dungannon, County Tyrone in 1782 and 1783, which had galvanised, respectively, the final assault on legislative subordination and the new campaign for Irish parliamentary reform, while sections on 'Irish parliamentary intelligence' became regular features of many papers from the later 1770s.[34] In at least one paper, moreover, James Donaldson's *Edinburgh Advertiser*, the Scottish reform cause was explicitly portrayed as part of a wider politics of liberty. In February 1783, a letter to the paper declared:

> The present moment, big with the fate of Liberty, should be grasped at, and improved. Our brethren in Ireland, and in America, just emerging into freedom and independence: those in England, beginning to say to the legislature, 'Give us our rights, restore to us our ancient privileges, which our ancestors purchased for us with their dearest blood'; shall Scotland, once so renowned for her firm attachment to the cause of Liberty, be the only place in the British Empire which will meekly crouch down until the yoke of slavery be so firmly wreathed about her neck, as that nothing will be left for her to do, but to drag her chains of infamy about her to the end of her existence?[35]

The same paper reprinted in its pages the letters of both the duke of Richmond and Richard Price to the Volunteers of Ireland.[36] The *Edinburgh Advertiser*, together with its Glasgow namesake, founded in 1783 by John Mennons, was the strongest supporter of reform within the Scottish press. More concretely, Scots burgh reformers recognised that their fortunes were heavily dependent on the vagaries of Westminster politics. Thus, they followed intently the fate of Pitt's reform bills of 1783 and 1785, the failures of which were interpreted as serious setbacks, although several voices in 1783 sought to counsel against the idea that they and the burgh reform cause were one and the same.[37] Again, one might view this as basically pragmatic: support at Westminster, whether from Pitt or the opposition Whigs, was key to their success (or lack thereof), as they were acutely aware in the later 1780s as they sought to navigate the treacherous waters of Westminster political rivalries and divisions. It went deeper than this, however; for it was indicative of how political debates and battles north of the border were increasingly refracted through a prism of Westminster politics.

Newspapers, which were steadily expanding in influence in Scottish society in the final third of the eighteenth century, were a very significant factor in this. English papers, especially metropolitan ones, were in the later eighteenth century circulating north of the border in ever-increasing volumes, a development facilitated by the increasingly quick and efficient postal service, the unintended effects of the Franking Act of 1764, which enabled MPs to send written orders to the Post Office allowing free mass delivery of newspapers in their names, and the streamlining of the systems for ordering them with the emergence of metropolitan newsagents who specialised in exporting London newspapers to the provinces.[38] The growth from the 1780s of subscription and commercial reading rooms in most of the larger towns – the grand Glasgow tontine coffee room led the way in this context – and quite a few smaller ones – Rothesay in Bute, for example, or Stranraer – ensured the wider availability of not just the metropolitan press, but English provincial, Irish and Scottish papers as well. The significance of this is reinforced by the fact that by the 1780s battles and debates at Westminster dominated the reporting of the Scottish and English press in a way that had not been the case earlier; for the very good reason that before 1771 the Commons had remained willing and able to defend its privileges over the reporting of its proceedings. From the early 1770s, however, with the Commons and then the Lords relinquishing these in the face of intense political and commercial pressures to do so, coverage of the major parliamentary debates came to occupy a remarkable number of newspaper column inches. Scottish newspapers, like newspapers across Britain, competed to bring the fullest, most accurate and speediest coverage of parliamentary debates to their readers.[39] When parliament was in session, the reports of the debates squeezed other coverage from their pages. The Scottish papers also increasingly had their own sources of information and news in London, who regularly reported back on events at Westminster, including the voting of Scots MPs and the fortunes of legislation with a particular Scottish interest or dimension.[40] By the 1780s, lists of how Scots MPs voted on the important political questions at Westminster were becoming a much more common feature of reporting.[41]

Quite how far party divisions at Westminster were coming to shape and influence Scottish political debate was revealed in 1783–4, when several Scots burghs and counties got drawn into battles and arguments over the issue of whether to address George III in support of his dismissal of the Fox–North coalition and dissolution of Parliament elected in 1780 with its majority opposed to Pitt. This was a political and constitutional crisis of the first order, and it served to divide very starkly many contemporaries. And, while focused undoubtedly on constitutional issues – whether George III's actions in using the Lords to defeat Fox's East India bill were consistent with liberty and whether his right to choose his ministers trumped the rights

Above. Professor Dugald Stewart. By Sir David Wilkie, chalk on paper, 1824. Lord Daer was one of the influential moral philosopher's first boarding pupils at the University of Edinburgh. [By permission of the Scottish National Portrait Gallery]

Left. Sir James Hall of Dunglass. By Angelica Kauffmann, oil on canvas, 1785. This portrait of Daer's close friend, and from 1786 his brother-in-law, was painted in Rome when Hall was travelling in Europe following a period of study at the University of Edinburgh, where Daer and he almost certainly met for the first time, probably in 1782. Hall and Daer shared an intense curiosity about the world and very lively, wide ranging intelligences. [By permission of the Scottish National Portrait Gallery]

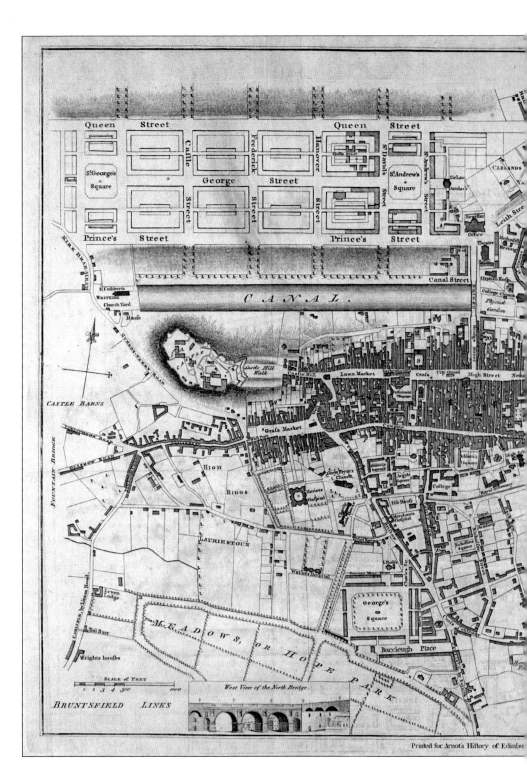

Queen Street

St. George's Square

Church

Castle Street

Frederick Street

George Street

Hanover Street

St. David's Street

St. Andrew's Square

Queen Street

St. Andrew's Street

Register Office

CLELANDS

Leith Street

Prince's Street

Prince's Street

Canal Street

KIRK BRAE HEAD

St. Cuthberts WESTKIRK Church Yard

Manse

Bridge Street

Theatre
Methodist Meeting

Orphan Hosp.

College Church

Physick Garden

C A N A L.

QUEENSFERRY ROAD

Castle Hill Walk

Castle Hill

Lawn Market

Cross

City Guard

High Street

Nether

CASTLE BARNS

GLASGOW ROAD

Grass Market

Grey Friars Church

Heriots Hospital

Parliament House

Brown's Square

Mint's Square

College

Argyle Square

Royal Infirmary

FOUNTAIN BRIDGE

HIGH

RIGGS

LAURIESTOUN

Watson's Hospital

Fife House

Merchants Hospital

Bristo Row

George Square

St. Hogs

Charles Str.

Nicolson's Square

Leven Lodge

Toll Barr

Wrights houses

CAUSEWAY by Linton Road.

M E A D O W S,   O R   H O P E   P A R K

George's Square

Buccleugh Place

SCALE OF FEET
1 2 3 4 500   1000

West View of the North Bridge.

B R U N T S F I E L D   L I N K S

Printed for Arnot's History of Edinbu

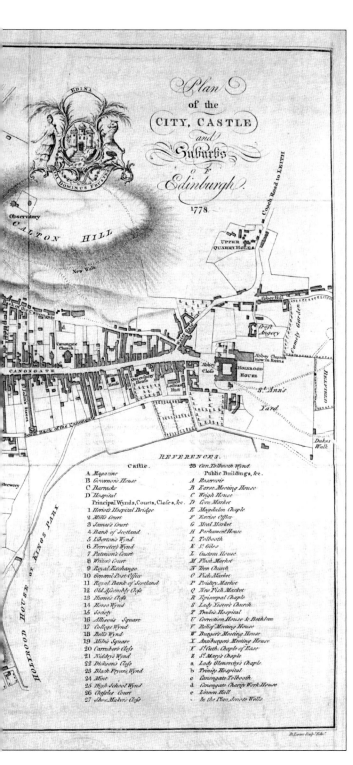

Plan of the City, Castle and Suburbs of Edinburgh, 1778. From Hugo Arnot, *History of Edinburgh* (1788 edn). [By permission of the National Library of Scotland]

Plan
of the
CITY, CASTLE
and
Suburbs
of
Edinburgh.

1778.

Coach Road to LEITH

Observatory

CALTON HILL

New Walk

UPPER
QUARRY HOLES

Abbey Hill

Croft
Angery

Canongate
Church

Abbey Church
now in Ruins

Countey Garden

CANONGATE

Abbey
Close

HOLYROOD
HOUSE

St Ann's

HOLYROOD

South Back of the Canongate

Yard

Dukes
Walk

Brewery

HOLYROOD HOUSE or KING'S PARK

REFERENCES.

Castle.

A Magazine
B Governors House
C Barracks
D Hospital
Principal Wynds, Courts, Closes, &c.
1 Heriots Hospital Bridge
2 Mills Court
3 James's Court
4 Bank of Scotland
5 Libertons Wynd
6 Forresters Wynd
7 Patersons Court
8 Writers Court
9 Royal Exchange
10 General Post Office
11 Royal Bank of Scotland
12 Old Assembly Close
13 Hume's Close
14 Horse Wynd
15 Society
16 Mison's Square
17 College Wynd
18 Bells Wynd
19 Milns Square
20 Carrubers Close
21 Niddry's Wynd
22 Dickson's Close
23 Black Fryars Wynd
24 Mint
25 High School Wynd
26 Chessels Court
27 Shoe Makers Close

28 Can Tolbooth Wynd
Public Buildings, &c.
A Reservoir
B Earse Meeting House
C Weigh House
D Corn Market
E Magdalen Chaple
F Excise Office
G Meal Market
H Parliament House
I Tolbooth
K St Giles
L Custom House
M Flesh Market
N Tron Church
O Fish Market
P Poultry Market
Q New Fish Market
R Episcopal Chaple
S Lady Yesters Church
T Trades Hospital
U Correction House & Bethlem
V Relief Meeting House
W Burgers Meeting House
X Antiburgers Meeting House
Y St Cuth. Chaple of Ease
Z St Mary's Chaple
a Lady Glenorchy's Chaple
b Trinity Hospital
c Canongate Tolbooth
d Canongate Charity Work House
e Linnen Hall
· In the Plan denote Wells

D. Lizars Sculp. Edinr.

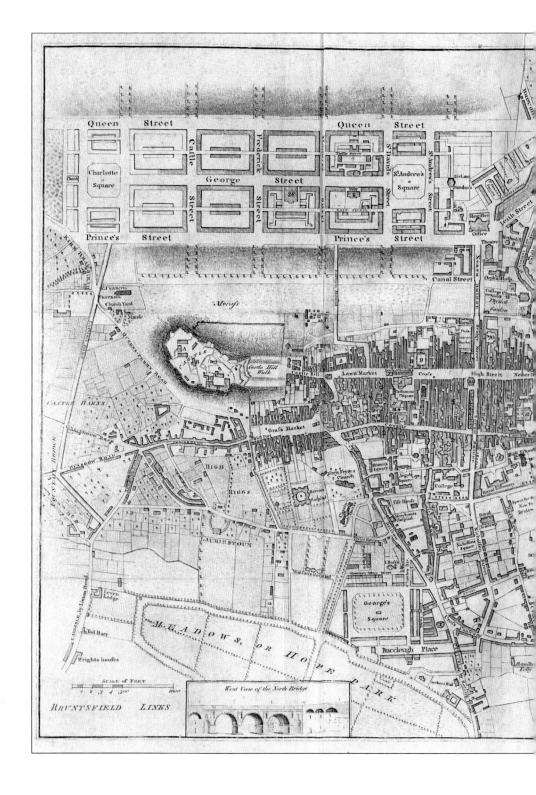

Queen   Street   Queen   Street

Charlotte   Castle   Frederick   Thistle Street   St Andrew's   St Andrew's
Square   Street   Street   Square   Street

George   Street   28   Register
                                          Rose Street   Office

Prince's   Street   Prince's   Street

Canal Street

Meadow

CASTLE BARNS

Castle Hill
Walk   Castle Hill   Lawn Market   High Street

Grass Market

HIGH
RIGGS

LAURISTOUN   College

George's
Square

Buccleugh   Place

M E A D O W S,   O R   H O P E   P A R K

SCALE of FEET

West View of the North Bridge

BRUNTSFIELD   LINKS

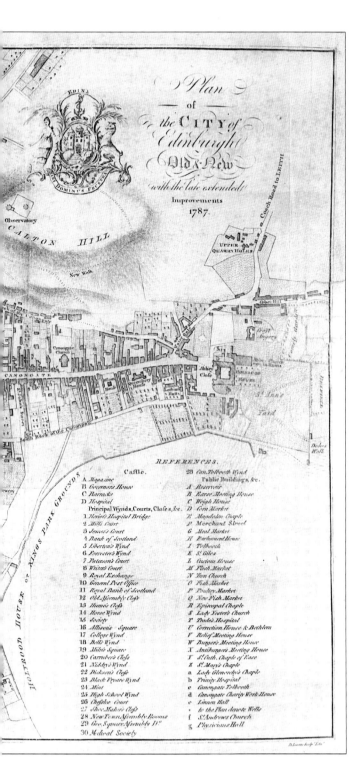

Plan of the City of Edinburgh Old & New, with the late extended improvements, 1787. From Hugo Arnot, *History of Edinburgh* (1788 edn). This and the 1778 map illustrate the extent of building in the new town and many of the main improvements to the city in the 1780s, notably the Mound and associated communication between the Lawnmarket and Princes Street, and the South Bridge. Paul's Work, the proposed site for the new flesh market, sat at the junction of Leith Wynd and the back of the Canongate. It is notable that the 1787 map included the new assembly rooms in George Square and the new town – unlike the earlier one. [By permission of the National Library of Scotland]

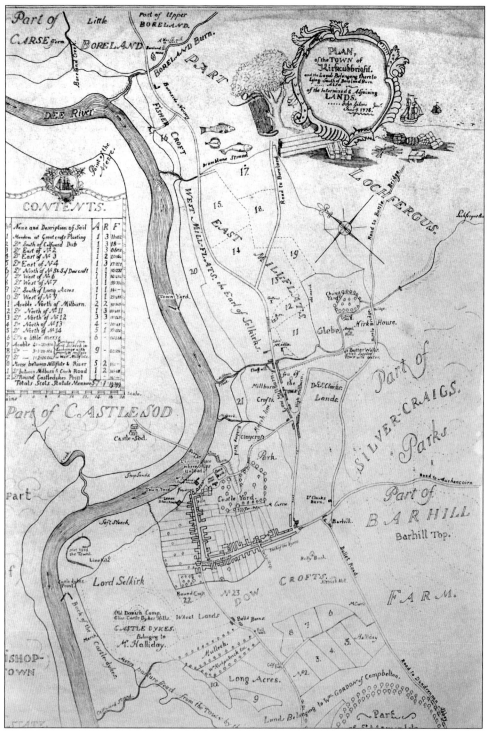

Copy of the Plan of the Town of Kirkcudbright, and the Lands Belonging thereto. Original by John Gilone, 1776. The town council employed the land surveyor John Gilone to produce several maps of the burgh and burgh lands, indicative of its careful stewardship of the burgh's 'common good'. [Courtesy of the Stewartry Museum, Kirkcudbright]

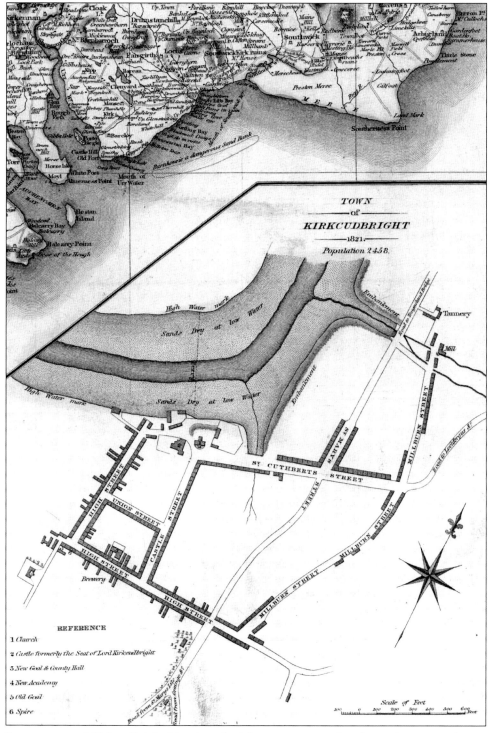

Inset on map of Kirkcudbrightshire. By John Thomson, 1821. This shows the extent of
building by this date on new streets laid out since the 1790s, including the earliest of these,
Castle Street, which almost certainly originated in a plan of Daer's. [By permission of the
National Library of Scotland]

Castle Street, Kirkcudbright (1860). The modest, but uniform appearance of the street was dictated by careful feuing conditions laid down first by the 4th earl of Selkirk when he disposed of plots of land for building on the street. [Courtesy of the Stewartry Museum, Kirkcudbright]

St Mary's Isle (n.d., but prob. late nineteenth century). This was the family home of the earls of Selkirk, and its unimposing appearance may well reflect, in part, the stance of political 'independence' assumed by the 4th earl and his sons. [Courtesy of the National Trust for Scotland, Broughton House Collection, Kirkcudbright]

of the Commons as the 'voice of the people' – the arguments bore a clear party imprint. At an Ayr county meeting held on 17 March 1784, as well as addressing the King, a vote of thanks to Pitt was passed, and the vote of thanks to the county MP, Sir Adam Fergusson, was for his conduct only during the 'present session', thereby very deliberately maintaining what can only be described as a resounding silence over his support for the North ministry *before* 1782.[42] In Glasgow, John Millar, the opposition Whig Professor of Civil Law, and those labelled by one contemporary as the 'Republicans', who were supporters of the Foxite Whigs, battled against a pro-Pitt address.[43] A similar set of issues resurfaced in 1789 during the so-called Regency crisis, caused by the first major illness of George III, when the question was whether to address the Prince Regent in support of his assuming power but subject to limitations defined by the parliament. This posed a particular dilemma for the burgh reformers, who, while ostensibly independent, were by the later 1780s moving ever-more clearly into the orbit of the opposition Whigs; although this was partly because there was no obvious alternative political destination for them, and certainly not the Scots MPs, who overwhelmingly opposed political reform, even the odd independent such as George Dempster, the MP for Perth burghs. Accordingly, while in favour of addressing the Prince Regent, they opposed addresses of thanks to Pitt. The leading burgh reformer, Archibald Fletcher, wrote in a personal capacity to make clear to other prominent burgh reformers in Perth, Dundee, Aberdeen and Glasgow the nature of their predicament, but also their dependency on Fox and his followers. One Irvine reformer, evidently opposed to the burgh reformers appearing to be the 'tools of party', was informed by Fletcher: '[Y]our aversion to the name of Party is too strong, if not, in the present instance, altogether misplaced.'[44] In 1791, Lord Sempill was drawing to the notice of the duke of Portland, the leader of the opposition Whigs, the support that the burgh reformers had shown for addressing in 1789 as a reason for his party to commit themselves to backing the burgh reform cause. Ministers, he went on, had 'few friends' in Glasgow, outside of the ruling 'Junto', also claiming that two-thirds of the inhabitants of Scotland's burghs were ready to support the opposition Whigs.[45] Clearly, such claims must be read mainly in terms of the author's wish to persuade. Nevertheless, it illustrates well how new party alignments were beginning to take shape in Scottish politics in the 1780s. These would become clearer in the 1790s, partly because the identity of the Scottish opposition Whigs sharpened in the face of Dundas and his supporters' fierce hostility to them, and because of the strongly polarising effects of the French Revolution and revolutionary wars, but also because of their shrinkage to a small, defiant rump led by the lawyer and, before he was deliberately not reappointed to the post in 1796, Dean of Faculty of Advocates, Henry Erskine.[46] In the early nineteenth century, the emergence of Fox and Pitt clubs in the Scottish capital and several other Scots burghs, including, for example, Dundee and Aberdeen, underlined the new salience of *British* party divisions.[47]

If there was, thus, a dynamic of convergence at work, we need to be careful not to exaggerate its strength or effects. The Scottish reform movements remained essentially separate from reform movements south of the border, and they developed in different ways. The rise of the campaign to reform county elections was largely a spontaneous reaction to the increasingly flagrant and obvious manufacture of fictitious votes; and there had been intermittent attempts to tackle it from the beginning of the eighteenth century, including the imposition of a qualifying oath on electors from 1708; further legislation seeking to define more tightly the property qualification for county electors in 1743; a major legal challenge to fictitious qualifications in 1768; and a proposed parliamentary bill in 1775.[48] In 1782, a new campaign began when three northern counties – Inverness, Moray and Caithness – issued resolutions calling for a co-ordinated national campaign to eliminate fictitious and nominal voters,[49] and it continued throughout the next decade, focused nationally on a legislative solution, but also producing challenges to fictitious and nominal voters at county level,[50] and a series of high-profile cases in the Court of Session concerning the legality of challenges to the credentials of voters, which eventually produced a ruling in the House of Lords in 1790 that the use of so-called interrogatories (investigations into the status of voters) was expressly permitted. Daer and his father were involved in discussions about county reform in 1782 in the Stewartry of Kirkcudbright, and almost certainly at other times and places for which no record exists. Daer attended the county reform conventions that met in Edinburgh in July 1792 and again in December of that year, presumably as a delegate from the Stewartry.[51]

The politics of county reform did not, moreover, divide simply along party lines of any kind, although opposition Whigs, such as Sir Thomas Dundas (mentioned earlier), often took the lead at the national level, and the cause drew on notions of freeholder and wider political independence. The fact that lines of support crossed party and factional divisions was why Robert Dundas, the Lord Advocate, could be found attending the county reform conventions in July and December 1792; he did not want to be seen directly to oppose a campaign that was building a head of steam and which appeared, briefly, as if it might achieve success.[52] In the end, what derailed the campaign was partly a failure to agree on precisely what measure of reform should be implemented – it was easy to agree that liferent and wadset voters should be abolished; much less easy to settle on whether to specify a new qualification for the franchise and at what level of property ownership. More immediately, the momentum building behind the campaign was brought to a sudden halt in the winter of 1792–3 by the rise of the anxious loyalism that swept through the Scottish propertied classes under the impact of the radicalisation of the French Revolution in 1792 and the emergence and spread of the domestic parliamentary reform movement in Scotland.[53] County reform was, in short, another of the victims of loyalist reaction and the underlying conservatism of most of the Scottish landed classes.

The origins of burgh reform, meanwhile, are, in the absence of a modern study of the movement, poorly understood at present. At one level, however, they were rooted in conflicts and traditions that had very deep historic roots – as, indeed, the reformers were not slow to point out in their anxiety to present themselves as seeking only the *restoration* of ancient rights. The forces of oligarchy in Scots burgh life had gained a clear ascendancy by the end of the seventeenth century; but sporadic resistance to this was evident in many burghs throughout the eighteenth century, although the full story remains to be pulled out of the records of relevant Court of Session cases. These battles were usually between the town councils and on occasion merchant guilds, but more often the trades incorporations, as for example in Dundee at the end of 1750s where the town's Nine Incorporated Trades sought legal backing for their claims to a direct voice in the appointment of two stipendiary ministers [i.e. ministers appointed in addition to the parish minister], the election of principal and town clerks, and the management and disposal of town lands.[54] The Trades were battling against their firmly subordinate position in urban government, the system of self-election employed by town councils, and the council's control of the election of other key burgh officers, such as, most importantly, the Dean of Guild, who in earlier periods had been elected by the Trades. As the Trades complained: 'the few have encroached upon the privileges of the many; so that the Government of almost all our burghs is become for the greater part oligarchical.'[55] In Stirling, such were the depth of the divisions and bitterness of the disputes by 1773 that the Court of Session felt compelled to suspend the burgh sett (i.e. constitution). When a committee of the privy council issued a new one in 1781, it significantly diluted the power of the local merchant oligarchy.[56] In Aberdeen and Glasgow, and to a rather lesser extent in Edinburgh, the incorporated trades acted as a focus for resistance to oligarchy, and in Glasgow they were part of a politics of contestation that formed a fairly continuous element in Glasgow civic life throughout the eighteenth century.[57]

Viewed more broadly, rising urban prosperity and growing expectations of urban government by the later eighteenth century led to new demands for making burgh councils properly accountable to their citizens. Accusations of council malfeasance, or misapplication of revenues, were fairly common-place throughout the eighteenth century, but it was almost certainly the rising expectations of councils by the 1780s in respect of direction of the burghs and improvement of their townscapes that brought them into much sharper focus. From 1785, the focus of the burgh reform campaign was no longer on parliamentary representation, but on the self-election of councils and their financial accountability, with the courts (in this case the Court of Exchequer as well as the Court of Session) again becoming key sites of political battle. What is hard to discern in any of this, however, is that the American war made a great deal of difference, or provided in the majority of places new divisions that might have helped focus these issues and demands. Much more impor-tant was almost certainly the fierce, and very widely supported anti-Catholic agitation of 1779, which was mobilised to defeat suspected plans to extend the Catholic Relief Act of 1778 to Scotland. Much of the energy and concern about British liberties galvanised by this campaign seems to have fed into the emergent burgh reform campaign and the revived anti-patronage campaign that gathered momentum in 1782.

Nevertheless, there was one way in which the American war *was* directly relevant to burgh reform and indeed the wider dynamic of convergence. Paradoxically, moreover, this was in large part a product of the fact that, unlike elsewhere in the British Isles, the war was *not* a source of major polit-ical division.

Supporters in Scotland of the American cause can be found. They included John Millar, for example, referred to earlier, and several of his colleagues at the University of Glasgow; William Thom, the popular minister of Govan, whose pamphlets in the 1770s were probably the most radical and critical of the existing ruling order of any published in later eighteenth-century Scotland; and several of the clergy in Edinburgh, notably John Erskine.[58] In Montrose, the anti-war fast-day sermons of the Rev. Charles Nisbet thoroughly discon-certed the local burgh elite.[59] The earl of Selkirk was an opponent of the American war, although he does not appear to have voiced this very publicly at the time. While several historians have sought to highlight the presence of this oppositional element, such individuals were, however, almost certainly part of a distinct minority. As the minister for the parish of Stevenston in Ayrshire, the Rev. James Wodrow reported at the beginning of October 1775: 'In Scotland I am sure nineteenth twentyeth [sic] parts [. . .] of the people are on the side of Gov.t in the present unhappy Quarrel', a view he repeated in the spring of 1778, then also noting that 'people of better education had given up the American cause since the Declaration of Independence'.[60] Other contemporaries made similar observations.

However, if most Scots appear to have viewed the war against the American colonists as legitimate, and, indeed, entirely necessary, albeit they were probably initially overly complacent about the likelihood of a quick military victory against unprofessional and improvised forces, this provided new opportunities for highly visible displays of Scots loyalty to the British state, which, in turn, further fuelled Scotto-British patriotism. In 1778, for example, subscriptions were enthusiastically raised in many places to support recruitment to new regiments required to fight in the widening conflict; France entered the war in that year, and Spain would do so in the following one. From Dundee, it was reported that the duke of Atholl, who was recruiting for a regiment in the town, was the 'darling of all ranks', though there was a sting of sorts in the tail: 'But North Britain will, by all its efforts, only drain itself of its money and inhabitants in vain, unless South Britain shall be timely roused to exert itself in proportion to its superior riches and numbers, in a cause which we stand or fall as a nation.' [61] Note, it is as 'a nation' – or rather, as they might easily have said, the *British nation*. In the following summer, Henry Dundas referred to the 'zeal manifested by all Ranks of people in this country for the public service'.[62] British military victories, such as at Charlestown in 1780, were greeted with outbursts of raucous popular celebration in Edinburgh and other towns. And, while a Scots militia bill was rejected by parliament in 1782 – the bill was also opposed by many Scots, particularly those involved in manufacturing – the earl of Shelburne did allow Scots coastal burghs in the winter of 1781–2 to raise defensive volunteer companies, and the government provided these with arms. The significance of this was that this was the first time in the eighteenth century that a London ministry had decided to trust Scots to organise their own defence. It was also only a few years previously (in 1779) that the earl of Suffolk, as the responsible secretary of state, had turned down offers from Scots burghs to form defensive associations such as had been formed in a number of English boroughs. As General Hugh Mackay noted in January 1781, when the plans for defence were again under discussion: '[The] national temper of the country,' was such, that, 'if they see a line drawn, and that they don't share in the confidence of the crown, they will feel it sincerely.'[63] In other words, they would have taken hard another rebuff to their patriotic credentials.

It was not coincidence at all, therefore, that a prominent feature of Scottish politics in the 1780s was concern with ensuring that English liberties were properly extended to the Scots. Not a new dynamic; this had first emerged very clearly in the agitation for a Scots militia at the end of the Seven Years War, a campaign that briefly revived in 1775–6 and again in the early 1780s, as alluded to above.[64] If the English had a militia, so should the Scots, doubly so since this was in part what defined them as a free people. The burgh reformers argued that what they were seeking was full access to English liberties, while the anti-patronage campaigners often deployed similar rhetoric. As the delegates of the royal burghs convened in Edinburgh to consider burgh reform in the spring of 1784 resolved: 'That by the spirit and principles of the British constitution, it is the indubitable right of the people to possess a share in the legislative power [. . .]'[65] Or, as the Dundee burgh reformers had put it in the previous year: '[it is] a self evident maxim, that English liberty is a good thing, and there no reason why Scotchmen shall be exempted from it.'[66] McGrugar and other burgh reformers quite happily talked of the notion of natural rights, without any sense of a possible contradiction, an ideological eclecticism that was entirely characteristic of reformers in this period. Nevertheless, the cause of reform was about redeeming the political dignity of the Scots burgesses and tradesmen, which might be expressed in terms of a restoration of ancient rights, but also, and if anything more readily, in terms of redeeming the promise of union. As one memorial for the burgh reformers declared, until reform of burgh elections and government was achieved 'it cannot with justice be said that the Scottish Nation has experienced, in their full extent, those fortunate and brilliant consequences which were expected from the union.'[67]

It was still eminently possible of course to play a very different patriotic card – a more narrowly Scottish one – as Boswell did in opposing the proposed reduction in the number of judges in the Court of Session in 1785.[68] As had occurred earlier in the century, the cry of breaching the Treaty of Union as an argument against unwanted measures was often heard, although there could be a highly rhetorical and political edge to this. Given this, it is hard to interpret such instances as being inspired by patriotic indignation or even genuine patriotic feeling. The terms of the Treaty of Union were, in short, a very useful bargaining counter within an essentially *British* legislative and political arena, one that certainly did not guarantee success, but was not easily ignored either.

There is one further context in which this deepening pattern of convergence and assimilation, albeit always partial, can be understood – one implicit in much of what has already been said. This is the extent to which the Westminster parliament was becoming relevant to the lives of many Scots in a way that had hitherto not been the case. In the first six decades or so of the eighteenth century, there was remarkably little legislation passed at Westminster specific to Scotland; Westminster was just not that important to Scots, except at moments of crisis, such as in the aftermath of the final major Jacobite rising of 1745–6.[69] The picture in this respect began to change from the 1760s, one simple measure of which was the growing body of Scottish legislation, especially local legislation – road acts, improvement acts of various kinds, police acts; or, measures might be British rather than specifically Scottish in their impact and significance, such as corn laws and various fiscal and economic measures – changes to licensing of distilleries, taxes on various objects or goods (carts, shops, windows and so on). The development of the Scottish linen industry was powerfully aided and influenced by legislative support, in the form principally of bounties on linen exports (first imposed by Westminster in 1742) and a prohibition from 1745 on imports of French cambrics and lawns (types of linen cloth). Whatever the particular issue, an increasing amount of public and press discussion focused on legislation and the legislative process, which naturally promoted comparison with the rest of Britain but also, in many cases, further integration into 'British' forms of politics. This was most evident with respect to the corn laws – legislation governing the circumstances under which foreign grain might be imported – an issue which periodically consumed the attention of many people from the early 1770s, creating new divisions in Scottish political life between the 'landed interest' and the manufacturing and commercial interests, and serving to begin to recast political debate north of the border as more transparent and open. Rather less dramatically, but cumulatively significant, private bill legislation had similar effects at the local level, as, for example, evident in Glasgow and Aberdeen in the late 1780s in relation to various proposals for police bills or in Edinburgh a few years earlier with respect to the series of police and improvement bills which were discussed in chapter 2.

Lobbying on economic and fiscal issues – many of which were not so much national as industry or sector specific, and which gained a new prominence in the 1780s with Pitt's fiscal innovations and new commercial diplomacy – was a further aspect of relations with the Westminster parliament that encouraged relationships and co-operation with bodies and groups elsewhere in Britain. New lobbying bodies such as the Glasgow and Edinburgh chambers of commerce, founded in 1783 and 1785 respectively, were less Scottish than British in their modes of operation and they quickly looked to develop connections with chambers or similar bodies in Liverpool, Manchester, Birmingham, Leeds, Cork and Belfast and so on.[70] Again, while not without precedent, habits of co-ordination and co-operation with those beyond the country's borders were significantly reinforced and broadened.

One might draw from this several more fundamental conclusions. The early phases of industrialisation, while following a distinct national pattern, drove deeper-lying processes of convergence within the British Isles, which is partly why we may even talk of a *British* industrial revolution. Increasingly rapid urbanisation in Scotland, and thickening lines of communication with other parts of the British Isles – in addition to the mighty beast that was London – were other factors promoting what Keith Robbins has very aptly described in a nineteenth- and twentieth-century context as the 'blending of Britain'.[71] So too at the apex of society sharply rising rental incomes after 1760 helped to promote the deepening Anglicisation of the Scots nobility, with more and more of them resident south of the border, choosing to educate their children there, and spending large amounts of time in London and Bath. Unlike earlier in the century, therefore, the new areas of political convergence increasingly evident in the 1780s were underpinned by important economic, social and cultural changes.

We now need to turn to see where Daer and his father fitted within this developing picture. In 1788, the earl of Selkirk was described, in a survey of leading political interests in the Stewartry of Kirkcudbright drawn up to aid the opposition Whigs in their electoral ambitions, as 'a very independent man, *attached* to no party, but who has hitherto acted with the Opposition from conviction. A large family. He has never interested himself in politicks, or affected to be at the head of any interest in the County'.[72] Selkirk consciously distanced himself, therefore, from the normal patterns of Scottish political competition, from the intricate manoeuvres and careful deal-making that accompanied most Scots electoral politicking. As such, he joined a rare group of individuals for whom political independence was their lodestar.

Yet, while Selkirk may have carefully and very deliberately eschewed involvement in party or electoral politics, from 1770–1 he showed his political hand clearly in one particular sphere – the Scottish peerage elections. Selkirk was very strongly committed to opposing ministerial intervention in these elections, in the form of a so-called 'King's list' – in other words, a list of approved ministerial candidates – a practice which his fellow independent peer, the earl of Buchan described as making a 'mockery of an election'.[73] From 1768, the practice had even developed of the responsible minister in London simply dispatching a list of preferred candidates to Scots peers asking for their support. In 1774, for example, Lord North wrote to the duke of Atholl, informing him that his name had been included among the list of sixteen peers proposed by the ministry for election. Atholl was asked to vote for all those listed, and to do all in his power to persuade other peers to vote for those on the official list.[74] While North might describe this procedure as 'necessary' – to whom and why went of course unspecified – a growing number of voices north of the border saw this as not just an attack on liberty, but on the dignity and standing of the Scottish peerage. As Selkirk complained in 1774, '[the] continued persistence in sending these letters marks a determined resolution to annihilate independence, and reduce the Peerage election to the despicable state of a *conge-d'elire*'.[75]

Particularly offensive was not just that ministers were making decisions about Scottish peerage representation without consulting the Scots peers, but they were seemingly deaf to the resultant protests. In 1770, for example, the earl of Weymouth, as the secretary of state for the northern department – the offices of home and foreign secretaries only emerged in 1782 – initially chose a peer without any Scottish property, the earl of Dysart, as the ministerial candidate, although, faced with an incipient revolt, he was swiftly dropped in favour of Lord Stair, who at least did have such property and was more likely to be approved by many Scots peers.[76] This belated, clumsy switch of candidates was itself unprecedented. Yet the deeper problem was the lack of a Scottish manager similar to the second and third dukes of Arygll between 1725 and 1761, the year of the third duke's death. The two brothers had acted as the conduit between London and Scotland, salving Scottish pride by having a Scot manage the elections for the administration who was able to discriminate between the claims of different individuals. The third duke often attended the elections in person. The absence of a replacement, apart briefly from James Stuart Mackenzie before 1765, left a vacuum, therefore, thereby also creating a destabilising fluidity in Scottish affairs. Not that opposition to ministerial influence in the peerage elections was new. Buchan had raised very vocal objections in 1768, and the issues had been fully aired much earlier than that, notably in 1734–5, and there had been proposals for reform as early as 1708.[77]

In the 1780s, Selkirk emerged as a leading figure amongst a group of 'independent peers' who stood on a platform of freedom and independence in the peerage elections. The emergence of this grouping was partly simply a product of the strengthening campaign from 1770 to eradicate undue influence in peerage elections, but it also grew directly out of the political crisis of 1783–4, and the battle between George III, Pitt and the Fox–North coalition. Following the collapse of the Fox–North coalition, Scottish opposition Whigs and peers committed to free elections began to compile their own list of candidates as an alternative to the ministerial list.[78] The 1784 elections were unusual, both because they were a genuine contest, and because the administration failed to secure the return of all the peers on their list. This challenge to ministerial ambitions and interest was sustained for the rest of the 1780s and during the 1790 election, which was again very closely contested, and in which the independents were able, eventually after a series of protests, to return five of their candidates. Dundas and the ministry, however, acted swiftly thereafter to regain the ministerial ascendancy, first moving to have overturned a 1709 order that debarred peers with British peerages from voting in the elections; such individuals were normally rewarded for political reasons, such as in the case of the fourth duke of Atholl in 1786, although his political agent, George Farquhar was gilding the lily somewhat when he congratulated his patron, declaring that the government had bestowed the honour on him because of their 'fear' of him and his importance in Scotland and his 'steady judicious manly conduct', not as 'gratitude for services rendered'.[79] The real truth was that Atholl expected his services to be rewarded, and had been fishing for the honour for some time. The impact of the French Revolution and rise of domestic radicalism aided the reassertion of ministerial control. A straw in the wind here was the decision of the former independent, the earl of Hopetoun, who was elected to a vacant seat in 1794, to support Dundas in return for his promise not to interfere in the election. At the general election of 1796, Dundas was able to secure the return of all of the candidates on the ministerial list.[80]

The 'independent peers' were a slightly strange mix, therefore, of opposition Whigs, such as Lord Kinnaird, former Northites, such as Viscount Stormont, and genuine independents such as Selkirk. Other 'true' independents included Lord Sempill, Lord Saltoun, the earl of Buchan, earl of Dumfries and, certainly in terms at least of patriotic motivation, the duke of Buccleuch. As Sempill declared to the earl of Morton in 1790:

> I may assure your lordship that I have, in no instance, exercised the rights of an elective peer, but in respect of what must be held to be equally for the honour & interest of the Peerage, the freedom of election; and I have solemnly pledged myself, that party shall never, in the smallest degree, influence my conduct where that interest is concerned.[81]

Sempill was closely connected to Glasgow's burgh reformers, and in the early 1790s became an important member of the Society for Constitutional Information. As we shall see in a later chapter, he was a key point of contact between the SCI and the Glasgow parliamentary reformers in 1791–3. One authority has described Buchan's intervention in the 1768 elections as no more than the vacuous posturing of a 'pompous and theatrical young man.'[82] That Buchan was possessed of a vastly inflated notion of his own dignity and worth is incontrovertible, and there was about his public life a marked sense of his playing the main part in a drama very much of his own scripting. But his patriotism was for all that deep-rooted and forms a continuous thread in his enthusiasms and activities. It was, for example, entirely characteristic of the man that he sent George Washington a box made from the oak which supposedly sheltered William Wallace after the Battle of Falkirk. Nor did he quickly drop his stance on the peerage elections. Buchan may have flirted constantly with appearing faintly ridiculous, but he had tenacity. In 1780 he made his own proposals for reform of the elections – seats, he contended, should rotate among the eligible peers – depicting the Union as a disastrous blow to the rights and privileges of the Scottish noble order.[83] In 1782, he stood in a special election against the earl of Lauderdale, who he insisted, despite Lauderdale's protestations to the contrary, was a ministerial candidate. Buchan, who saw this election as a test of the political credentials of the new ministry led by Shelburne, took the unusual step of reading a circular letter to the peers at the election, which was subsequently published in the press and which he seems to have circulated widely, declaring his separation politically from the Scots peerage. Whether his fellow peers took this at all seriously is moot, but it certainly won him praise from one group of Edinburgh independents, members of a shadowy body that went under the name of the 'Orange Club' and which may well have had links to McGrugar's burgh reformers.[84]

Selkirk, meanwhile, was elected as a representative peer in 1787, when he and Lord Kinnaird defeated the ministerial candidates in special elections called because the duke of Queensberry and earl of Abercorn had been required to vacate their seats. Both had recently been awarded British peerages, which led to their status as representative peers being challenged in the Lords by the earl of Stormont. The Lords, with the support of ten of the twelve representative peers present, had voted to uphold Stormont's challenge, which declared that possession of a hereditary right to representation was incompatible with a seat dependent on election. In the following year, the independents came within a single vote of winning another special election. Selkirk was defeated in the 1790 election and while he challenged this outcome in the Lords, it was eventually confirmed in 1793.[85]

The cause of 'free and independent election' was, moreover, not merely confined to the peerage elections themselves. Selkirk chaired repeated meetings of the Scots peers in Edinburgh and London, which sought to produce proposals to reform and regularise electoral procedure and the list of eligible peers.[86] His group may well have been sitting in London in 1786, when the third earl of Stanhope was preparing his own bill to reform the peerage elections, an initiative that, for reasons that are unclear, proved abortive.[87] Stanhope, Selkirk and Daer shared many interests, not least their enthusiasm for the French Revolution in the early 1790s; and it is very plausible that they came into contact in the mid- to late 1780s over the issue of reform of Scottish peerage elections.

This campaign might seem a rather narrow one, and of marginal relevance to the wider currents reshaping Scottish political debate in the later eighteenth century. Yet, as we have already begun to see, this would be a false conclusion, for the connections were substantial. We know that Selkirk had a residence in London from 1787, in Upper Brook Street in Westminster; and this and his election as a representative peer in the same year seem to have confirmed and deepened his opposition to ministerial power and the politics of control with which it was often associated. Even before that, in 1786 he warned a young Lord Morton 'to be at all times on your Guard against the sinister designs of Ministers'.[88] In May 1791, Sempill, who had approached the so-called 'Independent Peers' for their support for burgh reform, noted that the only one already 'determined' in their favour was Selkirk, further reporting to Robert Graham of Gartmore:

> We have been joined by Lords Selkirk, (Breadalbane who for good reasons does not wish to appear) Dumfries, Lauderdale & Saltoun. Selkirk *whose zeal is unequal'd in whatever relates to the public good or liberties of the people*, agreed with me that we should tell the Duke of Portland the consequence of refusing the Burgesses his interest [. . .].[89] (my emphasis)

The politics of independence and the politics of liberty were natural bedfellows, and Selkirk's commitment to 'liberty' was a broadening one in this period. It is highly likely that the politics surrounding county reform were a further part of this.

At the same time, the growing presence of the two men in London – we know Daer was there, for example, in the spring of 1789 – and shared opposition to the administration in the peerage elections, drew Selkirk and

Daer into ever closer co-operation with the opposition Whigs. At the 1790 general election, Daer stood as a candidate in two English borough constituencies – Poole, where he stood in partnership with Lord Haddo on the popular interest in support of 'commonalty' against the freemen vote, and Canterbury, another freeman borough, where he stood with financial assistance from the opposition Whigs.[90] In both he was defeated, although his performance at Canterbury appears to have exceeded expectation. He stood again in Poole in March 1791 at a by-election necessitated by one of the MPs accepting a government office, although as in the previous year the votes of his supporters were rejected as invalid. In the next few years, Daer would be drawn ever further into opposition Whig politics, albeit always remaining separate from them.

The other key, however, was patriotism. It is surely significant that Selkirk had been a member of the Select Society, the foundation of which in 1754 in Edinburgh heralded the rise of 'improvement' as the pre-eminent patriotic project in Georgian Scotland. There are hints that, like the earl of Buchan, he was very interested in the militia question.[91] As we saw earlier, demands for a Scottish militia had first been widely agitated at the end of the Seven Years War, and the campaign had briefly revived at several moments during the American war. Underpinning these were concerns about liberty and independence, but also equality within the Union: the militia became a symbol of Scottish national dignity. It was, moreover, sensitivity about patriotism and national dignity that ultimately lay behind another, related campaign in which Selkirk and Daer became the key figures in 1789–92 – to remove the prohibition on the eldest sons of Scottish peers voting in or standing for election to the House of Commons in Scotland.

From a British perspective, the barring of the eldest sons of Scottish peers from acting as voters and candidates in Scottish elections was plainly anomalous. Eldest sons of English peers could vote and stand in English elections, as could eldest sons of Scottish peers; they just could not vote or stand in their own country. Nor was the constitutional logic for debarring eldest sons of Scots peers from Scottish elections very clear, insofar as there were no relevant acts of the Scottish parliament but only several parliamentary resolutions, and all of these dating from the end of the seventeenth and early eighteenth centuries and readily construed as products of partisan political battles. Such logic as did exist derived partly from the Acts of Union, which stated that such limitations on representation as had hitherto existed would continue after 1707, but which also implied that the Scots peers were represented solely by their sixteen representatives. In 1708, the new British parliament confirmed their exclusion when it voted to remove as MPs several eldest sons of Scots peers, the main stated reason being concerns about limiting noble influence north of the border. Where this, or the fact that peers did not sit in parliament by right like their English counterparts, left the status of Scots peers was clearly moot, which is why Buchan could depict 1707 as a moment of Scots noble capitulation and badge of inferiority. This was reinforced by the decision of parliament in 1711 to debar the duke of Hamilton from sitting in the Lords by virtue of a British peerage conferred after 1707. This particular anomaly was undone in 1782 by the House of Lords under a challenge from Hamilton's great grandson. As the earl of Mansfield declared to the duke of Atholl: 'After 70 years we have overturned that arbitrary, illegal & unjust Resolution which disabled Scotch from being created English peers', or more accurately British peers with rights equivalent to their English counterparts.[92] The rescinding of the earlier resolution of 1711 was an important element in the background to the developing challenge to the relatively inferior position of the eldest sons of Scots peers.

One might well view rectifying this position, therefore, as an extension of the politics of completing the Union – which is precisely how it was portrayed by Lord Saltoun in a pamphlet published in London in 1788. The immediate occasion of his writing was an event that arose from a very particular set of circumstances from the previous year. On the death of Lord Elcho on 29 April 1787, the father of Francis Wemyss Charteris, MP for Haddington burghs, had assumed the title of the fifth earl of Wemyss, despite the fact that the title had been under attainder since 1756, while Charteris himself had become Viscount Elcho. On 21 May, Sir John Sinclair gave notice that he would move for a new writ for Haddington Burghs, although Elcho declared that he would oppose it since he had not vacated his seat. The question was fully debated two days later, with Sinclair quoting precedents to prove that Elcho, having become the eldest son of a Scottish peer, was disqualified from representing a Scottish constituency. The opposition disputed Sinclair's interpretation of the Act of Union, and the discrimination that it exhibited between the eldest sons of Scottish and English peers. Elcho maintained that he was at least entitled to retain his seat until the general election, when on his re-election a petition could be presented against him. Sinclair's motion, however, was carried without a division, and Elcho was forced to vacate his seat.

Saltoun's pamphlet effectively rehearsed and extended the opposition case that had been made during the debate of 23 May. For Saltoun, restoring these rights to the eldest sons – for part of the case was historical, that such rights had been exercised in the distant past and could not legitimately be abrogated – was a matter of right *and* expediency. But it was also predicated on a particular view of the Union and what it meant for Scotland. Union represented Scotland's incorporation within an English – now British – constitutional history that was focused on liberty. It was a promise of further assimilation to secure liberty north of the border. The abolition of heritable jurisdictions in 1747 had been a key moment in this process – indeed, the key moment since it was from then that Scottish incorporation in the 'British constitution' could really be dated. 'It is from this period,' Saltoun declared, 'that the people in Scotland can be said to have been real partakers of the British constitution.'[93] Freedom meant, on this view, limiting the power of the 'great proprietors' or 'overbearing influence of the great aristocracy', an influence that had quickly reasserted itself after a brief ebullition of 'enthusiasm for liberty' at the time of the glorious revolution of 1689. The Union was thus a process as much as a fixed agreement. There was an ambiguity here about the status of the Treaty of Union, an ambiguity that accurately reflected the Scottish–British cross-currents that were beginning to transform Scottish politics in this period, and which Saltoun sought to navigate by drawing an incipient distinction between essential and inessential aspects of the Union, although on what real basis such a distinction was to be drawn was nowhere stated. But constitutions evolved, and properly so, Saltoun here showing himself to be a true son of the Scottish Enlightenment view of the Scottish and English pasts. 'Not only have men of speculation,' he counselled, 'found it impossible to frame a model of government equally adapted to all mankind, but the laws of the same nations necessarily change with their changing characters and circumstances.' What this meant for the Union was explained in words which have a peculiar salience for today's politicians: 'Were no alterations practicable in the treaty of Union, it would, in time, become a confused and unwieldy mass, and fall to pieces from its inconsistency.' To restore the eldest sons of Scottish peers to their rights was thus both to reinstate them in their historic rights, but also to render the Union more complete, which here meant more complete assimilation with English liberties. As Saltoun further explained:

> The truth is, by the Union, the government of Scotland was to sink into that of England. The two kingdoms were to be inseparable, and for ever joined. The principles of that constitution which had deviated least from its original basis, and which was most congenial to the rights of mankind, were to be leading features in the British government.[94]

The English and Scottish constitutions shared common, Gothic origins, but the English constitution had through its development retained most closely its original character – in protecting the rights and liberties of the freeholders; while the Scottish constitution had, for various reasons, deviated from this path. In a sense, 'British' history constituted this narrative, which culminated in the Union and the transformation of the English into the British constitution, a constitution that would continue to evolve. For Saltoun, restoring the rights of the eldest sons was, or should be, part of the natural effects of the 'progressive' spirit of the eighteenth century, a spirit that had abolished the Scottish privy council, heritable jurisdictions and which had made judges only removable for bad conduct, and that would, surely, in future be extended to the demands now before parliament for reform of county and burgh elections.[95]

Whether Daer or Selkirk saw their campaign in quite these terms is unknowable, although they were undoubtedly aware of Saltoun's pamphlet. The record of their views comes in the form almost entirely of a mass of dense legal argument, designed to persuade first the Court of Session and then the House of Lords of the correctness of their position. Daer also, however, wrote a pamphlet laying out his case, but in this he stuck close to the specific issue of legal and constitutional right and eschewed any concern with expediency.[96] The case was constructed, therefore, on a narrow basis; that recognising the right to vote and stand in Scottish elections of the eldest sons of Scots peers was an act of restoration; that no acts of the Scottish parliament had excluded them; and that the resolutions of the Scottish parliament and British parliament in 1708 which did so were challengeable on grounds of being narrowly politically motivated in the case of the Scottish parliament and as based on a misunderstanding and inadequate information in the case of the British one. Moreover, all the evidence pointed to their having exercised this right in the remote past. Of union and wider constitutional principles he said nothing.

As for the campaign itself, the first steps were taken in 1789, when Daer unsuccessfully sought admission to the register of voters for Kirkcudbrightshire and Wigtownshire at the Michaelmas head courts in preparation for the general election of the following year. In 1790, he was successfully enrolled as voter for Wigtownshire, but this act was challenged and overturned in the Court of Session, a decision that was appealed by Daer up to the House of Lords. The Lords upheld the decision of the Court in 1792. The costs of pursuing the case in the Court of Session and then appealing to the Lords were considerable – around £2,500 – and a subscription to defray these was launched at a meeting of Scots peers chaired in 1793 by the duke of Buccleuch, presumably largely the same group that had been meeting under Selkirk's chairmanship in the 1780s. Daer and Selkirk had all along, however, been acting in close concert with a wider group of Scots peers, who were aligned politically with the opposition.[97] And, it was not so much the defeat in the Lords that ended the campaign, but rather, as Selkirk noted in a letter to the earl of Leven, the futility of proceeding in the face of opposition from Dundas, then home secretary and a man with the ear of William Pitt; not that this indicated any diminution in the notion that right was on their side. As Selkirk observed:

> The right of eligibility to the house of Commons seems to counterbalance the exclusion from the other House, & tho the ministry of the day may run down a Scottish Peer, who has only one opening into Parliament, yet among the 658 doors into the House of Commons, some one or other may be found which they cannot slap into our face.[98]

By this time, moreover, the political horizons of Daer and Selkirk had widened very significantly, and the liberty that they were seeking was not simply that of members of the Scots peerage, but of the 'people'. For Daer at least, the politics of Union had also come to mean something altogether different, no less than replacing the narrow agreement of 1707 with a true union, a union of all the British people.

The cause, meanwhile, of reforming Scots peerage elections would be taken up in the early nineteenth century by Thomas, his younger brother, now the fifth earl of Selkirk. He proposed that the Scots adopt the new Irish model, introduced with the Anglo-Irish Union of 1800. Those chosen as representative peers would sit for life, while the others could seek election to the House of Commons. The proposal died through lack of support, and Thomas continued his slow transmogrification into a supporter of the administration. More and more Scots peers, meanwhile, sought and achieved elevation to the British peerage – eighteen of them between 1784 and 1815. Partly this was driven by political expediency – their political value to Dundas and successive ministries – and in that sense was a continuation of the machine politics that had long been a looming feature of the Scottish political landscape. But it was also a response on the Scottish side to the sharpened sense that the system of representative peers was degrading, and only full equality with their English counterparts would suffice to assuage this complaint. Even Lord Kinnaird, who had been an important member of the campaign for free and independent peerage elections in the 1780s, in 1806 'bombarded' Lord Grenville as head of the ministry of all the talents for a British peerage that would free him from the restraints and diminished status of the representative system. Yet, as has been pointed out elsewhere, the rise of a genuinely British elite did not mean that the Scots peers were abdicating their sense of responsibility for defending and forwarding Scottish interests; and one of the ironies was that the representative peers, even where they were generally supporters of the administration, tended to display more independence in this regard than those who were British peers. The political trajectories traced out by Selkirk and Daer must be seen against this broader background, although, as we shall see in the next chapter, under the impact of the French Revolution they were by this stage veering off in new, altogether bolder directions.

CHAPTER SIX

Witness to Revolution

D aer was a relatively frequent visitor to France, travelling there in 1783, 1786, 1789 and 1791. In the case of the two earlier visits pretty much all that we know about them is that they occurred.[1] In 1789 he set out for Paris with his former teacher, Dugald Stewart, their arrival being timed to coincide with the opening of the Estates General, which was marked by two grand ceremonial occasions, a procession of the Court on 4 May and the opening session of the States with the King presiding on the following day.[2] The momentous nature of the meeting was well understood, both for France and the rest of Europe. Yet nothing could have prepared Stewart and Daer for the astonishing spectacle that unfolded in front of them, or the experience of immersion in the dramatic, emotionally super-charged politics of revolution. While the main events are of course clear in retrospect, at the time they were surrounded with much confusion, a frenzy of speculation about what they portended, and, more than that, a sense of an unfolding drama, the script of which was being written as it proceeded by an ever-shifting balance of forces and actors. Spurred on by Emmanuel Joseph Sieyès *Qu'est-ce'que le tiers Etat? (What is the Third Estate?)* and the humiliations heaped on them from their arrival in the capital by what one foreigner called 'the habits of tyranny' of most of the Noble or First Estate and the Court,[3] on 17 June the Third Estate, the rising force in French politics, declared its transformation into the National Assembly, in other words, the assembly of the nation. Two days later, the majority of the clergy, parish priests, voted to join the new National Assembly. On 23 June, the Court staged a *séance royale* in which the King sought to reassert control over events, making several important concessions, but also ordering the Estates to resume their deliberations as separate orders. Events were being played out before a mobilised, restive and closely attentive people; and for Daer, familiar as he was with the robust, lively popular politics of London, the scenes must have been remarkable. As the Englishman and writer on agricultural affairs, Arthur Young, reported on 24 June: 'The ferment in Paris is beyond conception; 10,000 people have been all this day in the Palais Royal.' Paris was awash with political talk and expectation, stirred by a vigorous, teeming press; and increasing popular defiance. Two days later, Young noted:

> Every hour that passes seems to give the people fresh spirit: the meetings at the Palais-Royal are more numerous, more violent, and more assured: and in the assembly of electors, at Paris, for sending a deputation to the National Assembly, the language that was talked, by all ranks of people was nothing less than a revolution in the government, and the establishment of a free constitution.[4]

On 27 June the Court backed down in the face of the firm resolve of the Third Estate, and Louis XVI ordered the nobility and remaining dissident clergy to sit in the combined body. On 9 July, the Assembly decided that it should draw up a declaration of rights as a preliminary to forming a new constitution.

The Revolution, however, was not yet secure. With troops, many of which were Swiss and German, being concentrated around Paris and Versailles, and when liberal members of the King's council, including the Genevan Jacques Necker, were dismissed on 11 July, to be replaced by an ultra-conservative ministry, fears mounted that a conservative counter coup was being planned. The following day, in response, a new citizen militia was formed in Paris, the National Guard, and the government of the city was seized from old regime officials. Two days later occurred the event that above all others announced the victory of liberty to France and the rest of the world, when crowds of artisans, shopkeepers and journeymen forced the surrender of the fortress of the Bastille, symbol of Bourbon despotism, securing the future of the Assembly. The British ambassador reported to ministers in London on 16 July:

> Thus [. . .] the greatest Revolution that we know anything of has been effected, with comparatively speaking, if the magnitude of the event is considered, the loss of very few lives: from this moment we may consider France as a free country; the King a very limited Monarch, and the Nobility reduced to a level with the rest of the Nation.[5]

On the following day, the King was forced to come to Paris in a humiliating act of submission 'to the wishes of the nation'. And, in what one historian has described as 'the most radical single episode of the entire French Revolution',[6] on the night of 4 August, in a heady mood of 'patriotic intoxication', deputies voted the destruction of feudalism and noble privilege. The revolutionary dynamic had taken a firm hold, leading in directions that could not have been anticipated only a few months earlier. Daer had left Paris by this stage, however, departing on or around 17 July.[7]

Through Stewart, Daer was introduced in Paris in 1789 to Thomas Jefferson, one of the giants of the American Revolution and the future third President of the United States, who had succeeded Benjamin Franklin as American Minister to France in 1784. Twenty-one years later, Jefferson would recall, in a letter to another leading member of the revolutionary generation and the second President, John Adams: 'I became immediately intimate with Stuart, calling mutually on each other almost daily, during their stay at Paris, which was of some months.' In a striking appraisal of Stewart's travelling companion, coming especially from a man who, as Alan Ryan has recently remarked, had many ideas, 'perhaps too many and too little digested',[8] he declared: 'Ld. Dare was a young man of imagination, with occasional flashes indicating deep penetration, but of much caprice and little judgement [. . .]'[9] Perhaps Daer was simply more carried away by the momentous events that were occurring before his eyes – or rather this was how an older, more reflective Jefferson chose to remember things. For from June 1789 Jefferson had, in fact, become a strong supporter of the French Revolution. As early as 19 May, he had expressed his hopes for political change in France in a letter to the Welsh Dissenting minister and good friend of America, Richard Price: 'My hope is that the mass of the Bourgeoisie is too well in motion and too well informed to be resisted or misled, and ultimately that this great country will obtain a constitution and shew the rest of Europe that reformation in government follows reformation in opinion.'[10] When the Bastille fell, Jefferson was immersed in a café discussion with a group of intellectuals-turned-politicians, who joyously greeted the news with stamping of feet and dancing around the tables. Jefferson apparently declared: 'Eh Bien! oui, Messieurs, you are delighted by this triumph. But you must contend with the nobles and priests, and until you have dealt with them you will never have liberty.'[11] As one of his modern biographers has noted, the Revolution from the fall of the Bastille 'leapt forward, and Jefferson [. . .] went with it'.[12] On 25 July, he wrote to the Scot, Sir John Sinclair, of the 'late miracles of Paris', while in late August he declared to fellow American James Madison, with reference to actions of the National Assembly in rooting up feudalism and seeking to eliminate aristocratic privilege: 'It [the Assembly] has shewn genuine dignity in exploding adulatory titles; they are the offerings of abject baseness, and nourish the degrading vice in the people.'[13] It was, moreover, at around this moment, in September 1789, that Jefferson developed probably his most radical thought – the principle that generations, as well as individuals, have natural rights. Each generation thus possessed – contrary to Burke's notion of a 'partnership' between the living, the dead and those who have yet to be born – the right to forge their own political destiny. This was the message that another of Jefferson's friends, the radical publicist Thomas Paine would bring to England and the rest of the British Isles with the publication in March 1791 of Part I of his *Rights of Man*.

We also know that in 1789 Daer was in contact with Lavoisier, who he had probably met for the first time three years earlier.[14] It seems highly likely, moreover, that as a result of Stewart's freshly-minted friendship with Jefferson he would have met the marquis de Lafayette, whose version of the declaration of rights, although rejected by the Assembly, was drawn up in close discussion with Jefferson. Others he may well have met include the marquis de Condorcet, the leading *philosophe* and republican ideologue, who in 1793 would become principal author of the world's first fully democratic republican constitution; the duc de la Rochefoucauld-Liancourt, who became President of the National Assembly on 12 July; as well as other leading figures within the so-called French Patriot party, who had come to see themselves as inspirers of a political transformation – the first modern revolution – that would (or so they believed and hoped) reconstitute and regenerate France's political institutions and French society in a manner fully consistent with their egalitarian and politically liberal ideals.

In the early summer of 1791 Daer set out again for Paris, on this occasion in the company of his two brothers, John and Thomas, and his brother-in-law and friend, Sir James Hall. On the trip he met and befriended Paine. Paine had returned to France in April 1791, intoxicated by his success with Part I of the *Rights of Man*, and utterly convinced of his capacity to spread revolution to England. Hall simply recorded in relation to their first meeting, which took place on 29 May: 'He [Paine] considers himself as having made the revolution in America & seems to think he will make one in England.'[15] Others who came into contact with Paine at around this time, who were less well disposed, referred to his being puffed up with vanity and self-importance; 'He seems Cock-Sure of bringing about a revolution in Great Britain,' recorded the American Gouverneur Morris in his diary on meeting him in

London in February 1792.[16] Daer, meanwhile, together with his companions, found himself drawn into another of the Revolution's crucial episodes, a crisis precipitated by the French royal family's attempted flight to the border fortress of Monmédy and capture at Varennes on the night of 21 June. The ensuing political uproar culminated with decisions of the National Assembly on 13 and 15 July to promulgate the fiction that Louis had been kidnapped and to allow him to retain the crown subject to his accepting a new constitution. What followed on swiftly was the so-called Massacre of the Champs de Mars on 17 July, when troops from the National Guard under the command of Lafayette, and accompanied by the Mayor of Paris, Jean-Sylvan Bailly, acted to suppress a peaceful crowd of possibly around 50,000 who had convened on the Champs de Mars, an open space in the south-western part of the capital, today the site of the Eiffel Tower, many of them to sign a petition effectively demanding that France become a republic.[17] When, with martial law declared and being informed that the demonstration was illegal by Lafayette, the crowd failed to disperse, in a confused sequence of events one group of soldiers responded to being barracked and pelted by stones by first firing blanks and then live rounds into the crowd, while a second column charged from the opposite side of the field, which resulted in as many as fifty deaths and thirty to forty wounded.[18] It marked the first time during the Revolution when the National Assembly and the Paris crowd were in open opposition, and in the ensuing days and weeks a wave of repression followed aimed at suppressing the insurgent movement for democratic republican equality. The rift, one notable French historian of the Revolution has observed, ran deep between the Paris popular movement and a section of the bourgeoisie; and the Patriot party, which had hitherto largely managed to maintain a precarious unity, finally split apart.[19] While Hall and possibly his brothers were still in Paris in mid-July – they very prudently departed on the day after the 'massacre' (18 July) – Daer had left for England on 8 July, in the company of Paine, now anxious to follow events in England and Ireland more closely, and the Genevan Pierre Étienne Louis Dumont.

The main purpose of this chapter is to assess the impact on Daer's political thinking and outlook of his seeing and experiencing at first hand French revolutionary politics. We have, predictably enough, to approach this rather obliquely. Our principal source is a remarkably detailed account of the trip in 1791 – running to a full 800 octavo pages – penned by Sir James Hall.[20] Daer features, it must be said, rather infrequently, and most of Hall's references to him tend to be brief and restricted to matters of fact. So, for example, the entry for 22 April simply records that Hall met Daer and his brother in the Palais Royal, of which more below, and that later on that same day they had both called on Lavoisier. Using Hall's account we can, nevertheless, begin to reconstruct what Daer was doing in Paris, as well as identify some of the individuals with whom he came into contact. And from this we can start to infer a good deal, albeit most must necessarily be deduced from the clues afforded by Hall's record. Beyond dispute, however, is that the city Daer found himself in during the summer of 1791 was once again racked with acute political and social tensions, filled with rumour and uncertainty, and electrified by intense political argument and questioning, and that much of the debate and contestation was about republicanism. To put it more bluntly, the question, now that the King's attempted flight had publicly lifted the veil on his attitude towards the revolution, was whether the only real path to true liberty was to turn the country into a democratic republic. As Condorcet declared, although in his mind the answer to this was abundantly clear: 'La Constituante se trouve donc en face d'une situation très nette et très simple: La République est possible; elle est nécessaire'[21] ('The Constituent Assembly is thus faced with a very clear and simple situation. The Republic is possible; it is necessary'). Several historians have recently emphasised the importance of his French experience and connections, and French debates, to the evolution of Paine's republicanism at the beginning of the 1790s.[22] We need to examine whether Daer's experiences in Paris during the summer of 1791 pushed him towards or even led to his embracing democratic republicanism.

We begin, however, with the motivations for the trip. For these are crucial to understanding the nature of Hall's descriptions of it and thus what we can glean about Daer as a witness to French revolutionary politics.

To a significant degree, the trip in 1791 was driven and shaped by their shared interests in science (especially chemistry, mineralogy and geology), technology and agricultural improvement, but also, and more pertinently, a restless intellectual energy and deep curiosity about the world. Hall and Daer were cut from the same cloth; in a very real sense each acts as a mirror to the other. They appear to have first met when they were students at Edinburgh, probably in 1782. Four years later, Hall married Daer's sister, Helen, and the two men were much in each other's company in ensuing years, propelled, we can safely assume, by the closeness of the two families, but also their shared preoccupations.[23]

Hall's intellectual credentials are reasonably well known, and need only brief rehearsal here.[24] His main achievements lay in the new field of experimental geology. In the early 1800s, using apparatus of his own construction, he devised and conducted a series of experiments, concerning, respectively the effects of compression on the decomposition under the impact of heat of calcium carbonate, and the recrystallisation of minerals under cooling, that furnished empirical support to James Hutton's revolutionary theories about the formation of the earth. As we saw in an earlier chapter, Hall also played a crucial role in publicising the new French chemistry associated with Lavoisier in Edinburgh in the later 1780s, engaging in a series of debates with Hutton on this topic at the Royal Society of Edinburgh in 1787. Elected a fellow of the Edinburgh Royal Society in 1806, six years later he became its president, serving in this office until 1820. In 1813 he published a work on another of his long-standing preoccupations, Gothic architecture, *An Essay on the Origin, History and Principles of Gothic Architecture.*[25] His main contention – that the Gothic form derived ultimately from nature, 'the great and legitimate source of beauty' , and had a common origin in some 'rustic' form of building – is not well regarded by modern authorities. But it owed much to his avowedly 'conjectural' approach to the puzzle of origins – itself indicative of how deeply he had absorbed Enlightenment methods – and his commitment to proving his thesis, which extended as far as building, or rather having a local cooper construct, a miniature cathedral created from living willow trees on the grounds of his estate at Dunglass, East Lothian. In 1819, his son fondly, and perhaps a touch wryly, observed of his father, who was by then in his late fifties: 'He retains all his ardour for enquiry of every kind; he has generally some four or five topics on his hands, and they keep him sufficiently occupied and of course amused.'[26] In 1781, Hall had referred more simply to his own 'persevering curiosity'.[27] It was a compulsion that led to him attending a series of lectures on municipal law given by David Hume (Professor of Scots Law and nephew of the philosopher) in Edinburgh in the winter of 1787–8: 'I cannot help thinking,' he offered to his uncle by way of explanation, although perhaps not meant entirely seriously, 'that to have some guess beforehand of how a business is likely to turn out is the most effectual way to keep oneself clear of the calamity of a law suit.'[28] A few years later (during the winter of 1791–2) he would again attend a series of classes at the University, this time in anatomy. 'I have,' he reported in comments that came as close as any of his to boasting about the striking range of his knowledge, 'stuck close to my anatomy all winter. The class is now over & I have followed it with very great pleasure: if I could now get hold of a little botany I should be fit to attack dame nature in many shapes.'[29]

How and why Hall acquired this habit of fierce curiosity is hard to say. It was, to be sure, still an age of the gentleman (and woman) enthusiast, and distinctions between professionalism and amateurism in many areas, not just science, were incipient, although the balance was beginning to shift – for example, in the arts and music. Fairly easily uncovered are coteries and networks of enthusiasts for experimental farming, which overlapped and intersected with an essentially provincial culture of enlightenment that drew together manufacturers, scientists, professionals (including churchmen) and members of the landed classes. It so happened that the Hall family was part of such a coterie resident in south-eastern Scotland, who met either in one another's houses or in their Edinburgh residences. A neighbour and friend of his father's, Sir John Hall, was James Hutton, while his uncle, William Hall of Whitehall, was also a student of chemistry and early convert to Lavoisier's new chemical theories. Hall may have corresponded rather irregularly with his uncle, as he on occasion acknowledged, but when he did find the time and inclination to write it was usually at considerable length and on subjects concerning shared scientific interests, including Lavoisier's attacks on phlogiston theories. William also evidently knew Sir William Hamilton, from 1764 the British ambassador to Naples and famous vulcanologist, who also had interests in chemistry and the new science of electricity, and whom his nephew would meet in Naples in 1785. Another local resident was Patrick Brydone, a son of the Manse, who was elected a fellow of the Royal Society in 1773, contributing several papers to its *Philosophical Transactions* on electricity. Brydone was an enthusiastic traveller, and his *Tour through Sicily and Italy*, published in 1773, achieved considerable popularity in an era when travel writing was eagerly consumed by a fast expanding reading public. Brydone was very much the modern traveller. Not for him, or his charges, pursuit of 'finish', but rather visiting classical sites, geologising and recording ethnographical impressions.[30]

Perhaps more important than any of these connections, however, was the relationship with his great-uncle, the distinguished military physician, Sir John Pringle, president of the Royal Society in London from 1772 to 1778. It was Pringle, who on the death of Hall's father, took over much of the responsibility for the young James's education; and through his great-uncle Hall gained further access to a cosmopolitan world of intellectual and scientific enquiry. When he was in Vienna in 1784, to give just one example, Hall had a series of meetings with Jean Ingen-Housz. Ingen-Housz, formerly a close associate of Pringle's, in 1779 published details of his experiments that demonstrated the production of oxygen in plants exposed to sunlight, results that had been received sceptically by Priestley and Black. In Hall's presence, Ingen-Housz repeated the experiments, and Hall duly wrote a long, detailed missive to his uncle William describing these and his being persuaded of the truth of the conclusions derived from them.[31] In a subsequent letter, Hall wrote of this information, in terms which suggest how far his uncle and he saw themselves and were part of a distinct scientific community: 'I shall be sorry if it [the letter] is lost as I am curious to know how it will be received by you and the rest of the Edinburgh philosophers.' In the same letter, Hall entirely characteristically referred to the contemporary fascination with ballooning – '[all] philosophical heads are busy now about the *balon volant*' – asking if anything on that was being done in Scotland. 'Write,' he encouraged his uncle, 'and tell me all that is going on either in Politics Philosophy or dancing all will be very welcome –'.[32] Hall's keen interest in dancing we met briefly in an earlier chapter; the interest in politics is something to which we shall return later in the present one.

Pringle's initial view of his young charge seems to have been a somewhat underwhelmed one, although this may in part have reflected Hall's awkwardness in his new situation and the rather different, more formal manners expected of him in the London society of which Pringle had become a very well-established part. But his judgment began to shift as Hall quickly displayed a special talent for drawing at the academy in London, run by a Monsieur Blondel, who taught him mathematics and Latin, where he was placed for a number of weeks before going to the University of Cambridge.[33] Hall spent a good deal of time over the years sketching architectural details of churches and cathedrals; and the illustrations for his book on Gothic architecture were his own. Of his time in Cambridge, little is known, although he was there for two years; and we can fairly safely assume that he continued to study mathematics, a particular strength of teaching of natural philosophy at Cambridge and another life-long interest of Hall's, and probably chemistry. One person whom we know that he met there was Richard Watson, the future Bishop of Llandaff, who had been appointed Professor of Chemistry in 1764, holding the post until 1773, although his academic career continued until 1787.[34] Accompanied by a tutor, Hall then went to Holland, but a period at a Dutch university was ruled out because Hall's Latin was of an insufficient standard; lectures and teaching in Dutch universities were in Latin. Pringle decided that he should instead go to Geneva for a year, where the teaching was in French, and where, unlike Lausanne, there were relatively few British students and less chance of Hall getting into bad company.[35] The great inventor and former pupil of Joseph Black's, James Watt, dispatched his son, also called James – who we shall meet again later – to Geneva for much the same reasons (1784–5). One might well be tempted to suppose that it was the University of Edinburgh that provided the crucial locus for the development of his preoccupations, and to an extent no doubt this was true. Based, however, on the facts referred to above, and the survival of part of a journal describing his time in Geneva[36] – which contains, among other things, several quite detailed accounts of conversations he held with George-Louis Le Sage, the physicist and mathematician, and foreign correspondent of the London Royal Society, on his mechanical theory of gravity and ideas about perpetual motion – it was much more the case that already by 1781 his was a quick-silver mind fully ready to sponge up the teaching that was available in the Edinburgh lecture rooms, and armed with very distinct intellectual enthusiasms.

Hall's zest for knowledge and understanding is abundantly and richly documented in his journals and diaries. The practice of keeping a journal whilst on the grand tour was a fairly common one for people of Hall's background, and Hall certainly did this during a three-year sojourn on the continent between 1783 and 1786. There the typicality ended, however. For Hall's journals are more detailed than most, more expressive of his various preoccupations and sheer appetite for knowledge and experience, and, indeed, his formidable reserves of restless energy. Among other things, Hall was a great walker and keen pursuer of what he called 'the true taste for the beauties of nature', by which he meant spectacular natural scenery. The habit of keeping journals, moreover, remained with him, and may well have been a near constant practice. Not only do we have the diaries of the trip to France, but journals that cover his travels through Britain on his return and from several later years. Some exist, moreover, in rough and fair copies, and even more strikingly the entries in his diaries of his French trip were carefully categorised and indexed.[37] When the latter was undertaken is unclear. However, alongside each paragraph Hall drew a line, and each was annotated with either the letter M for 'Manners', H for 'Husbandry' or P for 'Politics'. And, at the back of each of the volumes Hall produced a contents page, with the events of the days duly noted, and with the category under which his observations fell also indicated. This raises the possibility at least that Hall was thinking of publishing his account, but more obviously it tells us a great deal about how carefully Hall thought about his text, and that the diaries were almost certainly envisaged with their future use in mind – as indeed seems to have been the case with many of his other journals.[38]

Writing came of course much more easily to the upper and middling ranks than today, and indeed to a perhaps surprising number of the artisanal classes; and literacy and epistolary skills were carefully formed and cultivated, performing a crucial role in the forging and sustaining of social, cultural and indeed intellectual networks.[39] And there were quite a few compulsive recorders of their own experiences – Boswell comes very readily to mind here. Boswell's journals, however, were essentially about him; Hall's, by contrast, focused squarely on his preoccupations and interests.

It would take more space than we have here to scrutinise this journalising habit in depth. What the journals and diaries reveal, apart from a very organised mind – and, fortunately, tidy, precise hand – is a deep interest in a wide variety of matters: mineralogy, chemistry, geology, manufactures, technology, experimental farming, to name but a few. Some of these were perhaps to be expected from a man of his background and social status, such as, for example, the farming. But again it is impossible on reading the journals not to be struck by the sheer extent of enthusiasm, the commitment to the practice of experiment, and depth in which he explored his interests. He was constantly experimenting with new methods on his estate and farms – particular techniques in arboriculture, or the use of gypsum as a fertiliser – and once he became interested in something his pursuit of it was relentless. In 1792, for example, a particular interest was methods of draining land and water management, with an eye to implementing these, or variation thereon, on his estate. This took him to view Lord Stafford's water meadows at Trentham, widely regarded as the most advanced in Britain. Fully thirty-six pages of his journal covering a trip through England in 1792 was taken up with a record of a conversation that he held with a Mr Eccleston of Scarisbrook, near Ormskirk, Lancashire, in which water management featured very heavily. 'I have met with no single man,' Hall noted, 'from whom I have learnt so much in so short a time & *I felt that I had still much more to get from him*' (my emphasis).[40] The same journal contains sketches and detailed descriptions of several different ploughs that Hall came across on his travels, also a notable feature of his French diaries, suggesting this was another matter much on his mind in 1791–2. In Naples in 1785, Hall climbed Vesuvius on five occasions, also visiting Stromboli and Mount Etna, while page upon page of his journal covering these visits records in minute detail the geological phenomena – the varieties of lava and so on – that he had observed. As one modern authority has noted, Hall's journals reveal 'a concern with understanding nature's works in the field to explain and verify theories arrived at a priori'.[41] Perhaps in its way, however, as striking and indicative of his personality is the record of his visit to the museum at Portici, at which the objects excavated from both Pompeii and Herculaneum were on display. Organised on a room-by-room basis the account extended to over fourteen pages.[42] It is not that journals and descriptions like these are unfamiliar; indeed, the

practice of travel writing was essentially imitative, and there are quite a few
elements that will be very familiar to those with even the most superficial
acquaintance with eighteenth-century travel literature – the quick and ready
appraisals of townscapes and of female pulchritude (or equally of course its
absence). Thus, Hall recorded of his visit to Lyon in early September 1784:
'In the evening went to see the public walks over the river – a prodigious
number of people of all ranks – the lower class are ugly & the better sort of
bourgeois well enough.' In an earlier journal, he recorded, in another fairly
typical comment: 'Set out for Berne – Crossed the Lakes. Dined at Arburg –
a fair with people dancing the Allemand Bernoise in good time – the women
very ugly.'[43] The sexualised gaze of the male tourist is met with in many a
travel journal, and is a timely reminder of what today would seem uncomfort-
able assumptions and prejudices which lay very close to the surface of elite
society, even if they were rationalised by their authors, as in Hall's case, under
the fashionable and often ultimately rather vacuous category of 'manners'.
But if all this is true, there is at the same time in Hall's journals a rich record
of what can only be described as an obsessive chasing of information and
knowledge that sat at the very core of his personality.

Much of this was apparent during the visit to France in 1791. In Paris Hall
pursued many of his scientific interests, attending several public meetings
of the Académie des Sciences. On 4 May, for example, he heard Lavoisier
read a paper there on animal economy.[44] Elsewhere, he records a conversation, almost certainly with the great French mathematician, Pierre-Simon
Laplace, in which Laplace itemised his objections to a paper by the Scottish
mathematician and close friend of Dugald Stewart, John Playfair, which Hall
had sent him; Hall wrote these down in French in his diary, suggesting that
they were transcribed from original notes.[45] He also spent a good deal of
time examining and working on furnaces, including with Lavoisier. On 12
June, he and Daer travelled south from Paris to Orléans, Tours, Limoges and
then on to Clermont in Auvergne, to study the state of agriculture. What is
noteworthy and entirely characteristic about this is that it was envisaged as a
systematic enquiry. As Hall recorded:

> Our object is to examine the state of the country in particular with regard to
> husbandry in particular in those parts where the petite culture prevails where
> the land is worked by oxen & the farms held by metayers [i.e. sharecroppers].
> *Our view in this is to see the wretched state of the country as present and to observe
> the change some years hence in consequence of the revolution.*[46] (My emphasis)

Apparently, they aimed to talk to people in these areas about their condition and their expectations of change created by the Revolution. While in Paris, Daer wrote to Sir John Sinclair, who was then seeking to establish the British Wool Society, and who two years later would become the first president of the newly formed Board of Agriculture, about the possibility of exporting to Britain some fine-wooled Spanish-bred sheep.[47] News, however, of the King's flight and capture, sent Hall and his companions scurrying back to Paris, where they arrived on 26 June, and where they met Daer's father, the fourth earl of Selkirk, who had recently arrived in the French capital.

Politics, in fact, had always been the main reason for the visit. This became very clear on their arrival in Paris. On their first morning, Hall called on successively the duc de la Rochefoucauld-Liancourt, possibly the marquis de Lafayette, and then Lavoisier, with the objective of gaining permanent tickets for admission to the National Assembly. The following day he met Madame Lavoisier in a coffee house on the Place Vendôme, accompanying her and another lady to the National Assembly, where they sat on the platform of the president, the 'tribunal'. In subsequent days and weeks, Hall was a very regular attender at the National Assembly, often going there on a daily basis.[48] The decision, moreover, abruptly to return to Paris on hearing news of the King's flight to Varennes was driven by the wish to discover and follow the fall-out from the crisis. As Hall's entry for 23 June, when they were at the Pont de Chateau, outside Clermont, records: 'After dinner we heard the news of the king being fled from Paris and we set out instantly for Clermont. The news was confirmed when we came there and we resolved to set out by daylight tomorrow for Paris.'[49] No doubt the fact they had found people in the provinces generally poorly informed about events in Paris was also an important factor. The National Assembly went into permanent session between 22 and 27 July – meeting night and day for some 128 hours – before resuming its normal sessions, and Hall and his companions were often in attendance. They frequented many of the other main sites of the revolutionary politicking and debate in Paris: the Tuileries gardens, at one end of which stood the royal palace and at the other the National Assembly; the Palais Royal, on the right bank just behind the Louvre, which in the 1780s had been turned into a public pleasure garden by the duc d'Orleans and from the winter of 1788–9 became a hive of pamphlet sellers, cafés, political clubs, political talk and activity – the great historian of the French crowd, George Rudé described it as the 'guiding centre' of the revolution, the place to which the 'angry, bewildered, but elated citizens [of Paris] looked for leadership and guidance';[50] and the Jacobin Club or, to give it its proper name, the Société des Amis de la Constitution (Society of the Friends of the Constitution), in its home in a former convent of the Dominicans on the Rue Saint Honoré, adjacent to the National Assembly, and described by one foreigner in May 1791 as the 'receptacle of the purest patriotism'.[51] As we shall see below, they were also regularly in the company of several of the key actors in the political drama of late June and early July 1791.

From what we can tell from the rather exiguous record of his activities provided by Hall, politics was always the main attraction for Daer. Daer, we can surmise, spoke and understood French well, as was certainly true of Hall. On 2 May, Hall and Daer visited the National Assembly, and Hall regretfully noted the divisions and intemperate exchanges which character-ised the debates, also observing that part of this could be explained by the impact of the Comte de Mirabeau's death. (Mirabeau had died on 2 April.) 'They had,' Hall went on, 'no idea (as some of them acknowledged to Daer) till he was gone, how much they were led by him.'[52] Sometimes, as on this above occasion, Hall and Daer were together, so we are unable to distinguish between them. On 15 May, to take another example, they had been walking in the Tuileries gardens, when they had observed a morose Louis XVI going to Mass – 'vacant and stupid looking' was Hall's very pointed description.[53] Yet on other occasions, Hall provides clear hints that Daer's appetite for witnessing political exchanges went rather beyond that of his companion, and he often seems to have been better informed than Hall. On 3 June, Hall records: 'Passing by the church of the Theatins, Daer saw a groupe and went into it.'[54] Hall on this occasion had continued walking with Thomas Douglas in the Palais Royal, before meeting Daer to return home. Two days later, Hall, Daer and Thomas were again walking in the Tuileries, but while Hall and Thomas returned home, Daer had gone again to the Jacobins. Daer it was who introduced Hall to the Jacobin club on 30 June.[55] On the next day, Hall had gone to the Jacobins but found Daer already there. Of later the same day, Hall wrote: 'Returned to the Jacobins and went with Daer to the Palais royale – We went into a famous black-guard place for politics called the Bercean Lyrique but we were too late and all our politicians had gone to bed.' In a perhaps surprising coda, given our usual images of revolutionary Paris, he observed: 'The Parisians are I think upon the whole regular people – there is little stir after ten o'clock.'[56] Or, perhaps revolutions really were daylight affairs.

If Daer's eagerness to follow political debates, especially at the Jacobin Club, thus begins to emerge quite clearly, can we say much more about the impact that this might have had on him? We need, in this context, to look more closely at those whom he was meeting, and to whom he was talking. On one occasion, Hall noted simply: 'The fact is that our acquaintances lies [sic] among the Democrates [. . .].'[57] More specifically, many of them were part of a democratic republican vanguard, the inheritors and bearers of a radical enlightenment, and a group who Jonathan Israel has recently argued exercised an influence between 1789 and 1793 on the process, trajectory and nature of the Revolution out of all proportion to their small numbers.[58] They included Condorcet, Dumont and the minor playwright and poetaster Philippe-Antoine Grouvelle. On 28 June Daer and Hall called on Mme de Condorcet – Sophie Condorcet – who presided over one of the leading republican and *philosophique* Parisian salons.[59] They had met her and her husband earlier in the month at the Lavoisiers, but the connection may well, as alluded to earlier, go back rather further.

The full extent and nature of Daer's relationship to Condorcet is hidden. It is surely significant, however, that when in March 1794, facing death, Condorcet wrote his testament on the flyleaf of a book, it included the recommendation that if, in case of necessity, his daughter were to go to England she should contact either his close friend of many years, Charles, third earl of Stanhope, or Daer.[60] Perhaps they recognised in each other what one of Condorcet's modern biographers had termed a 'passion for the public good', a deep conviction regarding the duty of pursuing this, and a profound, although not naïve, optimism about the future.[61] For Condorcet, as for Daer's teacher, Dugald Stewart, the roots of this optimism resided in a particular reading of the past; it was history that furnished the basis for confidence in future progress.

Condorcet and his wife were, Hall confided to his diary on 28 June, 'very keen republicans'. When news of the King's flight first arrived in the capital, they had rapidly convened a group that they called the Société des Républicains, a group who included Jacques-Pierre Brissot, Paine and Achille Duchastelet, a colonel who had fought in the American war, and who was a close friend of Condorcet's and Brissot's. Alongside the much more populist Cordeliers Club, these individuals launched a campaign to promote a republican solution to the political dilemma created by Louis XVI's attempted escape. Condorcet and Brissot were among the French Revolution's foremost advocates of internationalism, human rights and black emancipation. In early June, Hall recorded a conversation involving Brissot and various other republican intellectuals about Geneva.[62] The failed Genevan revolution of 1782 had brought a cluster of Genevan republicans to Paris, including Dumont, who we met at the beginning of this chapter accompanying Daer and Paine back to England, and Étienne Clavière, the financier and after 1791 one of Brissot's closest political associates. Once in Paris, they became very closely aligned to the French republican vanguard, and were to play an important part in debates on the kinds of republicanism compatible with a modern, commercial society such as France. On 5 July, Hall – we can't tell whether Daer was present on this occasion – dined with Brissot, Jérôme Pétion, who would follow Bailly as Mayor of Paris in October 1791, François Nicholas Buzot, Duchastelet and Robespierre, describing the last as a man of 'morose patriotism'.[63] On 5 July, the very day he was dining with Hall, Brissot published a republican confession of faith, calling for an end to monarchy in France. On 10 July, two days after Daer left Paris, Brissot sought to turn the tide of opinion in the Jacobins decisively against monarchy; Hall, who was present on this occasion, noted in his diary that 'this is the first time the Jacobins have fairly spoken out'.[64] Two days earlier, at the Cercle Social, which met in the Palais Royal, Condorcet declared the French monarchy to be corrupt and called for an elected national convention with the authority to turn France into a republic; monarchy, he argued, 'is not at all appropriate for the French nation in the current epoch'; 'Cet amour pour les rois,' he warmly continued, 'si longtemps reproché a la nation française [. . .] cette vielle erreur s'est évanouie comme un songe, donc le souvenir meme s'éfface au moment du réveil. Il faut, pour le salut public, instituer sans retard la République'[65] (This love for kings, for so long a reproach to the French nation [. . .] this old error has faded like a dream so the memory fades on awakening. It is necessary for the salvation of the public, to institute without delay the republic).

Not all of Hall's and Daer's French contacts were supporters of a republic in the summer of 1791. Most were, nevertheless, from a group of French intellectuals-now-politicians, who derived originally from the circle of the one-time reforming minister, Anne-Robert-Jacques Turgot, but subsequently became associated with Condorcet, Mirabeau, Lafayette, La Rochefoucauld and the Abbé Sieyès. What united them – or had done so at least up until now – was their rejection of the notion of distinct orders within a state; their commitment to the principle of the sovereignty of the people; and their complete disavowal of the British model of mixed or balanced government. Turgot famously wrote a letter to Richard Price in 1778 attacking the balance of powers incorporated in most of the state constitutions in North America. Many of these individuals had connections with America, going back to the American Revolution, and most had in 1789 been outspoken critics of noble privileges and the principle of aristocracy. On 7 May, Daer dined 'in company' with Sieyès, whose 'dominant passion', according to his friend Benjamin Constant, was hatred of the nobility.[66] On 10 June, dinner was with Bailly, the mayor of Paris. In early July, Daer and his father dined with Lafayette, who had been very much to the fore in attacking the nobility on the famous night of 4 August 1789. In the summer of 1791, Sieyès, Bailly and Lafayette were, however, part of the majority of opinion within the National Assembly and indeed the Jacobin Club convinced of the need to stabilise the Revolution, which meant retaining the monarchy, or at least, as the American chargé d'affaires, William Short, very shrewdly observed, its 'shadow',[67] and suppressing the democratic republicans and their populist allies. Another important member of this grouping, with whom Hall was in contact, was the Grenoble lawyer and powerful orator, Antoine Joseph Barnarve, one of three deputies sent by the National Assembly to accompany the King and royal family back to Paris in late June. On 15 July, Barnarve delivered one of the most influential speeches in the National Assembly in support of the principle of monarchy, and in the subsequent months he would help to lead a general crackdown on the republicans and republican press in the interests of re-establishing order and stability.

It is easy to grasp what drew Daer and his companions back time and again to the National Assembly and Jacobin Club, especially in late June and early July. The King's attempted flight detonated one of the major political crises of the early phases of the Revolution, one which was nationwide in its effects, but focused on Paris, and which reverberated through its streets, cafés, 'sections' – bodies created in the spring of 1790 and which had come to assume an ever-growing role in government in the city, and many of which went into permanent session on news of the King's flight – clubs and other meeting places, while rumour, denunciation and argument filled the city's prolific news-sheets. It was one of those moments when politics overwhelmed everything, or nearly all else. As Short observed of the popular newsprint: 'These journals are hawked about the streets, cried in every quarter of Paris and sold cheap and given to the people who devour them with astonishing avidity.'[68]

To understand properly the scale and nature of the crisis, we need briefly to consider the immediate context, and the fears and uncertainties that then pervaded Paris and much of the rest of France. As Timothy Tackett has observed, even before the news of the flight was known, Paris was in anxious, fissile mood. 'On the eve of Varennes, Paris was already in danger of exploding from one day to the next.'[69] Fears multiplied about the role of refractory priests – those clergy who refused to take the oath of allegiance to the new constitution and the civil constitution of the clergy – and suspected counter-revolutionary plots involving the armies of emigrés gathering across the border in Germany, made only more destabilising because of uncertainties regarding the loyalties of those army officers who remained. Waves of strikes and labour disputes heightened social tensions; and the Cordeliers Club was seeking to orchestrate the activities of proliferating popular political societies. People were profoundly shocked by the King's attempted escape, even though in April he and his family had been prevented by crowds of Parisians from leaving for an Easter visit to the palace of St Cloud, fearing that this was an excuse for a permanent departure. 'The event,' Short declared, 'has so astonished every body and is so unaccountable in itself that no probable conjecture is formed of the manner in which it was effected [. . .]'[70] Many were convinced that had the King's flight been successful, it would have been followed by a foreign invasion to crush the Revolution; indeed, that it only made sense insofar as Louis was counting on foreign support. That the escape had proceeded very smoothly at first must have only reinforced alarm, once it became known. Nor did the King's capture and return to Paris solve the crisis; rather, this was where it really began. On departing, Louis had left behind him a message in which he had repudiated all of the Revolutionary decrees which he had previously signed and sworn to uphold. The veil on his intentions was now fully lifted; and the question was could the Revolution proceed further with him. Faced with the predicament these events created – whether to uphold the monarchy, and how to secure the Revolution – the majority of the deputies voted to continue drafting the constitution and to present it to the King, with his acceptance of it being the condition of his return to power. They voted, in other words, for a tactic of prudential evasion.

Daer and his fellow travellers were not present to witness the King and his family's return to Paris, watched by vast numbers of Parisians lining the streets in ominous silence, refusing even to remove their hats in recognition of their monarch. The mood they encountered, however, as they rushed back from the provinces was a defiant and angry one among the Patriots. At one place, it was made clear 'that if a war takes place, [the local Patriots were] for throwing all the aristocrats into a prison and to take off their heads without scruple if any reverse of fortune takes place', words which have an ominous import given events of the subsequent autumn. At Fontainebleau, Hall recorded, 'The King is every where talked of by the name of <u>notre cochon</u>.' As they drove into the capital, what struck them was that on all the signs bearing words such as 'roi' etc. these words had been blotted out.[71]

In Paris, Louis's failed flight had produced a dramatic reaction against the monarchy. One individual, who was a child at the time, recalled:

> The populace were roving about the streets in frantic turbulence – effigies of the King and Queen were carried about and burnt, whilst the mob danced round [. . .] and wherever the word *Royal* was inscribed over theatres, lottery offices, tobacconists, etc. it was effaced with mud or paint, and every symbol of royalty was dashed to pieces, or torn down by the infuriated multitude.[72]

Republican posters, such as one in large type authored and signed by Duchastelet on 3 July, went up all over the streets and most frequented parts of the capital; and voices now openly scathing about the King and monarchy were increasingly making themselves heard amidst the political din; '*Louis Le Faux*' and '*Louis Le Parjure*' were the cries of a betrayed, disconcerted and angry populace. Fears about war added to the uncertainty, and minor events, such as the sighting of a small number of British vessels off the Brittany coast, sparked invasion alarms. There was at the same time a growing gap in perception and feeling between the people of Paris and the National Assembly. Short's report to his boss, Jefferson, on conditions in the capital on 29 June is worth quoting from at some length:

> It seems clear to me that a great opposition is forming in the spirit of the people without, to that of the members, within the assembly. The latter as I have said wish to support the form of a monarchy. The former are becoming every day under the influence of their clubs, leaders, and journals, more and more averse both to the substance and the form. You may judge the spirit of the people of Paris who have much influence on those of the provinces, from the popular journals which you will receive by the way of Havre [Le Havre] together with the usual papers [. . .] Should this spirit propagate itself as seems certain, the present assembly will be obliged to abandon the helm.[73]

As his words disclose, it appeared to some as if it were the Assembly that might be forced to bend to popular opinion, or, if not, lose its position. The Jacobin Club, whose meetings attracted around 1,000 people at this point, debated the position of the King on an almost daily basis, and while very few members who were deputies openly called for a republic, many non-deputies called for the trial of the King. Thousands gathered on the Champs de Mars in support of republican petitions – as many as seventeen may have been presented to the National Assembly between 21 June and 17 July – most of them summarily and brusquely rejected by the deputies. The Cordeliers Club in alliance with other popular political societies was behind much of this activity. These mobilisations, which involved parades through the streets of vast numbers

– men, women and children – often seven or eight abreast, were important moments in the deepening politicisation of the Parisian crowd. And, along with the uncertainty, and the growing divisions between popular opinion and the National Assembly, which sought stability and the end of the revolution, the threat of imminent violence hung in the air. Hall declared simply on 14 July: 'it is in the highest degree probable that some great commotion will take place and nothing can save the Assembly but a good fight by which it may be driven into a near approach to the public opinion'.[74] The day before he had witnessed Charles de Lameth and Barnave attacked by the 'mob' as they left the National Assembly. Plans were also being initiated for a mass petition calling for the Assembly to desist from determining the question of the fate of the King until it had been put to the people, a move that would end in confrontation and bloodshed on the Champs de Mars on 17 July.

If the mood positively crackled with tension, and apprehensions about a breakdown of order and stability stalked many peoples' imaginations, political choices had become starkly clarified. Condorcet, Brissot, Paine and the Cercle Social and its journal, the *Bouche de fer*, which was appearing daily, now advocated the creation of a republic. From 2 July, Condorcet, Paine and Duchastelet edited a new, openly republican paper, *Le Républicain, ou défenseur du gouvernement représentatif*, in which Paine published his riposte to an article by Sieyès which appeared in another paper (the *Moniteur*) supporting the principle of monarchy. The Cordeliers Club also began publishing their own republican news-sheet, the *Journal du club des Cordeliers*. On 3 July, Paine, who had been dining with Hall and the others, talked of the 'republican spirit in the act of rising'.[75] Behind the relatively brief entries in Hall's journal, we can sense, in short, an excited, fearful and anxious cacophony of voices engaged with the issue of whether the French monarchy and the French nation any longer had a future together.

Such debates were, like most that occurred during the Revolution, political, ideological and intellectual. There was profound uncertainty about how to proceed and what might be legal; and much debate concerned how to deal with the King and through what mechanisms. Neither the constitution nor precedent offered any guidance. But there were deeper, more fundamental questions. Was a republic suited to a large, modern, commercial state such as France? Republicanism might well work in the United States, but that country, with its abundant land and lack of nearby enemies, was singular and no template for Europe. (Dugald Stewart argued something similar in his famous lectures on political economy in the early 1800s.) France surely needed stability, security for property, and this was best achieved, as Montesquieu had famously argued in his famous treatise, *De l'Esprit de lois* (the *Spirit of the Laws*), by a monarchy, albeit one subject to strict constitutional limits. But what then was liberty? If the Declaration of the Rights of Man and the Citizen made all equal before the law, then the sovereignty of the nation – as Brissot harangued the Jacobins in his speech of 10 July – acknowledged no citizen to be above the rest. Those who argued for the inviolability of the King, as many did, were arguing against the constitution. Ancient republics were direct democracies, but it was 'representative democracy' that Condorcet, Paine and their allies maintained held out the possibility of a new, modern kind of republic. Behind these issues was that of what popular sovereignty really meant or entailed; or how it could be reconciled with the imperatives of stable government. And behind these was how much freedom was possible and how far this entailed changing society through education and some element of social redistribution. It was this collection of issues that Paine sought to answer in Part II of his *Rights of Man*, a work which has a definite French as well as British context. Indeed, for Paine, the point precisely was that these issues transcended national belonging; they were universal.

We are, admittedly, still some way from knowing what Daer absorbed from these events and debates, and what effects they had on him. The Revolution, as Tackett has emphasised recently, was experienced at a profoundly emotional, as well as rational level; indeed, abrupt transitions between joy and anxiety were very much intrinsic to the revolutionary process.[76] Daer was, of course, an outsider, distanced from the events, but at the same time identifying strongly with them and the cause of liberty in France. As we shall see further below, being a witness to these events and to the distinctive forms of French revolutionary politics constituted a schooling in the politics of liberty for Daer. Political style and substance were, in this context, inseparable. The National Assembly, and even more perhaps the Jacobin Club, were where he encountered a new kind of politics, one which was very self-conscious about its authenticity and the need for a new set of values to animate political life and give substance to liberty; although at the same time it frequently descended into denunciation and, very often, paranoia.

Hall, meanwhile, offers us plenty of hints about his own views, which may well have been fairly close at this stage to Daer's, and at the very least partly informed by Daer's reactions and views and the frequent conversations they must have had. As we might suspect from those with whom they were in contact, they were strongly sympathetic to a revolution, which by 1791 could no longer be understood simply as an imitation of the British political system, but had fully disclosed itself as something entirely different in character and significance. On one occasion Hall was present at a dinner with a M. Terray, recording: 'All that family violent aristocrats, M & Me Lavoisier who were there battled for the other side of the question, M. T. and M. L. got into a warm dispute about the new and old system of taxes and of government. M. L. spoke with perfect reason & truth tho' with a degree of heat [. . .]'.[77] At another point, he reported an intriguing conversation with Sieyès in which the latter expressed his strong confidence in the power of education as a force in society and of the ultimate political capacity of the lower orders. The traditional argument against democracy, derived from Aristotle and Polybius, was that the lower orders were governed by passion not reason and thus democracy was inherently turbulent and unstable, and certain to result in tyranny. Hall informed Sieyès of a notion attributed by him to Dugald Stewart that 'since false ideas take such hold of the mind, the reign of truth were it once known, may be expected to be of universal duration', an idea of which Sieyès strongly approved as being compatible with his own notions.[78] In early June Hall noted a conversation he had with Dr Richard Gem, physician at the British embassy in Paris, and also Condorcet's doctor, about the inequality of property. In what appears to have been a somewhat unfocused discussion, Hall floated the idea that if a man were to die intestate, his estate should be divided among the poor of the district.[79] Gem, a committed champion of the Revolution, who had links with Diderot, Turgot, Dupont, Condorcet and Morellet, and who had been part of the Baron d'Holbach's materialist circle before the latter's death in 1789, was almost certainly the source of Jefferson's new conviction in 1789 that one generation of men in civil society could not bind another.[80]

Hall was also made a member of the Société des Amis de Noirs, the abolitionist society established in February 1788 and presided over by Condorcet, Brissot, Clavière, Carra, Pétion and their allies in the Cercle Social. In May, several of the debates that he heard in the National Assembly concerned the issue of granting full citizenship rights to colonial natives in the French empire, and it is clear that he supported the idea that 'gens de couleur' – in other words, free blacks and men of mixed race – should be recognised as full citizens, something to which the French West Indian planters were vehemently opposed.

Hall never became active in reform politics in the 1790s; or there is no record of this. This does not mean, however, that he was uninterested politically or, as we are beginning to see, that he did not possess definite political sympathies. The diaries themselves provide ample testimony to his profound curiosity about politics, and he quite frequently included his own reflections on issues and debates. In the mid-1780s, he had discussed at some length with his uncle the battles between Fox and Pitt at Westminster; in 1790 he subscribed to the *Courier de Londres*, a French newspaper published in London, presumably for the information that it provided on events in France; while in 1792 he and the earl of Stanhope conversed about the role of juries in the context of Fox's Libel Bill, of which Stanhope was an important promoter and supporter in the House of Lords.[81]

I don't think we can say for certain if Hall became a republican, although what this means is in any case not simple. As one of the founders of the Society for Constitutional Information, John Cartwright, mischievously argued, it could mean no more than commitment to the interests of the 'commonwealth of England'; and on this basis George III might be deemed a republican![82] Or it could connote the kind of fully-fledged democratic political republicanism espoused by Paine and his French friends. Radical politics in the 1790s became from one perspective a practical interrogation of the meanings of the term 'republican', for the individual and society, an impulse that led in notably diverse directions, including in the case of the Scot and former army officer, John Oswald, to vegetarianism. In Paris in July 1791 Hall, nonetheless, appears to have edged decisively towards supporting republicanism, at least for France. His description of Brissot's speech at the Jacobins on 10 July reads: 'M. Brissot de Warville rose next and spoke one of the most elegant and certainly the most effectual speech I ever heard. He turned the inviolability [of the King to punishment] into ridicule. <u>He said it was a convenient doctrine set on foot by Charles the second in order to save himself from having his head [word illegible]</u> and he showed clearly that in justice and common sense he ought to be tried.' The comments here underlined have been crossed out; perhaps Hall later came to see them as dangerous, even if they were a report of someone else's utterance. Earlier Hall recorded his opinion of Duchastelet's republican poster: '[I]t is written with much energy and I rather think truth.' This poster breathed a spirit of pure Paineite republicanism. 'What kind of office,' it declared starkly,

> must be in government which requires neither experience nor ability to execute? that may be abandoned to the desperate chance of birth, that may be filled with an idiot, a madman, a tyrant, with equal effect as by the good, the virtuous, and the wise? An office of this nature is a mere nonentity: it is a place of show, not of use. Let France then, arrived at the age of reason, no longer be deluded by the sound of words, and let her deliberately examine, if a King, however insignificant and contemptible in himself, may not at the same time be extremely dangerous.[83]

Hall and presumably Daer had been forcibly struck by the antipathy to the French king they had met on their journey back to Paris at the end of June; and this certainly convinced Hall that a 'republican scheme' was the most probable, and indeed probably the best, outcome of the crisis.[84]

Hall's staunch support for the French Revolution did not, moreover, quickly fade on his leaving Paris. Indeed, it endured well into 1792, as revealed in a series of entries in his diaries covering his travels through England during the summer and autumn of that year. On 16 August Hall read a newspaper account – 'great news' was his description – of the rising of the militants within the Paris sections on 10 August, which finally overthrew the French monarchy, although the republic was not formally declared until 21 September. The deaths of a number of Assembly members and several hundred royal troops were recorded by Hall in a decidedly matter-of-fact fashion, who continued: 'The event is no more than what was to be expected & I hope will turn out well. *It is not the first time that the assembly have been forced into their duty by what is called the mob of Paris.* It only remains to be seen how the army will act: Paris has hitherto given the lead. I hope it will do so on this occasion'[85] (my emphasis). Several days later Hall again reported what he had managed to pick up from reading several newspapers: 'The Armies of Austria & Prussia on the point of entering France & the Nation [i.e. the French nation] on the point of dismissing their treacherous king.' Hall had read a letter published in one newspaper, purportedly from an English traveller, which commented on the superior spirit of the French citizen soldiers compared to the armies of the old regime. 'I have,' he declared, 'great reason to hope this is a true account as consider such a conduct as likely to take place in an army where every man fight[s] for a cause as personally concerned.' And, using some very striking language, he reassured himself that '[s]uch conduct must in the long run get the better of the most formidable body of *regular slaves*' (my emphasis), a reference to the conscripted armies of the old regime powers who fought at their masters' whim. Referring to the commander of the Austro-Prussian forces' menacing, provocative declaration of 25 July, Hall noted: 'I have great hopes that the Duke of Brunswick will soon repent his insolent and ferocious manefesto [sic].'[86] This was the document that promised 'ever memorable vengeance by delivering over the city of Paris to military execution and complete destruction' were any violence to be offered to Louis XVI and the Royal Family, the threat which provided the immediate context for the overthrow of the monarchy.

Of a visit, meanwhile, which followed to the Manchester textile firm of Richard and Thomas Walker, Hall observed: 'We saw Mr Walker brother to

Mr T. Walker who seems to have the same opinions – he read some letters from France giving a comfortable account of the state of the country – The letters are dated previous to the great insurrection & the whole is foretold.'[87] Thomas Walker was a leading figure in the Manchester Constitutional Society, which since its foundation in 1790 as a moderate reform body had by the spring of 1792 become a much more radical, Paineite organisation, although publicly at least still not openly republican.[88] The 'great insurrection' refers to the events of 10 August. The letters, meanwhile, were almost certainly written by James Watt junior, the firm's commercial representative, then in Paris. On his departure for the Continent, Walker supplied Watt with letters of introduction to several individuals, including Pétion, whom he had met in London in the autumn of 1791, while Priestley had given him an introduction to Lavoisier and his circle. Walker's letter to Pétion openly disclosed his private hopes for a republican revolution in Britain, hopes that had been powerfully reinforced by the impact of Part II of the *Rights of Man*: 'Aristocracy he [Paine] has wounded mortally, war he has put an end to; Taxes can go no further, and monarchy will not, I think, continue long in fashion [. . .].'[89] Watt seems to have anticipated that the overthrow of the monarchy would bring his new Brissotin friends back into power, and he experienced what can only be described as a rush of revolutionary enthusiasm in the summer and autumn of 1792. On 7 July Tom Wedgwood, son of Josiah, the pottery manufacturer, then lodging in the French capital with Watt, whom he described as a 'furious democrat', wrote to his father that 'Watt says that a new revolution must inevitably take place, and that it will in all probability be fatal to the King, Fayette, and some hundred others. The 14th of this month will probably be eventful.'[90] Watt's revolutionary ardour endured well into the autumn, and he was able even to justify the September massacres, when hundreds of prisoners in Paris gaols thought to be engaged in counter-revolutionary activities, including several hundred refractory priests, were brutally murdered by Parisian *sans-culottes*. Watt was almost certainly the author of several first-hand accounts of events in Paris published in the radical newspaper of the north-west, the *Manchester Herald*, in the summer and autumn of 1792, including one of the massacres that basically justified them all as regrettable but necessary.[91] Increasingly, however, Watt turned against the faction that opposed the Brissotins, the supporters of Robespierre, whose growing power in the Paris Commune and in the Convention would drive the Revolution in a new direction, and lead Brissot and his allies to expulsion from, first, the Jacobins in the autumn of 1792 and then the Convention in May of the following year. From there many of them went to prison and thence to the guillotine.

By early October Hall, meanwhile, was searching for newspapers in the Midlands – a task that was much harder than one might assume from modern accounts of the eighteenth-century newspaper press. His purpose was to confirm the defeat by General Dumouriez and his revolutionary army of the invading Prussian army at Valmy (20 September) in the Champagne-Ardèche and then over the Austrians at Jemappes (6 November) in the Austrian Netherlands (present-day Belgium). On 7 October, Hall recorded: 'I got a newspaper at last and was much delighted with the news from the continent.'[92] The revolution that had been earlier in grave peril of being crushed by an alliance of despots – as radicals saw it – had been saved, events that unleashed a mood of euphoric, near-millennial joy among radicals throughout the British Isles, a mood that is perhaps best captured in the radical songs which accompanied many of the celebrations. At stake had been, at least in their eyes, not just the fate of the revolution in France, but of liberty in Britain and Ireland, and indeed of 'general happiness' and peace across the globe. As the London Corresponding Society addressing the Jacobins declared, the French were the 'champions of human happiness.'[93] If there was a 'republican moment' in Britain in the early 1790s, this was that moment, although it turned out to be very short-lived, and its significance and nature is at best ambiguous.

To return, however, to Hall and Daer: we should see them, therefore, as part of that loose collection of overlapping networks of families and individuals, linked by shared intellectual concerns and interests – in England they were often (although far from exclusively) rational dissenters – who viewed the French Revolution with enthusiasm; and who, naïvely perhaps, saw in it the realisation of the universal values of the Enlightenment. As John Cartwright put it in late 1792, the revolution was a 'luminary mounting in the firmament of reason, to dispel the heavy clouds of superstition, misgovernment, and oppression.'[94] This no doubt also reflected the nature of their personal connections to France, which were to that group of French revolutionaries who espoused and promoted a politics that derived directly from the Enlightenment, a politics that spoke the language of universalism, international peace, human rights and democratic republicanism. This drove some, such as Walker, Watt Jnr and their fellow Manchester radical, Thomas Cooper, who joined Watt in Paris in 1792, in the direction of fully-fledged republicanism in a British context. Most reform-minded people in Britain did not go that far, certainly publicly; rather, they sought reform and political and social transformation *within* the existing structures of the British constitution.[95]

At this distance, it may seem puzzling that Hall and others, including Daer, could have continued to support the French Revolution in the face of its growing violence in 1792. We need to be wary of hindsight – they could not know that Robespierre and the Terror lay around the corner. It continued still to be readily possible in the summer and autumn of 1792 to rationalise the admittedly shocking outbursts of violence in terms of the scale and momentous significance of the transformation under way; or to explain it in terms of the effects on French society of the *ancien régime* and absolutist government, an argument that, in light of modern attempts to explain revolutionary violence in terms of continuities with and echoes of the old regime, we should probably not dismiss too lightly. As a group of Belfast reformers advised in July 1792: 'Fixing our view steadily on the great principle of Gallic emancipation, we will not be diverted from that magnificent object by the accidental tumults, or momentary ebullitions of popular fury.' People should not, they urged, judge the revolution 'from the accidental irregularities, which while we condemn them, we are compelled to pity, as feeling that they spring not merely from a spirit of licentiousness, but from a sense of injury working on a sanguine people, still galled with the recollection of recent tyranny and oppression and jealous of liberty but just recovered, and scarcely yet secure.'[96] What one perceived was strongly conditioned, unsurprisingly, by one's beliefs and convictions about what had occurred and was occurring in France; which is not to say that events could and did not shift these, but the influences went both ways. And, if the realities of revolution could be messy, anarchic and vicious, this did not necessarily mean, did it, that the *principles* of the revolution were wrong – if, that is, one could agree on what these really were. Moreover, who, after all, were the 'real friends of peace' when, as the London reformer George Rous asked, the enemies of the Revolution 'appeal to force' and its supporters to the force of reason?[97]

Of Daer directly we can say frustratingly little. He features in Hall's diaries in the summer of 1792 just once and rather tantalisingly. Hall records that there was a parcel of letters waiting for him from Daer at Liverpool in early August, as well as a letter to Daer from Pierre Louis Roederer. Roederer had been a prominent supporter in the National Assembly of Sieyès and Mirabeau in 1789–90, and in the summer of 1791 he was a powerful voice in the Jacobin Club speaking out against the idea of the King's inviolability, becoming an important ally of Brissot's in 1792. Daer almost certainly met Roederer at the Jacobin Club in June or July 1791. Daer had sent letters to Hall for two prominent Liverpool Dissenters – the Quaker William Rathbone, and the Dumfriesshire born and Edinburgh-educated Dr James Currie, now best remembered as the first biographer and editor of the collected works of Robert Burns. Both were frequently accused of being 'Jacobins', though that barely signifies given that all who resisted the dulling pressures of loyalist conformism were vulnerable to being so labelled. The significant thread linking them to Daer may well be their strong opposition to war with France in 1792, as well as their enthusiasm for the Revolution.

There are several further stray clues to Daer's views of the French Revolution, one being a series of remarks recorded in the diary of William Dickson, an agent of the London Abolition Society. Dickson met Daer's father in Scotland in March 1792. We need to recall that Selkirk was in Paris in July 1791, and had just arrived when Hall and his party returned to the city in a hurry on hearing news of the flight to Varennes. Dickson's comments are worth quoting in full, so sharply made (and surprising) are they:

> His Lordship is a very sensible man but swears a very little – is warm in his temper – his voice exactly Burke's – his political principles exactly the opposite – He is a great friend to Liberty and to the poor, whose rights he holds sacred & I love and venerate him – *He is for every man having some share of political weight* – he knows how the poor fare as also does Lady Selkirk – says not how they lived before potatoes introduced – will suffer no man to kill any on his Isle [i.e. St Mary's Isle] – Protects every thing that had life. (My emphasis.)

Selkirk, as we saw in the previous chapter, had a record as an independent in politics, and was a champion of freedom of voting in Scottish peerage elections. But these comments suggest that, rather like Jefferson in July 1789, his views had moved on rapidly under the impact of the Revolution and perhaps the rise of a domestic parliamentary reform movement. Selkirk strongly disapproved of the decision of the National Assembly not to depose Louis XVI, and, according to Hall, had subsequently been 'a violent friend of liberty'.[98] Nor, as Michael Brown notes, did he relinquish or disguise his new views on his return to Britain, which led to his being dropped or avoided by most of his former political friends.[99] Daer and his father were very close; and while fathers and sons do not always agree, and many obviously do the inverse, Daer was in some important ways, as emphasised in several places elsewhere in this book, both his father's close collaborator and the perpetuator of his ambitions. Who was now influencing whom is moot; perhaps most likely is that they had both travelled politically in the same direction.

The second of our clues is another diary entry, this one made by Katherine Plymley, the intellectually and politically curious sister of Joseph Plymley, archdeacon of Salop. Katherine, who helped look after Plymley's tribe of children (there were twelve of them), was an accomplished water-colourist and botanist – very much the coming science in provincial genteel circles in the late eighteenth and early nineteenth centuries. Joseph presided over a widely extended and rather diverse network of acquaintances, many of them frequent visitors to his house near Shrewsbury. They included local churchmen and ministers, including Dugald Stewart's friend and frequent correspondent, Archibald Alison, then the curate at Kenley, Shropshire; local ironmasters, including the Reynolds family – visited by Sir James Hall in the summer of 1792; professionals and experimental scientists; and others, including Thomas Clarkson of the London Abolition Society, who shared Plymley's firm commitment to abolition of the slave trade. In May 1792, Katherine recorded a visit of Archibald Alison and his wife. Also present on this occasion was Theophilus Houlbrooke. Plymley was impressed by Alison, but also evidently struck by his comments on French affairs. 'Mr Alison told us from his authority that the present national assembly, contrary to the general idea, is composed of men of ability.' He also attributed the quality of its decision making to the nature of the interaction between its deliberations and the operations of a public opinion manifest in Paris coffee houses. He continued: 'Lord Dare [sic] has been much in France. he is a member of the Jacobin club, whose opinions & proceedings he says are much misrepresented in England.'[100] Houlbrooke had given Daer a letter of introduction to Plymley, and Joseph had met him in Shrewsbury. We know that Dugald Stewart was corresponding with Alison in the early 1790s on events in France, and that around this time he was relaying views conveyed to him by Daer's brother, Thomas, who was again in Paris. This is the only reference I know of to Daer having become a member of the Jacobin Club; and if this was true it must have occurred in the previous summer. In July 1791, the Jacobins had been divided, preventing their playing any sort of guiding role in the crisis that followed on from the King's attempted escape, a fact that seems to have led Hall to view it with increasing frustration in the first few weeks of July. On 16 July, most of the deputies from the National Assembly had left the Club, to be followed by three-quarters of the Paris membership. This group then established themselves at the convent of the Feuillants, which gave its name to the new society and the conservative tendency that it represented. By October 1791, however, the Jacobins, with its meetings now fully open to the public, and led by Brissot, Condorcet and their friends, revived, while at the same time Brissot and his democratic republican grouping, helped by the self-denying ordinance of the previous legislature, which excluded the Feuillant leaders, came to prominence in the new Legislative Assembly, elected in September 1791, and assumed growing control of the Paris commune. By the spring of 1792, the Brissotins, albeit under the shadow of a growing, orchestrated populism led by Robespierre and Marat, were approaching the height of their influence, a development confirmed in March when three Brissotins were brought into the royal ministry. Were these the Jacobins Daer thought of as 'misrepresented' in Britain? The timing of Alison's report suggests that this was the case, and it seems very plausible, given Daer's contacts with Brissot and his political allies, including Roederer.

Finally, we may anticipate a little the next chapter. There was, as we shall see, something of the politically amphibious about Daer; he was able to straddle several, quite divergent political streams within reform politics. Similar things were, however, true of many reformers in the 1790s, as indeed had been the case in the 1780s, which serves as a useful warning about not staking too much on associations and personal relationships in terms of pinning down someone's political opinions in this period. More importantly Daer's politics became increasingly driven by egalitarian ideals, and he was extremely sensitive to his rank standing in the way of consummating a new form of radical politics that was fully democratic and transparent in its operation. Was this the result of a kind of revolutionary osmosis, an internalisation of the debates and rhetoric that he would have witnessed in Paris in the summer of 1791, or indeed on his earlier visit in 1789, when his friends Sieyès, Lafayette and others had led their assault on the nobility and its privileges, a commitment which also led them to reject fundamentally the idea that France should copy Britain's mixed system of government? The terms 'aristocracy' and the 'landed classes' had gained new definitions from 1789, with the former coming, in reformist and radical circles, to mean supporters and beneficiaries (they were the same) of the existing corrupt, parasitic system of government, a group that was often elided with the landed elites. Paine's *Rights of Man* further imported these new meanings into British political debate in 1791–2. In 1792, Daer joined a series of reform societies in London, notably the Society for Constitutional Information, the Revolution Society and the London Corresponding Society, that very publicly and loudly demonstrated their support for and solidarity with the revolutionaries in France through to at least the end of that year. Unlike a good many propertied reformers in Britain, he remained active in radical politics in the face of the loyalist and conservative onslaught and repression from late 1792, and as radicalism took on a more genuinely popular character. Daer was also present at the British convention of radicals held in Edinburgh in early

December 1793, when the Scottish and English delegates present openly adopted French revolutionary forms and modes of address. The Convention may not have been strictly republican in its immediate goals – these were universal male suffrage and annual parliaments – and the adoption of French terms of address and forms can, as some have claimed, be seen basically as a gesture of defiance in the face of government and official hostility. Whatever the truth, however, the Convention's debates and actions were infused with a thoroughly republican spirit; and the major inspiration behind this were the democratic politics and ideals of the French Revolution.

CHAPTER SEVEN

Union(s) and Liberty

During 1792–3, Daer became deeply involved in what developed into the first, properly 'British' campaign for parliamentary reform. While the hopes and ambitions of most radicals were focused on a new, consciously egalitarian vision of political liberty, a vision that had a strong cosmopolitan element, for some like Daer this offered an opportunity to reimagine the nature of the Anglo-Scots union, to transcend the 'corrupt' bargain contrived in 1707 by a tiny elite, and to replace it with a true union of 'the people'. Submerged within the radical politics of the 1790s there was, in short, a thread of unionist radicalism. Often overlooked in accounts of this period, it provides a further vital key to understanding Daer's politics.

There had of course been earlier parliamentary reform campaigns. None, however, had been British in scope or substance. In the 1760s and early '70s, that irrepressible gadfly of English politics John Wilkes stood forth as the figurehead of a libertarian protest politics out of which emerged the first radical political society, the Society of the Supporters of the Bill of Rights (1769) and first organised campaign for political reform. It was a politics which was focused on London and its environs, and which took root in other English urban communities. A more complex figure than is sometimes appreciated – educated at Leiden, an energetic libertine, with no obvious religious convictions, and thoroughly at home in the salons of the Parisian Enlightenment – politically he was, as his most recent political biographer Peter Thomas has argued, above all an old-style *English* patriot.[1] He was also deeply cynical in his exploitation of the crude anti-Scottish sentiment of the London crowd in the 1760s, as he sought to mobilise English public opinion against George

III's favourite and briefly Prime Minister, Lord Bute, and then to persuade them of the existence of an insidious plot against liberty. It was a platform that unsurprisingly made him very unpopular north of the border, and his effigy continued to be burnt in Edinburgh on the anniversary of the King's birthday into the early nineteenth century.[2] As we saw in chapter 5, against the background of failure in the war against the American colonists, and an acute sense of national vulnerability, the later 1770s and early '80s saw the rise of a further English reform movement, the so-called Association Movement, which overlapped with and developed a series of connections to the emergent campaigns north of the border for burgh reform and reform of Scots county elections. This was part of a wider impulse as reformers in different parts of the British Isles, including Ireland, looked to one another for support and advice, a move facilitated by their common political language and a sense of their laying claim to a shared political heritage. Such links as did exist, however, were at best fragmentary and of strictly limited influence, reflecting the fact that these were at bottom very different movements with distinct origins.

The movement for parliamentary reform as it took shape in the early 1790s was different. Partly, this can be explained in terms of simple opportunity; partly by the deepening integration of Scottish and British political life at the end of the eighteenth century; and partly in terms of the common experience of government hostility and repression north and south of the border. Combating or just surviving repression drew reformers together from different parts of the British Isles, as they came to see their fates as interdependent. Yet the mental and political horizons of radicals in the 1790s were broader, and their commitment to co-ordination and alliance deeper-rooted, strategically and politically. Scots in London and Edinburgh began in the early 1790s very deliberately to knit together the Scottish and English reform campaigns. Daer, with his links to both London and Scottish radical circles, played a crucial role in this process.

It is here also, in the crucible of a developing *British* radical politics, that we finally get to hear Daer in his own words, recorded in several minutes of radical meetings and groups, but much more expansively in a long and fascinating letter that he sent to the young opposition Whig reformer Charles Grey in the spring of 1793. For this reason alone, and because the letter has led to some misunderstanding, it needs careful examination. Before we do so, however, we need to establish the political circumstances in which it was written, and how it reflected an unfolding pattern of radical politics in Scotland in the second half of 1792 and a radical who politically-speaking had his feet firmly planted on both sides of the English–Scottish border.

We begin in London, a city that by virtue of its extraordinary size – with a population of near on one million by 1801, Paris was half its size, and Edinburgh well under a tenth – but also for concentration of wealth, mercantile expertise and political power, was without rival in the contemporary Western world. London was a city of immigrants and sojourners, as well as of myriad connections to other places within the British Isles, and an expanding world overseas; it was, indeed, from this that its wealth and creativity ultimately derived, as well as its remarkable capacity to draw to it human capital and expertise. And a good deal of this was Scots in origin. Among the Scots who pursued their fortunes in the British capital were professionals – including medics like Sir John Pringle, who we met earlier in this book, architects and artists; merchants and financiers, including bankers; military men; writers, journalists and bookmen; tradesmen; and, although sometimes overlooked, many artisans – shoemakers, tailors and so on. The figure of the needy, grasping Scot on the make in the capital was pervasive – one of the reasons why Wilkes's venomous Scotophobia had such a remarkable impact in the 1760s and early '70s – although it belies the deeper story, which by and large was one of successful integration. Indeed, this was why Bute's propaganda had such an impact, that and the habits of patronage, connection and co-operation that lay behind Scots' success in the British capital, which outsiders interpreted usually in crude cultural terms as Scots 'clannishness'. Among the members of the 'Protestant Association' who joined Lord George Gordon in June 1780 on St George's Fields and then processed through the capital to petition parliament to repeal the Catholic Relief Act of 1778 were several Scots divisions; and this may well be one of the subterranean routes through which men such as the shoemaker Thomas Hardy, a native of Stirling who had arrived in the British capital in 1774 at the age of 22, and the first secretary and one of the founders of the London Corresponding Society, the main popular and most enduring of the radical societies formed in the 1790s, were led to radical politics after 1789. Robert Watson, Lord George's secretary, was another to play a significant part in the early stages of the LCS, while the first assistant secretary of the society was another Scot, Robert Littlejohn, who was prominent in one of several early Scots divisions (or at least divisions with large numbers of Scottish members).[3]

The importance, more broadly, of London to Scotland and Scots fortunes in the eighteenth century is something that historians have explored patchily, but was very significant.[4] Much Scottish overseas trade, for example, was directed through London, especially coarse linen cloth manufactured in the east, in Angus and Perthshire, on its way to North America and the Caribbean, where it was used as sacking and to make clothes for the slave populations. Many at the uppermost heights of the Scottish landed elite were resident in London for most of the year, as they had been since at least the Union, if not rather earlier. As noted in chapter 5, Daer's father had a house in Upper Brook Street in Westminster, home to most of London's fashionable elite. As the centre of British publishing and the print industry, including newspapers and periodicals; through an increasingly rapid and extensive postal system; and by virtue of personal connection; London's cultural and political reach in the eighteenth century was almost certainly greater than at any time in its history, although the rise of large provincial cities, including in Scotland Glasgow and Paisley, in the second half of the eighteenth century was beginning cumulatively to challenge and erode this leadership. This context is crucial to understanding why and how a *British* campaign for political reform was possible in the late eighteenth century, and why to a significant degree it was created in London.

More specifically, we need to bring into focus a series of moves that were made in the spring of 1792 to draw together various London and the growing number of provincial radical societies into closer communication and co-operation with one another. At the core of these were the veteran radical, John Horne Tooke and the Society for Constitutional Information (SCI). Tooke's radical politics went back to the Wilksite years of the 1760s and '70s, and his Wimbledon home, which ironically sat close to that of Henry Dundas, played host to many a convivial radical gathering in the 1790s. Tooke played the role of something of a father figure in radical circles in this period. The SCI had been formed from a body of advanced reformers as long ago as 1780, but had run out of steam by around 1786; and it was only the French Revolution that regalvanised it and its activities.

The drive towards greater radical co-operation had both short term and longer-term roots. It went back at least to March 1791, when the SCI sought to publicise Part I of Paine's *Rights of Man* to those fellow radical bodies with which it was in contact. But it also derived from precedents set by earlier reform campaigns, including the Quintuple alliance, which emerged in 1782 to create firmer connections between reformers across the metropolis, and similar initiatives associated with the advanced reformer John Jebb, who before his death in 1786 played a very prominent role in the SCI.[5]

Circumstances strongly favoured renewed efforts in this direction in early 1792. In the first place, links were created with several of the new popular provincial radical societies, the first of these being the Sheffield Constitutional Society, which had emerged in October 1791. The Sheffield reformers suggested to Tooke that in order to ensure 'regular communication' some of its members should be made associate members of a metropolitan radical society. Twelve Sheffield reformers were duly made associate members of the SCI on 30 March 1791.[6] Directly influenced by this Sheffield example, the Norwich radical societies quickly followed along the same path.[7] The advantages and, indeed, imperatives of union and co-ordination became increasingly insistent themes in radical thinking and strategy in the coming months; and the impulses behind this had provincial as well as metropolitan origins.

Secondly, in a related development, at the end of January Hardy and a handful of fellow artisans established the London Corresponding Society (LCS). An important catalyst was contact between Hardy and the Sheffield Constitutional Society, on which the organisation of the LCS, with its divisions and committees, was modelled. Through Hardy the LCS increasingly assumed from late 1792 a co-ordinating role in national radical politics. More importantly for present purposes, Tooke and several of his very close political allies, the lawyer Felix Vaughan and John Richter, played a very important guiding role in its initial stages. From inception, moreover, 'union' and communication between radical societies was a key element in the political platform of the LCS; printed in red ink on its membership tickets was the motto 'Unite, Persevere & Be Free', a fairly good summary of its political strategy. Hardy wrote formally to the SCI in March 1792 with copies of his society's initial resolutions. On 14 June, Hardy wrote again, declaring, in direct reference to the relationships that had been already established with the Sheffield and Norwich radicals: 'The approbation and the encouragement which our feeble endeavours have met with from the Constitutional Society make us desirous of uniting more strongly and more immediately with you.' Twelve associate members from the LCS were quickly elected by the SCI.[8] Even before that, however, Hardy had been in communication with the Sheffield Constitutional Society, the Manchester Constitutional Society – who in turn had been in contact with Sheffield – and the Southwark Friends of the People, of whom more below.[9]

If a strategy of tighter co-ordination between various radical societies was thus beginning to take clear shape in the spring of 1792, this also reflected a consciousness of growing official and unofficial hostility to radical activities and goals, together with a marked hardening of opinion within the ranks of radicals, symptomatic of which was the willingness of the SCI, but also the Revolution Society – with the SCI the most prominent of the early metropolitan radical societies – enthusiastically to support the French Revolution long after the point at which this incurred a great deal of suspicion. Formed in 1788, on the centenary of the Glorious Revolution, the Revolution Society drew together reformers and radicals within the capital. The tendency to continue defiantly supporting the French Revolution had been evident for some time. On returning from France in early July 1791, both Paine and Daer had attended a large gathering of reformers – contemporary press reports say over a thousand people – held at the famous Crown and Anchor Tavern in the Strand, with its great room the scene of many political, including radical, gatherings in the 1790s, to mark the anniversary of the fall of the Bastille. Against a background of attacks on the organisers of this event and their intentions, the occasion was very carefully managed in a somewhat vain attempt to allay suspicions, including, at the suggestion of the chairman, George Rous – author of two ripostes to Burke's *Reflections on the Revolution in France* – having the diners depart quietly at 9 o'clock. Even so, the leading opposition Whigs, Charles James Fox and Richard Brinsley Sheridan stayed well away.[10]

Much more calculatedly defiant, however – and provocative – were events at another venue, the London Tavern, on 4 November 1791, when the Revolution Society convened to commemorate the Glorious Revolution of 1688 on the anniversary of William III's birthday, as it had done since its foundation. Chaired by the Manchester radical, Thomas Walker, one of the guests of honour was another of the individuals who we met in the last chapter, Jérôme Pétion, the Jacobin Club member who would be complicit in the overthrow of the French monarchy in the following summer and who, on his return from London to Paris, would on 16 November 1791 decisively defeat Lafayette in the election for mayor. Pétion's diary of his trip reveals how forcibly struck he was by the fact that toasts to the British royal family were drunk in a gloomy silence, in sharp contrast to the enthusiasm which greeted those to the French Revolution. As he recorded: 'When the toast to the Revolution of 1688 came, I noticed that it was very little celebrated: that of the king and his family was greeted with the most gloomy silence, that of the French nation was met with the most lively emotions and the band immediately followed it with the famous air *Ça Ira* [. . .].'[11] According to a contemporary newspaper report, when the band played the revolutionary tune 'Ça Ira', what was described as the 'greater part of the company' beat time to the music with hands and feet.[12] The toasts to Priestley and Paine were also greeted with, Pétion observed, 'demonstrations les plus vives de l'allegresse' ('demonstrations of the most lively high spirits').[13] Paine exuberantly responded to the toast to him with 'To the Revolution of the World'.

The publication in February 1792 of Part II of Paine's *Rights of Man* further hardened the views of advanced radicals, also serving to sharpen the

differences between them and moderate reformers. These differences were
very clearly exposed when on 11 April 1792 a group of youthful opposition
Whigs, led by Richard Brinsley Sheridan, Charles Grey and James Maitland,
eighth earl of Lauderdale, decided to form, to give it its proper title, 'The
Friends of the People; Associated for the Purpose of Obtaining a Parliamentary Reform'. While the origins of this new association lay in rivalry between
this group and Edmund Burke for the ear of the opposition Whig leader,
Charles James Fox, more importantly in the present context was that it was
an exclusive body – as made clear by the relatively high admission fee of 2½
guineas – but also a fundamentally conservative one; albeit its effects proved
to be the opposite of this, serving as it did to encourage a further accession
of numbers of the ranks of the radicals, including the LCS. The intention,
nonetheless, of Grey and his allies was decisively to assert a moderate,
aristocratic Whig leadership on wider reforming opinion; to which end it
established a co-ordinating committee which was to 'advise all Friends of
Parliamentary Reform, to form themselves into *similar Societies, on similar
Principles*, in all Parts of the Kingdom' (my emphasis).[14] The founding declaration was very widely reprinted in many London, English provincial and
indeed Scottish newspapers.[15] This, in short, was an explicit bid for direction
of the reform movement in Britain.

The Whig Association of the Friends of the People also decisively rejected
Paineite principles, claiming instead filiation with a moderate, practical and
conserving reforming tradition that stretched back – supposedly, for in
reality there was no such tradition, at least in the sense implied – to John
Locke and William Blackstone, and thence through the earl of Chatham,
Sir George Saville, the duke of Richmond, the marquis of Landsdowne, Pitt
and Fox. They were determined, the Friends of the People announced on
26 April in their *Address to the Nation*, 'to avert for ever from our country
the calamities inseparable from such convulsions' as had occurred in France
since 1789. Britain did not need another revolution. As they protested, with a
clumsy vehemence (manifest in the use of capitalisation): 'WE DENY THE
EXISTANCE OF ANY RESEMBLANCE WHATEVER BETWEEN THE
CASES OF THE TWO KINGDOMS; AND WE UTTERLY DISCLAIM
THE NECESSITY OF RESORTING TO SIMILAR REMEDIES.'[16] On 30
April, Charles Grey gave notice in the Commons of a parliamentary reform
motion to be made in the following parliamentary session. Daer was one of
a number of Scots signatories to the Association's founding declaration, who
also included, in addition to Lauderdale and his brother, Thomas Maitland;
the restless Scot on the make, William Fullarton, who would be elected for

the county of Ayrshire in 1796, and who in late 1792 beat a very hasty retreat from his reformist views;[17] the MP for Invernesshire, Norman Macleod, who became a very close ally of Daer's in Scottish reforming circles in the winter of 1792–3; Malcolm Laing, the historian who had been a fellow member of the Speculative Society at Edinburgh in the mid-1780s; the Dumfriessian Dr William Maxwell, purveyor of daggers to the French revolutionaries and friend of Robert Burns; the political writers, James Mackintosh and Thomas Christie; and at a bit of a stretch, perhaps, the opposition Whig journalist and editor of the *Morning Chronicle*, James Perry, a native Aberdonian and one of quite a number of Scots to find a home in the cut-throat world of eighteenth-century London newspapers and periodicals. In addition, several non-resident Scots signed the declaration, most notably the earl of Buchan, whose reformism was always more than matched by his startling self-regard, and John Millar, Professor of Civil Law at the University of Glasgow, while Lord Kinnaird became one of two treasurers of the society.[18] Most Scottish reform bodies in late 1792 sought to align themselves with this body and in support of Grey's anticipated Commons motion for reform.

It may seem odd that Daer, who, as we have seen, emphatically did not share Grey's conservative views, or the opposition Whig complacency about the superiority of the British constitution, nevertheless joined the Association. This is almost certainly best viewed, however, in terms of tactical flexibility – *not* as a guide to his political opinions. He was not alone in this, although it may also have reflected initial uncertainty about just what the opposition Whig founders of the society intended by its establishment.[19] Other signatories, for example, included Major John Cartwright, whose radical career stretched back to the 1770s and would stretch on into the 1810s, the radical poet Robert Merry, and Thomas Christie, the native Montrosian who was also a member of the LCS and who ended up in Paris in late 1792 being employed by the National Assembly on the English section of the proposed polyglot edition of the new French constitution. In the spring of 1793, meanwhile, Daer joined another essentially Whig extra-parliamentary body, 'The Friends of the Liberty of the Press', formed in late 1792 in response to the ministerial assault on the radical and reform press, and the trial of Paine for sedition.[20] A pattern of intermittent co-operation between the Whigs, radicals and reformers recurred in the 1790s, driven by common opposition to and alienation from Pitt's politics of war and political repression.

A better indication of Daer's views and radical affiliations is the fact that in April he joined the Revolution Society,[21] whilst in May he joined the Society for Constitutional Information and the London Corresponding

Society.[22] His proposers for SCI membership were Cartwright and Paine, and he was elected to the Society on 11 May. Daer was present at most of its meetings during the rest of May until at least 15 June, serving on a number of important committees.[23] He recommended John Millar and Malcolm Laing for membership, although the latter proposal was withdrawn, presumably because Laing decided not to proceed. Daer's membership of the SCI and LCS reflected how far in the spring of 1792 he was becoming drawn into advanced metropolitan radical politics.

On 27 April 1792, the chairman of the SCI, Major John Cartwright, wrote to the Whig Association, declaring that if they were going to live up to their title they would need to commit themselves publicly to 'a substantial reform in the representation of the people' and sponsor a 'Declaration of Rights' similar to that adopted by the SCI. And, in the kind of millennial language that could only serve to underline the very sizeable gap between their different perspectives, he counselled:

> When this Society, Sir, contemplates that flood of light and truth, which, under a benign Providence, is now sweeping from the earth despotism in all its forms, and infringements of rights in all its degrees; to make way for freedom, justice, peace, and human happiness; and when it sees your Society announce itself to the world, as the Friends of the People, it rests assured, that this new Institution abundantly partakes of that light, that it embraces that truth, and that it will act up to the sacredness of that friendship which it professes, by nobly casting from it with disdain all aristocratic reserves, and fairly and honestly contending, for the People's Rights in their full extent.

One can only wonder whether this letter was, in truth, designed to smoke out the differences between them. Whatever the case, the response, formulated at a meeting on 12 May, was peremptory and dismissive. Writing as chairman of the Whig Association, Lord John Russell was scathing about the welfare proposals of Paine and Cartwright's notion of obtaining the 'full extent of the Rights of the People'. This was the 'indefinite language of delusion'; it was to spirit up 'unbounded prospects of political adventure' and 'excite a spirit of innovation of which no wisdom can foresee the effects and no skill direct the course'. It was to invite, in other words, destruction of the constitution and anarchy where the association sought its preservation. Russell, therefore, declined 'all future intercourse' with the SCI.[24]

The foundation of yet another new metropolitan radical society on 2 May at the London Coffee House was – although not usually noticed as such – closely connected to these events; and it only reinforces suspicion that Cartwright fully anticipated the likely outcome of his letter to the Whig Association. Called the London Society of the Friends of the People, many of its members were also members of the SCI and the Revolution Society, and they included a good number of the metropolis's advanced radicals: Cartwright; the popular political lecturer and later LCS ideologue, John Thelwall; Paine; Thomas Brand Hollis, another veteran of reform campaigns; Thomas Yeates, an early secretary of the SCI; the engraver William Sharp; the Rev. Francis Stone, a Unitarian writer against Burke; and the author George Dyer, who had just moved to London and was another member of the SCI. The first resolution of its second meeting on 4 May was that Lord Daer be admitted to the society. On 9 May, Daer and Cartwright were added to a committee formed at its first meeting (on 2 May) to frame a declaration of the society's purposes and also to consider its organisation. Modelling itself on the rules of the SCI, and indeed the LCS, it was agreed that the 'number of Members shall be unlimited' and that when any party met with thirty present it should be sub-divided into smaller parties or sub-divisions of at least ten; that its purpose was 'the cultivation and diffusion of political knowledge and particularly for the attainment of parliamentary reform on the broad basis of equal liberty'. A committee was also formed to confer with the Southwark Society of the Friends of the People and 'others in the metropolis'.[25] The Southwark Friends of the People had been established on 19 April by Tooke, Thelwall – a resident of the borough – and the slop-seller and orthodox Dissenter Samuel Favell. Its initial declaration made clear that in its view the solution to current political ills lay in the 'United efforts of the nation'. 'We are,' the society declared, in words that can only have been directed at the Whig Association: 'wearied with the unmeaning names of WHIG and TORY, and of MINISTERIAL and OPPOSITIONAL parties, and having often – too often – been deceived by both, we can no longer implicitly confide in either.' And, in a final resolution, they stated their commitment to a political strategy of union:

> We are desirous, therefore, of uniting with the several societies already formed in various parts of the nation, for promoting an enquiry into, and asserting the Rights of the People [. . .] we recommend a general correspondence with each other, and the Society for CONSTITUTIONAL INFORMATION at LONDON, as the best means of cementing the common union, and of directing our united efforts with greater energy and effect.

This declaration was communicated to the SCI on the very next day (20 April), and at its next meeting (on 27 April) the SCI resolved:

That every Society desiring an union or correspondence with this, and which doth not profess any principles destructive to truth or justice, and subversive to the Liberties of our country; but which on the contrary seeks, as we do, the removal of corruption from the Legislature and abuses from the government ought to be, and we hope will be, embraced with the most brotherly affection and patriotic friendship by this society.

What then followed was the reading and acceptance of Cartwright's letter to be sent to the Whig Association.[26] In other words, the sequence of events suggests that they were carefully co-ordinated.

Further steps taken by these two societies in early May tend to confirm this. At a general meeting of the Southwark Society on 8 May, chaired by Favell, it was agreed to send an address to the London Friends of the People. The latter replied on 12 May with their 'Declaration of the constitutional Rights of KING, LORDS, and COMMONS, of Great Britain', which had, as already referred to, been agreed on 9 May, and which Daer and Cartwright had helped to draw up. This included commitments to universal suffrage – excepting infants, the insane, and those criminals 'who may have forfeited their Rights by the Commission of Crimes – so theoretically at least including women; and to annual parliaments. One admittedly hostile newspaper reported on 14 May:

A schism, it seems, has already been made in these clubs: Those under Mr Baker, at the Freemason's Tavern [the Whig Association], including some Members of Parliament, are regarded by the Society under Mr Favell, in the Borough [i.e. Southwark], as a sort of French Feuillants at Paris; while Favell's clubs, incorporating Pain, Tooke, Walker, Watts [William Watts], Towers [Joseph Towers, the dissenting minister and SCI member], Cooper [Benjamin Cooper of Clements Lane, secretary of the Revolution Society], Lord Daer and Major Cartwright, are recognised as the true disciples of the Jacobin Order.[27]

Already by May there may have been five divisions of the Friends of the People, including one in Whitechapel in the east end, and one presided over by Daer at the White Hart in Holborn. Daer was also being described as the president of the Friends of the People, although this may be a mistake or rather a misdescription since he may have been rather chair of the committee delegated to oversee the organisation of the societies or the general meeting of the divisions.[28] Hardy had written to the Southwark Society as early as 18 April, which suggests that he was aware of the plans behind its establishment, and, although its delegate committee appears not to have met for much of the summer, close co-operation between it and the LCS resumed in early September. By October 1792, the Southwark Society had spawned at least five divisions.[29]

For a few months in the spring of 1792, then, guided by Tooke, the SCI became the effective leader of the national democratic movement, its influence reaching out into other metropolitan radical societies, while stronger links were also being forged with provincial radical societies. Part symptom and part cause of this was an influx of new members, many of whom, such as Daer or the lawyer John Frost – jailed in early 1793 after being overheard saying in a Marylebone coffee house, 'I am for equality [...] Why, no kings!' – were outspoken in their pro-French views and quite a few of whom were republicans, at least in private. As Albert Goodwin stresses, during this period the Society, which was now meeting weekly, took over from the Revolution Society as the main channel of communication with the Paris Jacobins, a communication in which James Watt jnr and Thomas Cooper played key roles.[30] They were also to the fore in attacking the policy of repression initiated by Henry Dundas as Home Secretary in May, although official and unofficial hostility began to take its toll in the early summer, and the SCI, together with the LCS began to assume a more cautious line. On 20 July 1792, the SCI adjourned its meetings until the last Friday in September – exactly the same pattern as the Southwark Society, again indicative of the close links between them. It was at this point, with radical spirits temporarily dampened, and with an absence of leadership that the political initiative in radical politics in the British capital began to pass to Hardy and the London Corresponding Society.

By the autumn of 1792, however, the radicals' hopes had been completely reinvigorated. The main cause was events in France and Europe that were discussed in the last chapter; namely, the unfolding drama of France becoming a republic and the revolutionary armies fighting to rescue the revolution from invading Austrian and Prussian armies. Portrayed as a fight between liberty and despotism, on these events rested the fate, so the radicals convinced themselves, of the French Revolution and liberty throughout the world. When around 1,000 people met under the auspices of the Revolution Society on 4 November 1792, the mood was a defiant, even exultant one. The toasts included: 'The Rights of Man', which was accompanied again by 'Ça Ira'; 'May unjust power be opposed by the friends of just Government'; 'The sovereignty of the people acting by an equal representation'; 'May the people no longer confide in Apostacy, or lukewarmness, but rely on their own exertions for parliamentary reform'. Reading a report from the Society's committee, Favell declared of the revolutionaries in France:

No language can do justice to the sublime efforts of this great nation, their
exertions for the increase of human liberty and happiness are unconfined, and
we doubt not but millions yet unborn will bless their labours, and regard their
memory of their enemies with the same indignation as we now contemplate
that of the most barbarous nations; – without deciding on forms of government, we take this opportunity of expressing our avowal of the unalienable
right every country has to form, at any time, that system that shall appear the
best.[31]

In other words, Jefferson's notion, shared by Paine, that natural rights
were possessed by generations and that each one had the right to remake
its government anew. The gathering was also determined to address the
Constituent Assembly in France, changing its title from 'An Address to the
Empire of France' to 'An Address to the Republic of France', an amendment
which was 'received', one report said, 'with the most vehement acclama-
tion'.[32] This was one of several addresses to the French National Convention
presented by English radical societies in November and December 1792,
including from the SCI and a joint one from the London Corresponding
Society, Manchester Constitutional Society, Norwich Revolution Society
and the Westminster-based Constitutional Whigs.[33]

There was, however, another, much more neglected, factor behind the
reinvigorated radical movement in the autumn of 1792. This was the rise of a
parliamentary reform movement in Scotland; and it is to this that we must
now turn.

Prior to the summer of 1792, while Paine's Part I of the *Rights of Man* was
evidently quite widely read – one contemporary noting in June 1791 that the
work had 'had a great run & is much admired in this Country'[34] – there was
little sign that a major campaign for parliamentary reform, similar to that
which existed south of the border, was about to emerge in Scotland.[35] One
reason, although not the sole one, was that those who might have provided
leadership to such a campaign were otherwise preoccupied – with the repeal
of the Test Act as it affected Scotland, and in the early part of 1792 with burgh
reform and abolitionism. There was also a separate agitation for reform of
Scottish county elections, focused on so-called 'fictitious' or 'nominal' votes,
into which, as we saw in an earlier chapter, Daer was drawn in the early
1790s, and which in the summer and autumn of 1792, appeared to be making
headway.[36] The Scottish petitioning campaign in support of abolition in early
1792 was very widespread indeed, embracing all parts of society and all sides
of political and religious opinion. Daer and Sir James Hall were present at the
very large abolitionist meeting in Edinburgh on 4 March, and Daer may have

been much more prominent in this cause than we are able to recover.[37] In April Henry Dundas proposed an amendment in the Commons in favour of gradual abolition, which carried the day, but was effectively a way of burying the measure, although it could not then have been predicted that this would be for fully fifteen years. In Glasgow, battles over proposals for a police bill, which intersected with the agitation for burgh reform, occupied a great deal of press and public attention in 1790–2, in which issues of political liberty, accountability and independence were very fully and vigorously aired.[38]

Below the surface of events, however, opinion was beginning to shift. James Wodrow, the minister for the Ayrshire parish of Stevenston, declared at the end of May 1792:

> I think within these two years the sentiments of our common people are growing much more liberal both in religion & politicks than they formerly were not so much owing to any publications for very few of these are spread in this country, but chiefly to the French revolution which has awakened more attention than you could easily imagine among them, set them a reading the news papers thinking & talking about this and other matters connected with it.

He also noted that 'Paine's books' – presumably Part II of the *Rights of Man* – had been imported from Ireland 'almost for nothing & have a wonderful spread'.[39] (Smuggling of cheap copies of books between Scotland and Ireland was a common enterprise.) The Scottish newspapers, less polarised politically than many of their English counterparts at this stage and seeking to retain their impartiality for longer, were relatively sympathetic to the French Revolution certainly before the end of 1791, and, like their counterparts elsewhere, gave much coverage to events in Paris; many of them, for example, published in full, usually over a series of issues, a translated version of the new French constitution accepted by Louis XVI in September 1791.[40] All that was really required for the emergence of a popular parliamentary reform campaign was a catalyst; and this was provided by another series of defeats (on 18 and 30 April 1792) for the burgh reformers at Westminster, which, as Wodrow noted, 'hurt the minds & feelings of all who are not dependant on the court, from interest or hope'.[41] These latest blows fell hard on the burgh reformers, already wearied by eight years of near-continuous setbacks and lukewarm support at Westminster; and having narrowed their campaign to focus purely on reform of burgh government rather than representation in parliament. That they quickly followed the disappointment of hopes for immediate abolition of the slave trade only reinforced their impact. And, while some burgh reformers seem to have confined their irritation to expressions of bruised disappointment, and Archibald Fletcher and others vainly battled on for at least another year, in Perth, Dundee, Brechin and Aberdeen, and several other places, angry crowds burnt Dundas in effigy, while plans to 'roast the effigy of the Secretary [i.e. Home Secretary]' were a key part of the background to the famous King's birthday riots in Edinburgh in early June.[42] Their hopes for burgh reform and immediate abolition now stymied, a growing number of burgh reformers also began to turn to parliamentary reform, providing much of the early leadership of the reform cause. This was very much the case in Edinburgh, where the Edinburgh Friends of the People emerged at a meeting on 26 July, although the idea had been in the air in the preceding weeks; Glasgow, where a few days earlier, at the Prince of Wales's Tavern in the city, the 'Glasgow Society for the Purpose of Effecting Constitutional and Parliamentary Reform' was formed; Perth, where the local Friends of the People first met on 14 August; Dundee; and it was probably true also of quite a few other places. The resolutions of the Glasgow society, which included a declaration of support for 'equal representation, frequent elections, and the universal right of suffrage', made explicit the link between the society's establishment and the dashing again of hopes for burgh reform.[43]

Contemporary reports of the contagious spread of reform opinion throughout the Lowlands during the summer and autumn undoubtedly contain exaggeration, reflecting the fear and horror of many of the elites; but the rise of the Scottish reformers was very remarkable, nonetheless. Beginning quite slowly in July, in the four months between August and November reform societies emerged across much of Scotland, with particular concentrations in the main manufacturing areas of Glasgow and Paisley in the west, Dundee and Perth in the east, and in Edinburgh. From these and other manufacturing towns the tentacles of the reform cause reached out into neighbouring manufacturing villages. Any estimates of numbers are at best rough and ready guesses, or based on claims, probably deliberately inflated, by the reformers themselves and picked up by government informers; but in some places they probably ran from several hundred even into the low thousands. From Glasgow, it was reported that 'The Reformers are computed at 1200 [although] they probably amount to a far greater number, as it is said that the number of Reformers in the West amount to between 40 and 50 thousand.'[44] From Dysart, James St Clair wrote in late November of the 'extraordinary change' in the last two months 'particularly in the political opinions of the people at large', also noting that already there were fifty affiliated societies to the main reform society in Glasgow.[45] In early December, the Dundee reformers were described as consisting of 'about 2000 of the lowest sort of people'.[46] Most surprising, however, because completely unexpected, was the spread of support for reform in Edinburgh, which at the beginning of December was strikingly described by George Home, brother to the fiercely anti-reform MP Patrick Home of Wedderburn, as the 'Paris of Scotland', something which was attributed to the influence of reform-minded advocates and writers (i.e. lawyers) spilling out from the Parliament House and gathering people together in taverns to talk of the 'Rights of man and new doctrines of equality'.[47] A week earlier, this same George Home described a meeting of delegates of the Edinburgh reform societies which had met at an old dancing school under the chairmanship of Hugh Bell, the Edinburgh brewer, and had been addressed by Norman Macleod, the Inver-nesshire opposition Whig MP referred to earlier:

> [A]fter noticeing [sic] that his Majesty had been pleased to issue a Proclama-tion against certain Books that had been published for the Instruction of his Subjects, and that he should not say a word about any thing contained in these books, but there was one book against which the Proclamation did not extend and that was the Almanack of which he begged leave to read a few pages – He then read the names of all the different officers about the Court, their appoint-ments, and Employments, Interspersed with Commentaries suited to the occasion and to Show how the poor tradesmen manufacturers and Labourers were oppressed with Taxes to support the Pageantry of the Court.

'You cannot conceive,' Home commented, 'that effect the diffusion of these ideas has among the Common People. In consequence of it, The great body of the Journeymen in all the different Trades are now become so insolent their Masters dare not quarrel with them.'[48] The response of the Edinburgh elites was, amongst other things, to hit the radicals hard where they thought it would hurt the most – in their pockets, by withdrawing their custom from their businesses and shops.

There were, to be sure, parts of Scotland where reform made limited headway in 1792 or indeed thereafter – in the Lothians, the borders, or in the north-east with its Episcopalian-Jacobite traditions. From the remote parish of Canisby in Caithness, the local minister reported confidently (and with a somewhat ridiculous pride) in February 1793 that 'a drop of disloyal blood runs not in the veins of one single individual under my charge'.[49] Daer's home territory of the south-west was another generally unhappy hunting ground for the reformers, the provost of Kirkcudbright declaring to Robert Dundas, the Lord Advocate, in early December, 'No seditious publications [are] in circulation.'[50] Yet even in these parts the general absence of reform societies

was far from the full picture. In the Lothians and the borders, several societies flickered into existence in late 1793.[51] Even our minister in Caithness
noted that there 'may be a few in the north evil minded towards our happy
constitution'. Sir William Maxwell of Springkell in Dumfriesshire had worked
himself into quite some lather in November 1792: 'Paine's pamphlet or the
cream & substance of it is now in the hands of almost every Countryman
& which they purchase at so low a price as twopence.' As he informed the
duke of Buccleuch, so concerned was he that he had 'already employed two
or three sensible people in whom I can confide, to mix with the populace to
learn what are the grievances of which they complain, and to find out what
are their intentions [. . .]'; 'I have desired,' he continued, 'the same persons
to endeavour to convince them that they live under the best, the mildest &
happiest government that ever was in the World.'[52] Just how they were to do
this Maxwell did not say, although to him, as to many of his ilk, presumably
this was self-evident; and herein perhaps lay much of the problem.

Daer was in London in the early part of the summer of 1792, and it is
unclear where he was between July and December, although some of this
time was almost certainly spent in Scotland, perhaps at St Mary's Isle or
in Edinburgh. He was definitely in the Scottish capital, however, when the
Scottish Friends of the People met between 11 and 13 December for the
first of three national conventions of the Scottish reformers held between
1792 and 1793. Daer was a delegate to the convention from the Edinburgh
Portsburgh society, which suggests that he was probably active in Edinburgh
radical circles in the preceding weeks.

Daer played a leading role in the opening stages of the convention,
seeking to direct the delegates to establish forms of business and organisation that were in keeping with, as he put it, the 'great principles of liberty and
political equality'. To this end he opposed establishing permanent officers
or leaders. At the beginning of the second sitting of the convention, Daer
insisted on commencing with issues of organisation, which drew opposition
from Thomas Muir, who, along with Thomas Fyshe Palmer, became a victim
of Braxfield's High Court of Justiciary in the following summer, but also
from Glasgow and Paisley delegates. Daer was unrepentant, referring explicitly to his knowledge of the operations of the French National Assembly; and
again his goal was to prevent the power of decision-making being captured
by a minority.[53] He was also adamant that the Convention should take no
notice of an address from the Society of the United Irishmen, the author
of which was William Drennan, whose medical education had been at first
Glasgow and then Edinburgh in the 1770s, which Muir wished it to acknowl-

edge, an address which, intriguingly, contained an explicit nationalist dimension in appealing for Scotland to join Ireland in pursuit of true liberty.[54] Daer may well have been absent for most of the deliberations after the first two sessions, since he attended the Convention of County Reformers, which was taking place in Edinburgh at the same time. And he may well have been elsewhere, therefore, when during the final session Robert Fowler proposed that all present should take the French oath 'To live free or die', which they duly did as one. Despite Fowler insisting that he 'meant no more [...] than to impress upon the minds of all present uniformity and steadiness in the cause of freedom and virtue', it was decided that this should go unremarked in the published minutes.[55] Daer had earlier warned delegates about not referring to themselves as the 'National Convention [...] as the Convention could not merit that title unless all Scotland had sent up delegates';[56] these are words which, again, are susceptible of being read in conservative but also quite radical ways. For if it did have delegates from all of Scotland, did this mean that it was the embodiment of the will of the people?

Strongly influenced by voices of caution and prudent moderation, such as those of Colonel William Dalrymple and indeed at this point Daer's, and several young opposition Whig lawyers, notably Robert Fowler and John Morthland, the first Scottish reform convention is usually presented as evidence for the underlying conservatism of the emergent Scottish reform movement.[57] As referred to earlier, the delegates decided to confine their reform efforts to petitioning in support of Grey's anticipated reform motion, and much of the time at the convention was spent seeking – without, in truth, real hope of success – in different ways to defuse the rising tide of loyalist hostility and suspicion about their activities. Just as the convention was meeting, the main Edinburgh loyalist association, the so-called Goldsmith's Association (it met in the Goldsmith's Hall), was forming. Yet we need to be very careful about how we view the deliberations and actions of the convention. An entirely plausible reading would be to suggest that what it reflected was the delegates' acute consciousness of the sort of shrill hostility and alarmism manifested in letters such as Maxwell's, quoted from above, a mood only further stirred by a series of popular radical demonstrations and disturbances triggered by celebrations of French military victories in November 1792. Scotland was becoming a 'mob-governed' country; or so it seemed to quite a few in late 1792. Scottish reform organisations were also, in important ways, differently structured from their English counterparts, reflecting the different chronologies and circumstances of their emergence. They emerged as very broad alliances, often with moderate leaders schooled in the cautious, almost painfully reasonable, politics of burgh reform, but behind them there was gathering a more genuinely popular and ideologically charged radicalism and it was from here that a new leadership would begin to come to the fore in Scottish reform circles in 1793.[58] There were hints of this different temper at the convention in remarks made by several delegates about the need to show expedition in drawing up petitions for reform, and not waiting for the Whig Association of the Friends of the People to take the lead in this respect. Muir also openly argued at one point for support for universal suffrage.[59] And, while links to the Whig Association were to the fore in late 1792, connections to other radical societies in England were already being forged.

Daer was ideally placed to play an important role in this developing patchwork of communication and connection – although he was certainly not acting alone. Thomas Hardy, who had heard news of the foundation of several reform societies in Scotland, wrote in June 1792 to his uncle in Falkirk, sending him the declaration and resolutions of the LCS, and expressing the hope that he would respond at 'the first opportunity'.[60] And on 14 July, he wrote to Daer with news of the rapid progress of the LCS, also noting that he had just received 'another packet of capital information from Sheffield', and requesting that Daer send him news of the 'progress of liberty in Scotland'.[61] Several weeks later, he was writing again enclosing the third Address of the LCS to the Nation, also informing Daer that the Edinburgh radical bookseller, Walter Berry, had been introduced to the LCS by Thomas Christie and had been able to inform them about the advance of the reform cause in Scotland, declaring:

> If you judge it proper, and have the opportunity to promote a correspond-
> ence between any of the societies in Scotland and the London Corresponding
> Society it will tend to cement us together for by uniting we shall become
> stronger and three-fold cord is not easily broken.[62]

Daer could well have acted on this because Hardy was in September in corre-spondence with William Johnston, the president of the Edinburgh Friends of the People, inviting the Edinburgh reformers to join the LCS in addressing the French National Convention, an invitation that Johnston declined, although he told Hardy that the Scottish reformers were 'daily increasing, & shall appear very numerous in a short time'.[63] We know there were further letters to the LCS from Edinburgh as well as Paisley and Kilmarnock in December, and that the correspondence with Paisley continued in the early months of 1793.[64] The Friends of Reform in Paisley were, in contrast to most of the Scottish reform societies in 1792, openly advocating universal suffrage, annual parliaments, equal electoral districts and polls on a single day, also arguing that commercial and manufacturing towns required direct representation in parliament. There was a definite social edge to their emerging radicalism, which was also unusual at this point in Scotland, although becoming more common in the following year: 'The poor then,' they declared, 'have an equal right, but more need, to elect representatives than the rich. He that is free, possesses that which is more to be valued than riches: but, robbed of liberty, he is poor indeed.'[65] There were other important links between the LCS and Scottish reformers, including through Hugh, Lord Sempill. Sempill had been very close to Glasgow's burgh reformers in the late 1780s, and in the early 1790s he was an important member of the SCI, as well as joining the LCS at some point in 1792. Sempill continued to play a very active role in the SCI in 1793–4, and was frequently the point of contact between the city and the SCI, presumably also playing a similar role in respect of the LCS.[66] There were communications between the SCI and several Scottish reform societies, between the Manchester and Sheffield Constitutional societies and Edinburgh, and almost certainly between the LCS and Glasgow, Dundee and, more curiously, Banff.[67]

It is probably significant that the Sheffield reformers were among the strongest provincial English proponents of radical unanimity and the idea of a national convention as the best means to expedite the cause of reform.[68] In October 1792, Matthew Campbell Browne, the editor of the Sheffield radical periodical, the *Patriot*, wrote to the LCS informing them of the recent upsurge of radical activity in Edinburgh. The letter declared that the Sheffield radicals had been impressed by 'some most spirited communications' from Edinburgh, which led to the observation:

> We clearly foresee that Scotland will soon take the lead of this country, and conceive it will be necessary to take the greatest care that an universal communication should be constantly kept up between the several societies, however distant, and that all should determine to act upon the same principle, and move together, as near as may be, in regular and active union.[69]

In the spring of 1793, the Sheffield Constitutional Society would again be in contact with Edinburgh urging the desirability of a common radical front and united campaign.[70]

These, then, were the developing circumstances in which on 17 January 1793 Daer put pen to paper and wrote his lengthy missive to Grey. The Scottish reform movement, as it took shape in the second half of 1792, carefully aligned itself with the moderate reformism of the Whig Association of the

Friends of the People in London, committing itself to petitioning parliament in support of Grey's forthcoming reform motion. And the Edinburgh reformers at least were in close correspondence with opposition Whig reformers in London and the Whig Association.[71] Grey wrote several letters in early January to William Skirving, the secretary to the Edinburgh Friends of the People. Thomas Muir, who was arrested on 2 January but released on bail, had been in London and made contact with Grey and the Association, reporting back that the latter 'intended taking into consideration the opprest state of their friends in Scotland.'[72] Daer, together with Macleod, appears to have been present at meetings of the Edinburgh reformers during this period. However, Scots radicals were also at the same time being drawn into closer relationships to a democratic radical movement led from London and with strongholds in several of the English provincial manufacturing towns. So what did he write?

The letter was at one and the same time a warning, a lesson on union and a recommendation about how to pursue reform.[73] The warning was that the English should petition in support of Grey's motion, as the Scottish reformers intended to do; and that Grey should not on any account retreat from his intention of moving for a reform in parliament. This was necessary for morale. Scots reformers, Daer argued, may be relatively more numerous than their English counterparts, but they were also 'more oppressed', continuing, 'By every act implying favour to Reform the people here expose themselves either to the heavy hand of Government or to the unceasing weight of little aristocratical oppression. If set forward alone, the arbitrary attacks against them will be more pointed than if countenanced by their friends in England.' These were prescient words, for the petitions in support of reform in the spring of 1793 were, in the event, disproportionately from Scotland, although the reasons may well have been greater scepticism in English radical circles about the possible efficacy of petitioning parliament. Whatever the cause, the dismal failure of Grey's motion was undoubtedly a powerful factor behind the rapid demoralisation of Scottish reformers in the spring and summer of 1793, although it also reflected the impact of the war, a sharp economic downturn which it triggered, and, as Daer had feared, fierce official and loyalist hostility.

Not to petition also risked, however, making 'The Tweed appear a boundary in national sentiment and action.' This was where the lesson about union became relevant; and while not entirely straightforward, its underlying message is quite readily grasped, although at least two historians have been strongly misled.[74]

Daer's portrayal of the Union was emphatically a negative one; and it was also in certain respects rather surprising. Scotland's 'bondage', he asserted, could be dated to the Union of the Crowns of 1603, and the Union of 1707 had done little to remedy this. To those, and there were a good number of them, including Adam Smith and most of Scottish Enlightenment literati, who argued that union meant progress and prosperity, Daer protested, in a pointed reference to the Navigation and Alien Acts of the seventeenth century, that union played little real role in any economic progress since 1707 'except removing a part of the obstacles which your greater power had posterior to the first union thrown around us'. Modern historians of the Union have in some ways supported Daer here, insofar as they commonly emphasise the role of asymmetries of state power as a key context for debates about union from the end of the seventeenth century, although Allan Macinnes in particular has documented the very considerable enterprise and success of many Scots merchants in circumventing the effects of the Navigation Acts, also seeking to stress the damage that this caused the English 'fiscal-military state'.[75] Yet what would it mean in any case, if union had delivered more in this context; merely, Daer suggested, that 'we bartered our liberty and with it our morals for a little wealth'. Thus far, this is perhaps not particularly novel, for faced with complacent English views about union as a kind of beneficent gift from a prospering England to a decrepit Scotland, other Scots responded in somewhat similar ways, as, to take one very well known example, did Smollett in his 1771 novel *The Expedition of Humphrey Clinker*. Smollett's great epistolary novel can be read as principally a very clever effort to induce the English to reimagine Britain and Britishness as more than simply Englishness writ large, to disclose and anatomise the web of prejudice that stood in the way of this goal. Indeed, its underlying theme is precisely one of prejudice and blinkered visions.

If economic progress and prosperity, and political stability, were the most frequently offered defences of the Union, another was liberty; and liberty here meant especially the freeing of Scotland from feudal tyranny. This case had been articulated by defenders of union in 1705–6, and subsequent destruction of feudal survivals, such as, most obviously, the abolition of heritable jurisdictions in the aftermath of the final Jacobite rising of 1745–6, were commonly portrayed at the time in terms of completing the Union. Daer was having none of this, however. For, as he told Grey, had there been no union, Daer believed 'most deliberately [. . .] we should probably have had a progression towards Liberty and no less than yours.' His confidence in this proposition appears to have been partly historical – he refers to the 'grievances' before 1603, which 'were of a kind [...] [which] must before this time have been annihilated', and to the legislative activism of the Scottish parliament in its final days. 'Even to the last of our separate parliaments,' he declared, 'they were always making laws for us and now and then one would remedy a grievance.' But it was also based, and here he was surely echoing Dugald Stewart's teaching, on a belief in the power of reason as a force for change, although he only hinted at this in a brief reference to 'a people acquiring knowledge'. The British parliament created in 1707 had proved itself anything but a parliament for Britain – generally ignoring Scotland and its interests and needs. Into the vacuum had stepped the Scottish courts of law, and presumably he had in mind here principally the Court of Session. It is worth recalling here that it was the Court of Session that ruled against Daer being enrolled on the register of voters for the Stewartry of Kirkcudbright in 1790, and probably this had a strong bearing on his view. On the other hand, the judgments of the Court of Session undoubtedly did play a large role in the governance of eighteenth-century Scotland, one that historians have yet really to grasp fully or at least examine systematically, although one might well think about its role in the evolution of poor relief, but also jurisdictional conflicts between, say, burgh councils and county administration, and indeed burgh government and county electoral politics.

The essence, however, of Scotland's predicament was not the principle of union, but the nature of the union that was created in 1707. The Union was a union of states, but herein lay its fundamental weakness in Daer's eyes. His case is worth quoting at length:

> Kept out of view by your [i.e. the English] greater mass so as never to make our concerns the principal objects even to our own representatives, at a distance so as not to make our cries be heard in the capital which alone awes an arbitrary government; our laws and customs different so as to make our grievances unintelligible; our law establishment distinct so as to deprive us of the benefit of those constant circuits from the capital which by rendering the learned and spirited defender of the laws, dwelling at the source of actual power, acquainted with the lesser transactions of the remotest corner of the country, provides perhaps the greatest remedy to a half free state against some of the bad consequences of an extended territory. Our civil establishment distinct, so as to isolate the petty tyranny of office; even our greed and national vanity working to retain all these offices to natives so as still more to leave you (our then only protectors, although oppressors) ignorant of our internal situation. *We have suffered the misery which is perhaps inevitable in a lesser and remote country in a junction where the Governing powers are united but the Nations are not united.* (My emphasis.)

If such was the problem, the solution was obvious, 'a closer Union of the Nations'. Parliamentary reform was the means in part to bring this about, whilst it would also, and here Daer's words are very striking, and suggestive of the degree to which he had become himself alienated from the Scottish establishment, 'relieve you [Grey and the English] from that vermin from this country who infect your court, your parliament, and every establishment'.

In the final section of the letter, Daer, meanwhile, laid out his prescription for expediting reform. The Scottish reformers had led the way in convening a national convention of delegates from reform societies in Edinburgh. Daer acknowledged the frailties of the Scottish reform movement, but he also declared that 'by the folly of the measures of government', by which he meant their strategy of repression and refusal to embrace reform, and through its co-ordination it might 'grow to a great strength'. England now needed to follow Scotland's lead and convene a similar convention. This was a matter of expediency – it was the only effective means of co-ordination and communication between 'scattered friends'. And here Daer alluded to his acute consciousness of a difference of view with Grey:

> As to such assemblies I believe you and I differ and you dread the magnitude of power which I look upon as necessary to withstand and prevail over the immense power of the Opposers of Reform and which I think might be more safely entrusted to a delegated, renovating body even tho' sent from self-elected Societies, than to any Self-elected body like the Jacobins in France, like the Society for Constitutional Information, or even like ourselves at Free Mason's Tavern.

His words are difficult to interpret definitively. What does 'renovating' mean in this context, and what political and constitutional standing did he envisage for such a body? There is an ambiguity here that may be entirely deliberate given to whom he was writing, although notions of a radical convention were, as already alluded to, often clothed in this kind of slippery language. But on another aspect of the convention he was entirely unambiguous. What Daer was really recommending was not an English convention, but a British one. 'If in England,' he wrote, 'any such Convention or Assembly should take place and not in separate delegated Meetings for different districts in England but in one meeting for all England, I look upon it as of the highest consequence [. . .] to get Scotland to unite in the same Assembly *without sending its Delegates thro' any intermediate Assembly for Scotland alone*' (my emphasis).

Daer ended on a note of warning. Continued Scottish co-operation with an English reform movement was not inevitable, and indeed it was precariously balanced. Currently, the Scots were looking to England and London for a lead, but if this were not forthcoming then, Daer declared, 'many may be for bidding you farewell'. On the other hand, if Grey and his allies could demonstrate that they 'think of us' and 'exert yourselves for us' it would 'help to rivet us to you'. Again, it is quite hard to know how exactly to construe this warning; but it does seem to indicate at least the pressure of patriotic and national sensitivities on Scottish radical politics in the 1790s, sensitivities that often lay just under the surface of debates.

In the event, a British convention of reformers, at least of the sort envisaged by Daer in his letter to Grey, was not forthcoming. The British convention that did take place met in Edinburgh for a start, in late 1793, and involved several English radical societies sending delegates north-wards, not the other way around. The story of this convention has been very well told elsewhere, and does not require retelling here in detail.[76] We should, however, pick up several threads: the origins of the initiative; the place within it of the politics and promise of union; and of course Daer's contribution.

The idea for the British convention, insofar as it had specific origins, came almost certainly on the Scottish side from William Skirving, the secretary of the Edinburgh Friends of the People. Skirving had been promoting the idea of a British convention at least from the time of the first Scottish reform convention in December 1792, and it seems highly likely that it was an idea that he had discussed with Daer before the latter wrote to Grey on 17 January. The LCS and Skirving were in renewed correspondence in May, and in July Skirving wrote to the Whig Association proposing a 'plan of delegates', which they predictably rejected. The idea was resurrected, however, in early October in private correspondence between Skirving and Hardy, in the context of preparation for the third convention of Scottish radicals, which was to meet later that month in Edinburgh.[77] This resulted in a formal letter of invitation from Skirving as secretary to the Edinburgh Friends of the People to the English reform societies to send delegates to the convention. In the event, the LCS, SCI and Sheffield Society for Constitutional Informa-tion appointed delegates to attend.[78]

The Scottish reformers who met in Edinburgh in late 1793 were of a different stripe from those who had met a year previously: their radicalism had been tempered and sharpened by the experience of harsh repression, which included the sentences of transportation handed down by Braxfield and his bench of judges to Muir and Fyshe Palmer in the summer of 1793. Braxfield's treatment of Muir and Fyshe Palmer had shocked the radicals, but also served to harden the resolve of a good number of them. Both men were still in Scotland at the time of the meeting of the third convention, being swiftly removed to London in October by officials fearful that there might be a plan to rescue them, in preparation for their voyage to Botany Bay. (Hardy visited both men on their transport ship, *The Surprise*, at Gosport in January.)[79] The overwhelming majority of the delegates who attended these final Edinburgh conventions were from the artisan and tradesmen classes, men such as the weavers Robert Sands and George Mealmaker from Perth and Dundee respectively; the Glasgow shopkeeper Walter Hart; the Paisley baker Archibald Hastie; the Linlithgow stocking weaver, William Henshelwood, described to Robert Dundas, the Lord Advocate, as a man of 'neither of Circumstances or Character – violent in the association & ready its thought to go any length having nothing to lose';[80] and the Strathaven weaver James Wilson, who would be executed in 1820 for his involvement in the so-called 'Radical War'.[81] Even before the English delegates arrived, they had, meeting as the third convention, agreed without any demur on support for universal suffrage and annual parliaments. As Robert Dundas, the Lord Advocate's informer, 'J. B.' – whose identity remains hidden – told his employer, the resolution was passed '*nem. con.* Whereupon all present shook hands, as if a Bill had actually passed both houses [i.e. of parliament] establishing it as law'.[82] The mood of the reformers was embattled, but defiant; and the arrival of the English delegates in Edinburgh on 7 November served to reinforce this defiance, but also (crucially) to impart a revived sense of political direction and possibility.

We know that Daer did not attend the third convention, although he may well have been in Edinburgh at the time. The absence of both him and Norman Macleod was a source of concern to those who were present, and the decision was taken to send delegations to both to see if they remained true to the radical cause, although in Daer's case this was rescinded, presumably because it was subsequently viewed as unnecessary.[83] Daer and Skirving were among the few delegates from 1792 who were again present for the beginning of the recalled third convention (on 14 November), which became the British convention, although owing to illness Daer attended only a few of the sessions. Captain William Johnston attended, but not as a delegate. Daer was present as the delegate from Wigtown; but there is no other record of a Wigtown radical society, which is not to say that it did not exist, but if it did it was a shadowy, evanescent body.

Responsibility for the incautious politics of the British convention is usually laid squarely at the door of the English delegates, especially Joseph

Gerrald and Maurice Margarot of the LCS. This included imitation of French styles of address, and French methods of business, although, as we saw earlier, there were echoes of this in the first convention, and again Daer was an important promoter of this. But it went much further in December 1793, including addressing each other as 'Citizen', and dating their minutes 'First Year of the British Convention'. The delegates also met in 'sections', which sent reports to the afternoon sittings. The purpose, Daer explained, was to establish a model for future conventions, to produce 'greater regularity' in debate, but also, and most importantly, to create a structure that would enable all to participate. As Daer explained, in words that testify once more to his deep commitment to an egalitarian politics: 'In certain classes of mankind, which had of late been much despised and abused, great abilities were frequently to be found.' The convention also began to put in place plans, including the appointment of a secret committee, for a 'Convention of Emergency', which was to be called in the event that parliament or the government took one of several specific steps which in their eyes would finally break the compact between people and government. This latter move reflected the pervasive sense in radical circles that relations between government and the radicals were in late 1793 moving rapidly to a crisis point, in which British liberty was under threat of being extinguished, a mood powerfully informed by events in Ireland, where the government had moved decisively to crush the main Irish radical society, the Society of the United Irishmen, including passing a convention act outlawing such meetings.[84]

The Scottish delegates were, nevertheless, very willing to be led in the directions suggested to them by their English colleagues; and this was because they were already moving on trajectories that were convergent with these. It was on the issue of 'union', moreover, that this was perhaps most apparent. Plans, in fact, for closer co-operation between radicals across Britain appear to have been widely aired in the autumn of 1793. In September, a radical from Cromarty wrote of the advantages which union promised to their cause: 'This union betwixt the two nations,' he enthused, 'shall not, like the former [ie the Union of 1707] be effected by the distribution of sordid gold; but result from the genuine impulses of Patriotism, uniformly tending to one centre.' Many of the commissions which the delegates brought with them to the reconvened meeting were accompanied with what were described by 'J. B.' as 'lengthy' letters in favour of union, reflecting the enthusiasm which had greeted the English delegates not just in Edinburgh but also in other places where they had visited between 7 and 14 November, and no doubt some they had not.[85]

During the convention itself, the proposals for union met with unanimous support, albeit there were differences about how best to call further British radical conventions. One of the reconvened convention's first actions was to establish a committee to draw up a plan of union, and Daer was one of thirteen delegates elected to this by the divisions.[86] As with other proposals, the plan for a union was closely debated in the various sections, and one of these drew up a document entitled 'Hints on the Question of Union', the first of which read:

> That the people of Great Britain, (disclaiming every distinction of Scots & English) from this Period, & forever; doe unite themselves into one Mass & in an indissoluble Union, Boldly appeal to this Island & to the Universe, that they demand the restoration of the Rights, from which demand they shall never depart.

In order to achieve this end, the section recommended, moreover, that delegates from national conventions in England and Scotland meet twice yearly on the banks of the River Tweed. This would be a symbolic meeting place 'where the Ashes of their Ancestors now lye', ancestors who had been condemned to die because of the 'caprice of the few in the Paltry Feuds of Court Etiquette'. It was also suggested that a weekly communication be opened up between 'South' and 'North' either by letter or in person so that 'Occurrences may be known from one end of the Kingdom to the other' in order to 'strengthen & Instruct every individual of this great but one indivisible Mass'.[87] The idea that the appropriate meeting place of a next convention was in the Borders was repeated by the LCS delegate, Joseph Gerrald, in a major speech defending the notion of calling another convention.[88] The motion, meanwhile, for bringing about a union of reformers was passed unanimously, following which the members of the convention rose and joined hands to mark the moment. Matthew Campbell Browne, the Sheffield delegate, expressed the hope that 'the distinction of North Britain and South Britain will soon be forgotten, and that these countries shall only be known by the common name of Britain'.[89] That the term 'South Britain' was, in contrast to 'North Britain', almost never used by contemporaries only makes his words more freighted with meaning. And Charles Sinclair, the delegate from the SCI, then proposed that the convention change its title henceforth to 'The British Convention of Delegates of the People, Associated to Obtain Annual Parliaments and Universal Suffrage', which again passed unanimously. It was not just the addition of 'British' that was and is significant, but also the shift from 'Delegates of the Societies of the Friends of the People in Scotland' to 'Delegates of the People'. This was a body that might well grow to speak the voice of the people – to become, in short, a true national convention – or so the radicals now hoped.

The British Convention and the ensuing few months represent the high point of British radical co-operation in the first half of the 1790s, with the English delegates corresponding frequently with their fellow radicals in London, and with the London radicals defending their colleagues' conduct in Edinburgh. Many of the LCS ideologue, John Thelwall's public lectures that so worried the authorities in the early months of 1794 dwelt on the treatment of Margarot, Gerrald and other radicals by the High Court in Edinburgh and on the dangers posed to freedom by the abuse of the law.[90] The suppression of the convention and subsequent trials of radicals for treasonable activities all but destroyed, however, the Scottish reform campaign as an open, constitutional force for the rest of the 1790s; and it appears to have been Daer's final involvement in radical politics.

The suppression of the convention was also followed by a period of deep alienation and anger among the Scottish radicals. In London, prompted by Gerrald, who had been released on bail, plans for a further British convention were laid by Hardy and the LCS, which went as far as elections being held of delegates in parts of England and Scotland, a scheme which was forestalled by a further round of arrests in March of leading London radicals, including Hardy. In Scotland a plan was concocted to seize Edinburgh Castle, ransack the banks, and arrest the Lord Provost and the leading judges. The hope was that simultaneous risings would take place in London and Dublin. A key architect of this plan was the Edinburgh wine merchant and former government informer, Robert Watt, who would pay for it with his life, being the only British radical to be executed on British soil in the 1790s in a grisly display of the awesome authority of the state in Edinburgh in early October 1794.

So fantastical has this plan seemed that historians have generally not taken it very seriously. Yet there may have been more going on than has been generally realised, as John Barrell has recently suggested.[91] Scots who were involved did get to London and make contact with representatives of the English radical societies. The most notable were the mysterious John Edmonds Stock and Alexander Scott, the former editor of the Edinburgh radical newspaper, the *Edinburgh Gazetteer*, who had fled the Scottish capital under threat of arrest. Scott may well have become a spy for ministers, and what he learnt or passed on may have informed their belief in an Anglo-Scottish conspiracy, a conviction that drove their unsuccessful prosecution of Hardy for treason. In June, a spy report on one division of the LCS referred to a 'very violent democrat' from Scotland who claimed that Scots would 'long ago have proceeded to violent measures' but had been encouraged to wait by 'favourable Reports they had heard of the London Corresponding Society'.[92] This may well have been the Paisley weaver poet James Kennedy, assistant secretary to the British convention, who fled Edinburgh following the exposure of the Watt plot. Officials in Edinburgh lacked ready means to penetrate the world of the radical artisans in Paisley, whence Kennedy hailed, and other artisan communities who were in contact with Watt; they were substantially in the dark. And yet they did make efforts to uncover what was going on; and the results, of which previous historians seem to have been unaware, cannot have been reassuring, involving as they did rumours of arming, drilling and a good deal of treasonable talk. In early January 1794, the Paisley reformers had been forced to meet on the open street when magistrates took possession of the hall in which they were due to meet; and they probably retreated behind closed doors from that point.[93] Several weavers from Paisley and Barrhead respectively and some others were interrogated in May by the Paisley Sheriff Court about military drilling and efforts to procure arms, which it appears had been taking place, although the numbers involved were relatively small – between forty and fifty. An innkeeper at Barrhead declared that one of those involved had told him around five weeks earlier 'that he did not think the King's health would be drunk or rather that the King's birth day would not be kept in London this year'.[94] Such talk was apparently quite widespread in different parts of lowland Scotland in the spring of 1794. Smeaton's bridge over the Tay at Perth was in April discovered to be covered in graffiti, which included the words, 'Damn all Kings, God damn the King, Curse all Tyrants, Who would want a King to eat the bread of twenty five thousand men, Britain must be a Republic, Liberty and Equality'.[95] From Montrose, the innkeeper Susan Bean was reporting that the 'republicans' were 'still very violent in a private way';[96] while there was also talk of arming in Dundee and Perth, and in East Lothian there were widespread rumours of a rising to coincide with the King's birthday in early June.[97] Talking of course was one thing, and doing another – and doing effectively and in properly co-ordinated fashion another again entirely. But Watt was not working alone, and there was almost certainly a good amount of talking and imagining of treason in popular radical circles in parts of Scotland in the opening months of 1794. Well might William McDowall write to Robert Dundas, the Lord Advocate, in 1800, when food disturbances were showing signs of politicisation in Paisley, that the 'spirit of 1794 has been set forth and politics is mixed with the present scarcity to excite the disaffected to tumult and insurrection'.[98]

Daer was by this stage battling the miserable effects of pulmonary tuberculosis, and played no role in these events. An obituary in the opposition
Whig paper, the *Morning Chronicle* in 1795 claimed that he had repudiated his
former political allies once they embraced violence.[99] There is no corrobora-
tion for this, and it certainly suited the opposition Whigs to make the claim,
for the failure of the Whig Association to expel Daer from its membership
was raised during Hardy's trial.

However, we should leave the final words of this chapter to William
Skirving, who, together with Daer, had been such a strong advocate of the
idea of a British radical union in 1792–3. Aboard the transport ship, the
Surprise that was to carry him to the penal colony at Botany Bay, Skirving
wrote to the SCI with the following advice: 'Uniting Love is the strength,
as well as solace of mankind.' 'Cement by reciprocal kind communications,'
he counselled, 'the Union of hearts, of interest, of measures, which have
solemnly been resolved. By so doing, you will escape the destruction which
is coming on all the earth.'[100] It was a sharply etched vision, and one that
showed how closely conjoined were optimism and desperate pessimism in
the radical mind in the 1790s. It was also a sentiment to which, although
probably without the apocalyptic element, Daer would almost certainly have
subscribed.

Conclusion

Daer was probably seriously ill by the end of 1793; within a year he would be dead. Whether he had any further involvement in radical politics after the British Convention is unknown. It seems, however, unlikely. The suppression of the British Convention by Robert Dundas and the Edinburgh authorities and subsequent judicial destruction of Scottish radicalism as an open, constitutional force must have been a thoroughly dispiriting spectacle, despite the calculated defiance of the English radicals Joseph Gerrald and Maurice Margarot in Braxfield's court room, as must the sweeping arrests of many of his radical comrades in London and elsewhere in the following spring. What he thought of the 'discovery' of the Watt Plot can only be surmise, although it was later claimed (rather unconvincingly) that this led him to separate from the radical cause. By the summer of 1794, almost certainly suffering from advanced symptoms of pulmonary tuberculosis, he was in search of relief from his debilitating condition. His plan was to travel overseas to Lisbon and a warmer climate, following a route well-travelled by sufferers of consumptive disorders in the eighteenth century.[1]

Daer would never depart Britain's shores. En route he found his way to the door of Thomas Beddoes – the *'philosophe'* doctor, as Roy Porter has dubbed him.[2] Beddoes, who had trained in Edinburgh in the mid-1780s, had recently left Oxford, where since 1788 he had taught chemistry under the rather curious title of 'Chemical Reader'. (The University of Oxford has always liked such baubles and still does.) He left before he was pushed, for, as Trevor Levere and Dorothy Stansfield have been able to show, his outspoken political radicalism had by 1792 become an insurmountable barrier to his appointment to a proposed statutory chair in chemistry, which would have secured his position.[3] Rather than remaining in the thickly conservative political atmosphere that had formed in Oxford, he departed for the Bristol Hotwells district, one of the many spas and resorts that proliferated in an eighteenth-century England that nurtured a vibrant, diverse medical marketplace, to set up as a physician. There he could anticipate a steady flow of well-heeled patients. His deeper purpose, however, was to pursue an idea that would occupy him for most of the rest of the 1790s – that the breathing of gases might offer a cure for consumption as well as an array of other illnesses. It derived from the astounding breakthroughs in the chemistry of gases in the 1780s which gripped the minds of young Edinburgh students; the growing understanding of respiration as a process – Beddoes conducted experiments on this in Edinburgh and Oxford; and an idea, associated with the heterodox Edinburgh physician Dr John Brown, that disease fell into two broad categories according to whether they were caused by excessive or insufficient excitement of the nervous system. The corollary was that diseases might be counteracted by either a depressant or stimulant. As Jan Golinski has observed, Beddoes was not a 'consistent devotee of Brunonianism', but it provided him with a useful theory with which to promote his faith that science might furnish the 'key' to unlocking the mystery of the body and its disorders, and helped perhaps further to convince him of, as Larry Stewart puts it, the 'vast hope lurking in the new gas chemistry'.[4]

Whether Beddoes genuinely believed that he could vanquish consumption is not entirely clear. Certainly this is what he claimed in print in 1793. This was quite deliberate; he after all was seeking to drum up support for a scheme that would require financial backing. There was, nevertheless, an obvious tension between his willingness to invoke speculative theories, such as Brown's theory of disease, an edition of whose works Beddoes published in 1795, and his insistence on the priority of experimental knowledge, and of immediate sensory experience as of ultimate persuasive value. Science for Beddoes was a purely empirical enterprise. He thought progress would depend on the dissemination of experimental information, and he collected and published reports of the experiences of other medics and chemists in the use of gases as treatments. What he envisaged for his proposed Pneumatic Institute was a space for establishing the demonstrative proof for a new medical order.[5]

This is not quite the full story, however. The notion that 'factitious airs' might provide a cure for all sorts of conditions was one that, as Stewart and others have described, was 'in the air' in the 1780s.[6] If Beddoes was seduced by it, so were a good number of other physicians and chemists, many of them, like Beddoes, trained in Edinburgh under the guidance of Joseph Black and William Cullen. The distinguished chemist, Thomas Henry, who taught at the Manchester Academy, was another, as were the Manchester physicians, Thomas Percival and John Ferriar.[7] James Lind, the Windsor-based physician-in-ordinary to the royal household may have been deeply suspicious of the politics of some of the enthusiasts for the new pneumatic medicine, but was not prepared to dismiss its potential benefits:

> Indeed there seems to have been such a wonderful coincidence in sentiments of some of the modern Chemists in this country that I have declined taking a part in the Pneumatical practice of Medicine from a detestation of having any connexion with such a set of miscreants notwithstanding I am induced to believe from several reasons that in many Diseases the practice to be of real use.[8]

The London physician Robert John Thornton may have been one of those 'miscreants' who Lind had in mind, although his politics were in fact strictly loyalist. Thornton's Cambridge thesis was on 'oxygen air imbibed by the blood', and Beddoes relied heavily on reports of Thornton's cases in his publications. In 1794, Thornton treated patients with deafness and blindness with oxygen, apparently successfully. As Beddoes reported to James Watt: 'A boy so deaf for 15 months that he did not hear the tower guns, though close to them has nearly recovered his hearing by oxygenation.' 'The credit of pneumatic medicine,' Beddoes positively trilled, 'is daily rising.'[9] Perhaps there was something here of that familiar pattern in the medical world of early successes fuelling heady expectations and hopes.

Beddoes was a natural enthusiast caught up in the excitement of natural science at the end of the eighteenth century. His career, like that of Daer's brother-in-law, Sir James Hall, exemplifies the openness and internationalism of late Enlightenment science. Fluent in French and German, he was responsible for bringing out translations and editions of works by several eminent Continental naturalists and experimentalists. In 1787 he visited Guyton de Morveau in Dijon, where he met the travelling party of Antoine Lavoisier, Antoine Fourcroy and Claude Louis Berthollet. Beddoes's respect for experimental science as defined by its British practitioners was absolute, and there was about his mind a wonderful promiscuity, a failure to be deterred by setbacks, and an ability to transfer his belief from likely cure to likely cure. Thus, if it was fixed air, or hydrogen, that held out most hope in 1794 for curing consumption, it was digitalis or foxglove that he put his faith in a little while later, and then the so-called 'cow-cure', living side-by-side with a cow, by the end of the decade. But Beddoes's enthusiasm was political and social, as well as medical. Beddoes believed that medical reform, political reform and social reform were inextricably intertwined, links that he made explicit as he promoted his ideas in 1793. As he declared:

[N]ow, when the human mind seems, in so many countries, about to be roused from that torpor, by which it has been so long benumbed, we may reasonably indulge the expectation of a rapid progress in this, the most benefi- cial of all the sciences. An infinitely small portion of genius has hitherto been exerted in attempts to diminish the sum of our painful sensations; and the force of society has been exclusively at the disposal of Despots and Juntos, the great artificers of human evil. Should an entire change in these two respects, any where take place, every member of society might soon expect to experi- ence, in his own person, the consequence of so happy an innovation.[10]

He was here consciously linking evidence of intellectual progress – the breakthroughs of Priestley, Lavoisier and other lesser figures – and political revolution. The new era of democracy, then dawning in France and spreading to Britain in the form of the rise of political radicalism, would not just banish poverty, as Paine had promised, but disease and suffering as well. If knowl- edge was power, then knowledge in a democratic society was real power.

That Daer turned to Beddoes in 1794 may be fairly easily explained, although again this must be speculation. It is highly likely that Daer met him first in Edinburgh, when they were both medical students. Beddoes was in Edinburgh studying medicine between 1784 and December 1786. Possibly the encounter took place as they sat in Joseph Black's lecture room. Beddoes remained in close contact with Black; he was another who fell deeply under his spell as a teacher – 'Black's course is the best I have ever heard or ever shall hear.'[11] His chemistry lectures at Oxford were explicitly modelled on Black's, including the emphasis placed on experimental demonstration. Beddoes greatly admired Black's experimental virtuosity and technical inventiveness. Daer, or possibly Sir James Hall, with their close links to Edinburgh's scien- tific community, and wider British and European scientific circles, would certainly have heard about Beddoes's experiments on respiration and using gases to treat consumption and other diseases. Beddoes publicised these in any case in three pamphlets published in 1793. (The quotation above comes from the preface to one of these.) Beddoes's principal supporters in his scheme were the Birmingham-based engineer James Watt, Derby's Erasmus Darwin, the chemist and manufacturer James Keir, the Ketley ironmaster William Reynolds and their circles of Enlightened English provincial intel- lectuals, although Watt and Keir were of course Scots.[12] As was stressed in chapter 1 and at several later points in this book, Daer almost certainly had his own close links to these networks or to those who were in regular contact with them, who would include Black and Hall. Hall would later be one of the subscribers to Beddoes's Pneumatic Institution, as would many members of the Edinburgh scientific community.[13] It is also just possible that the connection to Beddoes was provided by James Watt jnr whose fervent support for the French Revolution Daer had shared in 1792, with whom he appears to have been corresponding in 1794.[14]

Pulmonary tuberculosis is an awful disease, a chronic, epidemic condition which usually extinguishes life slowly as the body's defences weaken, and the cause – *Mycobacterium tuberculosis* – was only identified in the early 1880s by the German bacteriologist Robert Koch. Amongst its common symptoms are haemoptysis – the coughing up of haemorrhaged blood – cough producing sputum, fever, night sweats, weight loss with wasting, and difficult, laboured breathing.[15] The representations of consumptive disorders in the eighteenth century as a condition of the fashionable and refined, a tendency that would only deepen in the first half of the nineteenth century, may have served to disguise the terror which it brought, but to Beddoes, with experience of treating the condition, they threatened to promote an irresponsible passivity.[16] As this was the single largest killer of adults in the eighteenth century, killing more and more people through the decades, to hold out the promise of a cure was to offer, therefore, a rare hope. Having read one of his treatises of 1793, Erasmus Darwin wrote to Beddoes: '[I] am glad to find you are about to combat this giant malady; which has hitherto baffled the skill and withstood the prowess of all ages; and which in this country destroys whole families, and, like war, cuts off the young in their prime of life, sparing old age and infirmity.'[17] The peculiar cruelty of consumption was, as Darwin here underlined, that it struck down the young. Of Daer and his brothers, only Thomas would survive into older age. Daer and John would die from consumption, John in 1797, while yellow fever would account for Dunbar whilst on naval service in the West Indies.

The bitter limits of existing medical help are, moreover, all too apparent in correspondence between parents and physicians. Darwin in 1794 was treating James Watt's daughter, Janet, or 'Jessie' as she was commonly known. As she slipped towards death, Darwin tried everything that he could think of to relieve her symptoms: opium, a regime of exercise – bell-ringing was one of his more curious suggestions here – exposure to cold air, emetics and swinging her to induce sickness so that she might better absorb the substances that Darwin hoped might eradicate the 'ulcers on her lungs' that he believed were killing her.[18] Watt and his wife were beside themselves and Darwin even at one stage chose to talk of Jessie's condition as a 'general debility', clearly not wanting to name it as consumption.[19] 'Decline' was another euphemism often associated with the disease. Watt eventually turned to Beddoes and his 'airs', but to no better effect. On 9 June 1794, Watt wrote to his old friend, Joseph Black in Edinburgh – who himself appears to have suffered from consumption-like symptoms and who had been advising Watt on possible treatments for his daughter, mostly consisting of regimes designed to strengthen the constitution – of the unavailing efforts to save Jessie. Watt's words are perhaps all the more moving for his inability or unwillingness to change his ingrained habit of exact, careful description:

> My Amiable and lovely daughter expired on Friday morning after a long suffering, the fever she had when I wrote you last proved a hectic of the most violent kind, which perhaps we might have seen sooner if we had not been misled by her violent hystericks. On perceiving a change in the expectorated matter I sent for Mr Darwin, who gave little hopes but prescribed for the fever and other urgent symptoms. I then had Dr Beddoes who attended her daily for a week, but also seemed to think the case desperate, she breathed fixt air from effervescing mixtures placed near here and some times inhaled it mixt with atmospheric, but without other apparent effect then its being grateful to her. The violence of her fever the hystericks and the great weakness prevented our trying the effect of other airs and of some active medicines which were proposed. Yeast seemed to moderate very much the hot fit of fever and I think she owed some <ease> to the use of it. It has a tendency to purge which is easily counteracted by ipecuanha [. . .] The irritation to cough, sometimes convulsive, with a fever and rapid pulse of 120 to 130, brought on a hemorrage in the lungs of which she expired in a few minutes.

Culminating in the massive pulmonary haemorrhage, which led almost certainly to shock and asphyxia, the picture presented is bleak, and Watt's additional words do little to alleviate this: 'We have only the consolation to think that we did all to save her which was in our power, or the very able physicians we consulted could suggest was proper.'[20]

To assuage his grief for the loss of his daughter, Watt became Beddoes's greatest collaborator in 1794–6, spending a huge amount of time and energy in devising apparatus for producing and administering the gases, and making endless suggestions about which gases might be tried. Watt also experimented on himself with various gases, some of which had alarming effects – nausea, giddiness, head-aches, even loss of consciousness – although in chemistry self-experiment was quite normal in this period. More disturbingly perhaps, he showed little hesitation in trying out gases on several of his servants who were ill. There are over fifty letters between Watt and Beddoes for this period, testifying to his determination to turn his personal tragedy into something positive.

Did Daer believe that Beddoes might be able to cure him? The answer seems to be not. Yet as with Watt in the case of his beloved daughter, he was desperate enough by late 1794 to grasp at a possible cure. Beddoes and his gases appeared to offer the most hope.

Beddoes seems to have displayed what with hindsight is astonishing conviction that he was, indeed, Daer's best bet; in fact, his only one. As he wrote on 14 October 1794: 'Daer is certainly in confirmed consumption. His physicians hitherto have doubted; but I suppose this disease has become more distinct. I am afraid by going soon to Lisbon he will lose his only chance.'[21] This chance was to be achieved through the breathing of 'fixed air' (hydrogen), Beddoes's current theory being that consumption was a product of hyper-oxygenation. Although largely speculative, it was a theory that he sought to provide some evidence for by breathing oxygen and cataloguing its effects. On 24 October, Beddoes was reporting to Watt: 'Consumption must be curable if we can apply our power [. . .]', continuing:

> Lord Daer bears fixed air astonishingly. He takes as 1 to 3 in atmospheric [air] – with[ou]t the least <titillation?> [i.e. the sense of itching or tickling] or disagreeable effect or feeling. I wish he was not going to Lisbon; for having brought him to this standard, I c.d continue him f[ixed] a[ir] constantly. But he goes to certain death from a possibility of help.[22]

But Daer was of several minds, Beddoes writing in another letter to Watt in a manner which again betrays an unattractive impatience, but also deep absorption in his project: 'Lord Daer has not done himself justice. Poor Man he is distracted between inconsistent plans.' Beddoes was administering ever stronger concentrations of hydrogen to his patient. Having started with a mixture of about one to three parts hydrogen to normal air, Daer was now breathing one part hydrogen and one part air for periods of twenty to thirty minutes, almost certainly through an early version of Watt's breathing apparatus. The portable version of this was not perfected until 1796. The idea was that wealthier patients able to purchase the apparatus would be able to self-administer their gases; so the scheme had a neat commercial dimension. Daer was now, however, refusing another treatment recommended by Beddoes – to have his room filled with fumes from 'effervescing mixtures with vinegar'. It appears that he was unable to decide whether to continue with the original plan of travelling to Lisbon, Beddoes commenting that 'he was [. . .] incessantly occupied in trifles, as buying tools & laying in useless stores.'[23]

At this point Daer disappears from Beddoes's correspondence, although his breathing machine gets several later mentions since Beddoes had a purchaser for it, but its return to Clifton was delayed.[24] As far as we can tell, Daer's condition quickly deteriorated. Whether he continued in his plans to depart for the Continent is unknown. Almost certainly his illness, like Jessie Watt's, was too far advanced for any contemporary medical intervention to have made any significant difference, whatever Beddoes believed. This is hinted at in a letter which Sir James Hall wrote on 11 November 1794 on hearing of Daer's death: 'We this morning received information of the death of Ld Daer – a loss never to be repaired. The last accounts we had were such as to make us wish that all were easily over, and there is reason to believe that his end at last was sudden, tho' we have not yet learnt any particulars.'[25] It is very likely that Daer drowned in his own blood after a severe lung haemorrhage.

That Daer made his way to Beddoes in 1794 is in one sense poignantly ironic; in the rise and eventual collapse of Beddoes's ambitions for the new pneumatic medicine are obvious echoes of the rise and fall of the hopes of a new era of liberty which at the beginning of the 1790s gripped Daer and fellow political reformers and radicals, Beddoes included. Conservative critics of Beddoes, following Burke and his assault on Priestley, had all-too-predictable fun with airy metaphors and the dissolution of common sense in pursuit of fatuous dreams. The later focus at the Pneumatic Institute on experiments with inhaling nitrous oxide, associated with his talented assistant, the young Humphry Davy, furnished a gift so rich in comic possibility as to be impossible to resist in this context, but comedy infused with destructive and hostile intent. Beddoes and his ilk were condemned as dangerous quacks, flirting with hysteria, strange sensations, and, since young women were among their patients, sexual impropriety. The early promethean hopes of Beddoes were unrealisable, but their implosion was powerfully aided by the political and cultural polarisations of the 1790s.

*   *   *

Daer was not, as was said at the outset of this book, a front-rank figure in the politics of the early 1790s, and many of his friends and contacts are today much better known than he. Daer's memory would be completely eclipsed by that of his younger brother, Thomas, although not in Kirkcudbright and the south-west of Scotland, where it burned with an intense luminosity well into the nineteenth century. Daer was regionally long remembered for his far-reaching schemes of improvement which had become, quite literally, inscribed on the shifting local landscape and townscape. Sometimes, in the course of this book, it may have seemed that Daer's principal claim on our attention is those whom he knew or with whom he came into contact. Yet, in some ways a bit like Thomas Beddoes, Daer was a remarkable individual, one who made a profound and enduring impression on those who met him. Anna Letitia Barbauld would not forget him, and neither would his other great teacher, Dugald Stewart. Anna Letitia's modern biographer has described Daer as his subject's 'favourite pupil', noting that she long treasured a pair of leather balls of the kind used by printers to ink type 'because', as she wrote to her brother, John Aikin, 'you must know Lord Daer made them himself & gave them me & therefore I should be very sorry to lose them'.[26]

Daer's egalitarianism and his advanced political radicalism pose fascinating challenges for the historian. They partly resulted, as we have seen, from a combination of influences – educational, intellectual, political and ideological – and of a moment or series of moments that held within them multiple possibilities for these influences to combine in very different ways. At the core of his personality were an unshakeable commitment to the public good and an equally deep conviction that it was his duty to promote this. For Daer the 'public good' was identified very strongly with an idea of progress; that knowledge is power; and that its measure was the 'happiness' of the people. It was a conception of patriotic citizenship to which he was probably introduced first by the Barbaulds at their Palgrave academy. Underpinning it was a clear moral obligation, one that, if anything, fell more heavily on the rich. As Anna Letitia would later write: 'Every man owes to the state one good citizen [. . .] If he is rich he <u>must</u> consider himself under a strict moral obligation to pay off his great debt [to [the] society that has given him riches] by every attention to the interests of the community which leisure, an enlightened mind, and the command of property, can enable him to give.' To serve one's country was to serve the whole of society – 'all ranks and professions'. And, as Richard Price would argue in his famous sermon 'On the Love of Country', delivered to the Revolution Society on 4 November 1789, true patriotism was focused on 'all humankind'. Private interests and prejudices, even patriotism itself, would ultimately dissolve in 'universal philanthropy'.[27]

Such ideas and convictions were formed within particular currents of the Enlightenment. In Daer's case they derived from at least two separate, but overlapping Enlightenments – the Scottish and the provincial English one. Historians debate whether there was a 'British' Enlightenment. Whether you think such a thing existed depends ultimately on how you define 'The Enlightenment'.[28] There was, nevertheless, very definitely a *British culture* of enlightenment – one that was both practical and idealistic at the same time; and which was forged from the interactions between the two, and indeed with a wider world of European enlightenment learning and intellectual exchange. This was the Enlightenment of Lord Daer. It was also what linked his activities as a practical improver on the family estates, as an ingenious, innovative, and determined road builder in the south west, and as an urban planner of sorts in the tiny burgh of Kirkcudbright, and his wider outlook on public life and duty.

Why Daer became quite so convinced of the prospects for political transformation in the early 1790s, and willing to pursue this as a goal after many, probably most, propertied reformers had distanced themselves from the new popular *re-distributive* political radicalism that developed from 1791, is harder to pin down. William Roscoe was puzzled by the latter, leading him to demand in a letter to Lord Lansdowne (the former prime minister Lord Shelburne): 'Why has he committed himself in such a business, and nipt his usefulness in the bud?' His explanation lay in the snare as he now saw it of an inflexible principle: 'Great harm has been done by the doctrine, so industriously inculcated by a sect of which I am a professing member, that whatever is ultimately right is to be pursued at all times.'[29]

Daer's sense of political duty and convictions owed much to his education, not just at Palgrave but also under the direction of Dugald Stewart in Edinburgh. Stewart's main influence seems to have been strongly to reinforce Daer's progressive idea of civic duty and his faith in progress as one of the defining features of the modern, as opposed to ancient, world. Stewart taught that this progress was predicated, in large part, on a democratisation and internationalisation of the intellect made possible by the combined effects of global trade and print. One might view Stewart in this context as a very early theorist of the 'public sphere'. For progress in his eyes was the consequence of the rise of a new economy of knowledge made possible by globalisation and the ability to store and communicate knowledge in print. Through his father, Daer inherited a posture of political independence. It was another kind of politics of virtue, one that rejected the servility and corruption that appeared to pervade Scottish politics and political culture. Independence, liberty and patriotism were different facets of the same political stance, although here liberty might mean many things, from reforming the elections of the Scottish representative peers, to electoral reform, or, indeed, to the complete reinvention of political life.

More crucial still to Daer's developing political outlook and activities was how far he became drawn into the excitement and intoxicating hopes and dreams of French revolutionary politics between 1789 and 1792. As with a good many other British reformers and radicals in this period, he was utterly convinced of the immediate relevance to British politics of the lessons and goals of the fundamental political transformation under way in France. Witnessing key events in the Revolution, immersing himself in the frenzied debates of the Paris Jacobin Club, the National Assembly and the Palais Royal, served to cement and deepen this conviction. His French Revolution – if we can talk in such terms – as it was for Paine and most other British supporters of the French Revolution, was the version associated with Jacques-Pierre Brissot and the republican vanguard of 1791–3, politicians who sought the creation of a modern, commercial republic and, ultimately, the spread of liberty and peace across the globe. That this is not what came about is beside the point here; hindsight is a treacherous thing in seeking to understand people such as Daer. Daer was in Paris in 1789 to witness the start of the Revolution, and in Paris again in the summer of 1791 he became very close to those revolutionaries – the marquis de Condorcet and Sophie Condorcet, Brissot, Pierre Louis Roederer – who, in response to Louis XVI's flight, openly spoke of and argued for a republic. And he sought to apply directly the models of French politics and of politics that he witnessed in person in the National Assembly and Jacobin Club to guide British radicals in their pursuit of 'true liberty' in 1792–3. Daer, like Paine and an assortment of other British, European and American radicals, was part of that cosmopolitan moment in French revolutionary politics that waxed most strongly in 1790–2, but was crushed under the terrible weight of war and revolutionary violence in 1793.

Possibilities within moments may present themselves, but whether they are perceived and acted upon will depend on education and outlook in the broadest sense, but also on personality and disposition. Whether through upbringing or education, or because of the nature of the times in which he came to adulthood, or the combination of these things, Daer seems to have apprehended the world with a marked restlessness, an appetite for improvement and change, and for new ideas. Towards the end of his life Dugald Stewart would give Charles Babbage a plan for the construction of a calculating machine drawn up by Daer thirty-five years previously, which has led one modern scholar to suggest that Daer may even have been 'something of a visionary'.[30] Perhaps so; the evidence is slight. His intellect, however, was certainly a very active one, and one intently focused on the possibilities of producing change, as his road schemes in the south-west illustrate very powerfully.

In this there may have been a generational dimension, and perhaps a distinctively Scottish one. The 1780s in Scotland were a decade characterised

by a broadly progressive spirit – although there were, to be sure, contradictions and contrary forces, most obviously the extraordinary upsurge of
popular anti-Catholic feeling in 1779–81. But the position was more complex
than this implies, because the impulse to reform often had conservative roots
in later Georgian Britain. Conservatism and challenge and change were not
necessarily in opposition. There was a growing sense in the 1780s of a society
in the throes of rapid change and transformation. The new streets, the South
Bridge scheme and the renewed drive to enhance the amenity and efficiency
of the Scots capital were one expression of this, as were the renewed hopes
for the transformation of the Highlands symbolised by the de-annexation of
the Forfeited Estates and establishment of the Edinburgh Highland Society
in 1784. In 1793, that apostle of improvement, James Anderson, would depict
its possibilities as almost limitless. 'The French,' he wrote in his periodical,
The Bee,

> have an excellent expression, which they apply to the exertions of men who go
> beyond whatever was expected of them; *il fait l'impossible*. In the same spirit,
> we may say these are a few of the *impossible* things that we have actually seen
> executed, with a few others that are in view. But there are an infinity of others
> that our descendants will see executed, (if they shall be wise enough to be
> contented with liberty and property,) which we have not even got a glimpse
> of as yet.[31]

The scientific achievements of the 1770s and '80s, especially in chemistry and
the closely linked sciences of mineralogy and geology, powerfully informed
the attitudes of Daer and his generation. This was certainly not incompatible
with basically conservative views, as would become very clear from 1791 to
1792, and as we saw in relation to the membership of the Spec in the 1780s.
A belief in the potential of improvement to transform society was in no way
a monopoly of radicals or reformers, as the example of George Dempster
nicely illustrates, or indeed that of his fellow Sutherland landowner, Sir
John Sinclair of Ulbster, whose *Statistical Account* provides an immensely
rich record of the sense of dynamism within Scottish society at the beginning of the 1790s. And it is very plausible that it was precisely the experience of movement and progress, and the degree to which Scotland's elites
were invested in this, that helped to inoculate Scotland against 'revolutionary
contagion' in the 1790s, certainly among the propertied classes. But one can
also argue that the shifts in mood and attitude between the 1780s and 1790s
were experienced more starkly in Scotland because the 1780s stand out
as more sharply distinct than in England and Wales. Probably this cannot

be pushed too far as an idea, not least because what you see in the world depends so much on *disposition* and indeed *position*.

Where Daer was unusual was not so much in the breadth and intensity of the interests and commitments, or indeed that his reformist politics could incubate in the Edinburgh of the 1780s – this would be true, for example, of the much better known James Mackintosh or indeed Thomas Addis Emmett, the Irish radical – but in his immersion in popular radical politics in London, Edinburgh *and* Paris. It is easier to describe how this happened than to explain it, although circumstantial factors were important; some of his story is simply about contingency and chance, and about relationships forged along the way, although friends choose one another of course.

Daer's politics were 'British' or rather Scotto-British, as well as cosmopolitan; they were necessarily framed by the consequences and implications of the Union. The Union state as it was created in 1707 was one that Daer came to wish to destroy. Not to restore Scottish independence, however, for nationalism, as has been emphasised repeatedly, was entirely alien to his outlook and indeed to the late Enlightenment world that conditioned this. Instead, his goal was to see the squalid memory of its making – as he saw it – effaced in a much wider and deeper political transformation that would make the people and the political nation truly one and the same, and that would at the same moment bind together Scots and English in a genuine union of interests and sentiment. His vision was of a much closer union – a true union of peoples, in short. This was still an essentially civic vision of the state, one predicated on a notion of political rights and duties and not cultural identities. Political unity did not require a cultural unity other than a common commitment to an expansive vision of political liberty. But it was a dream every bit as striking in its way as Beddoes's one of disease vanquished by the promise of pneumatic chemistry and systematic experiment with the respiration of gases; and it was probably only imaginable in the particular circumstances and conditions of the early 1790s.

How seriously should we, then, view it? We might after all argue that it was a vision associated with a small, embattled group of political radicals who grasped at the idea of a British radical union simply because there was in 1792–3 nowhere else for them to turn. The radical hopes of late 1793 which came to a head at the British Convention in Edinburgh were hopes born of desperation and the conviction that the complete suppression of radicalism, perhaps the violent suppression, was only a matter of time. Plans for an emergency convention, first proposed in Edinburgh, that Thomas Hardy and his fellow radicals in London continued to seek to implement in early 1794, were conceived in response to a sense of imminent and developing crisis in radical politics. The irony is that Pitt and his supporters saw in these plans the threat of violent revolution. The radicals were anticipating, however, that Pitt's government would inevitably act to destroy their cause, perhaps even using military force to do so, extirpating at the same time what remained of English and British 'liberty'. Yet if a vision of radical union was the product of hope and desperation in equal measure, it does not fully answer the question of why there was a clear British thread to radical politics in the 1790s, one that can be traced back at least to the very early phases of the emergence of a Scottish parliamentary reform movement from the summer of 1792.

The most influential explanation for this is Linda Colley's, which is to see this as another symptom of the rise of 'Britishness' in the long eighteenth century.[32] Colley portrays this Britishness as a form of identity superimposed on existing national identities, one forged in the crucible of a century of frequent warfare and fierce international rivalries. In truth, however, Britishness was never a unitary thing, and her view of British identity underplays the tensions, divisions, miscomprehension and mute indifference that stood in the way of a single, over-arching British national feeling in this period. English puzzlement and, frankly, hostility to Scots patriotic sentiment have a very long history.

As has been argued in this book, we might in any case be better to see the British radicalism of the 1790s as mainly a Scottish creation, deriving in part from the experiences of living with the Union and emerging from developing structures of politics that were increasingly taking on a British dimension. The strategy of union, the impulse towards co-ordination and forging of links, also, to be fair, developed from within radical politics in London and the English provinces, and the notion of a convention as the salvation and hope for radicalism was taking clear shape in the minds of radicals throughout Britain in 1792. Links between radicals in, on the one hand, London, Sheffield and Manchester, and on the other, Edinburgh and Glasgow were quickly forged in 1792, facilitated by the circulation of radical newspapers and periodicals, but also the presence of Scots south of the border, such as in Sheffield the radical printer John Crome and journalist and writer James Montgomery, or in London Thomas Hardy and his fellow Scottish artisans. How many radicals in England who were not native Scots were thinking before 1793 in consciously British terms, however, is debatable, although sadly unanswerable.

Daer's short political life coincided with the rise of the politics of British liberty in Scotland, which reflected, in turn, a pattern of deepening conver-

gence and assimilation with English politics in the final third of the eighteenth century. This did not mean the eradication of Scottish difference,
but it was symptomatic of a new phase in the history of the Union and its
political operation. Semi-autonomy in the form it had operated in the first
half century or so of the Union was being replaced by something different;
and what was producing this was not so much pressures from England as the
ambitions of the Scots themselves. The radicalism of the 1790s grew directly
from the reformist and popular currents at work in Scottish society in the
previous decade – burgh reform, opposition to patronage in the Kirk, even
opposition to Catholic relief – all of which, in their different ways, were about
ensuring that Scotland participated fully in English liberties, or, as the earl
of Buchan might have seen it, ensuring that there was something that could
genuinely be called the *British constitution*, as opposed to simply persistence
of the English one.

Daer's far-reaching vision of British liberty was destroyed almost as
soon as it began to be created. Yet he and his collaborators left an important legacy, a vivid and carefully nurtured memory and tradition of *British*
radical aspiration which would endure in Scottish society throughout the
nineteenth century, through the political convulsions of the post Napoleonic
war era, the era of the Chartists, and from thence through popular liberalism
to the modern Labour movement. This drew on Scottish patriotic feeling
and symbols, but in a way that usually reinforced its broader ambitions
and horizons. Daer's politics expressed themselves in Scottish, British *and*
universal terms. To be a patriotic Scot, British and cosmopolitan were for
him entirely compatible, as they would be for many who lived within the
radical tradition throughout the nineteenth and twentieth centuries.

However, it may well be that national identity is not and never really has
been the essential issue in the politics of the Union. This may have begun to
change in the recent past as the politics of 'identity' have come to challenge,
and even at times, overwhelm that of class. This, surely, is one of the most
striking changes of recent decades, and one that is causing profound
upheavals in the nature of contemporary cultural and political life. Taking
the long view, however, union has always been about interest and definitions
of this, and this still to a very significant extent is the case. Does, in other
words, the Union work for Scotland, or, as Daer would have expressed it
more pertinently, does it work for the Scots people, their liberty, prosperity
and happiness conceived in the broadest sense, and perhaps for the English
people (rather than the elites)? On the other hand, Daer would almost
certainly have argued that, as was the case for its first three hundred years

the Union needs to be flexible to endure and prosper. This, as Alvin Jackson has reminded us recently in his parallel history of the two unions that have underpinned the United Kingdom state, has been a distinguishing feature of the Anglo-Scots union, its capacity for periodic reinvention.[33] Unionism and nationalism were also never, partly as a result, at polar extremes from one another. Yet, as importantly, or more importantly perhaps, responsibility for the health of the Union lies with the English and Scots together. This, in the end, may be why Daer has something still to say to us. It could be that it is the English who really need to sit up and take note, as Daer was intimating to Charles Grey in 1793. For unionist radicals' dreams truly to prosper you require English as well as Scots unionist radicals. For if they do not act together, and with common and equal purpose, then the Scots must and will look elsewhere for the realisation of their ambitions.

Appendix

1. Robert Burns, 'Lines on Meeting with Lord Daer'

> This wot ye all whom it concerns,
> I, Rhymer Robin, alias Burns,
>   October twenty-third,
> A ne'er-to-be-forgotten day,
> Sae far I sprachled up the brae,
>   I dinner'd wi' a Lord.
>
> I've been at druken writers' feasts,
> Nay, been bitch-fou' 'mang godly priests,
>   Wi' rev'rence be it spoken:
> I've even join'd the honour'd jorum,
> When mighty squireships of the quorum,
>   Their hydra drouth did sloken.
>
> But wi' a Lord — stand out, my shin!
> A Lord — a Peer — an Earl's son! —
>   Up higher yet, my bonnet!
> And sic a Lord! — lang Scotch ells twa,
> Our Peerage he o'erlooks them a',
>   As I look o'er my sonnet.
>
> But, oh! for Hogarth's magic pow'r!
> To show Sir Bardie's willyart glow'r,
>   And how he star'd and stammer'd,
> When goavan [vacant], as if led wi' branks,
> An' stumpan [walking stupidly] on his ploughman shanks,
>   He in the parlour hammer'd.

I sidling shelter'd in a nook,
An' at his lordship steal't a look,
    Like some portentous omen;
Except good sense and social glee,
An' (what surpris'd me) modesty,
    I marked nought uncommon.

I watch'd the symptoms o' the great,
The gentle pride, the lordly state,
    The arrogant assuming;
The fient a pride, nae pride had he,
Nor sauce, nor state, that I could see,
    Mair than an honest ploughman.

Then from his lordship I shall learn,
Henceforth to meet with unconcern
    One rank as weel's another;
Nae honest worthy man need care
To meet with noble youthful Daer,
    For he but meets a brother.

2. Letter from Lord Daer to Charles Grey, Edinburgh, 17 Jan. 1793

Dear Sir

    I write to you in some alarm from a passage in your letter of the 13th inst. to our Secretary Skirving [i.e. William Skirving, secretary of the Edinburgh Friends of the People]. You there say 'In this part of the country I am afraid our supporters are not sufficiently numerous to render the attempt to secure petitions at present adviseable'. I am desired by several Gentlemen to ask an explanation. You must tell us explicitly whether you mean to petition or not, for if you dont in England, neither (say they) will we in Scotland. I deprecate the idea of your not petitioning. Were your petitioners as few in number as the members of your societies, you should petition. When you talk of not petitioning do you think likewise of not moving in Parliament for a Reform? If so, many will consider it almost treachery in you & your friends. Not that I or anyone who knows you can think so. Nor do I mention it to influence you personally, for I trust to God that in the great line you have taken up you have set your mind above being influenced even by the disapprobation of your personal friends. But I mention it because I look upon it as of great consequence to keep our leading men and societies in London high in the estimation of the supporters of freedom at a distance. If you begin to petition in England, I am convinced from my local knowledge of several parts that a great body of the common people are inclined to petition and that it may very probably take a run amongst them. At any rate the strength of the Cause both here and in England consists more in its goodness, in the vigour of the men who support it and in the numbers who we are sure hereafter must join it than the numbers who have already declared. It is curious to see the error which prevails amongst the supporters of freedom in every place in England & in Scotland where I have been, that the declared friends of freedom are more numerous everywhere else. Our folks here are astonished at your information that you are not innumerable about London as perhaps you may be surprised when I say that the declared friends of Reform in Scotland are most contemptible in the view of counting noses, what ever they may be in counting heads. This I aver to be the fact, tho' I believe immense numbers of non-declarants would sign a petition. Every reason you urge for petitioning to keep up the spirit etc applies equally to England as to Scotland, but I ought perhaps to apologise for being carried away to speak of what should be done in England, instead of what is the likely consequences to result from it in Scotland. If the idea gets abroad that the friends of Reform in any place, or at least any leading place, are to lye by for any reason whatever, I believe it will in every place for the moment damp the ardor of their coming forward, if not extinguish it. You wish us in Scotland to come forward because we are more numerous. I believe that small as our numbers are, they are greater in proportion than in England, but far from enough to command protection from the Executors of the forms of law. If we are more numerous I believe also we are much more oppressed. By every act implying favor to Reform the people here expose themselves either to the heavy hand of Government or the unceasing weight of little aristocratical oppression. If set forward alone, the arbitrary attacks against them will be more pointed than if countenanced by their friends in England: at least, they may think so which is the same, and they will feel all the bitterness of desertion in distress. It may even have a national bad effect, if this should go so far, or anything else should take such a turn as to make the Tweed appear a boundary in political sentiment or action, it requires more confidence in the good sense of our countrymen than even I can reasonably have not to believe that it is possible (though I do not think probable) that a fatal national jealousy may arise. Scotland has long groaned under the chains of England and knows that its connection there has been the cause of its greatest misfortunes. Perhaps you may shrug your shoulders at this and call it Scot's prejudice, but it is time at moments like these when much may depend on suiting measures to the humour of the people, that you Englishmen should see this rather as it is or at least be aware of how we Scotsmen see it. We have existed a conquered province these two centuries. We trace our bondage from the Union of the Crown and find it little alleviated by the Union of the Kingdoms. What is it you say we have gained by the Union? Commerce, Manufactures, Agriculture. Without going deep into the principles of political economy or asking how our Government or any country can give these to any nation, it is evident in this case that the last Union gave us little assistance in these except removing a part of the obstacles which your greater power had posterior to the first union [i.e. the Union of Crowns (1603)] thrown around us. But if it did more what would that amount to, but to the common saying that we bartered our liberty and with it our morals for a little wealth? You say we have gained emancipation from feudal tyranny. I believe most deliberately that had no Union ever taken place we should in that respect have been more emancipated that we are. Left to ourselves we should probably have had a progression towards Liberty and not less than yours. Our grievances prior to the accession of the Stewarts to your throne were of a kind which even had that event not taken place, must before this time have been annihilated. Any share of human evil that might have awaited us we are ignorant of, whereas we feel what we have undergone. Even to the last of our separate parliaments they were always making laws for us and now and then one to remedy a grievance. And a people acquiring knowledge must have compelled a separate legislature to more of these. Since the parliaments were united scarcely four acts have been passed in as many score of years affecting Scots law or merely the incongruities which must arise betwixt old laws and modern manners. As our courts of law found something of this to be necessary they instead of applying to the parliament at London have taken upon themselves with a degree of audacity which can hardly be made credible to a stranger, to make under pretence of regulating of court Little Laws (acts of parliament as they call them) materially affecting the liberty of the subject. Kept out of view by your greater mass so as never to make our concerns be the principal objects even to our own representatives, at a distance so as not to make our cries be heard in the capital which alone awes an arbitrary government; our laws and customs different so as to make our grievances unintelligible; our law establishment distinct so as to deprive us of the benefit of those constant circuits from the capital which by rendering the learned and spirited defender of the laws, dwelling at the source of actual power, acquainted with the lesser transactions of the remotest corner of the country, provides perhaps the greatest remedy to a half free state against some of the bad consequence of an extended territory. Our civil establishment distinct, so as to isolate the petty tyranny of office; even our greed and national vanity working to retain all these offices to natives so as still more to leave you (our then only protectors, although oppressors) ignorant of our internal situation. We have suffered the misery which is perhaps inevitable to a lesser and remote country in a junction where the Governing powers are united but the Nations are not united. In short, thinking we have been the worse of every connection hitherto with you, the Friends of Liberty in Scotland have almost universally been enemies to the Union with England. Such is the fact, whether the reasons be good or bad. I for one should still be of opinion did I not look upon it that a thorough Parliamentary Reform would necessarily place us in a much better situation and higher in the political sphere whilst at the same time it would relieve you from that vermin from this country who infect your court, your parliament and every establishment. I, therefore, wish a closer Union of the Nations, but many here differ from me, some through principle, others through prejudice or pique, for these cannot at once be thrown off even by the rapid progress of philosophy and philanthropy amongst us. Perhaps we may require to be treated with delicacy and tenderness as a Nation whose temper is somewhat sour, who have sometimes met with insults & always felt the degradation of artificial inferiority. A steady watch ought to be kept and regard paid to every circumstance in our political progress which may be made a means further to cement or sever the two nations. Of these a possible one of the most important kind has long hung upon my mind and seems fast approaching. The keen Friends of Liberty here have commenced a plan of a Convention for Scotland of Delegates from all the Societies for Reform throughout this part of the Kingdom. It is this Convention who addressed our Society at Free Masons' tavern and with whom you correspond, and most properly, for their declarations are strong, explicit, and strictly constitutional and their conduct, under provoking circumstances, firm and temperate. But though weak in its infancy it may, especially by the folly of the measures of Government, grow to a great strength. I doubt that you in England will never make great progress till you adopt something similar. It is requisite for keeping up that degree of knowledge and concert amongst your scattered friends, which the acquaintance by letters is inadequate to. It may even be necessary to save them from temporary extinction. As to such assemblies I believe you and I differ and you dread the magnitude of power which might thereby be accumulated, a degree of power which I look upon as necessary to withstand and prevail over the immense power of the Opposers of Reform and which I think might more safely be entrusted to a delegated, renovating body even tho' sent from self-elected Societies than to any self-elected body like the Jacobins in France, like the Society for Constitutional Information, or even like ourselves at Free Mason's Tavern. But without pretending to convince, I will speak hypothetically. If in England any such Convention or Assembly should take place and not in separate delegated Meetings for different districts in England but in one meeting for all England, I look upon it as of the highest consequence (though perhaps very difficult in the management) to get Scotland to unite in the same Assembly without sending its Delegates thro' any intermediate Assembly for Scotland alone. In this and every view, I should wish the particular Societies to be encouraged to correspond directly with yours and others in London. One of the greatest bonds of union betwixt the two nations at present is that the Reformers here feel that they have need to lean upon you. If it be possible once to teach them that they can take the lead many may be for bidding you farewell. The very grievance of our present persecution may be thus turned to account. Were you to neglect us, it might excite the worst spirit of indignation and despair and even if contrary to our information, you are as much persecuted as us, but still show that you think of us and that you exert yourselves for us; tho' it should be in vain, it will help to rivet us to you. Whilst I speak thus you will readily believe how particularly pleased I was as well as with others most grateful for the reception your Society gave to Mr. Thomas Muir and the interest you took in his relation of the proceedings in Scotland. Should a case ever happen to occur when a man thus appears before you, whose manner even disgusts and whose conduct cannot be approved of as wise or prudent, yet I trust the good sense of your Society will recollect only that he is a Martyr or an Envoy from Brethren in distress

> Yours with the greatest regards
> Daer.

P.S. May I request your immediate answer about petitioning as I lost yesterday's post before I had got half done the first page. I then let myself out a little & beg pardon for imposing the trouble of reading eight such pages on you. But I would rather do that as take the trouble to abridge them or without perhaps making matters better by writing it a second time, lose the claim to some excuse by sending the words as they originally fell from me.

Notes

Introduction

1 Quoted in Guy Ortolano, *The Two Cultures Controversy: Science, Literature and Cultural Politics in Postwar Britain* (Cambridge, 2009), p. 10.

2 The family home and library on St Mary's Isle was destroyed by fire in 1940.

3 E. P. Thompson, *The Making of the English Working Class* (London, 1963).

4 Alexander Murdoch, 'The Importance of Being Edinburgh: Management and Opposition in Edinburgh Politics 1746–1784', *Scottish Historical Review*, 62 (1983), 1–16.

5 Emma Vincent Macleod, 'The Scottish Opposition Whigs and the French Revolution', in Bob Harris (ed.), *Scotland in the Age of the French Revolution* (Edinburgh, 2005), pp. 79–98.

6 On which, see esp. Richard B. Sher, *The Enlightenment & the Book* (Chicago and London, 2006).

7 Mark R. M. Towsey, *Reading the Scottish Enlightenment: Books and their Readers in Provincial Scotland, 1750–1820* (Leiden, 2010); David Allan, *A Nation of Readers: The Lending Library in Georgian England* (London, 2008); *The Edinburgh History of the Book in Scotland, vol. 2, Enlightenment and Expansion, 1707–1800*, ed. Stephen Brown and Warren McDougall (Edinburgh, 2011).

8 Robert Darnton, *The Forbidden Bestsellers of Pre-Revolutionary France* (New York and London, 1995) and more recently, Darnton, *The Devil in the Holy Water, or the Art of Slander from Louis XIV to Napoleon* (Philadelphia, 2009).

9 Huntingdon Library, California, William Pulteney Papers, Pu138, George Dempster to William Johnstone, 9 Feb. 1762. Dempster was here contrasting Edinburgh to London with its much more pluralistic and diverse cultural world. I am very grateful to Andrew Mackley for bringing this letter to my attention.

10 Roger Emerson, 'Overseas Contacts and Influences: The Shaping of the Scottish Enlightenment, 1730–1790' (unpublished paper), p. 4.

11 See Dennis C. Rasmussen, *The Problems and Promise of Commercial Society: Adam Smith's Response to Rousseau* (University Park, PA, 2008).

12 Quoted in Thomas A. Horne, *Property Rights and Poverty: Political Argument in Britain, 1605–1834* (Chapel Hill and London, 1990), p. 109.

13 See the discussion in Brian Bonnyman, *The Third Duke of Buccleuch and Adam Smith: Estate Management and Improvement in Enlightenment Scotland* (Edinburgh, 2014), pp. 66–8.

14 T. C. Smout, *A History of the Scottish People 1560–1830* (London, 1998), p. 483.

15 Horne, *Property Rights and Poverty*, p. 94.

16 Stewart is best approached through Gordon Macintyre, *Dugald Stewart: The Pride and Ornament of Scotland* (Sussex, 2003), although this book has very little to say in detail about his thinking and ideas.

17 University of Edinburgh, Special Collections, Gen 874/IV/19–20, Lord Daer to Dr Joseph Black, London, 9 Aug. 1785.

18 Thomas J. Schlereth, *The Cosmopolitan Ideal in Enlightenment Thought* (Notre Dame, IN, 1977), pp. 25–46.

19 Quoted in Schlereth, *Cosmopolitan Ideal*, p. 26.

20 For which, see Paul Wood and Charles J. Withers, 'Introduction: Science, Medicine and the Scottish Enlightenment: An Historiographical Overview', in Withers and Wood (eds), *Science and Medicine in the Scottish Enlightenment* (East Linton, 2002), pp. 1–16.

21 J. M. Bumsted, *Lord Selkirk: A Life* (East Lansing, MI, 2009).

22 See Appendix.

23 James Currie, *The Works of Robert Burns; with an Account of his Life, and a Criticism on his Writings*, 4 vols (Montrose, 1816), i, p. 108.

1 A 'Liberal' Education

1 Christopher Wyvill, *Wyvill Papers*, 6 vols (York, 1794–1806), i, pp. 322–7. See also the relevant comments in Joanna Innes, 'Politics and Morals: The Reformation of Manners Movement in Later Eighteenth Century England', in Eckhart Hellmuth (ed.), *The Transformation of Political Culture: England and Germany in the Later Eighteenth Century* (Oxford, 1990), pp. 59–60.

2 Henry Roscoe, *The Life of William Roscoe*, 2 vols (London, 1833), i, p. 113.

3 The importance of these Sunday lectures in understanding Hutcheson's thought has been recently emphasised by Thomas Anhert in his *The Moral Culture of the Scottish Enlightenment, 1690–1805* (New Haven and London, 2014).

4 T. D. Campbell, 'Francis Hutcheson: "Father" of the Scottish Enlightenment', in R. H. Campbell and Andrew S. Skinner (eds), *The Origins and Nature of the Scottish Enlightenment* (Edinburgh, 1982), pp. 167–85; Michael Brown, *Francis Hutcheson in Dublin, 1719–30: The Crucible of his Thought* (Dublin, 2002).

5 Quoted in *The Writings and Papers of Thomas Douglas, 5th Earl of Selkirk, vol. 1*, ed. J. M. Bumsted (Manitoba Record Society Publications, 1984), p. 5.

6 National Library of Scotland, MS 3420/171, Lord Selkirk to Lord Camden, 3 June 1789.

7 See chapter 4, below.

8 See esp. J. M. Bumsted, *Lord Selkirk: A Life* (East Lansing, MI, 2009), on which the following section is heavily dependent.

9 See the very useful discussion in Fredrik Albritton Jonsson, *Enlightenment's Frontier: The Scottish Highlands and the Origins of Environmentalism* (New Haven, 2013).

10 Thomas Douglas, fifth earl of Selkirk, *Observations on the Present State of the Highlands of Scotland, with a View of the Causes and Probable Consequences of Emigration* (Edinburgh, 1805), p. 58. Quoted in Albritton Jonsson, *Enlightenment's Frontier*, p. 251.

11 Joseph Priestley, *Lectures on History, and General Policy: To which is Prefixed, An Essay on a Course of Liberal Education for a Civil and Active Life* (Birmingham, 1788). Priestley's *Essay* was first published in 1760.

12 William McCarthy, 'The Celebrated Academy at Palgrave: A Documentary History of Anna Letitia Barbauld's School', *The Age of Johnson: A Scholarly Annual*, 8 (1997), 345–67.

13 McCarthy, 'The Celebrated Academy', pp. 279–392.

14 Anthony Fletcher, *Gender, Sex, and Subordination in England, 1500–1800* (New Haven and London, 1995), p. 305.

15 Fletcher, *Gender, Sex, and Subordination*, p. 301.

16 Fletcher, *Gender, Sex, and Subordination*, p. 302.

17 John Cannon, *Aristocratic Century: The Peerage of Eighteenth Century England* (Cambridge, 1987), pp. 37–44.

18 Dancing masters based in towns quite commonly sought clientele from gentry families in the neighbourhood.

19 John Warden Robberds, *A Memoir of the Life and Writings of the Late William Taylor*, 2 vols (London, 1843). Dancing masters taught correct posture as well as the fashionable dances.

20 For an earlier period, see Keith M. Brown, *Noble Society in Scotland: Wealth, Family and Culture from Reformation to Revolution* (Edinburgh, 2000), pp. 183–7.

21 For Montrose, see I. Cumming, 'The Scottish Education of James Mill', *History of Education Quarterly*, 2 (1962), 152–67.

22 Martin Fitzpatrick, 'Heretical Religion and Radical Politics', in Eckhart Hellmuth (ed.), *The Transformation of Political Culture: England and Germany in the Later Eighteenth Century* (Oxford, 1990), pp. 339–72, esp. pp. 346–7.

23 Joseph Priestley, *The Proper Objects of Education in the Present State of the World: Presented in a Discourse, Delivered on Wednesday, the 27th of April, 1791, at the Meeting House in the Old Jewry, London; to the Supporters of the New College at Hackney* (London, 1791), p. 6.

24 Lucy Aikin (ed.), *The Works of Anna Letitia Barbauld. With a Memoir by Lucy Aikin*, 2 vols (London, 1825), i, pp. ix–xi.

25 David L. Wykes, 'The Contribution of the Dissenting Academy to the Emergence of Rational Dissent', in Knud Haskonssen (ed.), *Enlightenment and Religion: Rational Dissent in Eighteenth-Century Britain* (Cambridge, 1996), pp. 99–139.

26 McCarthy, 'The Celebrated Academy'; McCarthy, *Anna Letitia Barbauld: Voice of the Enlightenment* (Baltimore, MD, 2008).

27 Robberds, *Memoir of the Life and Writings of William Taylor*, i, p. 9.

28 Joseph Priestley, *Miscellaneous Observations Relating to Education* (Cork, 1780), p. 42.

29 Priestley, *Miscellaneous Observations*, p. 211.

30 David A. Reid, 'Rational Dissent and the Rhetoric of Educational Philanthropy in the Dissenting Academies of Lancashire, Hackney and Exeter', *Northern History*, 47 (2010), 116.

31 Priestley, *Miscellaneous Observations*, p. 57.

32 McCarthy, 'The Celebrated Academy', n. 39, p. 383.

33 See the discussion in David A. Reid, 'Science for Polite Society: British Dissent and the Teaching of Natural Philosophy in the Seventeenth and Eighteenth Centuries', *History of the Universities*, 21/2 (2006), 117–18.

34 Quoted in McCarthy, 'The Celebrated Academy', p. 367.

35 McCarthy, 'The Celebrated Academy ', p. 367.

36 John Seed, *Dissenting Histories: Religious Divisions and the Politics of Memory in Eighteenth-Century England* (Edinburgh, 2008).

37 Reid, 'Science for Polite Society', 140–1.

38 Quoted in McCarthy, 'The Celebrated Academy', p. 360.

39 Alison Kennedy, 'Historical Perspectives in the mind of Joseph Priestley', in Isabel Rivers and David L. Wykes (eds), *Joseph Priestley: Scientist, Philosopher and Theologian* (Oxford, 2008), pp. 172–202.

40 McCarthy, 'The Celebrated Academy', p. 361.

41 McCarthy, 'The Celebrated Academy', p. 307.

42 Daniel John Dewispelare, 'Spectacular Speech: Performing Language in the Late Eighteenth Century', *Journal of British Studies*, 51 (2012), 858–82.

43 McCarthy, 'The Celebrated Academy ', pp. 292–3.

44 Quoted in McCarthy, 'The Celebrated Academy', p. 352.

45 David Chandler, '"The Athens of England": Norwich as a Literary Centre in the Late Eighteenth Century', *Eighteenth Century Studies*, 43 (2010), 171–92.

46 Harriet Guest, *Unbounded Attachment: Sentiment and Politics in the Age of the French Revolution* (Oxford, 2013), p. 126.

47 Robberds, *Memoir of the Life and Writings of the Late William Taylor*, i, pp. 68–9.

48 See esp. John Seed, '"A Set of Men Powerful Enough in Many Things": Rational Dissent and Political Opposition in England 1770–1790', in Haakonssen (ed.), *Enlightenment and Religion*, pp. 40–68.

49 Lucy Aikin, *Works of Anna Letitia Barbauld*, i, p. xlviii.

50 *Poetical Works of the Late F. Sayers, M.D. To which have been Prefixed the Contested Disquisitions on the Rise and Progress of English Poetry, and on English Metres; And also Some Biographical Particulars of the Author, Supplied by W. Taylor, of Norwich* (London, 1830), p. xxii.

51 University of Keele, Wedgwood Archives, 17651–20, 1761A–20. I am very grateful to Professor Trevor Levere for supplying this reference and for personal communication on Daer's possible links to the Priestley circle.

52 G. Kitteringham, 'Science in Provincial Society: The Case of Liverpool in the Early Nineteenth Century', *Annals of Science* (1982), 329–48.

53 Fitzpatrick, 'Heretical Religion and Radical Politics', in Hellmuth (ed.), *The Transformation of Political Culture*, p. 350; Jon Mee, *Conversable Worlds: Literature, Contention and Community 1762–1830* (Oxford, 2011); Mark Philp, *Godwin's Political Justice* (London, 1986).

54 Andrew Kippis, *A Sermon Preached at the Old Jewry [. . .] on Occasion of a New Academical Institution, among Protestant Dissenters, for the Education of Their Minister and Youth* (1786), p. 29.

2 'The Lyceum of Britain'

1 The chapter title is from T. Hutchins, used in a letter to Joseph Black (University of Edinburgh, Special Collections, Gen 873/11/167–8, Hutchins to Black, 10 Apr. 1784).

2 Ayrshire Archives, Hunter Blair of Blairquhan Papers, bundle 1a, item 10(iii), William Robertson to James Hunter Blair, 19 Feb. 1785.

3 See notice of its sale in the *Edinburgh Advertiser*, 10 Feb. 1784; *A Directory for Edinburgh, Leith, Musselburgh and Dalkeith: Containing the Names and Places of Abode of Public & Private Gentlemen* [. . .] *By Thomas Aitchison* [. . .] (Edinburgh, 1794), p. 163. By the early 1790s, his father's Edinburgh residence was 44 Queen Street.

4 Ayrshire Archives, Blair of Blairquhan Papers, bundle 109, item 1941, John Grieve to James Hunter Blair, 8 Mar. 1784.

5 Vincent Lunardi, *An Account of Five Aerial Voyages in Scotland. With an Introduction by Alexander Law* (Edinburgh, 1976), p. 5.

6 *To the Highlands in 1786: The Inquisitive Journey of a Young French Aristocrat*, ed. Norman Scarfe (Woodbridge, 2001), p. 114.

7 Birmingham Central Library, James Watt Papers, MS 3219/4/120, James Watt to Joseph Black, 25 Sept. 1783.

8 *A Guide for Gentlemen Studying Medicine at the University of Edinburgh. By J. Johnson Esq.* (London and Edinburgh, 1792), pp. 2–3.

9 As emphasised by Charles McKean in his, 'Twinning Cities: Modernization Versus Improvement in the Two Towns of Edinburgh', in Brian Edwards and Paul Jenkins (eds), *Edinburgh: The Making of a Capital City* (Edinburgh, 2005), pp. 42–63.

10 *Scots Magazine* (1759), 383, quoted in Dorothy Bell, *Edinburgh Old Town: The Forgotten Nature of Urban Form* (Edinburgh, 2008), p. 132.

11 Hugo Arnot, *The History of Edinburgh* (reprint of the first edn of 1779, Edinburgh, 1998), 'A View of the New Bridge of Edinburgh with Adjacent Buildings of the Old and New Town, from the West', p. 181.

12 See e.g. R. A. Houston, *Social Change in the Age of Enlightenment Edinburgh 1660–1760* (Oxford, 1994) and, more recently, W. W. Knox, 'The Attack of the "Half-Formed Persons": The 1811–12 Tron Riot in Edinburgh Revisited', *Scottish Historical Review*, 91 (2012), 287–310.

13 National Library of Scotland [hereafter NLS], MS 3288, J. Drummond to David Blair, Esq., Edinburgh, 21 Feb. 1786.

14 Henry Cockburn, *Memorials of his Time* (Edinburgh, 1856), p. 212.

15 NLS, MS 196, Minutes of the 'Monthly Club'. Original members of this body included many of the leading magnates and landed improvers of the period. Attendance quickly became patchy, however, and the body seems to have fallen into abeyance in the mid-1790s before an attempt at revival was made in 1803. More generally, see Bob Harris, 'Parliamentary Legislation, Lobbying and the Press in Eighteenth-Century Scotland', in Jason Peacey (ed.), *The Print Culture of Parliament 1600–1800* (Edinburgh, 2007), pp. 76–95.

16 See esp. the detailed listing of shops, giving details of names, occupations and places of residence contained in the records of the shop tax for the city, 1786–7 (National Records of Scotland [hereafter NRS], Exchequer Records, E326/4/4). The preponderance of shops in the capital was one reason for the strength of Edinburgh's

opposition to Pitt's shop tax. By 1788–9, 968 of the capital's shops were paying the shop tax, compared to Glasgow's 680 (E326/4/8).

17 As late as the early 1800s, the English MP and parliamentary diarist, Nathaniel Wraxall, noted when visiting Glasgow: 'But, carriages, I see none in the streets, & the crouds of people assembled, or walking about, are all mechanics.' (NLS, MS 3108, Diary of a Tour into Scotland, 12 July–27 Sept. 1813, vol. 2, f. 18.)

18 NRS, Exchequer Records, E326/8/4, carriage tax, 1786–7: burghs, which reveals that Edinburgh inhabitants were paying tax on 105 carriages, compared to Glasgow's 63. E326/5/8, male servants tax, 1786–7: burghs reveals that the tax was paid in the capital on 413 male servants as compared to Glasgow's rather paltry 125.

19 NRS, Exchequer Records, E326/3/63, inhabited house tax, 1786–7: burghs, which show that Edinburgh residents paid tax on 2,640 houses with a total rentable value of £38,039. Glasgow, by comparison, paid tax on 1,984 houses with a total rentable value of £24,530. The number of houses in the highest tax bracket in Edinburgh (i.e. those with an annual rentable value of above £40) was more than 2½ times that in Glasgow. The remarks on insurance values are based on a sampling of records from the policy books of the Sun Fire Insurance Company, held in the Corporation of London Record Office, Guildhall Library, London.

20 Bell, *Edinburgh Old Town*, p. 284.

21 Bell, *Edinburgh Old Town*, p. 226. Bell also notes (on p. 235) that the south side remained 'essentially separate' from the city proper.

22 Stewart was to move out of Edinburgh to Kinneil House in 1803, seemingly because of the constant morning interruptions from visitors.

23 See *Extracts from the Records of the Burgh of Edinburgh 1665 to 1680*, ed. Marguerite Wood (Edinburgh and London, 1950).

24 Edinburgh City Archives [hereafter ECA], SL1/1/32, Edinburgh town council minutes, 1686–9.

25 ECA, SL1/1/30, Edinburgh town council minutes, 1681–4.

26 Leona Jayne Skelton, 'Environmental Regulation in Edinburgh and York, c. 1560–c. 1700. With reference to several smaller Scottish burghs and northern English towns', unpublished PhD thesis, University of Durham, 2012, esp. pp. 110–42.

27 ECA, SL1/1/34, Edinburgh town council minutes, 1692–4.

28 *Extracts from the Records of the Burgh of Edinburgh 1665–1680*, ed. Marguerite Wood (Edinburgh and London, 1950), pp. 298–9.

29 Innes Macleod, *Sailing on Horseback: William Daniell and Richard Ayton in Cumbria and Dumfries and Galloway* (Dumfries, 1988), p. 74.

30 *Extracts from the Records of Edinburgh 1701–1718*, ed. Helen Armet (Edinburgh and London, 1967), pp. 2–3; *Notes from the Records of the Assembly Rooms of Edinburgh* (1842), p. 49.

31 See e.g. NLS, MS 1955, proposals for keeping the streets, lanes & passages of Edinburgh neat & clean by a voluntary subscription (n.d., but mid-1730s). This complained about the ease with which inhabitants circumvented the regulations created in the 1680s regarding maintaining the cleanliness of the streets, and called, in pursuit of 'efficiency, order and civility', for a voluntary subscription to employ scavengers to collect waste placed in dedicated vessels.

32 Thus, the instructions to George Warrender, the city's MP in 1715 declared: 'Ye shall

to your utmost assist in the legall dissolution of the Union soe destructive to the City ye represent and grievous to all good Scotsmen.' ECA, McLeod Collection, bundle 1, item 10, List of instructions to the Member of Parliament for the City of Edinburgh, 1715.

33 *Extracts from the Records of Edinburgh 1701–1718*.

34 A. J. Youngson, *The Making of Classical Edinburgh, 1750–1840* (Edinburgh, 1966), p. 241.

35 *Notes from the Records*, p. 33. By 1772, there were 266 lamps (ECA, McLeod Collection, Bundle 129, item 5, a list of the city of Edinburgh lamps, 1772).

36 NLS, Acc 5779, 'Reminiscences of Edinburgh 60 Years Ago (1794) by John Howell (1854)'.

37 One of the reasons was the mounting cost of repairing the old road surface owing to the wear and tear inflicted by carriages. Bob Harris and Charles McKean, *The Scottish Town in the Age of the Enlightenment, 1740–1820* (Edinburgh, 2014), p. 250.

38 Other ports were removed in the 1780s.

39 Separate police commissions were created for South Leith (1771); the Southern Districts (1771); and Canongate (1772).

40 ECA, McLeod Collection, bundle 60, item 32, report by Baillie Trotter anent keeping the streets clean, 1769; bundle 60, item 32, recommendation to Trotter and his committee to consider other acts of the council on the subject that whole regulations may be ingrossed in one act, 1770; bundle 10, item 83, regulations for keeping the streets of Canongate clean, 1770. See also bundle 121, item 3, copy of act for lighting etc., Canongate, 1772.

41 ECA, McLeod Collection, bundle 88, item 9, packet of reports and estimates for cleaning and lighting the streets, 1768–1783.

42 Henry Skrine, *Three Successive Tours in the North of England, and Great Part of Scotland* (London, 1795), p. 159; *To the Highlands in 1786*, ed. Scarfe, p. 111.

43 Alexander Murdoch, '"The Importance of Being Edinburgh": Management and Opposition in Edinburgh Politics, 1746–1784', *Scottish Historical Review*, 62 (1983), 1–16.

44 There were hopes that money for the reversion of the forfeited estates could be used to defray the costs of the bridewell, for which see Ayrshire Archives, Blair of Blairquhan Papers, Bundle 43, 1557, John Grieve to James Hunter Blair, 7 June 1784. These, however, came to nothing.

45 ECA, SL 1/1/1/, 103, Edinburgh town council minutes, 1782–3, 11 Dec. 1782.

46 Ayrshire Archives, Blair of Blairquhan Papers, Bundle 35, 2023, Lord Galloway to James Hunter Blair, House of Lords, 14 June 1782. For details on the battles with the trades over the bill, see Bundle 35, 2036, John Grieve to James Hunter Blair, 16 May 1782. Archibald McDowall described the bill in March 1782 as 'the most unpopular Bill that ever the Town Councill was concerned in' (Bundle 35, 2041, McDowall to James Hunter Blair, Edinburgh, 17 Mar. 1782).

47 *Caledonian Mercury*, 10 Mar. 1783.

48 ECA, SL1/1/111, Edinburgh town council minutes, 3 Feb. 1788–1789, ff. 150–63 [10 Sept. 1788].

49 *Edinburgh Advertiser*, 27 Sept., 11, 14, 18, 28 Oct., 1, 8 Nov. 1785; ECA, SL1/1/107, Edinburgh town council minutes, 26 Oct. 1785–24 May 1786, ff. 14 [28 Oct. 1785], 28–39 [9 Nov. 1785, act containing agreement with the proprietors anent lowering the

street]. For the importance of reducing the gradient on the High Street and removal of the Guard House, see *A New Guide to the City of Edinburgh* (Edinburgh, 1790), p. 34.

50 ECA, SL1/1/109, Edinburgh town council minutes, 20 Dec. 1786–4 July 1787.

51 Bell, *Edinburgh Old Town*, n. 20, p. 405. I have not been able to confirm this since the council accounts are far from easy to make sense of for this period. However, the council did arrange for a £6,000 credit from the banks in 1786 in order to defray the costs of purchasing properties on the north side of the Lawnmarket as part of this project (SL1/1/107, f. 147 [8 Feb. 1786]).

52 The origins of this measure may well lie in 1775, when it was agreed by the council that a book should be furnished in which to record annually the number of lamps in the city and any additional ones ordered by the council.

53 ECA, SL217/1 and 2, sederunt books of the commissioners for lighting, 1785–1810.

54 John Carr, *Caledonian Sketches* (London, 1809), p. 169.

55 *Edinburgh Advertiser*, 14 June 1785.

56 *Edinburgh Advertiser*, 22 Nov. 1782.

57 *Edinburgh Advertiser*, 8 Mar. 1783.

58 Edinburgh Central Library, Edinburgh Room, YML 28A G36159, *Notes from the Records of the Assembly Rooms of Edinburgh* (Edinburgh, 1842).

59 Edinburgh Central Library, B18749, Regulations for George's Square Assemblies, Anno 1785.

60 *Edinburgh Advertiser*, 11 Dec. 1781, 1 Jan. 1782, 11 Feb. 1786; *Boswell: The Applause of the Jury 1782–1785*, ed. Irma S. Lustig and Frederick A. Pottle (London, 1981), p. 280.

61 *Williamson's Directory for the City of Edinburgh, Canongate, Leith and Suburbs: From June 1780 to June 1781* (Edinburgh, 1780), p. 29.

62 Creech's letters were first published in the *Edinburgh Evening Courant* and rapidly found their way into other Edinburgh papers.

63 For the Pantheon, see Rosalind Carr, *Gender and Enlightenment Culture in Eighteenth-Century Scotland* (Edinburgh, 2014), pp. 85–92.

64 For Graham, see Roy Porter, 'James Graham (1745–1794), *Oxford Dictionary of National Biography*, Oxford University Press, online edn, 2006 [http://www.oxforddnb.com/view/article/41993, accessed 21 Jan. 2015]. Graham's publicity features in many of the Edinburgh papers in August 1783. He also used the press in his tussles with the burgh magistrates who sought to prohibit his lectures on the ground of indecency.

65 Tytler's main talent was for writing quickly and for clever abridgement, which partly explains why he has tended to be overlooked by historians.

66 Sir James Fergusson, *Balloon Tytler* (London, 1972); Lunardi, *Account of Five Aerial Voyages in Scotland*.

67 See notice for sale in *Edinburgh Advertiser*, 20 Jan. 1784.

68 See e.g. *Edinburgh Advertiser*, 17 Feb. 1784.

69 Trotter and Young's premises were, from 1777, at 5 Princes Street.

70 NRS, GD113/5/33e, item 13, receipt for payment by Gilbert Innes of Stow, Esq. of £11.15.0 by Young & Trotter, for 10 mahogany wheel backed chairs covered in haircloth, and £3.1.0 for two elbow chairs; item 18, receipted account for payment by Gilbert Innes of Stow, Esq. of £9.10.0 by Young & Trotter, upholsterers, for purchase and hanging of 5½ quires of long cartridge paper, 7 pieces of fine green paper, 5 doz. borders, 26 pieces of stone ground paper and canvass.

71 NRS, GD113/5/105, 12, Gilbert Innes of Stow to Jane Innes, London, 5 Jan. 1791.

72 NRS, GD113/5/105, 21, Gilbert Innes of Stow, London, to Jane Innes, 23 Apr. 1791.

73 *Boswell's Edinburgh Journals, 1767–1786*, ed. Hugh M. Milne (Edinburgh, 2001).

74 NLS, MS 3108, f. 37r. Wraxall's response to Edinburgh, a city he described as 'half finished', reflecting the slow progress of building from the 1790s, is fascinating, not least since he was hardly sympathetic to the Scots, but then he was hardly sympathetic to anything other than the British metropolis.

75 NRS, GD113/4/164, William Tytler to Gilbert Innes of Stow, 3 Nov. 1791.

76 Michael Fry, 'McQueen, Robert, Lord Braxfield (1722–1799)', *Oxford Dictionary of National Biography*, Oxford University Press, 2004, online edn [http://www.oxforddnb.com/view/article/17738, accessed 21 Jan. 2015].

77 K. J. Logue, *Popular Disturbances in Scotland 1780–1815* (Edinburgh, 1979), pp. 41, 50–1.

78 The full story of this, including the operation of the bread assize, has yet to be traced, but some of it can be followed in the town council minutes. Relevant evidence for the 1790s and early 1800s is surveyed in Bob Harris, *The Scottish People and the French Revolution* (London, 2008), pp. 188–95.

79 NLS, Saltoun Papers, MS 17602, ff. 175–6, 'Memorial on Methods to be Pursued for the Future to Prevent Complaints on Account of the Scarcity or Dearth of Oatmeal in the Markatts [sic] of Edinburgh and Leith, 30 Nov. 1763'.

80 Very illuminating in the context is the record of sedulous intervention described in University of Edinburgh, Special Collections, Laing Collection, La. III 552, police memorandums by John Hutton, superintendent, 1793–6, vol. 1st.

81 ECA, McLeod Collection, Bundle 129, items 81 and 82.

82 *General Heads of a Plan for New Prison and Bridewell in the City of Edinburgh, Offered to the Consideration of the Public* (Edinburgh, 1782).

83 *Edinburgh Advertiser*, 13 Jan. 1784.

84 Thomas Gilbert, *Plan for the Better Relief and Employment of the Poor* (London, 1781).

85 ECA, McLeod Collection, Proclamation anent Beggars, 1784.

86 Ayrshire Archives, Blair of Blairquhan Papers, A1/5, 2552, copy of A Bill for Providing a Fund for the Relief of the Poor of the City of Edinburgh (1786). The bill failed because of opposition to levying of poor rates, especially by residents of the southern districts and the Faculty of Advocates and Society of Writers to the Signet, but also demands that the council be more transparent in its provision of financial information. There were also those who argued that while a system such as the one proposed might have been appropriate for towns such as Glasgow and Paisley, it was ill suited to a place such as Edinburgh with its large population of transients. The council instead levied an assessment of 2% on valued rents to help fund the charity workhouse, the financial condition of which was parlous.

87 See esp. William Porteous, *A Letter to the Citizens of Glasgow, Containing a Short View of the Management of the Poors Funds, under the Administration of the General Session* (Glasgow, 1783). Glasgow was also the first place to see the introduction of Sunday schools, in 1787, though it was closely followed by a number of other places, including Dundee in the following year.

88 John Hope to Matthew Boulton, 22 May 1784, as quoted in Jan Golinski, *Science as Public Culture: Chemistry and the Enlightenment in Britain, 1760–1820* (Cambridge, 1992), pp. 40–1. In attendance on this occasion were James Hutton, Joseph Black,

Henry Cort, the iron manufacturer, and Lord Dundonald, who in the 1790s would establish a major salt manufacturing concern.

89 University of Edinburgh, Special Collections, Dc. 5. 126, Minutes of the Poker Club, 1774–1784.

90 NLS, Acc 10,000/2 and 3, Minutes of the Royal Society of Edinburgh.

91 M'Farlan, *Tracts on Subjects of National Importance* (Edinburgh, 1786).

92 *Inquiries Concerning the Poor. By John M'Farlan* (Edinburgh, 1782). See also *Observations on Dr M'Farlan's Inquiries Concerning the State of the Poor. By T. Tod, merchant, Treasurer to the Orphan Hospital* (Edinburgh, 1783).

3 Dugald Stewart and the 'Spec'

1 See University of Edinburgh, Special Collections, Dc. 8.178, 8, tours in England and Scotland, 1797–1803.

2 For evidence that Daer was taught by Black, see University of Edinburgh, Special Collections, Gen. 874/IV/19–20, Daer to Black, 9 Aug. 1785, in which Daer recommended a Frenchman to Black's notice, ending his letter: 'I shall esteem as a particular favour any attentions you may be able to shew him. I hope you will pardon this trouble from your late pupil.'

3 Dennis Wood, *Benjamin Constant: A Biography* (London and New York, 1993), p. 47.

4 Quoted in Wood, *Constant*, p. 47.

5 J. B. Morrell, 'Professors Robison and Playfair, and the "Theophobia Gallica": Natural Philosophy, Religion and Politics in Edinburgh, 1789–1815', *Notes and Records of the Royal Society of London*, 26 (1971), 45–6.

6 National Library of Scotland [hereafter, NLS], MS 1567, papers relating to claim of Joseph Mason, carpenter of Wiltshire, and student of medicine at the University for £500 damages for assault arising from disturbances at the Theatre Royal. The defenders presented plenty of evidence, including the posting of handbills in the University, that the actions in the theatre had been planned, and also pointed to the involvement of George Ross, who had been employed in the office of the leading Edinburgh radical newspaper, the *Edinburgh Gazetteer*.

7 *An Address to the Lately Formed Society of the Friends of the People. By John Wilde, Esq., Advocate, Fellow of the Royal Society, and Professor of Civil Law in the University of Edinburgh* (Edinburgh and London, 1793).

8 Jonathan Israel, *The Dutch Republic: Its Rise, Greatness, and Fall 1477–1806* (Oxford, 1995), pp. 1049–50; Esther Mijers, 'The Netherlands, William Carstares, and the Reform of Edinburgh University, 1690–1715', *History of Universities*, 25/2 (2011), 111–42; Mijers, 'Scottish Students in the Netherlands, 1680–1730', in Alexia Grosjean and Steve Murdoch (eds), *Scottish Communities Abroad* (Leiden, 2005), pp. 301–31.

9 Israel, *Dutch Republic*, p. 1050.

10 *A New Guide to the City of Edinburgh* (Edinburgh, 1790), p. 60.

11 Robert D. Anderson, Michael Lynch and Nicholas Phillipson, *The University of Edinburgh: An Illustrated Guide* (Edinburgh, 2003), p. 83.

12 Insofar as work has been done on this, it relates mainly to medical students, who came from North America, the West Indies, as well as many European countries, and from throughout the British Isles, including Ireland. See, most notably, Lisa Rosner, *Medical Education in the Age of Improvement: Edinburgh Students and Apprentices*

1760–1826 (Edinburgh, 1991).

13 M. D. Eddy, 'The University of Edinburgh Natural History Class Lists, 1782–1800', *Archives of Natural History*, 30 (2003), 2; *The Correspondence of Joseph Black*, ed. Robert G. W. Anderson and Jean Jones, 2 vols (Farnham, 2012), i, pp. 536–7, letter from John Maitland, Excise Office, to John Thomson, Secretary of Excise, Edinburgh, 9 Oct. 1782, concerning the deserving son of a Mrs Gibb from Dundee and asking Thomson to recommend to Black for a 'Gratis Ticket' for the boy.

14 University of Southampton, Special Collections, Broadlands Papers, BR23AA/8/3, Dugald Stewart, Edinburgh, to the second Viscount Palmerston, 10 May 1801; J. Johnson, *A Guide for Gentlemen Studying Medicine at the University of Edinburgh* (London, 1792), p. 69.

15 *Edinburgh Advertiser*, 7 Nov. 1783.

16 *Edinburgh Advertiser*, 11 Nov. 1783.

17 Henry Brougham, *Lives of the Philosophers of the Time of George III* (London and Glasgow, 1855), p. 19, cited in *Correspondence of Joseph Black*, ed. Anderson and Jones, i, p. 43.

18 Quoted in Jan Golinski, *Science as Public Culture: Chemistry and the Enlightenment in Britain, 1760–1820* (Cambridge, 1992), pp. 11–49.

19 National Records of Scotland [hereafter, NRS], GD206/2/300, 6, Hall to his uncle, 5 Dec. 1781; same to same, 1 Mar. 1782; 10, same to same, 23 Nov. 1782. In 1782–3, Hall was entered for the following classes: Natural Philosophy, Moral Philosophy and Rhetoric.

20 University of Southampton, Special Collections, Broadlands Papers, BR12/1/4/1, second Viscount Palmerston to Dugald Stewart, 13 June 1800.

21 University of Southampton, Special Collections, Broadlands Papers, BR24/4/3, Henry Temple to Fanny Temple, 28 Feb. 1803.

22 His drawing master was Alexander Nasmyth, who had been a successful portrait painter in the 1780s but whose commissions dried up in the 1790s owing, it seems, to his liberal political opinions and hostility towards the measures of the Pitt ministry.

23 University of Southampton, Special Collections, Broadlands Papers, BR19/13/2, Helen D'Arcy Stewart to Mary Mee, Viscountess Palmerston, 29 Oct [n.d., but prob. 1800].

24 *Boswell: The Applause of the Jury 1782–1785*, ed. Irma S. Lustig and Frederick A. Pottle (London, 1981), p. 204. Boswell had met Burke in London, and both were members of the Literary Club presided over by Samuel Johnson.

25 University of Southampton, Special Collections, Broadlands Papers, BR6/7/16, Mary Mee, Edinburgh, to Frances, 16 Oct. 1800; BR6/7/23, Mary Mee to Elizabeth Temple, 31 Oct.–1 Nov. 1800.

26 See esp. Jane Rendall, 'Adaptations: History, Gender, and Political Economy in the Work of Dugald Stewart', *History of European Ideas*, 38 (2012), 143–61.

27 University of Southampton, Special Collections, Broadlands Papers, BR24/4/4, Henry Temple to Elizabeth, 6 Mar. 1803.

28 Rendall, 'Adaptations', 145.

29 University of Southampton, Special Collections, Broadlands Papers, BR6/7/16, Mary Mee, Edinburgh, to Frances, 16 Oct. 1800.

30 This is the conclusion reached by Michael Brown based on marginalia to Stewart's copy of Ferguson's *Institutes of Moral Philosophy*, which are dated from November

1784. (Michael Brown, 'Dugald Stewart and the Problem of Teaching Politics in the 1790s', *Journal of Irish and Scottish Studies*, 1 (2007), n. 19, p. 92).

31 For which, see below, pp. 84–5.

32 As noted in University of Southampton, Special Collections, Broadlands Papers, BR23AA/8/4.

33 Bruce Lenman, *Integration, Enlightenment and Industrialisation: Scotland 1746–1832* (London, 1981), p. 110.

34 For Millar, see W. C. Lehmann, *John Millar of Glasgow, 1735–1801* (Glasgow, 1960); while for Stewart's membership of the Royal Midlothian Volunteer Artillery Company, see NRS, Buccleuch Papers, GD224/676/1/26, List of the Gentlemen who have Agreed to Form Themselves into a Corp for the Purpose of Receiving Instructions to Qualify them to Serve as a Company of Artillery, 1797.

35 Richard B. Sher, *Church and University in the Scottish Enlightenment: The Moderate Literati of Edinburgh* (Edinburgh, 1985), pp. 312–13.

36 See the very illuminating comments on this in relation to the lectures of William Cullen and Joseph Black in Golinski, *Science as Public Culture*, pp. 11–49.

37 University of Edinburgh, Special Collections, DC.4.97, Archibald Bell, 'Lectures on Moral Philosophy by Dugald Stewart Esq. Delivered in the University of Edinburgh in the Years 1793–4', p. 25.

38 NLS, MS 3771, George Strickland, 'Notes on Political Oeconomy From Prof: Stewart's Lectures at Edinburgh from Nov.r 1803 to April 1804', f. 10.

39 Quoted from Emma Vincent MacLeod, 'The Scottish Opposition Whigs and the French Revolution', in Bob Harris (ed.), *Scotland in the Age of the French Revolution* (Edinburgh, 2005), p. 83. See also Bob Harris, *The Scottish People and the French Revolution* (London, 2008), pp. 115–45.

40 D. B. Horn, *A Short History of the University of Edinburgh, 1556–1889* (Edinburgh, 1967), p. 40.

41 Henry Cockburn, *Memorials of his Time* (Edinburgh, 1856), pp. 85, 175.

42 For the most recent discussion of this battle, see Charles Bradford Bow, 'In Defence of the Scottish Enlightenment: Dugald Stewart's Role in the 1805 John Leslie Affair', *Scottish Historical Review*, 92 (2013), 123–46.

43 Morrell, 'Professors Robison and Playfair', 55.

44 Thomas Anhert, *The Moral Culture of the Scottish Enlightenment, c. 1690–1805* (New Haven and London, 2014), pp. 126–37.

45 Quoted in Gordon Macintyre, *Dugald Stewart: The Pride and Ornament of Scotland* (Sussex, 2003), p. 91. The reference to 'insanity' was almost certainly to John Wilde, the Professor of Civil Law.

46 University of Edinburgh, Special Collections, MS Gen 2023, Josiah Walker, 'Abbreviations from Lectures on Moral Philosophy Delivered by Dugald Stewart Professor of Mathematics in the University of Edinburgh', f. 442.

47 Walker, 'Abbreviations, 1778/9', ff. 353–4.

48 Walker, 'Abbreviations, 1778/9', ff. 353–6.

49 Walker, 'Abbreviations, 1778/9', ff. 384, 400, 426.

50 Drennan's political ideas have only been partially examined by historians, and his later political writings have all but been ignored. However, they reveal a very strong Enlightenment framework and a notably progressive outlook.

51 The relationship with Drennan is discussed in Brown, 'Dugald Stewart and the Problem of Teaching Politics', 87–9.

52 The phrase is quoted from Robert J. Mayhew, *Malthus: The Life and Legacies of an Untimely Prophet* (Cambridge, MA and London, 2014), p. 27.

53 *The Papers of Thomas Jefferson, Vol. 15, 27 Mar. 1789–30 Nov. 1789*, ed. Julian F. Boyd (Princeton, NJ, 1958), pp. 90–7, 279–80, 329–81.

54 Brown, 'Dugald Stewart and the Problem of Teaching Politics', 119.

55 The letters are reprinted in John Veitch, 'Memoir of Dugald Stewart', in *The Collected Works of Dugald Stewart*, ed. William Hamilton, 10 vols (Edinburgh, 1854–60), x, pp. cxxii–cxxxvi.

56 Quoted in J. M. Bumsted, *Lord Selkirk: A Life* (East Lansing, MI, 2009), p. 48. The incident Thomas witnessed almost certainly took place after news had arrived of the failure of a parliamentary motion in support of burgh reform, which Dundas had opposed.

57 Edinburgh Central Library, DA 1861.789, journal of Andrew Armstrong, 1789–93, f. 27.

58 *Edinburgh Herald*, 31 Mar. 1790.

59 *Edinburgh Advertiser*, 12–16 Feb. 1790.

60 *Edinburgh Advertiser*, 27–31 Aug. 1790.

61 *Edinburgh Herald*, 22 Nov. 1790.

62 University of Edinburgh, Special Collections, Speculative Society Minute Book, vol. 3, 1787– .

63 Bob Harris, 'Scotland's Newspapers, the French Revolution, and Domestic Radicalism (*c.* 1789–1794)', *Scottish Historical Review*, 84 (2005), 38–62.

64 NRS, GD206/2/300, f. 50, Sir James Hall, Paris, to his uncle, 12 June 1791.

65 Paul Wood, 'Reid, Thomas (1710–1796)', *Oxford Dictionary of National Biography*, Oxford University Press, 2004, online edn 2006 [http://www.oxforddnb.com/view/article/23342, accessed 21 Jan. 2015].

66 For Hall's steadfast antipathy to the contemporary war fever, see NRS, GD206/317, f. 55, Hall to his uncle, 3 Feb. 1793.

67 David Hume, *Essays, Moral, Political and Literary. Part II* (1752), esp. the essays entitled 'Of Commerce' and 'Of the Populousness of Ancient Nations'.

68 Strickland, 'Notes on Political Oeconomy', f. 12.

69 Strickland, 'Notes on Political Oeconomy', f. 13.

70 On which see the recent discussion in Christopher J. Berry, *The Idea of Commercial Society in the Scottish Enlightenment* (Edinburgh, 2013).

71 *The Works of Adam Smith, LLD*, 5 vols (London, 1811), v, p. 481.

72 *Collected Works of Dugald Stewart*, ed. Hamilton, ii, p. 243.

73 Stewart to Lord Craig, 20 Feb. 1794, in *Collected Works of Dugald Stewart*, ed. Hamilton, x, pp. lxxii–lxxv.

74 *Collected Works of Dugald Stewart*, ed. Hamilton, ii, p. 229.

75 'Notes on Political Oeconomy', f. 59.

76 'Notes on Political Oeconomy', f. 103.

77 'Notes on Political Oeconomy', f. 59.

78 'Notes on Political Oeconomy', f. 59.

79 On which, see Brown, 'Dugald Stewart and the Problem of Teaching Politics in the 1790s', esp. 114–18.

80   Bell, 'Lectures on Moral Philosophy', pp. 339–40.

81   As recently stressed in Rendall, 'Adapations', 154–5.

82   Strickland, 'Notes on Political Oeconomy', f. 64.

83   Strickland, 'Notes on Political Oeconomy', f. 82.

84   Bell, 'Lectures on Moral Philosophy', pp. 25.

85   Bell, 'Lectures on Moral Philosophy', pp. 159–60.

86   'Dissertion: Exhibiting the Progress of Metaphysical, Ethical, and Political Philosophy, since the Revival of Letters in Europe, with Numerous and Important Additions Now First Published', in *Collected Works of Dugald Stewart*, ed. Hamilton, i, p. 491.

87   See T. R. Malthus, *A Letter to Samuel Whitbread, Esq, M.P., on his Proposed Bill for the Amendment of the Poor Laws* (London, 1807), esp. pp. 11–12.

88   Strickland, 'Notes on Political Oeconomy', ff. 4–5.

89   James Kendall, 'The First Chemical Society, the First Chemical Journal and the Chemical Revolution', *Proceedings of the Royal Society of Edinburgh*, 63A (1952), 344–68.

90   See esp. the discussion in Golinski, *Science as Public Culture*, pp. 130–52; Carleton E. Perrin, 'Joseph Black and the Absolute Levity of Phlogiston', *Annals of Science*, 40 (1983), 109–37.

91   V. A. Eyles, 'The Evolution of a Chemist', *Annals of Science*, 19 (1963), esp. 171–2.

92   University of Edinburgh, Special Collections, Gen. 873/111/153–4, Thomas Charles Hope to Dr Joseph Black, Glasgow, 14 July 1789.

93   Eddy, 'University of Edinburgh Natural History Class Lists', 104.

94   See esp. Steven Shapin, 'Property, Patronage, and the Politics of Science: The Founding of the Royal Society of Edinburgh', *British Journal for the History of Science*, 7 (1974), 1–41.

95   This is very clearly traced in Golinski, *Science as Public Culture*, pp. 11–49.

96   See on this, Steven Shapin, 'The Audience for Science in Eighteenth Century Edinburgh', *History of Science*, 12 (1974), 95–121.

97   Quoted in Margaret C. Jacob and Larry Stewart, *Practical Matter: Newton's Science in the Service of Industry and Empire* (Cambridge, MA, 2004), pp. 116–17.

98   *Correspondence of Joseph Black*, ed. Anderson and Jones, i, pp. 345–7, 477–80, 484–8, 511–13, 543–51, 612–17, 649–52, 665–75, 692, 718, 723–9, 730, 771; ii, 820–2, 825, 835–7.

99   C. J. Withers, 'A Neglected Scottish Agriculturalist: The "Georgical Lectures" and Agricultural Writings of the Rev. Dr John Walker (1731–1803)', *Agricultural History Review*, 33 (1985), 132–46.

100   C. J. Withers, '"Both Useful and Ornamental": John Walker's Keepership of Edinburgh University's Natural History Museum, 1779–1803', *Journal of the History of Collections*, 3 (1993), 65–77. Edinburgh City Archives, McLeod Collection, Extract of Act of Council agreeing to give Professor Walker £25 yearly on account of the Museum, 1785. Daer was also a subscriber for the purchase of further materials for this museum in 1794 (University of Edinburgh, Special Collections, Laing Collection, La. III. 352/2, list of subscribers for the purchase of Mr Weir's Museum).

101   Margaret C. Jacob, *The First Knowledge Economy: Human Capital and the European Economy, 1750–1850* (Cambridge, 2014).

102   *Works of Adam Smith*, v, p. 463.

103   *Boswell: The Applause of the Jury*, ed. Lustig and Pottle, p. 8.

4 Heroic Improver

1 T. C. Smout, 'Problems of Nationalism, Identity and Improvement in Later Eighteenth Century Scotland', in T. M. Devine (ed.), *Improvement and Enlightenment* (Edinburgh, 1989), pp. 1–21.

2 For urban improvements, which were cumulatively very significant, although individually much less dramatic, see Bob Harris and Charles McKean, *The Scottish Town in the Age of the Enlightenment, 1740–1820* (Edinburgh, 2014), esp. ch. 2.

3 R. H. Campbell, 'The Landed Classes', in T. M. Devine and R. Mitichison (eds), *People and Society in Scotland, Vol. 1, 1760–1830* (Edinburgh, 1988), esp. p. 100. Campbell fully acknowledges the varying motives behind 'improvement', but underlines both the 'simple practical case for improvement' of estates and the deeper and more fundamental change which he argues was the commercialisation of land use. See also R. H. Campbell, 'The Enlightenment and the Economy', in R. H. Campbell and A. S. Skinner (eds), *The Origins and Nature of the Scottish Enlightenment* (Edinburgh, 1982), p. 16; T. M. Devine, 'The Great Landlords of Lowland Scotland and Agrarian Change in the Eighteenth Century', in T. M. Devine (ed.), *Clearance and Improvement: Land, Power, and People in Scotland 1700–1900* (Edinburgh, 2006), pp. 45–6; I. H. Adams, 'The Agents of Agricultural Change', in M. L. Parry and T. R. Slater (eds), *The Making of the Scottish Countryside* (London, 1980), p. 173.

4 Andrew Monro Lang, *A Life of George Dempster, Scottish MP of Dunnichen (1732–1818)* (Lewiston, NY and Lampeter, 1998).

5 George McGilvary, *East India Patronage and the British State: The Scottish Elite and Politics in the Eighteenth Century* (2008), esp. pp. 140–5.

6 For Dempster's improvements on the Dunnichen estate, which included the foundation of the industrial village of Letham in 1788 and the use of calcinated marl, produced according to a method prescribed by Dr Joseph Black, Daer's chemistry teacher from the University of Edinburgh, see *The Statistical Accounts of Scotland, 1791–99*, vol. 1, pp. 419–34 [http://stat-acc-scot.edina.ac.uk/link/1791-99/Forfar/Dunnichen/419-34, accessed 26 Nov. 2014].

7 The pamphlet was entitled *Observations on the Present State of the Highlands of Scotland, with a View of the Causes and Probable Consequences of Emigration* (Edinburgh, 1805).

8 On which, see Eric Richards, *Debating the Highland Clearances* (Edinburgh, 2007).

9 University of Toronto Library, Dempster Letter, 1777–1854, Microfilm 61, vol. 8, 1, 'Some Observations on Lord Selkirk's Late Publication', 1808; ibid., 2, another reply to Selkirk, signed 'A. B., once a small Highland proprietor'. Dempster was an opponent of the creation of large sheep runs in the Highlands. Rather his prescription was to confer independence on the Highlander, through changes in the terms under which land was leased from landowners, and to plant manufactures in the region.

10 University of Toronto Library, Dempster Letters, 1777–1854, Microfilm 61, vol. 4, Forbes of Pitsligo to Dempster, Edinburgh, 14 Feb. 1797.

11 *The Statistical Accounts of Scotland, 1791–99, Vol. 8*, p. 380 [http://stat-acc-scot.edina. ac.uk/link/1791-99/Sutherland/Criech/380, accessed 26 Nov. 2014].

12 On which, see the very valuable discussion of this in Brian Bonnyman, *The Third Duke of Buccleuch and Adam Smith: Estate Management and Improvement in Enlightenment Scotland* (Edinburgh, 2014), where the author offers if anything a more positive view of landowner paternalism than that provided here.

13 For the background to this drive, and why the imperative of compliance recommended itself so strongly to landowners, see C. A. Whatley, *Scottish Society, 1707–1830: Beyond Jacobitism, Towards Industrialisation* (Manchester, 2000), esp. pp. 149–58.

14 [Lord Gardenstone], *Letter to the People of Laurencekirk* (Edinburgh, 1780), pp. 52–3.

15 Edward J. Cowan, 'Agricultural Improvement and the Formation of Early Agricultural Societies in Dumfries and Galloway', *Transactions of the Dumfriesshire and Galloway Natural History and Antiquarian Society*, ser. III, 53 (1977–8), 157–67.

16 [James Anderson] 'Thoughts on the Progressive Improvements in Scotland', in *The Bee, Or Literary Weekly Intelligencer, Consisting of Original Pieces, and Selections from Performances of Merit, Foreign and Domestic. A Work Calculated to Disseminate Useful Knowledge Among All Ranks of People at a Small Expence. By James Anderson*, 13 (1793), 140–6.

17 The stated goals of the Highland Society were to enquire into the present state of the Highlands and Islands and the condition of their inhabitants; and to examine the 'state of their improvement'.

18 Huntingdon Library, Pulteney Papers, Box 26, Pu55, James Anderson to William Pulteney, 17 Nov. 1784. I am grateful to Andrew Mackley for bringing this letter to my attention.

19 Lorna J. Philip, 'The Creation of Settlements in Rural Scotland: Planned Villages in Dumfries and Galloway, 1739–1850', *Scottish Geographical Journal*, 119 (2003), 93.

20 Robert Heron, *Observations Made in a Journey through the Western Counties of Scotland in the Autumn of 1792*, 2 vols (Perth, 1793), ii, p. 216.

21 Bonnyman, *The Third Duke of Buccleuch and Adam Smith*, p. 103.

22 A. J. Warden, *Angus or Forfarshire, The Land and People, Descriptive and Historical*, 5 vols (Dundee, 1880–5), i, p. 264.

23 David McClure, *Tolls and Tacksmen* (Ayr, 1994). The first general road act for Ayrshire was passed in 1766, but first discussed in 1758.

24 Under legislation passed by the Scots Parliament in 1696, the Commissioners of Supply had the powers to raise a modest levy to support the upkeep of roads.

25 Bonnyman, *The Third Duke of Buccleuch and Adam Smith*, esp. pp. 104–5.

26 James Robertson, *The Public Roads and Bridges in Dumfriesshire 1650–1820* (Melksham, 1993).

27 Lt-Col C. A. S. Maitland, *Commissioners of Supply for the Stewartry of Kirkcudbright 1728–1828* (1933), pp. 82–94; Ann E. Whetstone, *Scottish County Government in the Eighteenth and Nineteenth Centuries* (Edinburgh, 1982), p. 86.

28 Alex D. Anderson, 'The Development of the Road System in the Stewartry of Kirkcudbright, 1590–1890', *Transactions of the Dumfriesshire and Galloway Natural History Society*, ser. III, 44 (1967), 205–22.

29 Robertson, *Public Roads and Bridges of Dumfriesshire*, pp. 95–111.

30 The story in relation to the Dumfriesshire road act of 1777 can be followed in correspondence in the Pulteney Papers in the Huntingdon Library, which shows just how fierce could be the battles. Town councils regularly took their cases against county road measures and acts to the Court of Session, although this was in reality partly shadow boxing or politics by another means; the goal was the same – to ensure that towns were not unduly burdened financially or that urban magistrates found their powers infringed upon.

31 National Records of Scotland [hereafter, NRS], GD206/2/506/203, James Hall to William Hall, 1 Oct. 1794.

32 Whetstone, *Scottish County Government*.

33 *Edinburgh Advertiser*, 22–5 Feb., 22–5 Nov. 1785.

34 Samuel Smith, *General View of the Agriculture of Galloway: Comprehending Two Counties, viz. the Stewartry of Kirkcudbright and Wigtownshire* (1813), p. 54.

35 Rev. George Ogilvy Elder, *Kirkcudbright: The Story of an Ancient Royal Burgh* (Castle Douglas, 1898), p. 33.

36 See T. M. Devine, *The Transformation of Rural Scotland: Social Change and the Agrarian Economy 1660–1815* (Edinburgh, 1994), pp. 60–1; T. C. Smout, 'Scottish Landowners and Economic Growth, 1650–1850', *Scottish Journal of Political Economy*, 9 (1962), 218–34; Smout, 'A New Look at the Scottish Improvers', *Scottish Historical Review*, 91 (2012), 125–49.

37 Alexander Fenton and Bruce Walker, *The Rural Architecture of Scotland* (Edinburgh, 1981), p. 116.

38 T. C. Smout, 'The Improvers and the Scottish Environment', in T. M. Devine and J. R. Young (eds), *Eighteenth Century Scotland: New Perspectives* (East Linton, 1999), p. 216.

39 James Webster, *General View of the Agriculture of Galloway, Comprehending the Stewartry of Kirkcudbright and Shire of Wigton* (Edinburgh, 1794), p. 6.

40 Smout, 'The Improvers and the Scottish Environment', pp. 219–20.

41 *The Statistical Accounts of Scotland, 1791–99*, vol. 11, p. 8 [http://stat-acc-scot.edina.ac.uk/link/1791-99/Kirkcudbright/Kirkcudbright/8, accessed 26 Nov. 2014].

42 Another symptom of this was the widespread foundation of Horticultural Societies across Scotland in this period. We must remember also that weaving cottages at this time quite often had small plots of garden, and weavers were keen horticulturalists as part of a wider culture of artisan improvement.

43 Ewart Library, Dumfries, R. C. Reid Collection, vol. 179, 'Memorandum of a Journey into Scotland, June 1800', pp. 24–5.

44 *The Statistical Accounts of Scotland, 1791–99*, vol. 11, p. 8 [http://stat-acc-scot.edina.ac.uk/link/1791-99/Kirkcudbright/Kirkcudbright/8, accessed 26 Nov. 2014].

45 Ibid.

46 Ewart Library, Dumfries, W2/1/1, minutes of the Wigtown road trustees, 1786–92.

47 Huntingdon Library, Pulteney Papers, Pu1617, John Maxwell to William Pulteney, 4 Oct. 1776. Bonnyman records that the third duke of Buccleuch spent 'upward of £7,000' on road subscriptions between 1769 and 1795 (Bonnyman, *The Third Duke of Buccleuch and Adam Smith*, p. 104).

48 Ewart Library, R.C. Reid Collection, vol. 179, 'Memorandum of a Journey', p. 44.

49 Advocates Library, Court of Session Papers, Campbell Collection, vol. 6, Magistrates of Paisley v. Road Trustees, paper no. 85.

50 First Report from the Committee on the Highways of the Kingdom, 1807–12; 1808 (225), Appendix 14, pp. 107–9.

51 Daer's copy of the draft bill with amendments written on it survives in the minutes of the Commissioners of Supply.

52 Usually this consensus was created prior to presenting a petition for legislation at Westminster. Where this did not happen, and there was division and counter-petitioning, the costs associated with any legislation would climb rapidly, and often

the result was frustration and failure.

53 Smith, *General View*, p. 318.

54 Although see Paula Martin, *Cupar: The History of a Small Town* (Edinburgh, 2005).

55 See esp. Harris and McKean, *The Scottish Town*.

56 The figure for 1821 is given on John Thompson's map of Kirkcudbrightshire, with its inset plan of the town. The 1792 figure comes from the *Statistical Accounts, 1791–99*.

57 NRS, CC13/6/126/4922, TDI of Andrew Muir, merchant, Kirkcudbright, 1804.

58 There was considerable trade also with Europe from an early stage, legal and illegal, for which, see C. Hill, 'The Mechanics of Overseas Trade: Dumfries and Galloway, 1600–1850', *Transactions of the Dumfriesshire and Galloway Natural History and Antiquarian Society*, ser. III, 80 (2006), 81–104. Coastal trade consisted of exports of grain, potatoes, livestock etc. and imports of coal, lime, timber and general goods.

59 See T. M. Devine, *To the Ends of the Earth: Scotland's Global Diaspora 1750–2010* (London, 2012), pp. 47–9.

60 *The Statistical Accounts of Scotland, 1791–99*, vol. 11, p. 16 [http://stat-acc-scot.edina.ac.uk/link/1791-99/Kirkcudbright/Kirkcudbright/16, accessed 26 Nov. 2014].

61 The best sources for the local occupational profile are the stent rolls, which can be found in the Stewartry Museum, but also a census of the population undertaken in 1819. A part of this, covering one side of the eastern leg of the High Street, is in the Stewartry Museum. The Hornel Library in Broughton House appears to have another part.

62 Heron, *Observations*, ii, p. 194.

63 David Allan, 'Provincial Readers and Book Culture in the Scottish Enlightenment: The Perth Library, c. 1784–1800', *The Library*, 4 (2002), 367–89.

64 http://stat.acc.scot.edina.ac.uk/link/1791-99/kirkcudbright/kirkcudbright/11/23/. A catalogue for the library dating from 1824 largely confirms Muter's assessment. Hornel Library, *Catalogue of Books Belonging to the Library at Kirkcudbright* (Kirkcudbright, 1824).

65 It does or rather did hold the minute books for the Kirkcudbright Subscription Library, but these were, as of the summer of 2013, missing. I am very grateful, therefore, to Dr Mark Towsey of the University of Liverpool for very kindly sending me his notes from these taken during his research for his important study of these libraries *Reading the Scottish Enlightenment: Books and their Readers in Provincial Scotland 1750–1820* (Leiden, 2010).

66 On which, see Mark R. M. Towsey, 'First Steps in Associational Reading: Book Use and Sociability at the Wigtown Subscription Library, 1795–9', *Papers of the Bibliographical Society of America*, 103 (2009), 455–95.

67 For action against 'ruinous houses', see Stewartry Museum, Kirkcudbright burgh court papers, BC 02/6503, ruinous houses, 1726–51. These records show action against seven properties in 1732, and another five in 1737. An entry in the town council minutes for 25 July 1759 would appear to indicate action against ruinous properties in the burgh as early as 1722.

68 See Hornel Library, Broughton House, Kirkcudbright, MS6-S, Samuel Cavan, 'Lecture on Kirkcudbright in the Eighteenth Century, 17 Mar. 1885'.

69 Hornel Library, MS4/31, revenue and expenditure of the burgh of Kirkcudbright for the year ending 31 Oct. 1815; David Brewster, *Edinburgh Encyclopedia*, 18 vols

(Edinburgh, 1814–30), xii, 464–6. By 1818, the town's revenue stood at £1,198.

70 The following paragraphs are based on the town council minutes held in the Stewartry Museum in Kirkcudbright. I am enormously grateful to David Devereaux and his staff for enabling me to have access to these records, and for all their assistance.

71 For which see Harris and McKean, *The Scottish Town*, ch. 2.

72 Edinburgh City Archives, McLeod Collection, SL 30, bundles 238–42. Kirkcudbright petitioned for support to rebuild its ruinous Kirk in 1730, a petition granted in 1731, and again in 1735 for a reduction in their quota of the cess tax payable, which led to a report on the state of the burgh in 1737.

73 NRS, B42/3/1, burgh register of sasines, Kirkcudbright, vol. 1. Sasines, of course, only reveal such activity with a transfer in ownership of property.

74 Heron, *Observations*, ii, p. 186.

75 Joseph Robison, *Kirkcudbright* (Dumfries, n.d.), pp. 37–42.

76 This was 117 High Street.

77 NRS, CS96/4256, sederunt book of William McClure, 1817. McClure also owned two sloops. He was mainly trading with calico printers in Manchester and merchants in Whitehaven and elsewhere in Cumberland.

78 There was development of some houses along the Milnburn, especially from the later 1780s. Further land along the Milnburn was feued for building in 1810. The feuing conditions were quite modest, but clearly designed to ensure a regular building line, slate or metal roofed, with sash windows and stone lintels etc. The dwellings could be one storey, which is what was built, most of these houses being occupied by weavers.

79 NRS, Court of Session papers, CS235/B/12/7, Alexander Birtwhistle v. Lord Daer, 1791.

80 Bob Harris, 'Landowners and Urban Society in Eighteenth Century Scotland', *Scottish Historical Review*, 92 (2013), 231–54.

81 See J. Robison, 'Kirkcudbright Incorporated Trades 1744–1799. Being the Second of Two Lectures given to Members of the Six Incorporated Trades', 1920, who wrote: 'If there is one name above another that ought to be venerated by Kirkcudbright people it is that of the "noble, youthful Daer"'.

82 Stewartry Museum, Kirkcudbright town council minutes, 28 Mar. 1789, refer to a letter from Daer repeating an offer of £50 towards the repair of the harbour and the building of a quay. In 1793, Daer sought to get Kirkcudbright Bay surveyed as part of a government survey of harbours in Galloway designed to render some of them more suitable for the accommodation of a cutter employed in preventing smuggling or naval vessels (7 Nov. 1793).

83 The agreement was reached in January 1790 and executed as contracts between the council and Selkirk on 24 May and 1 June 1790. See the excellent description of these events in David Marsden, 'The Development of Kirkcudbright in the Late 18th Century: Town Planning in a Galloway Context', *Transactions of the Dumfriesshire and Galloway Natural History and Antiquarian Society*, ser. III, 72 (1997), 89–96.

84 See David Marsden, 'The Development of Kirkcudbright in the Early 19th Century by the Emergence of Voluntarism', *Transactions of the Dumfriesshire and Galloway Natural History and Antiquarian Society*, ser. III, 81(2007), 109–114. The minute book of the New Building Society is held in Broughton House, Kirkcudbright.

85 Rev. W. Mackenzie, *The History of Galloway, from the Earliest Period to the Present Time*, 2 vols (Kirkcudbright, 1841), ii, p. 495.

86 Brewster, *Edinburgh Encyclopedia*, xii, pp. 464–6.

5 The Politics of 'North Britain'

1 Bruce Lenman, *Integration, Enlightenment and Industrialization: Scotland 1746–1832* (London, 1981), p. 16.

2 T. Oldfield, *History of the Original Constitution of Parliaments, from the Time of the Britons to the Present Day [. . .] to which is Added the Present State of Representation* (London, 1797), p. 491.

3 David J. Brown, 'The Government of Scotland under Henry Dundas and William Pitt', *History*, 83 (1998), 265–79.

4 J. S. Shaw, *The Political History of Eighteenth-Century Scotland* (Basingstoke, 1999), p. 28.

5 R. H. Campbell, 'The Landed Classes', in T. M. Devine and R. Mitchison (eds), *People and Society in Scotland, Vol 1, 1700–1830* (Edinburgh, 1988), esp. p. 97.

6 A point first emphasised by William Ferguson in his 'Dingwall Politics and the Parliamentary Franchise in the Eighteenth Century', *Scottish Historical Review*, 38 (1959), 89–108. See also R. M. Sunter, *Patronage and Politics in Scotland, 1707–1832* (Edinburgh, 1986).

7 National Records of Scotland [hereafter, NRS], Buccleuch Papers, GD224/31/6/1, Sir William Maxwell to the third duke of Buccleuch, Springkell, 15 Nov. 1789.

8 NRS, Home Office Papers (Scotland), RH 2/4/387, esp. ff. 208–9, Thomas Miller to the earl of Suffolk, 25 Jan. 1779; ff. 230–1, same to same, 27 Feb. 1779.

9 For a very detailed investigation into the anti-Catholicism of one London petty official, the constable William Payne, a Calvinistic Anglican, which illustrates the strength of anti-Catholicism in London in this period, see Joanna Innes, 'The Protestant Carpenter – William Payne of Bell Yard (*c.* 1718–82): The Life and Times of a London Informing Constable', in Joanna Innes, *Inferior Politics: Social Problems and Social Policies in Eighteenth-Century Britain* (Oxford, 2009), pp. 279–341.

10 R. K. Donovan, *No Popery and Radicalism: Opposition to Roman Catholic Relief in Scotland 1778–1782* (New York, 1987).

11 Quoted in Henry Meikle, *Scotland and the French Revolution* (Glasgow, 1912), pp. 37–8.

12 James Boswell, *A Letter to the People of Scotland, on the Alarming Attempt to Infringe on the Articles of Union and Introduce a Most Pernicious Innovation, by Diminishing the Number of Lords of Session* (London, 1785), p. 4.

13 The best narrative account remains Ian. R. Christie, *Wilkes, Wyvill and Reform: The Parliamentary Reform Movement in British Politics 1760–1785* (London, 1962).

14 For which, see esp. Troy O. Bickham, *Making Headlines: The American Revolution as Seen Through the British Press* (De Kalb, IL, 2009).

15 S. J. Connolly, *Divided Kingdom: Ireland 1630–1800* (Oxford, 2008), ch. 10.

16 Padhraig Higgins, *A Nation of Politicians: Gender, Patriotism and Culture in Late Eighteenth Century Ireland* (Madison, WI, 2010).

17 James Kelly, 'Parliamentary Reform in Irish Politics, 1760–1790', in David Dickson et al. (eds), *The United Irishmen: Republicanism, Radicalism and Rebellion* (Dublin, 1993), pp. 74–87.

18 The English–British component of the Irish Patriot viewpoint is emphasised in Connolly, *Divided Kingdom*, esp. pp. 388–9.

19 *A Collection of the Letters which have been Addressed to the Volunteers of Ireland, on the Subject of Parliamentary Reform, by the Earl of Effingham, Doctor Price, Major Cartwright, Doctor Jebb, and the Rev. Mr Wyvill* (London, 1783).

20 Anthony H. Page, *John Jebb and the Enlightenment Origins of British Radicalism* (Westport, 2003), pp. 254–9.

21 British Library, Westminster Committee minutes, Add MSS 38595.

22 National Library of Ireland, Dublin, MSS 10,713.3, letters from John and Ann Jebb to John Forbes; MSS 2251, letters to Francis Dobbs from John Cartwright and John Jebb. By 1785 it was a view expressed by the Society for Constitutional Information, possibly owing to Jebb's influence, for which see *At a Meeting of the Society for Constitutional Information [. . .] on Friday, January 14th 1785 [. . .] A Third Address from the Society for Constitutional Information to the People of Great Britain and Ireland* (London, 1785), p. 22.

23 C. Wyvill, *Wyvill Papers*, 6 vols (York, 1794–1806), i, pp. 322–7, the earl of Buchan to William Gray jun., Edinburgh, 20 Apr. 1781.

24 University of Edinburgh, Special Collections, Gen 1736, 5, Wyvill to Buchan, Burton Hall, 22 Nov. 1782; 15, Wyvill to Dr Gilbert Stuart, 14 Nov. 1782.

25 Wyvill, *Wyvill Papers*, iii, pp. 1–14, 20–3.

26 *Caledonian Mercury*, 27 Jan. 1783.

27 My emphasis. University of Edinburgh, Special Collections, Gen 1736, 3, McGrugar to Buchan, 12 June 1783. A letter from Wyvill to the Edinburgh reformers of 21 Dec. 1784 was reprinted in the *Edinburgh Advertiser*, 28 Dec. 1784.

28 Wyvill, *Wyvill Papers*, iii, pp. 20–3, esp. 22.

29 *Aberdeen Journal*, 13 Feb. 1784; *Scots Mag.*, Apr. 1784, 179–80; *Edinburgh Advertiser*, 17 Feb. 1784.

30 Quoted in Paul Langford, *A Polite and Commercial People: England 1727–1783* (Oxford, 1989), p. 328.

31 *An Address to the Public from the Society for Constitutional Information* (London, 1780).

32 Society for Constitutional Information, *Constitutional Tracts*, 2 vols (London, 1783), ii, pp. 59–62.

33 Page, *John Jebb*, pp. 252, 262.

34 See e.g. *Caledonian Mercury*, 24 Apr. 1792; *Edinburgh Advertiser*, 20 Sept. 1783; *Glasgow Mercury*, 17 Feb., 3 Mar. 1785. On occasion, the *Edinburgh Advertiser* also included extracts from the *Volunteers Journal or Irish Herald*.

35 *Edinburgh Advertiser*, 14 Feb. 1783.

36 *Edinburgh Advertiser*, 24, 28 Oct. 1783. The *Caledonian Mercury* reprinted Wyvill's and Richmond's responses to the Belfast volunteers (*Caledonian Mercury*, 15, 20, 27 Oct. 1783).

37 *Edinburgh Advertiser*, 17 May 1783; *Caledonian Mercury*, 12 May 1783.

38 Bob Harris, 'Scotland's Newspapers, the French Revolution, and Domestic Radicalism, c. 1789–1794', *Scottish Historical Review*, 84 (2005), 41–2; Victoria Gardner, 'Newspaper Proprietors and the Business of Newspaper Publishing in Provincial England 1760–1820', unpublished DPhil thesis, University of Oxford, 2008, pp. 118–19.

39 Bob Harris, *Politics and the Rise of the Press: Britain and France 1620–1800* (London, 1996), pp. 42–3.

40 Bob Harris, 'Parliamentary Legislation, Lobbying and the Press in Eighteenth Century Scotland', in Jason Peacey (ed.), *The Print Culture of Parliament 1600–1800* (Edinburgh, 2007), pp. 76–95.

41 *Caledonian Mercury*, 31 Mar. 1784; Grayson Ditchfield, '"How Narrow the Limits of this Toleration Appear": Dissenting Petitions to Parliament, 1771–1773', in Stephen Taylor and David L. Wykes (eds), *Parliament and Dissent* (Edinburgh, 2005), p. 98.

42 *Aberdeen Journal*, 29 Mar. 1784.

43 Dr Williams's Library, London, D W L MSS 24: 157 (74), James Wodrow to William Kenrick, 15 Apr. 1784.

44 NRS, Graham of Gartmore Papers, GD22/1/315/26 (2), copy of a letter from Archibald Fletcher to [George] Meliss [of Perth], [John] Ewen [of Aberdeen], [Robert] Bisset of Dundee & <Donald> of Glasgow, n.d., but 1789; 34 (1–2), copy of a letter from Archibald Fletcher to Mr Tod of Irvine, 9 Feb. 1789. At a Stirling county meeting in January 1789 a resolution for an address of thanks to Pitt was rejected by a considerable majority (*Aberdeen Journal*, 17 Jan. 1789).

45 NRS, GD22/1/315, copy of a letter from Lord Sempill to the duke of Portland, 12 May 1791.

46 Emma Vincent Macleod, 'The Scottish Opposition Whigs and the French Revolution', in Bob Harris (ed.), *Scotland in the Age of the French Revolution* (Edinburgh, 2005), pp. 79–98.

47 T. E. Orme, 'Toasting Fox: The Fox Dinners in Edinburgh and Glasgow, 1801–1825', *History*, 99 (2014), 588–606.

48 William Ferguson, 'The Electoral System in the Scottish Counties before 1832', in D. Sellar (ed.), *The Stair Society, Miscellany II*, Stair Society Publications, 35 (Edinburgh, 1984), pp. 261–94.

49 NRS, GD22/1/315/1, printed circular letter from Alexander Keith to Robert Graham of Gartmore, 20 Aug. 1782, covering copies of advertisements from the counties of Inverness, Moray and Caithness.

50 In the 1790 general election, nominal and fictitious voters were summarily excluded from the voting rolls in Invernesshire, Aberdeenshire and Moray. That it did not happen elsewhere was normally because all parties to the elections did not agree on this.

51 Wyvill, *Wyvill Papers*, iii, pp. 36–40.

52 Dundas, in fact, won a tactical victory at the December meeting when rather than considering immediately Henry Erskine's proposed reform bill, on a motion of the Lord Advocate's, the delegates voted that counties should consider it at their 30 April meetings with a view to a further convention in May. The proposal was effectively killed at the county meetings, when those in attendance voted not to send delegates to a further convention.

53 See *Letter from an Old Freeholder to his Fellow Freeholders. Refuting the Principles of the Bill Approved by the Meeting of Delegates Held at Edinburgh, in December Last, for Regulating the County Election Laws in Scotland* (Edinburgh, 1793).

54 NRS, Court of Session Papers, Dundee Corporations v. Dundee Magistrates, 1759.

55 NRS, Court of Session Papers, Sessional Papers 61; 7 (1757–61), The Petition of the Deacon Convenor of the Several Corporations in Dundee, 24 Nov. 1761.

56 *Caledonian Mercury*, 20 Nov. 1773; *A General History of Stirling* (Stirling, 1794), p. 97.

57 Hisashi Kuboyama, 'The Politics of the People in Glasgow and the West of Scotland, 1707–*c*. 1785', unpublished PhD thesis, University of Edinburgh, 2011.

58 D. F. Fagerstrom, 'Scotland and the American Revolution', *William and Mary Quarterly*, 11 (1954), 252–75.

59 Samuel Miller, *Memoir of the Rev. Charles Nisbet D.D.; Late President of Dickenson College* (New York, 1840), pp. 74–9.

60 Dr Williams's Library, D W L MSS 24: 157 (58), James Wodrow to William Kenrick, 1 Oct. 1776; (60), same to same, 16 Mar. 1778.

61 *Caledonian Mercury*, 11 Apr. 1778.

62 NRS, RH2/4/387, ff. 290–1.

63 NRS, RH2/4/387, ff. 103.

64 John Robertson, *The Scottish Enlightenment and the Militia Issue* (Edinburgh, 1985).

65 *Caledonian Mercury*, 27 Mar. 1784.

66 *Caledonian Mercury*, 10 Feb. 1783.

67 Wyvill, *Wyvill Papers*, iii, p. 33.

68 James Boswell, *A Letter to the People of Scotland, on the Alarming Attempt to Infringe the Articles of the Union, and to Introduce a Most Pernicious Innovation, by Diminishing the Number of the Lords of Session* (London, 1785).

69 Joanna Innes, 'Legislating for Three Kingdoms: How the Westminster Parliament Legislated for England, Scotland, and Ireland 1707–1830', in Julian Hoppit (ed.), *Parliaments, Nations, and Identities in Britain and Ireland, 1660–1850* (Manchester, 2003), pp. 15–47.

70 R. J. Bennett, *Local Business Voice: The History of Chambers of Commerce in Britain, Ireland, and Revolutionary America, 1760–2011* (Oxford, 2011); Bob Harris, 'Towards a British Political Economy: An Eighteenth-Century Scottish Perspective', in Perry Gauci (ed.), *Regulating the British Economy, 1660–1850* (Farnham, 2011), pp. 83–105.

71 Keith Robbins, *Nineteenth-Century Britain: Integration and Diversity* (Oxford, 1989).

72 Charles Adam, *View of the Political State of Scotland in the Last Century: A Confidential Report on the Political Opinions, Family Connections, or Personal Circumstances of the 2662 Voters in 1788* (Edinburgh, 1887), p. 195.

73 *Edinburgh Advertiser*, 21 May 1782.

74 Blair Castle, Atholl Papers, Box 54 (5), 195, Lord North to the duke of Atholl, 5 Oct. 1774.

75 Quoted in M. W. McCahill, *The House of Lords in the Age of George III* (Chichester, 2009), p. 49.

76 McCahill, *House of Lords*, p. 48.

77 McCahill, *House of Lords*, pp. 48–9; Roger L. Emerson, *An Enlightened Duke: The Life of Archibald Campbell (1682–1761), Earl of Ilay, 3rd Duke of Argyll* (Kilkerran, 2013), pp. 255–61.

78 McCahill, *House of Lords*, pp. 51–2; NRS, GD150/2378/3, earl of Selkirk to Lady Morton, 6 Mar. 1784.

79 Blair Castle, Atholl Papers, Box 65 (5), 113, George Farquhar to the duke of Atholl, Edinburgh, 21 July 1786.

80 McCahill, *House of Lords*, pp. 53–4.

81 NRS, GD150/2379, Lord Sempill to the earl of Morton, 12 June 1790.

82 James Fergusson, *The Sixteen Peers of Scotland: An Account of the Elections of the Representative Peers of Scotland, 1707–1959* (Oxford, 1960), p. 81.

83 *Speech of the Earl of Buchan in which his Lordship Proposes a Plan for the Better Regulation of the Peerage of Scotland* (Edinburgh, 1780).

84 University of Edinburgh, Special Collections, Gen 1736, 16, vote of thanks of the Orange Society, 'one of the first Patriotic Clubs instituted for free discussion of Political sentiment'; 17, letter from William Hutchison, praeses, to the earl of Buchan, 4 Nov. 1782.

85 McCahill, *House of Lords*, pp. 52–3.

86 NRS, GD150/2378, earl of Selkirk to Lord Morton, London, 25 May 1785; same to same, 7 June 1785.

87 G. M. Ditchfield, 'The Scottish Representative Peers and Parliamentary Politics 1787–1793', *Scottish Historical Review*, 60 (1981), 14–31.

88 NRS, GD150/2378, earl of Selkirk to Lord Morton, St Mary's Isle, 12 Sept. 1786.

89 NRS, GD22/2/315 (40), Sempill to Graham of Gartmore, May 1791.

90 Donald E. Ginter, *Whig Organization in the General Election of 1790: Selections from the Blair Adam Papers* (Cambridge, 1967), pp. 201–2, 221–3, 255–6.

91 *Edinburgh Advertiser*, 22 Oct. 1782 [notice of county meeting at Kirkcudbright chaired by the earl of Selkirk, where Selkirk and Daer were both appointed to the county committee to meet with other such bodies on the issue of the militia]; NLS, MS 6332, Diary of Sir James Hall of Dunglass, f. 99, which notes a conversation between Hall and Selkirk in Paris on the latter's 'militia scheme'.

92 Blair Castle, Atholl Papers, Box 65, 4 (45), earl of Mansfield to the duke of Atholl, 7 June 1782.

93 earl of Saltoun, *Thoughts on the Disqualification of the Eldest Sons of the Peers of Scotland, to Elect, or to be Elected from that Country to Parliament* (London, 1788), p. 13.

94 Saltoun, *Thoughts on the Disqualification*, p. 107.

95 Saltoun, *Thoughts on the Disqualification*, p. 124.

96 Basil William Douglas, Lord Daer, *The Right of the Eldest Sons of Peers to Represent the Commons of that Part of Great Britain in Parliament, Considered* (Edinburgh, 1790).

97 NRS, GD26/17/1956, minute of meeting at Bayll's Tavern, Edinburgh, 16 Sept. 1793. An accompanying letter from Robert Hill to Lord Balgonie refers to a meeting in London on 31 May 1790 that Balgonie had attended, which was taken as an indication that he concurred in the campaign. Daer was appointed treasurer of the subscription, and given the power to draw on the sums subscribed. See also NRS, GD150/2378/15, sederunt of meeting chaired by the the duke of Buccleuch [. . .] Edinburgh, 24 Oct. 1789. This refers to searches undertaken by Daer regarding the rights of eldest sons. A committee, chaired by Daer, was to undertake further searches, but also to pursue these rights in the courts. Copies of invitations to the meeting were sent to all peers and eldest sons, as were the minutes of the meeting on 24 Oct.

98 NRS, GD26/17/1956, letter from Lord Selkirk to the earl of Leven, St Mary's Isle, 8 Jan. [n.d., but prob. 1794].

6 Witness to Revolution

1 See National Records of Scotland [hereafter, NRS], Hall of Dunglass Papers, GD206/2/315/1, ff. 3–5, where Hall records travelling to Calais with Daer in June 1783, the latter en route to Paris, while Hall was going to Germany. When Burns met Daer in 1786 at Dugald Stewart's Ayrshire home at Catrine, Daer was returning from France.

2 As testified to in a letter written by Richard Price to Thomas Jefferson, 4 May 1789, where he writes: 'This letter will, I hope, be convey'd to you, by Mr Dugald Stewart, Professor of Moral Philosophy at Edinburgh and a very able man who is this day setting out for Paris with Lord Dare [sic] *in order to be present there at the time of the meeting of the three estates*' (my emphasis). (*The Papers of Thomas Jefferson, Vol. 15, 27 Mar. 1789–30 Nov. 1789*, ed. Julian P. Boyd (Princeton, NJ, 1958), pp. 90–7.)

3 *Papers of Thomas Jefferson, Vol. 15*, p. 111, Thomas Jefferson to John Jay, 9 May 1789.

4 Quoted in Peter Burley, *Witness to the Revolution: American and British Commentators in France 1788–94* (London, 1989), pp. 52–3.

5 J. M. Thompson (ed.), *English Witnesses of the French Revolution* (Oxford, 1938), p. 53.

6 William Doyle, *Aristocracy and its Enemies in the Age of Revolution* (Oxford, 2009), p. 212.

7 *Papers of Thomas Jefferson, Vol. 15*, p. 279, Thomas Jefferson to Richard Price, 17 July 1789, where Jefferson notes that Daer had offered to carry this letter to Price.

8 Alan Ryan, *On Politics: A History of Political Thought from Herodotus to the Present* (London, 2012), p. 611.

9 *The Adams–Jefferson Letters: The Complete Correspondence between Thomas Jefferson and Abigail and John Adams*, ed. Lester J. Capper (New York, 1971), p. 561, Jefferson to John Adams, Monticello, 16 Mar. 1820.

10 *Papers of Thomas Jefferson, Vol. 15*, p. 111.

11 Jonathan Israel, *Revolutionary Ideas: An Intellectual History of the French Revolution from 'The Rights of Man' to Robespierre* (Princeton, NJ, 2014), p. 62.

12 Merrill D. Peterson, *Thomas Jefferson and the New Nation* (New York, 1970), p. 382.

13 *Papers of Thomas Jefferson, Vol. 15*, pp. 306, 367.

14 For which, see chapter 3, p. 80.

15 National Library of Scotland [hereafter NLS], MSS 6330, f. 131.

16 *A Diary of the French Revolution by Gouverneur Morris 1752–1816: Minister to France during the Terror*, ed. Beatrice Cary Davenport, 2 vols (London, 1939), ii, p. 368, 12 Feb. 1792.

17 Timothy Tackett, *When the King Took Flight* (Cambridge, MA and London, 2003), p. 147.

18 Historians give different sets of figures; I am here following Tackett, *When the King Took Flight*, p. 150.

19 Michel Vovelle, *The Fall of the French Monarchy 1787–1792* (Cambridge, 1984), p. 144.

20 NLS, MSS 6329–32.

21 Léon Cahen, *Condorcet et La Révolution Française* (Paris, 1904), p. 260.

22 Gary Kates, 'From Liberalism to Radicalism: Tom Paine's *Rights of Man*', *Journal of the History of Ideas*, 50 (1989), 659–87; Richard Whatmore, 'A Gigantic Manliness: Thomas Paine's Republicanism in the 1790s', in Stefan Collini, Richard Whatmore and Brian Young (eds), *Economy, Polity, and Society: British Intellectual History 1750–1950*

(Cambridge, 2000), pp. 135–57; Mark Philp, 'Revolutionaries in Paris: Paine and Jefferson', in Mark Philp, *Reforming Ideas in Britain: Politics and Language in the Shadow of the French Revolution, 1789–1815* (Cambridge, 2014), pp. 187–209.

23 The evidence for this is contained in various letters sent to James's uncle, William Hall. See e.g. NRS, GD206/2/300/27, 28, James to William Hall, 5 Jan., 21 Jan. 1787; 45, same to same, 1 Mar. 1789; GD206/2/317/6, Helen Hall to William Hall, 16 Jan. 1791.

24 V. A. Eyles, 'The Evolution of a Chemist', *Annals of Science*, 19 (2006), 153–82. What follows owes a clear debt to Eyles's article.

25 Hall first revealed his ideas on this topic in a paper he read to the Edinburgh Royal Society in the spring of 1797 (*Essay on the Origins and Principles of Gothic Architecture. By James Hall. From the Transactions of the Royal Society of Edinburgh. Read April 6, 1797.*)

26 NLS, MS 3649, Basil Hall to Dr Marcet, 18 Jan. 1819.

27 NRS, GD206/2/315/18, transcript of Diary of Sir James Hall, Bt, Geneva, 7–15 Apr. 1781, p. 3.

28 NRS, GD206/2/300/35, James to William Hall, Edinburgh, 6 Dec. 1787.

29 NRS, GD206/2/300/53, James to William Hall, Edinburgh, 28 Apr. 1792.

30 James Epstein, *Scandal of Colonial Rule: Power and Subversion in the British Atlantic during the Age of Revolution* (Cambridge, 2012), p. 49.

31 NRS, GD206/2/300/14, James to William Hall, Vienna, 17 Dec. 1783.

32 NRS, GD206/2/300/15, James to William Hall, Vienna, 18 Mar. 1784.

33 NRS, GD206/2/507/3, Sir John Pringle to William Hall, 15 Sept. 1777. Hall boarded with Blondel, but attended Pringle's Wednesday and Sunday 'companies'.

34 As revealed in NRS, GD206/2/315/6, diary of Sir James Hall, 2–15 Aug. 1792, f. 53. Watson was appointed Regius Professor of Divinity at Cambridge in 1771.

35 NRS, GD206/2/428/11, Sir John Pringle to William Hall, London, 5 Aug. 1779.

36 NRS, GD206/2/315/18.

37 The indexing and annotation of the French diaries is stressed by Michael Brown in his 'A Scottish Literati in Paris: The Case of Sir James Hall', *Journal of Irish and Scottish Studies*, 2 (2008), 73–100, esp. 82. I am grateful to Professor Brown for sending me a copy of his article.

38 That Hall did in fact refer to them in later years is indicated by a note in one of them dated 20 Oct. 1825 (NLS, MS 6330, f. 80).

39 For the compelling argument that literacy needs to be conceived of as a repertoire of skills in this period and not a simple facility, see Susan E. Whyman, *The Pen and the People* (Oxford, 2012).

40 NRS, GD206/2/315/6, Diary of Sir James Hall, 2–15 Aug. 1792, ff. 87–123, quotation on f. 123. Eccleston had drained a very large lake on his land.

41 Stuart Hartley, 'Appealing to Nature: Geology "in the Field" in Late Enlightenment Scotland', in Charles W. J. Withers and Paul Wood (eds), *Science and Medicine in the Scottish Enlightenment* (East Linton, 2002), p. 290, cited in Brown, 'A Scottish Literati in Paris', 77.

42 NRS, GD206/2/315/4, ff. 4–16.

43 NRS, GD206/2/315/3, f. 39; GD206/2/315/2, f. 86.

44 NLS, MS 6329, ff. 136–7.

45 NLS, MS 6332, f. 149.

46 NLS, MS 6331, f. 47. In a letter to his uncle written on 12 June (NRS, GD206/2/300/50),

he explained it slightly differently: 'Our object is to see those parts of France that are famous for their wretched culture in consequence of oppression of every kind & we have a kind of plan of returning some years hence to see the change produced by the revolution.' This plan may well have originated in a conversation that took place on 7 June at a dinner with Condorcet, Sieyès, Roederer and Grouvelle about the rural economy, including the nature of the *petit culture* (NLS, MS 6330, f. 173).

47 *Farmers' Magazine*, 6 (1805), 301–2.
48 The National Assembly at this point is well described by Henry, Viscount Palmerston, who was in France between 6 July and 31 August 1791: 'The room is very long, fitted up with rows of benches something like our House of Commons or perhaps something more like Westminster Hall during a trial, though infinitely inferior. The president sits in the middle of one side and the tribune or desk from which reports and regular speeches are made is opposite him. At each end are great galleries raised which hold large numbers and are filled with very low people. On the sides are smaller galleries which are rather more select in their company and more difficult to get admittance to. The confusion and want of order is extraordinary at first and the president's bell has a very odd effect.' (*The Despatches of Earl Gower, English Ambassador at Paris from June 1790 to August 1792*, ed. Oscar Browning (Cambridge, 1885), p. 286.)
49 NLS, MS 6331, f. 194.
50 G. Rudé, The Crowd in the French Revolution (Oxford, 1959), p. 51, cited in Darrin M. McMahon, 'The Birthplace of the Revolution: Public Space and Political Community in the Palais-Royal of Louis-Philippe-Joseph D'Orléans 1781–1789', *French History*, 10 (1996), 26.
51 *The Papers of Thomas Jefferson, Vol. 20, 1 April–4 August 1791*, ed. Julian P. Boyd (Princeton, NJ, 1982), p. 351, William Short to Thomas Jefferson, 2 May 1791.
52 NLS, MS 6329, f. 119.
53 NLS, MS 6330, f. 35.
54 NLS, MS 6330, ff. 146–7.
55 NLS, MS 6332, f. 36. The following sentence in the diary has been heavily scrawled out, but seems to refer to Daer.
56 NLS, MS 6332, ff. 44–5.
57 NLS, MS 6330, f. 35.
58 Israel, *Revolutionary Ideas*.
59 NLS, MS 6332, f. 28.
60 Ghita Stanhope and G. P. Gooch, *The Life of Charles, Third Earl of Stanhope* (n.p. 1914), p. 111. If she were to go to America, she was to get in contact with either Jefferson or Franklin's grandson. A translated version of Condorcet's 'testament' is reproduced in *The Political Theory of Condorcet II*, ed. Fiona Sommerlad and Iain McLean, University of Oxford, Social Studies Faculty Centre, Working Paper (Oxford, 1991), p. 232.
61 Keith Michael Baker, *Condorcet: From Natural Philosophy to Social Mathematics* (Chicago, IL and London, 1975), esp. p. 24.
62 NLS, MS 6331, ff. 38–9.
63 NLS, MS 6332, f. 62.
64 NLS, MS 6332, f. 96. The speech is reproduced in F. A. Aulart, *Recueil de documents pour l'histoire du club des Jacobins de Paris, Vol. II* (Paris, 1891), pp. 608–26.
65 Cahen, *Condorcet*, p. 260.

66 Doyle, *Aristocracy and its Enemies*, p. 305.

67 *Papers of Thomas Jefferson, Vol. 20*, ed. Boyd, p. 585, William Short to Thomas Jefferson, Paris, 29 June 1791.

68 Quoted in Tackett, *When the King Took Flight*, p. 92.

69 Tackett, *When the King Took Flight*, p. 96.

70 Quoted in Burley, *Witness to the Revolution*, p. 139.

71 NLS, MS 6332, ff. 9, 15, 16.

72 Quoted in *English Witnesses*, ed. Thompson, p. 125.

73 *Papers of Thomas Jefferson, Vol. 20*, ed. Boyd, p. 585.

74 NLS, MS 6332, f. 121.

75 NLS, MS 6332, ff. 49–50.

76 Timothy Tackett, *The Coming of the Terror in the French Revolution* (Cambridge, MA, 2014).

77 NLS, MS 6330, f. 35.

78 NLS, MS 6330, ff. 168–9.

79 NLS, MS 6330, f. 39.

80 *Papers of Thomas Jefferson, Vol. 15*, ed. Boyd, pp. 384–98.

81 NRS, GD206/2/300/23, James to William Hall, Paris, 9 Mar. 1786; 300/47, James to William Hall, Dunglass, 10 May 1790.

82 John Cartwright, *A Letter to the Duke of Newcastle [. . .] respecting his Grace's Conduct in the Disposal of Commissions in the Militia; Together with Some Remarks Touching the French Revolution, a Reform of Parliament in Great Britain, and the Royal Proclamation of 21st of May* (London, 1792), p. 34.

83 Quoted in *English Witnesses*, ed. Thompson, p. 130.

84 NLS, MS 6332, ff. 6–15, 45.

85 NRS, GD206/2/315/6, Diary of Sir James Hall, 2–15 Aug. 1792, ff. 21, 23.

86 NRS, GD206/2/315/6, f. 69.

87 NRS, GD206/2/315/7, Diary of Sir James Hall, 15–27 Aug. 1792, ff. 43, 45.

88 On 29 August 1792, Thomas Cooper had declared to John Horne Tooke, in relation to the founding of the newspaper, the *Manchester Herald*, 'We shall immediately set up a paper among ourselves [. . .] we shall at first be gently, but always decidedly *democratic*' (TNA, Treasury Solicitor's Papers, TS 11/966, Papers relating to the London Corresponding Society and the Constitutional Society: meetings held on 9 Dec. 1791–9 May 1794, Thomas Cooper to John Horne Tooke, 29 Aug. 1792).

89 Quoted in Albert Goodwin, *The Friends of Liberty: The English Democratic Movement in the Age of the French Revolution* (London, 1979), p. 201.

90 Quoted in David V. Erdman, *Commerce des Lumières: John Oswald and the British in Paris, 1790–1793* (Columbia, NY, 1986), p. 162.

91 *Manchester Herald*, 30 June, 25 Aug., 1 Sept., 15 Sept. 1792.

92 NRS, GD206/2/315/9, Diary of Sir James Hall, 29 Sept.–15 Oct. 1792, entry for 7 Oct.

93 *London Corresponding Society, 1792–1799*, ed. Michael T. Davis, 6 vols (London, 2002), i, p. 29.

94 Cartwright, *Letter to the Duke of Newcastle*, p. 84.

95 John Dinwiddy, 'Conceptions of Revolution in the English Radicalism of the 1790s', in Eckhart Hellmuth (ed.), *The Transformation of Political Culture: England and Germany in the Late Eighteenth Century* (Oxford and New York, 1990), pp. 535–60.

96 *Manchester Herald*, 28 July 1792.

97 Letter from George Rous to James Mackintosh, 10 July 1792, published in the *Manchester Herald*, 14 July 1792.

98 NLS, MS 6332, ff. 164–5.

99 Brown, 'A Scottish Literati in Paris', 96.

100 Shropshire Archives, Diary of Katherine Plymley, 1066/10, 24 Apr.–11 May 1792, ff. 13–14. I am very grateful to Professor Jon Mee for supplying me with photocopies of the relevant entries from this source.

7 Union(s) and Liberty

1 P. D. G. Thomas, *John Wilkes: A Friend to Liberty* (Oxford, 1996).

2 National Library of Scotland, Acc 5779, 'Reminiscences of Edinburgh 60 Years Ago (1794), by John Howell (1854)'.

3 Bob Harris, 'Scottish–English Connections in British Radicalism in the 1790s', in T. C. Smout (ed.), *Anglo-Scottish Relations from 1603 to 1900* (Oxford, 2005), p. 198. Another prominent early Scottish member was Alexander Grant, who was expelled from the society in 1793 for his lack of prudence in directing William Carter to post LCS bills up during daylight, for which he was prosecuted. Grant was an important witness at the trial of Hardy for treason in 1794.

4 Although see Stana Nenadic (ed.), *Scots in London in the Eighteenth Century* (Lewisburg, PA, 2010).

5 For Jebb, see ch. 5, above, pp. 115, 118.

6 The National Archives, Kew [hereafter TNA], Treasury Solicitor's Papers, TS 11/962, Minute Book of the Society for Constitutional Information, 1791–4, ff. 53, 55.

7 TNA, TS 11/962, f. 66, minute for meeting of 4 May 1792.

8 TNA, TS 11/962, ff. 87v–88r, Thomas Hardy to the Society for Constitutional Information, 14 June 1792.

9 TNA, TS 11/965/3510A (1), letter from the Manchester Society for Constitutional Information to Hardy, 7 Apr. 1792; Hardy to the Southwark Friends of the People, 18 Apr. 1792; Hardy to Sheffield Society for Constitutional Information, 9 Mar. 1792; letter from Sheffield Society for Constitutional Information to Hardy, 19 Mar. 1792.

10 For reports of this meeting, see *The Morning Post & Daily Advertiser*, 15 July 1791.

11 Marcel Reinhard, 'Le Voyage de Pétion à Londres 24 Octobre–11 Novembre 1791', *Revue d'histoire diplomatique*, 84 (1970), 54–5.

12 *The Star*, 5 Nov. 1791.

13 Reinhard, 'Le Voyage', 55.

14 *Proceedings of the Society of the Friends of the People; Associated for the Purpose of Obtaining a Parliamentary Reform, in the Year 1792* (London, 1793), p. 9.

15 See e.g. *Caledonian Mercury*, 2 May 1792; *Edinburgh Evening Courant*, 3 May 1792; *Glasgow Courier*, 5 May 1792; *The Derby Mercury*, 10 May 1792.

16 *Proceedings*, p. 16.

17 For Fullarton, whose life intersected with Daer's and Hall's at quite a few points, see esp. James Epstein, *Scandal of Colonial Rule: Power and Subversion in the British Atlantic during the Age of Revolution* (Cambridge, 2012), pp. 46–89.

18 Daer was also one of nine appointed on 19 May to a committee of the Whig Association

to enquire into the state of parliamentary representation in Scotland. (Notice in the *Gazetteer and New Daily Advertiser*, 21 May 1792.)

19 The LCS, perhaps significantly, only broke with the Whig Association at the beginning of 1793 when the latter refused to clarify exactly what particular measures of parliamentary reform they favoured.

20 *Proceedings of the Friends of the Liberty of the Press* (London, 1793). On 15 March 1793, Daer was among those nominated as members of the committee of this body. For Daer's presence and contribution to debates at a meeting on 20 April 1793, see the *Morning Post*, 22 April 1793.

21 British Library [hereafter BL], Add MS 64814, minute book of the Revolution Society, 1788–91.

22 For his membership of the LCS, see BL, Francis Place Papers, Add MS 27,814, f. 36.

23 TNA, TS 11/962, esp. ff. 66–86.

24 *Proceedings of the Society of the Friends of the People*, pp. 25–34.

25 BL, Francis Place Papers, Add MS 27, 817, ff. 22–5.

26 TNA, TS 11/962, ff. 59–63.

27 *Public Advertiser*, 14 May 1792. See also 26 May 1792.

28 *Public Advertiser*, 17 May 1792, which noted that Dr O'Connor had been elected president of the London division, Favell of the Southwark division, and Daer president of the 'Delegates of the Association'.

29 *Southwark Friends of the People. At a Meeting of the General Committee holden Oct. 2, 1792 at the Three-Tuns-Tavern* (London, 1792), p. 4. These societies remain rather shadowy, and the relationship between various groups sharing the name 'The Friends of the People' is unclear, such as the 'Holborn Society, of the Friends of the People; Instituted 22d November 1792, for the Purpose of Political Investigation'. However, their similarities are very striking.

30 Albert Goodwin, *The Friends of Liberty: The English Democratic Movement in the Age of the French Revolution* (London, 1979), p. 239.

31 *The Morning Chronicle*, 6 Nov. 1792.

32 Ibid.

33 The Constitutional Whigs have received very little attention from historians. They almost certainly emerged from the Foxite campaigns of 1784–90, and before that the Wilkesite struggles of the 1760s and '70s; and they provide an important link between the 1780s and the renewed political and radical activism of Westminster's tradesmen and artisans in the early 1800s. The Southwark Friends of the People decided to address the French Convention separately (TNA, TS 11/965/3510A, John Frederick Schiefer, secretary to the general committee in Southwark, to Thomas Hardy, 18 Nov. 1792).

34 Dr William's Library, London, D W L MSS 24: 157, Wodrow–Kenrick Correspondence *c.* 1750–1810, 164, James Wodrow to William Kenrick, 16 June 1791.

35 A straw in the wind may have been the formation of the so-called Universal Liberty Club in Edinburgh in February, whose aims included the extension of liberty and rights of man; abolition of the slave trade; and repeal of 'various oppressive and disgraceful laws'. The only reference that I have so far found to this body is a paragraph in *The Derby Mercury*, 11 Feb. 1792.

36 See e.g. the confidence expressed in the letters from Norman Macleod to Charles Grey

of 4 July, 13 Aug. and 30 Nov. 1792 (Edward Hughes, 'The Scottish Reform Movement and Charles Grey 1792–94: Some Fresh Correspondence', *The Scottish Historical Review*, 35 (1956), 27–9, 31–3).

37 *The Star*, 9 Mar. 1792 [for a report on the Edinburgh meeting, which notes the presence of Daer and Hall].

38 This can be followed in the pages of the main Glasgow newspapers – the *Glasgow Advertiser* and the *Glasgow Courier*.

39 D W L MSS 24: 157, 174, Wodrow to Kenrick, 30 May 1792.

40 See e.g. *Glasgow Courier*, 13, 15, 17, 22, 24 Sept. 1791; *Edinburgh Advertiser*, 16, 20, 23, 27, 30 Sept., 7, 14 Oct. 1791. For the role of the press, see my 'Scotland's Newspapers, the French Revolution and Domestic Radicalism, *c.* 1789–1794', *Scottish Historical Review*, 84 (2005), 38–62.

41 D W L MSS 24: 157, 174, Wodrow to Kenrick, 30 May 1792.

42 The phrase quoted comes from Blair Castle, Atholl Papers, Box 65, Bundle 10 (33), George Farquhar, Edinburgh, to the duke of Atholl, 2 June 1792. For popular political and radical disturbances in 1792 more generally, see my 'Political Protests in the Year of Liberty', in Harris (ed.), *Scotland in the Age of the French Revolution* (Edinburgh, 2005), pp. 50–78.

43 *Glasgow Courier*, 24 July 1792.

44 National Records of Scotland [hereafter NRS], Home Office Papers (Scotland), RH2/4/209, f. 23.

45 NRS, GD 164/1729/15, James St Clair, Dysart, to [Robert D?], 29 Nov. 1792.

46 NRS, RH2/4/209, f. 13.

47 NRS, Home of Wedderburn Papers, GD267/1/16, f. 10, George Home to Patrick Home of Wedderburn, Edinburgh, 3 Dec. 1792.

48 NRS, GD267/1/16, ff. 7–8, George Home to Patrick Home of Wedderburn, Edinburgh, 25 Nov. 1792.

49 NRS, Melville Papers, GD51/5/9, John Morison, minister of Canisby, Caithness, to Robert Dundas [?], n.d. but almost certainly Feb. 1793.

50 NRS, RH2/4/66, f. 261, David Sproat, provost of Kirkcudbright, to Robert Dundas, 10 Dec. 1792.

51 As reported by Skirving to the Edinburgh general committee on 15 Nov. 1793, for which see, TNA, HO102/9, f. 192v.

52 NRS, RH2/4/65, ff. 54–8, copy of a letter from Sir William Maxwell to the duke of Buccleuch, Springkell, 19 Nov. 1792.

53 Henry Meikle, *Scotland and the French Revolution* (Glasgow, 1912), Appendix A, The Minutes of the Proceedings of the Delegates from the Societies of the Friends of the People throughout Scotland at their several sittings in Edinburgh on the 11th, 12th, and 13th, 1792, as contained in spy reports, Public Record Office, London, pp. 241–2, 244–5.

54 Ibid., pp. 246, 259.

55 Ibid., p. 272.

56 Ibid., p. 247.

57 See esp. John Brims, 'From Reformers to "Jacobins": The Scottish Association of the Friends of the People', in T. M. Devine (ed.), *Conflict and Stability in Scottish Society* (Edinburgh, 1991), pp. 31–50.

58 On which, see Bob Harris, *The Scottish People and the French Revolution* (2008), pp. 92–105.

59 Meikle, *Scotland and the French Revolution*, Appendix, Proceedings, pp. 252–3, 258, 269–70.

60 BL, Add MS 27,817, f. 12, Thomas Hardy to J. Walker, 4 June 1792. See also TNA, TS11/965/3510A, James Walker to Thomas Hardy, Falkirk, 23 June 1792.

61 BL, Add MS 27,817, f. 15.

62 BL, Add MS 27,814, f. 184, copy of private letter from Hardy to Daer, 8 Sept. 1792.

63 TNA, TS 11/965/3510A, Johnston to Hardy, 31 Oct. 1792.

64 In early November at a meeting of the United Societies of Paisley, one of the resolutions agreed was to 'act in conjunction with the Society of the Friends of the People in London, *and other Societies in Britain* [. . .]' (*Caledonian Mercury*, 5 Nov. 1792).

65 *A Declaration of Rights and An Address to the People. Approved by a Number of the Friends of Reform in Paisley*, n.d., but prob. late 1792 or early 1793.

66 For Sempill's prominent role in the SCI in this period, see TNA, TS 11/962.

67 Harris, 'Scottish–English Connections', pp. 199–200.

68 See the letter they sent the Whig Association on 14 May 1792 (*Proceedings of the Society of the Friends of the People*, pp. 38–42, esp. p. 42).

69 *The Second Report from the Committee of Secrecy of the House of Commons*, copy of a letter from the editors of the *Patriot* to the secretary of the London Corresponding Society, Sheffield, 15 Oct. 1792, in M. T. Davis (ed.), *The London Corresponding Society, 1792–1799*, 6 vols (London, 2002), vi, pp. 69–70.

70 NRS, Court of Justiciary Papers, JC27/102, Bundle 1, Item 2, William Camage, Sheffield, to William Skirving, 17 Apr. 1793; Item 12, same to same, 27 May 1793. The latter referred to a communication from the Edinburgh Friends of the People of 10 May, which had contained a copy of the radical paper, the *Caledonian Chronicle*, in which the resolutions of the recent second general convention of delegates from the various Scottish societies of the Friends of the People had been published.

71 NRS, RH2/4/209, ff. 27, 31.

72 NRS, RH2/4/209, ff. 32.

73 The letter is reproduced in full in Hughes, 'The Scottish Reform Movement and Charles Grey', 33–7.

74 P. Beresford Ellis and S. Mac a'Ghobhainn, *The Scottish Insurrection of 1820* (Edinburgh, 2001), pp. 56, 299–300.

75 Allan I. Macinnes, *Union and Empire: The Making of the United Kingdom in 1707* (Cambridge, 2007).

76 John Barrell, *Imagining the King's Death: Figurative Treason, Fantasies of Regicide 1793–1796* (Oxford, 2000), pp. 252–84.

77 Harris, 'Scottish–English connections', p. 200.

78 They were Maurice Margarot and Joseph Gerrald from the LCS; Charles Sinclair from the SCI; and Matthew Campbell Brown from the Sheffield Society for Constitutional Information. The SCI also elected Henry Redhead Yorke as a delegate but he did not travel to Edinburgh. During the convention, Brown was adopted as a delegate by the Leeds Constitutional Society and Margarot by the United Societies at Norwich.

79 TNA, TS 11/966.

80 TNA, HO 102/9, ff. 100–1, William Scott to Robert Dundas, Edinburgh, 31 Oct. 1793.

81 The *Edinburgh Herald* helpfully identified the occupations of the majority of delegates in its issues for 2 and 7 Dec. 1793.

82 TNA, HO 102/9, f. 182r.

83 TNA, HO 102/9, f. 175v.

84 The United Irishmen, Simon Butler and Archibald Hamilton Rowan, were present in Edinburgh in November impressing on the Edinburgh radicals the parlous condition of liberty in Ireland.

85 NRS, JC27/102, bundle 1, item 22, letter from Calder, Cromarty, to William Skirving, 4 Sept. 1793; NRS, RH2/4/73, ff. 192–5, report from 'J.B.', 15 Nov. 1793, which reported that Sinclair and one other London delegate had gone to Glasgow, Perth, Dundee and Montrose.

86 NRS, RH2/4/73, f. 214 v, report from 'J.B.', 22 Nov. 1793.

87 NRS, JC27/102, loose papers, 'Hints on the Question of Union suggested by Class No. 3'.

88 *An Account of the Proceedings of the British Convention: Held in Edinburgh, the 19th of November, 1793. By a Member* (London, 1793), p. 17.

89 *An Account*, p. 21.

90 TNA, TS11/965/3510A(3), document entitled 'Report on Sedition', which includes evidence drawn from spy reports on Thelwall's lectures.

91 John Barrell, '11 May 1794', *Bodleian Library Record*, 24 (2011), 19–24.

92 Mary Thale (ed.), *Selections from the Papers of the London Corresponding Society 1792–1799* (Cambridge, 1983), p. 177.

93 Harris, *The Scottish People*, p. 104.

94 NRS, Paisley Sheriff Court Processes, SC58/22/95, 19 May 1794, precognition for sedition. This is filed out of place, in a bundle of processes from 1801, which may explain why it has not hitherto come to light.

95 Perth and Kinross Council Archives, B59/32/109, declarations of William Wedderspoon and David Buist relative to some persons writing on the bridge, 24 Apr. 1794.

96 NRS, Graham of Fintry Papers, GD151/11/2, Susan Bean to Robert Graham of Fintry, 30 Jan. 1794.

97 Harris, *The Scottish People*, p. 105.

98 NRS, RH 2/4/86, f. 283, William McDowall to Robert Dundas, 6 Nov. 1800.

99 *Morning Chronicle*, 16 Mar. 1795. Amelia Alderson met Charles Sinclair in Daniel Isaac Eaton's bookshop in early 1794. Sinclair claimed that Daer had absented himself from the final stages of the British Convention, thereby avoiding arrest, at the request of his mother and sisters. He also suggested that it was Daer's social rank that had protected him from prosecution. Sinclair, who was critical of what he thought was Daer's failure of political nerve, did acknowledge that 'Lord D. is supposed to be dying'. It is hard to know what credence to give to Sinclair's comments, not least because the abandonment of his trial at Edinburgh led to his being suspected of being a government informant. Daer was also indeed very ill by this stage. Celia Lucy Brightwell, *Memorials of the Life of Amelia Opie* (2nd edn, Norwich, 1854), pp. 43–4.

100 TNA, TS 11/962, ff. 176–7, copy of letter from William Skirving, on the *Surprise* transport, 17 Apr. 1794.

Conclusion

1 National Records of Scotland, Hall of Dunglass Papers, GD206/2/300/58, James Hall of Dunglass to Sir William Hall, 21 Aug. 1794, where the author notes: 'I have been for a week [in Edinburgh] along with Ld Daer who is preparing to go abroad for his health.' Three days later he wrote to the same correspondent: 'Will lie in town till Daer sets out which may be in a week' (GD206/2/300/59).

2 Roy Porter, *Doctor of Society: Thomas Beddoes and the Sick Trade in Late-Enlightenment England* (London, 1992), p. 5, where Porter writes 'he is, was, in every important respect, a central late-Enlightenment figure [. . .]'

3 Dorothy A. Stansfield and Ronald G. Stansfield, 'Dr Thomas Beddoes and James Watt: Preparatory Work 1794–96 for the Bristol Pneumatic Institute', *Medical History*, 30 (1986), 276–302; Trevor H. Levere, 'Dr Thomas Beddoes: Chemistry, Medicine and the Perils of Democracy', *Notes & Records of the Royal Society*, 63 (2009), 215–29.

4 Jan Golinski, *Science as Public Culture: Chemistry and Enlightenment in Britain, 1760–1820* (Cambridge, 1992), p. 159; Larry Stewart, 'His Majesty's Subjects: From Laboratory to Human Experiment in Pneumatic Chemistry', *Notes & Records of the Royal Society*, 63 (2009), 232.

5 Golinski, *Science as Public Culture*, pp. 155–6.

6 Larry Stewart, 'His Majesty's Subjects', 233.

7 Birmingham Central Library [hereafter BCL], Watt Papers, MS3219/4/27, James Watt to Thomas Percival, 24 Nov. 1794; Thomas Henry, Manchester, to James Watt, 16 Apr. 1795; MS3219/4/29, James Watt to John Ferriar, 19 Dec. 1794.

8 BCL, MS3219/4/27, James Lind to James Watt, Windsor, 20 Feb. 1795.

9 BCL, MS3219/4/27, Beddoes to Watt, 5 Nov. 1794. For Thornton, see Martin Kemp, 'Thornton, Robert John (1768–1837)', *Oxford Dictionary of National Biography*, Oxford University Press, 2004 [http://www.oxforddnb/view/article/27361, accessed 6 Feb. 2015].

10 Beddoes, *Observations on the Nature and Cure of Calculus, Sea Scurvy, Consumption, Catarrh, and Fever: Together with Conjectures on Several Other Subjects of Physiology and Pathology* (London, 1793), p. iv, quoted in Golinski, *Science as Public Culture*, p. 158.

11 Quoted in Dorothy A. Stansfield, *Thomas Beddoes M.D. 1760–1808* (Dordrecht, 1984), p. 23.

12 On which, see esp. Levere, 'Dr Thomas Beddoes: Chemistry, Medicine, and the Perils of Democracy'.

13 The subscribers are listed at the end of Thomas Beddoes and James Watt, *Medical Cases and Speculations; Including Parts IV and V of Considerations on the Medicinal Powers, and the Productions of Factitious Airs* (Bristol and London, 1796).

14 For which, see BCL, MS3219/4/27, Thomas Beddoes to James Watt, Clifton, Oct. 1794, where Beddoes writes: 'I said to him [i.e. Daer] "You have received a letter from James Watt Junior." He said "Yes" but neither mentioned the contents to me nor Dr <Home?>.' The Dr Home referred to may well be Dr Francis Home, the first Edinburgh Professor of Materia Medica.

15 Helen Bynum, *Spitting Blood: The History of Tuberculosis* (Oxford, 2012), pp. xxii–xxiii.

16 Beddoes, *Essay on the Causes, Early Signs, and Prevention of Pulmonary Consumption, For the Use of Parents and Preceptors* (Bristol and London, 1799), pp. 1–6.

17 *The Collected Letters of Erasmus Darwin*, ed. Desmond King-Hele (Cambridge, 2007), pp. 413–15, Erasmus Darwin to Thomas Beddoes, 17 Jan. 1793.

18 *Collected Letters of Erasmus Darwin*, ed. King-Hele, pp. 424–5, 426–7, 431–2, 434–5, 436–7, 437–8, 439.

19 It may be that this coyness was induced by his writing to Jessie's mother, Ann (ibid., pp. 431–2).

20 *Partners in Science: Letters of James Watt and Joseph Black*, ed. Eric Robinson and Douglas McKie (London, 1970), pp. 203–4, Letter 144, Watt to Black, Birmingham, 9 June 1794.

21 BCL, MS3219/4/27, Thomas Beddoes to James Watt, Clifton, 14 Oct. 1794.

22 BCL, MS3219/4/27, same to same, 24 Oct. 1794.

23 BCL, MS3219/4/27, same to same, Oct. 1794 [no day given, but certainly after 24 Oct.].

24 BCL, MS3219/4/27, same to same, 9 Jan. 1795; same to same, 20 May 1795.

25 National Records of Scotland, GD206/2/300/61.

26 William McCarthy, *Anna Letitia Barbauld: Voice of the Enlightenment* (Baltimore, MA, 2008), p. 185.

27 McCarthy, *Anna Letitia Barbauld*, p. 171.

28 John Robertson, 'The Scottish Contribution to the Enlightenment', in Paul Wood (ed.), *The Scottish Enlightenment: Essays in Reinterpretation* (Rochester, NY, 2000), pp. 37–62.

29 Henry Roscoe, *The Life of William Roscoe*, 2 vols (London and Edinburgh, 1833), i, p. 113.

30 British Library, Letters of Charles Babbage, Add MS 37183, f. 72.

31 *The Bee, Or Literary Weekly Intelligencer, Consisting of Original Pieces, and Selections from Performances of Merit, Foreign and Domestic. A Work Calculated to Disseminate Useful Knowledge Among All Ranks of People at a Small Expence. By James Anderson*, 13: 112 (1793), p. 142.

32 Linda Colley, *Britons: Forging the Nation 1707–1837* (London and New York, 1992).

33 Alvin Jackson, *The Two Unions: Ireland, Scotland, and the Survival of the United Kingdom, 1707–2007* (Oxford, 2012).

Bibliography

MANUSCRIPT SOURCES

Advocates Library, Edinburgh
Court of Session Papers

Ayrshire Archives, Auchencruive
Hunter Blair of Blairquhan Papers

Birmingham Central Library
James Watt Papers

Blair Castle
Atholl Papers

British Library
Add MSS 38595, Minutes of the Westminster Committee
Add MSS 64814, Minute Book of the Revolution Society, 1788–91
Francis Place Papers
Letters of Charles Babbage

Dr Williams's Library, London
D W L MSS 24: 157, Correspondence of James Wodrow and William Kenrick

Edinburgh City Archives
Edinburgh Town Council Minutes
McLeod Collection
Convention of Royal Burghs, Moses Collection
SL217/1&2, Sederunt Books of the Commissioners for Lighting, 1785–1810
Treasurers' Account Books

Edinburgh Central Library

YML 28A G36159 *Notes from the Records of the Assembly Rooms of Edinburgh* (1842)
B18749, Regulations for George's Square Assemblies, Anno 1785
DA 1861.789, Journal of Andrew Armstrong, 1789–93

Ewart Library, Dumfries

R. C. Reid Collection, vol. 179, Memorandum of a Journey into Scotland, June 1800
Minutes of the Wigtown Road Trustees

Hornel Library, Broughton House, Kirkcudbright

Catalogue of Books Belonging to the Library at Kirkcudbright (Kirkcudbright, 1824)
Samuel Cavan, 'Lecture on Kirkcudbright in the Eighteenth Century, 17 Mar. 1885'
Minute Book of the New Building Society
Revenue and Expenditure of the Burgh of Kirkcudbright for the Year Ending 31 Oct. 1815

Huntingdon Library, California

William Pulteney Papers

The National Archives, Kew

Treasury Solicitor's Papers

National Library of Ireland, Dublin

MSS 10,713.3, Letters from John and Ann Jebb to John Forbes
MSS 2251, Letters from John Cartwright and John Jebb to John Forbes

National Library of Scotland

Acc 5779, Reminiscences of Edinburgh 60 Years Ago (1794), by John Howell (1854)
Acc 10,000/2&3, Minutes of the Royal Society of Edinburgh
MS 196, Minutes of the Monthly Club
MS 1567, Papers Relating to a Claim of Joseph Mason, carpenter of Wiltshire and student of medicine at the University for [. . .] Damages Arising from Disturbances at the Theatre Royal, 1794
MS 1955, Proposals for Keeping the Streets, Lanes & Passages of Edinburgh Neat & Clean by Voluntary Subscription, n.d. but prob. mid-1730s
MS 3288, Miscellaneous Letters
MS 3771, George Strickland, 'Notes on Political Oeconomy From Prof: Stewart's Lectures at Edinburgh from Nov.r 1803 to April 1804'
MS 3108, Nathaniel Wraxall, Diary of a Tour into Scotland, 12 July–27 Sept. 1813
MS 6329–23, Travel Diaries of Sir James Hall of Dunglass, 1791
MS 17602, Saltoun Papers

National Records of Scotland

Commissary Court Records
CC13, Kirkcudbright

Court of Session Papers

CS96, Productions of Processes
CS235/B/12/7, Alexander Birtwhistle v. Lord Daer, 1791
Dundee Corporations v. Dundee Magistrates, 1759–61

Court of Justiciary Papers

JC27/102, Papers of William Skirving, tried for sedition on 6–7 Jan. 1794

Sheriff Court Records

SC58 Paisley Sheriff Court

Exchequer Records

E326/4/4, Shop Tax Records, Royal Burghs, 1786–7
E326/4/8, Shop Tax Records, Royal Burghs, 1788–9
E326/8/4, Carriage Tax, Royal Burghs, 1786–7
E326/5/8, Male Servants' Tax, Royal Burghs, 1786–7
E326/3/63, Inhabited House Tax, Royal Burghs, 1786–7

Gifts and Deposits

GD22, Graham of Gartmore Papers
GD26, Leven and Melville Papers
GD51, Melville Papers
GD113, Innes of Stow Papers
GD150, Morton Papers
GD151, Graham of Fintry Papers
GD206, Hall of Dunglass Papers
GD224, Buccleuch Papers
GD267, Home of Wedderburn Papers

Other

RH2/4, Home Office Papers (Scotland)
Burgh Register of Sasines, Kirkcudbright, vol. 1

Perth and Kinross Council Archives, Perth

B59, Perth Burgh Records

Shropshire Archives

Diary of Katherine Plymley

Stewartry Museum, Kirkcudbright

Burgh Court Papers
Kirkcudbright Town Council Minutes

University of Edinburgh, Special Collections

Correspondence of Joseph Black
DC.4.97, Archibald Bell, 'Lectures on Moral Philosophy by Dugald Stewart Esq. Delivered at the University of Edinburgh in the Years 1793–4'

Dc. 5.126, Minutes of the Poker Club, 1774–84

Dc.8.178, 8, Dugald Stewart, Tours in England and Scotland, 1797–1803

MS Gen 1736, Material Relating to the Earl of Buchan

MS Gen 2023, Josiah Walker, 'Abbreviations from Lectures on Moral Philosophy Delivered by Dugald Stewart Professor of Mathematics in the University of Edinburgh, 1778/9'

Laing Collection

Speculative Society Minute Books

University of Keele

Wedgwood Archives

University of Southampton, Special Collections

Broadlands Papers

University of Toronto

Dempster Letters, 1777–1854

PRINTED PRIMARY SOURCES

Adam, Charles, *View of the Political State of Scotland in the Last Century: A Confidential Report on the Political Opinions, Family Connections, or Personal Circumstances of the 2662 Voters in 1788* (Edinburgh, 1887)

An Account of the Proceedings of the British Convention: Held in Edinburgh, the 19th of November, 1793. By a Member (London, 1793)

The Adams–Jefferson Letters: The Complete Correspondence between Thomas Jefferson and Abigail and John Adams, ed. Lester J. Capper (New York, 1971)

Aikin, Lucy (ed.), *The Works of Anna Letitia Barbauld. With a Memoir by Lucy Aikin*, 2 vols. (London, 1825)

Arnot, Hugo, *The History of Edinburgh* (Edinburgh, 1779)

Aulart, F. A., *Recueil de documents pour l'histoire du club des Jacobins de Paris, Vol II* (Paris, 1891)

Beddoes, Thomas, *Essay on the Causes, Early Signs, and Prevention of Pulmonary Consumption, For the Use of Parents and Preceptors* (Bristol and London, 1799)

Beddoes, Thomas and Watt, James, *Medical Cases and Speculations: Including Parts IV and V of Considerations on the Medicinal Powers, and the Productions of Factitious Airs* (Bristol and London, 1796)

Boswell: *The Applause of the Jury, 1782-1785*, ed. Irma S. Lustig and Frederick A. Pottle (London, 1981)

Boswell's Edinburgh Journals, 1767–1786, ed. Hugh M. Milne (Edinburgh, 2001)

Boswell, James, *A Letter to the People of Scotland, on the Alarming Attempt to Infringe on the Articles of Union and Introduce a Most Pernicious Innovation, by Diminishing the Number of Lords of Session* (London, 1785)

Brewster, David, *Edinburgh Encyclopedia*, 18 vols (Edinburgh, 1814–30)

Carr, John, *Caledonian Sketches* (London, 1809)

Cartwright, John, *A Letter to the Duke of Newcastle [. . .] respecting his Grace's Conduct in the Disposal of Commissions in the Militia; Together with Some Remarks Touching the French Revolution, a Reform of Parliament in Great Britain, and the Royal Proclamation of 21st of May* (London, 1792)

Catalogue of Books Belonging to the Library at Kirkcudbright (Kirkcudbright, 1824)

Cockburn, Henry, *Memorials of his Time* (Edinburgh, 1856)

The Collected Letters of Erasmus Darwin, ed. Desmond King-Hele (Cambridge, 2007)

The Collected Works of Dugald Stewart, ed. William Hamilton, 10 vols (Edinburgh, 1854–60)

A Collection of the Letters which have been Addressed to the Volunteers of Ireland, on the Subject of Parliamentary Reform, by the Earl of Effingham, Doctor Price, Major Cartwright, Doctor Jebb, and the Rev. Mr Wyvill (London, 1783)

The Correspondence of Joseph Black, ed. Robert G. W. Anderson and Jean Jones, 2 vols (Farnham, 2012)

Currie, James, *The Works of Robert Burns; With an Account of his Life, and a Criticism on His Writings*, 4 vols (Montrose, 1816)

A Declaration of Rights and An Address to the People. Approved by a Number of the Friends of Reform in Paisley, n.d., but prob. late 1792 or early 1793

The Despatches of Earl Gower, English Ambassador at Paris from June 1790 to August 1792, ed. Oscar Browning (Cambridge, 1885)

A Diary of the French Revolution by Gouverneur Morris 1752–1816: Minister to France during the Terror, ed. Beatrice Cary Davenport, 2 vols (London, 1939)

A Directory for Edinburgh, Leith and Dalkeith: Containing the Names and Places of Abodes of Public & Private Gentlemen [. . .] By Thomas Aitchison (Edinburgh, 1794)

Douglas, Basil William, Lord Daer, *The Right of the Eldest Sons of Peers to Represent the Commons of that Part of Great Britain in Parliamentary, Considered* (Edinburgh, 1790)

Douglas, Thomas, fifth earl of Selkirk, *Observations on the Present State of the Highlands of Scotland, with a View of the Causes and Probable Consequences of Emigration* (Edinburgh, 1805)

English Witnesses of the French Revolution, ed. J. M. Thompson (Oxford, 1938)

Extracts from the Records of the Burgh of Edinburgh 1665–1680, ed. Marguerite Wood (Edinburgh and London, 1950)

Extracts from the Records of Edinburgh 1701–1718, ed. Helen Armet (Edinburgh and London, 1967)

Gardenstone, Lord, *Letter to the People of Laurencekirk* (Edinburgh, 1780)

A General History of Stirling (Stirling, 1794)

General Heads of a Plan for a New Prison and Bridewell in the City of Edinburgh, Offered to the Consideration of the Public (Edinburgh, 1782)

Gilbert, Thomas, *Plan for the Better Relief and Employment of the Poor* (London, 1781)

Ginter, Donald E., *Whig Organization in the General Election of 1790: Selections from the Blair Adam Papers* (Cambridge, 1967)

Heron, Robert, *Observations Made in a Journey through the Western Counties of Scotland in the Autumn of 1792*, 2 vols (Perth, 1793)

Hughes, Edward, 'The Scottish Reform Movement and Charles Grey 1792–94: Some Fresh Correspondence', *Scottish Historical Review*, 35 (1956), 26–41

Hume, David, *Essays, Moral, Political and Literary. Part II* (London, 1752)

Johnson, J., *A Guide for Gentlemen Studying Medicine at the University of Edinburgh* (London and Edinburgh, 1792)

Kippis, Andrew, *A Sermon Preached at the Old Jewry [. . .] On Occasion of a New Academical Institution, among Protestant Dissenters, for the Education of Their Ministers and Youth* (London, 1786)

Letter from an Old Freeholder to his Fellow Freeholders. Refuting the Principles of the Bill Approved by the Meeting of Delegates Held at Edinburgh, in December Last, for Regulating the County Election Laws in Scotland (Edinburgh, 1793)

The London Corresponding Society, 1792–1799, ed. Michael T. Davis, 6 vols (London, 2002)

Lunardi, Vincent, *An Account of Five Aerial Voyages in Scotland. With an Introduction by Alexander Law* (Edinburgh, 1976)

Macleod, Innes, *Sailing on Horseback: William Daniell and Richard Ayton in Cumbria and Dumfries and Galloway* (Dumfries, 1988)

Malthus, T. R., *A Letter to Samuel Whitbread, Esq. M.P., on his Proposed Bill for the Amendment of the Poor Laws* (London, 1807)

M'Farlan, John, *Inquiries Concerning the Poor* (Edinburgh, 1782)

M'Farlan, John, *Tracts on Subjects of National Importance* (Edinburgh, 1786)

Miller, Samuel, *Memoir of the Rev. Charles Nisbet D.D.; Late President of Dickenson College* (New York, 1840)

A New Guide to the City of Edinburgh (Edinburgh, 1790)

Notes from the Records of the Assembly Rooms of Edinburgh (1842)

Oldfield, T., *History of the Original Constitution of Parliaments, from the Time of the Britons to the Present Day [. . .] to which is Added the Present State of Representation* (London, 1797)

The Papers of Thomas Jefferson, Vol. 15, 27 Mar. 1789–30 Nov. 1789, ed. Julian P. Boyd (Princeton, NJ, 1958)

The Papers of Thomas Jefferson, Vol. 20, 1 April–4 August 1791, ed. Julian P. Boyd (Princeton, NJ, 1982)

Parliamentary Papers, First Report from the Committee on the Highways of the Kingdom, 1807–12; 1808

Partners in Science: Letters of James Watt and Joseph Black, ed. Eric Robinson and Douglas McKie (London, 1970)

The Political Theory of Condorcet II, ed. Fiona Sommerlad and Iain McLean, University of Oxford, Social Studies Faculty Centre, Working Paper (Oxford, 1991)

Porteous, William, *A Letter to the Citizens of Glasgow, Containing a Short View of the Management of the Poors Funds, Under the Administration of the General Session* (Glasgow, 1783)

Priestley, Joseph, *Miscellaneous Observations Relating to Education* (Cork, 1780)

Priestley, Joseph, *Lectures on History and General Policy: To which is Prefixed, An Essay on a Course of Liberal Education for a Civil and Active Life* (Birmingham, 1788)

Priestley, Joseph, *The Proper Objects of Education in the Present State of the World: Presented in a Discourse, Delivered on Wednesday, the 27th of April, 1791, at the Meeting House in the Old Jewry, London; to the Supporters of the New College at Hackney* (London, 1791)

Proceedings of the Friends of the Liberty of the Press (London, 1793)

Proceedings of the Society of the Friends of the People; Associated for the Purpose of Obtaining a Parliamentary Reform, in the Year 1792 (London, 1793)

Reinhard, Marcel, 'Le Voyage de Pétion à Londres 24 Octobre–11 Novembre 1791', *Revue d'histoire diplomatique*, 84 (1970), 1–60

Robberds, John Warden, *A Memoir of the Life and Writings of the Late William Taylor*, 2 vols (London, 1843)

Roscoe, Henry, *The Life of William Roscoe*, 2 vols (London, 1833)

Saltoun, earl of, *Thoughts on the Disqualification of the Eldest Sons of the Peers of Scotland, to Elect, or to be Elected from that Country to Parliament* (London, 1788)

Skrine, Henry, *Three Successive Tours in the North of England, and Great Part of Scotland* (London, 1795)

Smith, Samuel, *General View of the Agriculture of Galloway: Comprehending Two Counties, viz. the Stewartry of Kirkcudbright and Wigtownshire* (1813)

[Society for Constitutional Information] *An Address to the Public from the Society for Constitutional Information* (London, 1780)

[Society for Constitutional Information] *Constitutional Tracts*, 2 vols (London, 1783)

[Society for Constitutional Information] *At a Meeting of the Society for Constitutional Information [. . .] on Friday, January 14th 1785 … A Third Address from the Society for Constitutional Information to the People of Great Britain and Ireland* (London, 1785)

Southwark Friends of the People. At a Meeting of the General Committee Holden Oct. 2, 1792 at the Three Tuns Tavern (London, 1792)

Speech of the Earl of Buchan in which His Lordship Proposes a Plan for the Better Regulation of the Peerage of Scotland (Edinburgh, 1780)

The Statistical Accounts of Scotland, 1791–99

Taylor, William (ed.), *The Collected Works of Frank Sayers* (London, 1823)

Thale, Mary (ed.), *Selections from the Papers of the London Corresponding Society 1792–1799* (Cambridge, 1983)

To the Highlands in 1786: The Inquisitive Journey of a Young French Aristocrat, ed. Norman Scarfe (Woodbridge, 2001)

Tod, T., *Observations on Dr M'Farlan's Inquiries Concerning the State of the Poor* (Edinburgh, 1783)

Webster, James, *General View of the Agriculture of Galloway, Comprehending the Stewartry of Kirkcudbright and Shire of Wigton* (Edinburgh, 1794)

Wilde, John, *An Address to the Lately Formed Society of the Friends of the People. By John Wilde, Esq., Advocate, Fellow of the Royal Society, and Professor of Civil Law in the University of Edinburgh* (Edinburgh and London, 1793)

Williamson's Directory for the City of Edinburgh, Canongate, Leith and Suburbs: From June 1780 to June 1781 (Edinburgh, 1780)

The Works of Adam Smith, LLD, with an Account of his Life and Writings by D. Stewart, 5 vols (London, 1811)

Wyvill, Christopher, *Wyvill Papers*, 6 vols (York, 1794–1806)

NEWSPAPERS AND PERIODICALS

Aberdeen Journal
[Anderson, James], *The Bee, or Literary Weekly Intelligencer*
Caledonian Mercury
The Derby Mercury
Edinburgh Advertiser
Edinburgh Evening Courant
Edinburgh Herald
Farmers' Magazine
Gazetteer and New Daily Advertiser
Glasgow Courier
Manchester Herald

Morning Chronicle
Morning Post
Public Advertiser
Scots Magazine
The Star

SECONDARY SOURCES

Adams, I. H. 'The Agents of Agricultural Change', in M. L. Parry and T. R. Slater (eds), *The Making of the Scottish Countryside* (London, 1980), pp. 155–75

Allan, David, 'Provincial Readers and Book Culture in the Scottish Enlightenment: The Perth Library, *c.* 1784–1800', *The Library*, 4 (2002), 367–89

Allan, David, *A Nation of Readers: The Lending Library in Georgian England* (London, 2008)

Anderson, Alex D., 'The Development of the Road System in the Stewartry of Kirkcudbright, 1590–1890', *Transactions of the Dumfriesshire and Galloway Natural History Society*, ser. III, 44 (1967), 205–22

Anderson, Robert D., Lynch, Michael and Phillipson, Nicholas, *The University of Edinburgh: An Illustrated Guide* (Edinburgh, 2003)

Anhert, Thomas, *The Moral Culture of the Scottish Enlightenment, c. 1690–1805* (New Haven and London, 2014)

Baker, Keith Michael, *Condorcet: From Natural Philosophy to Social Mathematics* (Chicago, IL and London, 1975)

Barrell, John, *Imagining the King's Death: Figurative Treason, Fantasies of Regicide 1793–1796* (Oxford, 2000)

Barrell, John, '11 May 1794', *Bodleian Library Record*, 24 (2011), 19–24

Bell, Dorothy, *Edinburgh Old Town: The Forgotten Nature of Urban Form* (Edinburgh, 2008)

Bennett, R. J., *Local Business Voice: The History of the Chambers of Commerce in Britain, Ireland, and Revolutionary America, 1760–2011* (Oxford, 2011)

Beresford Ellis, P. and Mac a'Ghobhainn, S., *The Scottish Insurrection of 1820* (Edinburgh, 2001)

Berry, Christopher J., *The Idea of Commercial Society in the Scottish Enlightenment* (Edinburgh, 2013)

Bickham, Troy O., *Making Headlines: The American Revolution as Seen Through the British Press* (De Kalb, IL, 2009)

Bonnyman, Brian, *The Third Duke of Buccleuch and Adam Smith: Estate Management and Improvement in Enlightenment Scotland* (Edinburgh, 2014)

Bow, Charles Bradford, 'In Defence of the Scottish Enlightenment: Dugald Stewart's Role in the 1805 John Leslie Affair', *Scottish Historical Review*, 92 (2013), 123–46

Brims, John, 'From Reformers to "Jacobins": The Scottish Association of the Friends of the People', in T. M. Devine (ed.), *Conflict and Stability in Scottish Society* (Edinburgh, 1991), pp. 31–50

Brown, David J., 'The Government of Scotland under Henry Dundas and William Pitt', *History*, 83 (1989), 264–79

Brown, Keith M., *Noble Society in Scotland: Wealth, Family and Culture from Reformation to Revolution* (Edinburgh, 2000)

Brown, Michael, 'Dugald Stewart and the Problem of Teaching Politics in the 1790s', *Journal of Irish and Scottish Studies*, 1 (2007), 89–126

Brown, Michael, 'A Scottish Literati in Paris: The Case of Sir James Hall', *Journal of Irish and Scottish Studies*, 2 (2008), 73–100

Brown, Stephen and McDougall, Warren (eds), *The Edinburgh History of the Book in Scotland, Vol. 2, Enlightenment and Expansion, 1707–1800* (Edinburgh, 2011)

Bumsted, J. M., *Lord Selkirk: A Life* (East Lansing, MI, 2009)

Burley, Peter, *Witness to the Revolution: American and British Commentators in France 1788–94* (London, 1989)

Bynum, Helen, *Spitting Blood: The History of Tuberculosis* (Oxford, 2012)

Cahen, Léon, *Condorcet et La Révolution Française* (Paris, 1904)

Campbell, R. H., 'The Enlightenment and the Economy', in R. H. Campbell and A. S. Skinner (eds), *The Origins and Nature of the Scottish Enlightenment* (Edinburgh, 1982), pp. 8–25

Campbell, R. H., 'The Landed Classes', in T. M. Devine and R. Mitchison (eds), *People and Society in Scotland, Vol. 1, 1760–1830* (Edinburgh, 1988), pp. 91–108

Cannon, John, *Aristocratic Century: The Peerage of Eighteenth Century England* (Cambridge, 1987)

Carr, Rosalind, *Gender and Enlightenment Culture in Eighteenth-Century Scotland* (Edinburgh, 2014)

Chandler, David, '"The Athens of England": Norwich as a Literary Centre in the Late Eighteenth Century', *Eighteenth Century Studies*, 43 (2010), 171–92

Christie, I. R., *Wilkes, Wyvill and Reform: The Parliamentary Reform Movement in British Politics 1760–1785* (London, 1962)

Colley, Linda, *Britons: Forging the Nation 1707–1837* (London and New York, 1992)

Connolly, S. J., *Divided Kingdom: Ireland 1630–1800* (Oxford, 2008)

Cowan, Edward J., 'Agricultural Improvement and the Formation of Early Agricultural Societies in Dumfries and Galloway', *Transactions of the Dumfriesshire and Galloway Natural History and Antiquarian Society*, ser. III, 53 (1977–8), 157–67

Cumming, I., 'The Scottish Education of James Mill', *History of Education Quarterly*, 2 (1962), 152–67

Darnton, Robert, *The Forbidden Bestsellers of Pre-Revolutionary France* (New York and London, 1995)

Darnton, Robert, *The Devil in the Holy Water, or the Art of Slander from Louis XIV to Napoleon* (Philadelphia, PA, 2009)

Devine, T. M., 'The Great Landlords of Lowland Scotland and Agrarian Change in the Eighteenth Century', in T. M. Devine (ed.), *Clearance and Improvement: Land, Power, and People in Scotland 1700–1900* (London, 1980), pp. 42–53

Devine, T. M., *The Transformation of Rural Scotland: Social Change and the Agrarian Economy 1660–1815* (Edinburgh, 1994)

Devine, T. M., *To the Ends of the Earth: Scotland's Global Diaspora 1750–2010* (London, 2012)

Dewispelare, Daniel John, 'Spectacular Speech: Performing Language in the Late Eighteenth Century', *Journal of British Studies*, 51 (2012), 858–82

Dinwiddy, John, 'Conceptions of Revolution in the English Radicalism of the 1790s', in Eckhart Hellmuth (ed.), *The Transformation of Political Culture: England and Germany in the Later Eighteenth Century* (Oxford, 1990), pp. 535–60

Ditchfield, Grayson, 'The Scottish Representative Peers and Parliamentary Politics 1787–1793', *Scottish Historical Review*, 60 (1981), 14–31

Ditchfield, Grayson, '"How Narrow the Limits of Toleration Appear": Dissenting Petitions to

Parliament, 1771–1773', in Stephen Taylor and David L. Wykes (eds), *Parliament and Dissent* (Edinburgh, 2005), pp. 91–106

Donovan, R. K., *No Popery and Radicalism: Opposition to Roman Catholic Relief in Scotland, 1778–1782* (New York, 1987)

Doyle, William, *Aristocracy and its Enemies in the Age of Revolution* (Oxford, 2009)

Eddy, M. D., 'The University of Edinburgh Natural History Class Lists, 1782–1800', *Archives of Natural History*, 30 (2003), 97–117

Elder, Rev. George Ogilvy, *Kirkcudbright: The Story of an Ancient Royal Burgh* (Castle Douglas, 1898)

Emerson, Roger L., *An Enlightened Duke: The Life of Archibald Campbell (1682–1761), Earl of Ilay, 3rd Duke of Argyll* (Kilkerran, 2013)

Emerson, Roger, 'Overseas Contacts and Influences: The Shaping of the Scottish Enlightenment, 1730–1790' (unpublished paper)

Epstein, James, *Scandal of Colonial Rule: Power and Subversion in the British Atlantic during the Age of Revolution* (Cambridge, 2012)

Erdman, David V., *Commerce des Lumières: John Oswald and the British in Paris, 1790–1793* (Columbia, NY, 1986)

Eyles, V. A., 'The Evolution of a Chemist', *Annals of Science*, 19 (1963), 153–82

Fagerstrom, D. F., 'Scotland and the American Revolution', *William and Mary Quarterly*, 11 (1954), 252–75

Fenton, Alexander and Walker, Bruce, *The Rural Architecture of Scotland* (Edinburgh, 1981)

Fergusson, James, *The Sixteen Peers of Scotland: An Account of the Elections of the Representative Peers of Scotland, 1707–1959* (Oxford, 1960)

Fergusson, Sir James, *Balloon Tytler* (London, 1972)

Ferguson, William, 'Dingwall Politics and the Parliamentary Franchise in the Eighteenth Century', *Scottish Historical Review*, 38 (1959), 89–108

Ferguson, William, 'The Electoral System in the Scottish Counties before 1832', in D. Sellar (ed.), *The Stair Society Miscellany II*, Stair Society Publications, 35 (Edinburgh, 1984), pp. 261–94

Fletcher, Anthony, *Gender, Sex, and Subordination in England, 1500–1800* (London, 1995)

Fitzpatrick, Martin, 'Heretical Religion and Radical Politics', in Eckhart Hellmuth (ed.), *The Transformation of Political Culture: England and Germany in the Later Eighteenth Century* (Oxford, 1990), pp. 339–72

Gardner, Victoria, 'Newspaper Proprietors and the Business of Newspaper Publishing in Provincial England 1760–1820', unpublished DPhil thesis, University of Oxford, 2008

Golinski, Jan, *Science as Public Culture: Chemistry and the Enlightenment in Britain, 1760–1820* (Cambridge, 1982)

Goodwin, Albert, *The Friends of Liberty: The English Democratic Movement in the Age of the French Revolution* (London, 1979)

Guest, Harriet, *Small Change: Women, Learning and Patriotism, 1750–1810* (Chicago, IL, 2000)

Guest, Harriet, *Unbounded Attachment: Sentiment and Politics in the Age of the French Revolution* (Oxford, 2013)

Harris, Bob, *Politics and the Rise of the Press: Britain and France 1620–1800* (London, 1996)

Harris, Bob, 'Political Protests in the Year of Liberty', in Bob Harris (ed.), *Scotland in the Age of the French Revolution* (Edinburgh, 2005), pp. 50–78

Harris, Bob, 'Scotland's Newspapers, the French Revolution, and Domestic Radicalism (c. 1789–1794), *Scottish Historical Review*, 84 (2005), 38–62

Harris, Bob, 'Scottish–English Connections in British Radicalism in the 1790s', in T. C. Smout (ed.), *Anglo-Scottish Relations from 1603 to 1900* (Oxford, 2005), pp. 189–212

Harris, Bob, 'Parliamentary Legislation, Lobbying and the Press in Eighteenth-Century Scotland', in Jason Peacey (ed.), *The Print Culture of Parliament 1600–1800* (Edinburgh, 2007), pp. 76–95

Harris, Bob, *The Scottish People and the French Revolution* (London, 2008)

Harris, Bob, 'Towards a British Political Economy: An Eighteenth-Century Scottish Perspective', in Perry Gauci (ed.), *Regulating the British Economy, 1660–1850* (Farnham, 2011), pp. 83–105

Harris, Bob, 'Landowners and Urban Society in Eighteenth Century Scotland', *Scottish Historical Review*, 92 (2014), 231–54

Harris, Bob and McKean, Charles, *The Scottish Town in the Age of the Enlightenment, 1740–1820* (Edinburgh, 2014)

Hartley, Stuart, 'Appealing to Nature: Geology "in the Field" in Late Enlightenment Scotland', in Charles W. J. Withers and Paul Wood (eds), *Science and Medicine in the Scottish Enlightenment* (East Linton, 2002), pp. 280–300

Higgins, Padhraig, *A Nation of Politicians: Gender, Patriotism and Culture in Late Eighteenth Century Ireland* (Madison, WI, 2010)

Hill, C., 'The Mechanics of Overseas Trade: Dumfries and Galloway, 1600–1850', *Transactions of the Dumfriesshire and Galloway Natural History and Antiquarian Society*, ser. III, 80 (2006), 81–104

Horn, D. B., *A Short History of the University of Edinburgh, 1556–1889* (Edinburgh, 1967)

Horne, Thomas A., *Property Rights and Poverty: Political Argument in Britain 1605–1834* (Chapel Hill and London, 1990)

Houston, R. A., *Social Change in the Age of Enlightenment: Edinburgh 1660–1760* (Oxford, 1994)

Innes, Joanna, 'Politics and Morals: The Reformation of Manners Movement in Later Eighteenth Century England', in Eckhart Hellmuth (ed.), *The Transformation of Political Culture: England and Germany in the Later Eighteenth Century* (Oxford, 1990), pp. 57–118

Innes, Joanna, 'Legislating for Three Kingdoms: How the Westminster Parliament Legislated for England, Scotland, and Ireland 1707–1830', in Julian Hoppit (ed.), *Parliaments, Nations, and Identities in Britain and Ireland, 1660–1850* (Manchester, 2003), pp. 15–47

Innes, Joanna, 'The Protestant Carpenter – William Payne of Bell Yard (c. 1718–82): The Life and Times of a London Informing Constable', in Joanna Innes, *Inferior Politics: Social Problems and Social Policies in Eighteenth-Century Britain* (Oxford, 2009), pp. 279–341

Israel, Jonathan, *The Dutch Republic: Its Rise, Greatness and Fall 1477–1806* (Oxford, 1995)

Israel, Jonathan, *Revolutionary Ideas: An Intellectual History of the French Revolution from the 'The Rights of Man' to Robespierre* (Princeton, NJ, 2014)

Jackson, Alvin, *The Two Unions: Ireland, Scotland, and the Survival of the United Kingdom, 1707–2007* (Oxford, 2012)

Jacob, Margaret C., *The First Knowledge Economy: Human Capital and the European Economy, 1750–1850* (Cambridge, 2014)

Jacob, Margaret C. and Stewart, Larry, *Practical Matter: Newton's Science in the Service of Industry and Empire* (Cambridge, MA, 2004)

Jonsson, Fredrik Albritton, *Enlightenment's Frontier: The Scottish Highlands and the Origins of Environmentalism* (New Haven and London, 2013)

Kates, Gary, 'From Liberalism to Radicalism: Tom Paine's *Rights of Man*', *Journal of the History of Ideas*, 50 (1989), 659–87

Kelly, James, 'Parliamentary Reform in Irish Politics, 1760–1790', in David Dickson et al. (eds), *The United Irishmen: Republicanism, Radicalism and Rebellion* (Dublin, 1993), pp. 74–87

Kendall, James, 'The First Chemical Society, the First Chemical Journal and the Chemical Revolution', *Proceedings of the Royal Society of Edinburgh*, 63A (1952), 344–68

Kennedy, Alison, 'Historical Perspectives in the Mind of Joseph Priestley', in Isabel Rivers and David L. Wykes (eds), *Joseph Priestley: Scientist, Philosopher and Theologian* (Oxford, 2008), pp. 172–202

Kitteringham, G., 'Science in Provincial Society: The Case of Liverpool in the Early Nineteenth Century', *Annals of Science*, 39 (1982), 329–48

Knox, W. W., 'The Attack of the "Half-Formed Persons": the 1811–12 Tron Riot in Edinburgh Revisited', *Scottish Historical Review*, 91 (2012), 287–310

Kuboyama, Hisashi, 'The Politics of the People in Glasgow and the West of Scotland, 1707–c.1785', unpublished PhD thesis, University of Edinburgh, 2011

Lang, Andrew Monro, *A Life of George Dempster, Scottish MP of Dunnichen (1732–1818)* (Lewiston, NY and Lampeter, 1998)

Langford, Paul, *A Polite and Commercial People: England 1727–1787* (Oxford, 1989)

Lehmann, W. C., *John Millar of Glasgow, 1735–1801* (Glasgow, 1960)

Lenman, Bruce, *Integration, Enlightenment and Industrialisation: Scotland 1746–1832* (London, 1981)

Levere, Trevor, 'Dr Thomas Beddoes: Chemistry, Medicine, and the Perils of Democracy', *Notes & Records of the Royal Society*, 63 (2009), 215–29

Logue, K. J., *Popular Disturbances in Scotland 1780–1815* (Edinburgh, 1979)

Macinnes, Allan I., *Union and Empire: The Making of the United Kingdom in 1707* (Cambridge, 2007)

Macintyre, Gordon, *Dugald Stewart: The Pride and Ornament of Scotland* (Sussex, 2003)

Mackenzie, Rev. W., *The History of Galloway, from the Earliest Period to the Present Time*, 2 vols (Kirkcudbright, 1841)

Macleod, Emma Vincent, 'The Scottish Opposition Whigs and the French Revolution', in Bob Harris (ed.), *Scotland in the Age of the French Revolution* (Edinburgh, 2005), pp. 79–98

Maitland, Lt-Col C. A. S., *Commissioners of Supply for the Stewartry of Kirkcudbright 1728–1828* (1933)

Marsden, David, 'The Development of Kirkcudbright in the Late 18th Century: Town Planning in a Galloway Context', *Transactions of the Dumfriesshire and Galloway Natural History and Antiquarian Society*, ser. III, 72 (1997), 89–96

Marsden, David, 'The Development of Kirkcudbright in the Early 19th Century by the Emergence of Voluntarism', *Transactions of the Dumfriesshire and Galloway Natural History and Antiquarian Society*, ser. III, 81 (2007), 109–114

Martin, Paula, *Cupar: The History of a Small Town* (Edinburgh, 2005)

Mayhew, Robert J., *Malthus: The Life and Legacies of an Untimely Prophet* (Cambridge, MA and London, 2014)

McCahill, M. W., *The House of Lords in the Age of George III* (Chichester, 2009)

McCarthy, William, 'The Academy at Palgrave: A Documentary History of Anna Letitia Barbauld's School', *The Age of Johnson: A Scholarly Annual*, 8 (1997), 345–67

McCarthy, William, *Anna Letitia Barbauld: Voice of the Enlightenment* (Baltimore, MD, 2008)

McClure, David, *Tolls and Tacksmen* (Ayr, 1994)

McGilvary, George, *East India Patronage and the British State: The Scottish Elite and Politics in the Eighteenth Century* (London, 2008)

McKean, Charles, 'Twinning Cities: Modernization Versus Improvement in the Two Towns of Edinburgh', in Brian Edwards and Paul Jenkins (eds), *Edinburgh: The Making of a Capital City* (Edinburgh, 2005), pp. 42–63

McMahon, Darrin M., 'The Birthplace of the Revolution: Public Space and Political Community in the Palais-Royal of Louis-Philippe-Joseph D'Orléans 1781–1789', *French History*, 10 (1996), 1–29

Mee, Jon, *Conversable Worlds: Literature, Contention and Community 1762–1830* (Oxford, 2011)

Meikle, Henry, *Scotland and the French Revolution* (Glasgow, 1912)

Mijers, Esther, 'Scottish Students in the Netherlands, 1680–1730', in Alexia Grosjean and Steve Murdoch (eds), *Scottish Communities Abroad* (Leiden, 2005), pp. 301–32

Mijers, Esther, 'The Netherlands, William Carstares, and the Reform of Edinburgh University, 1690–1715', *History of Universities*, 25/2 (2011), 111–42

Morrell, J. B., 'Professors Robison and Playfair, and the "Theophobia Gallica": Natural Philosophy, Religion and Politics in Edinburgh, 1789–1815', *Notes and Records of the Royal Society of London*, 26 (1971), 43–63

Morris, Marilyn, *The British Monarchy and the French Revolution* (New Haven and London, 1988)

Morris, Marilyn, *Sex, Money and Personal Character in Eighteenth Century British Politics* (New Haven and London, 2015)

Murdoch, Alexander, '"The Importance of Being Edinburgh": Management and Opposition in Edinburgh Politics 1746–1784', *Scottish Historical Review*, 62 (1983), 1–16

Nenadic, Stana (ed.), *Scots in London in the Eighteenth Century* (Lewisburg, PA, 2010)

Orme, T. E., 'Toasting Fox: The Fox Dinners in Edinburgh and Glasgow, 1801–1825', *History*, 99 (2014), 588–606

Page, Anthony H., *John Jebb and the Enlightenment Origins of British Radicalism* (Westport, 2003)

Perrin, Charles E., 'Joseph Black and the Absolute Levity of Phlogiston', *Annals of Science*, 40 (1983), 109–37

Peterson, Merrill D., *Thomas Jefferson and the New Nation* (New York, 1970)

Philip, Lorna J., 'The Creation of Settlements in Rural Scotland: Planned Villages in Dumfries and Galloway, 1739–1850', *Scottish Geographical Journal*, 119 (2003), 77–102

Philp, Mark, 'Rational Religion and Political Radicalism', *Enlightenment and Dissent*, 4 (1985), 35–46

Philp, Mark, *Godwin's Political Justice* (London, 1986)

Philp, Mark, 'Revolutionaries in Paris: Paine and Jefferson', in Mark Philp (ed.), *Reforming Ideas in Britain: Politics and Language in the Shadow of the French Revolution, 1789–1815* (Cambridge, 2014), pp. 187–208

Porter, Roy, *Doctor of Society: Thomas Beddoes and the Sick Trade in Late-Enlightenment England* (London, 1992)

Rasmussen, Dennis C., *The Problems and Promise of Commercial Society: Adam Smith's Response to Rousseau* (University Park, PA, 2008)

Reid, David A., 'Science for Polite Society: British Dissent and the Teaching of Natural Philosophy in the Seventeenth and Eighteenth Centuries', *History of the Universities*, 21/2 (2006), 117–58

Reid, David A., 'Rational Dissent and the Rhetoric of Educational Philanthropy in the Dissenting Academies of Lancashire, Hackney and Exeter', *Northern History*, 47 (2010), 97–116

Rendall, Jane, 'Adaptations: History, Gender, and Political Economy in the Work of Dugald Stewart', *History of European Ideas*, 38 (2012), 143–61

Richards, Eric, *Debating the Highland Clearances* (Edinburgh, 2007)

Robertson, James, *The Public Roads and Bridges in Dumfriesshire 1650–1820* (Melksham, 1993)

Robertson, John, *The Scottish Enlightenment and the Militia Issue* (Edinburgh, 1985)

Robertson, John, 'The Scottish Contribution to the Enlightenment', in Paul Wood (ed.), *The Scottish Enlightenment: Essays in Reinterpretation* (Rochester, NY, 2000), pp. 37–62

Robbins, Keith, *Nineteenth-Century Britain: Integration and Diversity* (Oxford, 1989)

Robison, John, *Kirkcudbright* (Dumfries, n.d.)

Robison, John, 'Kirkcudbright Incorporated Trades, 1744–1799. Being the Second of Two Lectures Given to Members of the Six Incorporated Trades' (1920)

Rosner, Lisa, *Medical Education in the Age of Improvement: Edinburgh Students and Apprentices 1760–1826* (Edinburgh, 1991)

Ryan, Alan, *On Politics: A History of Political Thought from Herodotus to the Present* (London, 2012)

Schlereth, Thomas J., *The Cosmopolitan Ideal in Enlightenment Thought* (Notre Dame, IN, 1977)

Seed, John, '"A Set of Men Powerful Enough in Many Things": Rational Dissent and Political Opposition in England 1770–1790', in Knud Haskonssen (ed.), *Enlightenment and Religion: Rational Dissent in Eighteenth Century Britain* (Cambridge, 1996), pp. 140–68

Seed, John, *Dissenting Histories: Religious Divisions and the Politics of Memory in Eighteenth Century England* (Edinburgh, 2008)

Shapin, Steven, 'Property, Patronage, and the Politics of Science: The Founding of the Royal Society of Edinburgh', *The British Journal for the History of Science*, 7 (1974), 1–41

Shapin, Steven, 'The Audience for Science in Eighteenth Century Edinburgh', *History of Science*, 12 (1974), 95–121

Sher, R. B., *Church and University in the Scottish Enlightenment: The Moderate Literati of Edinburgh* (Edinburgh, 1985)

Sher, R. B., *The Enlightenment and the Book* (Chicago, IL and London, 2006)

Shaw, J. S., *The Political History of Eighteenth-Century Scotland* (Basingstoke, 1999)

Skelton, Lorna Jayne, 'Environmental Regulation in Edinburgh and York, *c.* 1560–*c.* 1700: With Reference to Several Smaller Scottish Burghs and Northern English Towns', unpublished PhD thesis, University of Durham, 2012

Smout, T. C., 'Scottish Landowners and Economic Growth, 1650–1850', *Scottish Journal of Political Economy*, 9 (1962), 218–34

Smout, T. C., *A History of the Scottish People 1560–1830* (London, 1969)

Smout, T. C., 'Problems of Nationalism, Identity and Improvement in Later Eighteenth Century Scotland', in T. M. Devine (ed.), *Improvement and Enlightenment* (Edinburgh, 1989), pp. 1–21

Smout, T. C., 'The Improvers and the Scottish Environment', in T. M. Devine and J. R. Young (eds), *Eighteenth Century Scotland: New Perspectives* (East Linton, 1999), pp. 218–34

Smout, T. C., 'A New Look at the Scottish Improvers', *Scottish Historical Review*, 91 (2012), 125–49

Stanhope, Ghita and Gooch, G. P., *The Life of Charles, Third Earl of Stanhope* (n.p., 1914)

Stansfield, Dorothy, *Thomas Beddoes M.D. 1760–1808* (Dordrecht, 1984)

Stansfield, Dorothy and Stansfield, Ronald G., 'Dr Thomas Beddoes and James Watt: Preparatory Work 1794–96 for the Bristol Pneumatic Institute', *Medical History*, 30 (1986), 276–302

Stewart, Larry, 'Putting on Airs: Science, Medicine and Polity in the Late Eighteenth Century', in Trevor Levere and Gerard E. Turner (eds), *Discussing Chemistry and Steam: The Minutes of a Coffee House Philosophical Society, 1780–1787* (Oxford and New York, 2002), pp. 207–55

Stewart, Larry, 'His Majesty's Subjects: From Laboratory to Human Experiment in Pneumatic Chemistry', *Notes & Records of the Royal Society*, 63 (2009), 231–45

Sunter, R. M., *Patronage and Politics in Scotland 1707–1832* (Edinburgh, 1986)

Tackett, Timothy, *When the King Took Flight* (Cambridge, MA and London, 2003)

Tackett, Timothy, *The Coming of the Terror in the French Revolution* (Cambridge, MA, 2014)

Thomas, P. D. G., *John Wilkes: A Friend to Liberty* (Oxford, 1996)

Thompson, E. P., *The Making of the English Working Class* (London, 1963)

Towsey, M. R. M., 'First Steps in Associational Reading: Book Use and Sociability at the Wigtown Subscription Library, 1795–9', *Papers of the Bibliographical Society of America*, 103 (2009), 455–95

Towsey, M. R. M., *Reading the Scottish Enlightenment: Books and their Readers in Provincial Scotland, 1750–1820* (Leiden, 2010)

Vovelle, Michel, *The Fall of the French Monarchy 1787–1792* (Cambridge, 1984)

Warden, A. J., *Angus or Forfarshire: The Land and People, Descriptive and Historical*, 5 vols (Dundee, 1880–5)

Whatley, C. A., *Scottish Society 1707–1830: Beyond Jacobitism, Towards Industrialisation* (Manchester, 2000)

Whatmore, Richard, 'A Gigantic Manliness: Thomas Paine's Republicanism in the 1790s', in Stefan Collini, Richard Whatmore and Brian Young (eds), *Economy, Polity and Society: British Intellectual History 1750–1950* (Cambridge, 2000), pp. 135–57

Whetstone, Ann E., *Scottish County Government in the Eighteenth and Nineteenth Centuries* (Edinburgh, 1982)

Whyman, Susan, *The Pen and the People* (Oxford, 2012)

Withers, C. J., 'A Neglected Scottish Agriculturalist: The "Georgical Lectures" and Agricultural Writings of the Rev. Dr John Walker (1731–1803)', *Agricultural History Review*, 33 (1985), 132–46

Withers, C. J., '"Both Useful and Ornamental": John Walker's Keepership of the Edinburgh University's Natural History Museum, 1779–1803', *Journal of the History of Collections*, 3 (1993), 65–77

Wood, Dennis, *Benjamin Constant: A Biography* (London and New York, 1993)

Wood, Paul and Withers, Charles J. (eds), *Science and Medicine in the Scottish Enlightenment* (East Linton, 2002)

Wykes, David L., 'The Contribution of the Dissenting Academy to the Emergence of Rational Dissent', in Knud Haskonssen (ed.), *Enlightenment and Religion: Rational Dissent in Eighteenth-Century Britain* (Cambridge, 1996), pp. 99–139.

Youngson, A. J., *The Making of Classical Edinburgh, 1750–1840* (Edinburgh, 1966)

Index

Aberdeen 23, 121, 122, 123, 127, 184
Abercorn, James Hamilton, 8th earl of 131
abolitionism 182–3
Adam, William, MP 65
Aikin, Arthur 30
Aikin, John, snr 21, 23
Aikin, John 19, 23, 26, 29
Alison, Archibald 69, 71, 167
Ancram, William Kerr, Lord 62, 69
Anderson, James 90, 212
Angus Beef-Steak Club 92
Anti-Catholic agitation1779 112–13, 124
Arnot, Hugo, *History of Edinburgh* 37
Ashburnham, George, Lord 62
Association Movement 114–15
Atholl, John Murray, 4th duke of 94, 113,
    125, 129, 130, 134
Ayr 100, 103

Babbage, Charles 211
Bailly, Jean-Sylvan 155
Baldoon estate, Wigtownshire 94, 97
Banff 189
Barbauld, Anna Letitia 4, 18, 19, 21, 23, 24,
    25–7, 29, 209
Barbauld, Rev. Rochemont 4, 18, 23, 24,
    25, 29
Barnarve, Antoine Joseph 155

Barrell, John 198
Barrhead 199
Beddoes, Thomas 34, 201–8
Belfast 34
Bell, Dorothy 39, 46
Bell, Hugh185
Berry, Walter 188
Black, Joseph, professor of chemistry 10, 25,
    33, 34, 56, 59, 60–1, 79–81, 82, 146,
    202, 204, 206
Blackstone, Sir William 76
Blair, James Hunter, MP, provost of
    Edinburgh 33, 43–4
Blondel, Monsieur 147
Board of Trustees for the Improvement of
    Manufactures and Fisheries 81
Boerhaave, Herman, professor of medicine
    58
Boswell, James 35, 48, 49, 50–1, 58, 62, 85,
    113, 126, 149
Breadalbane, John Campbell, 4th earl of 113
Brechin 184
Brissot, Jacques-Pierre 153, 154, 160, 161,
    167, 211
Bristol Hotwells 201–2
British convention of radicals 168–9, 194–8,
    213–14
    idea for 116–17, 193, 194, 214

British Enlightenment 209–10
Brown, Dr John 202
Browne, Matthew Campbell 189, 197
Brydone, Patrick 146
Buccleuch, 3rd duke of 44, 91, 111, 130, 137
Buchan, David Steuart Erskine, 11th earl of
    13, 116, 129, 131, 177
Bull, Frederick, Alderman of City of Lon-
    don 113
Bumsted, J. M. 11, 16
Burke, Edmund 8, 57, 62, 116, 176
    Reflections on the Revolution in France, 8,
    69, 70–1, 77
Burns, Robert 3, 11–12, 57
Buzot, François Nicholas 154

Caledonian Hunt 92
Cambridge, University of 78, 147
Campbell, Archibald, 3rd duke of Argyll
    81, 129
Campbell, John, 2nd duke of Argyll 129
Campbell, John 116
Canisby 185
Cannadine, David 1
Cappe, Joseph 30
Carr, John 46
Cartwright, Major John 115, 118, 161, 164,
    177, 178, 179
chambers of commerce 128
Charteris, Francis Wemyss, MP 134
Christie, Thomas 28, 177, 188
Clavière, Étienne 154, 160
Clerk, Sir George, of Penicuik, 4th Bt. 97
Cockburn, Henry 4, 37, 66
Colley, Linda 214
Condorcet, marquis de 66, 74, 142, 144,
    153, 154, 158, 160, 167, 211
Condorcet, Sophie, Mme de 153, 211
Constant, Benjamin 57, 84
Constitutional Whigs 182
Cooper, Thomas 164, 181
Court of Session 46, 106, 122, 123, 124,
    126, 136, 192
Court of Exchequer 124
Cranstoun, George 63
Creech, William 48, 57

Crome, John 214
Cullen, William, professor of the practice of
    physic 34, 60, 81, 82, 202
Currie, Dr James 166

Dalrymple, Colonel William 187
Dalyell, James, provost of Kirkcudbright
    99, 106
Dalzel, Andrew, professor of Greek 62, 65,
    67
Darnton, Robert 5
Darwin, Erasmus 204, 205
Davy, Humphry 208
Davy, Martin 30
Dempster, George, of Dunnichen, MP 5, 70,
    86–8, 90, 91, 96, 121, 212
Denman, Thomas 19
Dickson, William, agent of the London
    Abolition Society 166
Dobbs, Francis 115
Doddridge, Philip 22
    Northampton academy 21–2, 23, 24
Donaldson, James *see under Edinburgh
    Advertiser*
Douglas, Alexander 15, 18
Douglas, Basil William, Lord Daer
    and abolitionism 11, 182–3
    in Edinburgh 53–5
    egalitarian disposition 11–12, 209
    family background 13–18
    French Revolution, influence on
        139–69, 210–11
    illness and death 204–8
    in London 132; *see also under* the radical
        politician
    and nationalism 3, 186–7, 213, 215
    politics to 1792 92, 122, 133–7, 210
    as provost, councillor, and baillie of
        Kirkcudbright 106
    the radical politician 13, 170–200
    as rural improver 10, 93–8
    schooling 18–31
    sincerity 13
    on the Union 83, 190–4, 213–5
    at university 9, 30, 35, 56–85, 210
    as urban improver 98–109

Douglas, Dunbar, 4th earl of Selkirk 20, 32, 54–5, 56, 89, 90, 92, 95, 100, 107, 108,124, 132
  education 13–14
  French Revolution, influence on 151, 155, 166
  political views 15, 122, 124, 133–8
Douglas, Dunbar 15, 205
Douglas, Helen, neé Hamilton 14, 18, 71, 97
Douglas, John 15, 18, 19, 30, 35, 71, 108, 205
Douglas, Thomas, 5th earl of Selkirk 11, 18, 19, 30, 31, 35, 62, 71, 108, 109
  and Canadian colonisation 15–16, 17
  political views 137; *see also* and French Revolution
  and the French Revolution 69–70, 71, 152
  views on highland emigration 16–17, 87
Drennan, William 68–9, 186
Drummond, George, provost of Edinburgh 42
Duchastelet, Achille 153, 154, 157, 158, 161
Dumfries 20, 44, 90, 103, 106
Dumfries, 6th earl of 130
Dumfries and Galloway Hunt 92
Dumont, Pierre Étienne Louis 143, 153
Dundas, Henry 4, 16, 44, 110, 113, 125, 130, 137, 183
Dundas, Sir Lawrence, MP 4, 43
Dundas, Robert, Lord Advocate, MP 122
Dundas, Thomas, MP 116, 122
Dundee 100, 103, 121, 122, 123, 125, 126, 183, 184, 185, 189, 199
  Whig club 70
Dunn, William 47–8
Dysart, 5th earl of 129

East Lothian 19
Edgeworth, Maria 63
Edinburgh 32–55
  assemblies 47–8, 53
  bridewell 44, 52
  Canongate 39, 40, 42–3, 45
  clubs and societies: Highland Society 90, 212; Musical Society, 50, 51; Orange Club 131; Oyster Club 53, 62; antheon Society 48, 70; Philosophical Society 10; Poker Club 54; Royal Society of Edinburgh 10, 54, 80, 145; Select Society 133
  culture 47–51
  fashionable life styles 38, 49–50
  fleshmarket 45
  High School 21
  improvement of 32–3, 36–47
    lighting 46–7, 52
  Linen Board 81
  literary world 5
  Luckenbooths 45
  new town 36, 38, 39, 42, 45, 46
  Police Act (1785) 46–7
  politics 4, 37–8, 57–8, 65–6, 123, 127, 131, 171, 182, 185, 214
  poor relief and social policy 44, 51–3
  Register House 39
  rioting, 51–2, 53
  sociability 5, 35–6
  southern districts 42, 44
  theatre 47, 57–8
Edinburgh Advertiser 117, 119
Edinburgh, University of 29–30, 33–5, 44, 56–7, 58–63, 66
  Chemistry Society 54
  Leslie affair 66–7
  Museum of Natural History 82
  Natural History Society 54, 80
  Speculative Society 30, 53, 57–8, 68, 71, 83–5
Effingham, Lord 115
Eglintoun, Archibald Montgomerie, 11th earl of 107
Elder, Rev. George Ogilvy 93, 95
Elocution 26–7
Emerson, Roger 5
Emmet, Thomas Addis 57, 58, 84
Enfield, William, 19, 23, 26, 28
Enfield, Richard, 19, 28
Enlightenment *see* Scottish Enlightenment *and* British Enlightenment
Erskine, Henry 4, 122
Erskine, Rev. John, minister of Edinburgh 124

Farquhar, George 130
Favell, Samuel, Southwark radical 179, 180, 181–2
Fenton, Alexander 93
Ferguson, Adam, professor of moral philosophy 63
Fergusson, Sir Adam, MP 121
Ferriar, John 202
Fletcher, Archibald 121
Fletcher, Anthony 20
Forbes, John 115
Forbes, William, of Pitsligo 88–9
Forfar Town and County Hall 92
Fowler, Robert 187
Fox, Charles James, MP 175, 176
Fox's Libel Act (1792) 83, 161
French Revolution, impact on domestic politics 58, 65–6, 70–1, 123
Friends of the Liberty of the Press 177
Frost, John 181
Fry, Michael, 51
Fullarton, William 176–7

Galloway, John Stewart, 7th earl of 93, 94, 99, 101
Gardenstone, Francis Garden, Lord 89
Garthshore, Dr Maxwell 19
Gatehouse of Fleet 90
Gem, Dr Richard 160
Geneva University 147
Gerrald, Joseph 196, 197, 198, 201
Gilbert, Thomas, MP 52
Gilone, John, land surveyor 97, 104
Glasgow, 43, 53, 112, 121, 123–4, 127, 131, 184, 189, 214
Glasgow, University of 13–14, 124
Glasgow Advertiser 119
Godwin, William 77
Golinski, Jan 202
Goodwin, Albert 181
Gordon, Sir Alexander, of Culvennan 96–8
Gordon, Lord George 112
Gordon, Jane, duchess of 37
Gordon, Robert 104
Graham, Dr James 48
Grattan, Henry 115

's Gravesande, Willem Jacob 58
Gregory, James 54
Grey, Charles, MP 171, 176, 190
Grieve, John, provost of Edinburgh 33
Guest, Harriet 28

Haddo, George Gordon, Lord 133
Hall, Sir James, of Dunglass 36, 53, 61, 71, 72, 80, 98, 182, 204, 208
    education and scientific interests 144–51
    An Essay on the Origin, History and Principles of Gothic Architecture 145
    journal keeping 148–50
    membership of the Bowmen of the Border 92
    political views 159–64
    trip to France 1791 143–69
Hall, Helen neé Douglas 36, 71
Hall, Sir John, of Dunglass 98, 146
Hall, William, of Whitehall 61, 71, 146–7
Hamilton, Sir William 146
Hardy, Thomas 4, 172, 180, 188, 194, 195, 198
Hart, Walter 195
Hastie, Archibald 195
Hawick 100
Henry, Thomas 202
Henshelwood, William 195
Heron, Robert 90, 100, 104
Home, George 185
Home, Henry, Lord Kames 6, 81
Hope, Charles, MP, Lord Advocate 58
Hope, Thomas Charles, professor of chemistry 62, 63, 80
Hope, John, professor of botany 53, 59
Hopetoun, James Hope, 3rd earl of 130
Houlbrooke, Rev. Theophilus 30, 167
Howard, John 52
Hume, David 5, 7–8, 54, 72, 75, 76
Hutcheson, Francis, professor of moral philosophy 13–14, 72
Hutton, James 53, 54, 80–1, 146

Independent Peers *see* Scottish peerage elections
Ingen-Housz 146

Innes, Gilbert, of Stow 49, 50
Irish Linen Board 81
Ireland
    independence of 84
    trading relationship with 83
    Patriot politics 115
Irvine 107
Israel, Jonathan 153

Jebb, John 115–16, 118, 173
Jedforesters 92
Jefferson, Thomas 11, 69, 141–2, 160
Jennings, John 21
Johnston, Captain William 188, 195
Joy, Henry 115–16

Keir, James 204
Kennedy, James 199
Kerr, Robert 80
Kilmarnock 188
Kinnaird, George Kinnaird, 6th Lord 130,
    137–8, 177
Kippis, Andrew 30
Kirkcaldy 104
Kirkcudbright 10, 19, 94–5, 97, 99–102, 185
    Blair House 104
    Broughton House 101, 103
    changing lifestyles in 105
    County and Town Hall 92, 105–6
    gaol and court house 108
    harbour 107
    Later Georgian improvement of 98,
        102–9
    New Building Society 109
    Old Building Society 101, 109
    seminaries 108
    subscription library 100

Lafayette, marquis de 142, 151, 155
Laing, Malcolm 57, 177, 178
Laplace, Pierre-Simon 150
Lauderdale, James Maitland, 8th earl of 131,
    176
Lavoisier, Antoine Laurent 142, 150, 151,
    203
    Scottish reactions to new theory of

chemistry 34, 79–80
    Traité Elémentaire de Chimie 80
Lavoisier, Madame 151
Leiden, University of 29, 58–9, 170
Leith 37
    Police Commissioners 81–2
    South Leith 42, 45
Lenman, Bruce 110
Lenox, William 99
    Le Sage, George Louis 148
Leslie, John 66
Levere, Trevor 201
libraries, subscription 100–1
Lind, John 202
Lindsey, Theophilus 22
Littlejohn, Robert 172
Liverpool, 22, 29, 30, 99, 165
Lolme, Jean-Louis de 76
London 49, 113, 172–3, 214
London Corresponding Society 3, 28, 164,
    168, 172, 174, 177–8, 180–1, 182,
    188, 189, 194, 198, 199
London Society of the Friends of the People
    178–81
Lunardi, Vicenzo 34, 49

McCarthy, William 24, 26
McClure, William 105
McDowall, William 199
McGrugar, Thomas 116–7
Macinnes, Allan 191
Mackay, General Hugh 125
Mackenzie, Henry 63, 70–1
Mackenzie, Rev. W 109
McKie, Mrs Jean 101
Mackintosh, James 30, 57, 177
Macleod, Norman MP 177, 185, 190, 195
McQueen, Robert, Lord Braxfield, Lord
    Justice Clerk 51, 66
Maitland, Thomas 176
Malthus, Thomas Robert 78, 82
    An Essay on the Principle of Population 78
Manchester 22, 214
    Manchester Constitutional Society 163,
        174, 182, 189
    Manchester Herald 163

Mansfield, William Murray, 1st earl of 134
Margarot, Maurice 196, 201
Marsh, Charles 28
Maxwell, Dr William 177
Maxwell, Sir William, of Monreith 101
Maxwell, Sir William, of Springkell, 111, 186
M'Farlan, Rev. John, minister of Canongate 54
Mealmaker, George 195
Mennons, John *see under Glasgow Advertiser*
Merry, Robert177
Millar, John, professor of civil law 62, 64, 121, 124, 177, 178
Miller, Thomas, Lord Justice Clerk 112
Mirrie, Thomas, provost of Kirkcudbright 101
Montgomery, James 214
Montrose 52, 100, 103, 124, 199
    grammar school 21
Morthland, John 187
Morris, Gouverneur 142
Morton, George Douglas, 16th earl of 130, 132
Muir, Andrew 99, 100
Muir, Thomas 186, 190, 194
Murray, Lord George 21
Murray, James 100
Murray, James, of Broughton 90, 101
Mure, William, provost of Kirkcudbright, factor on Selkirk estates 101
Muter, Rev. Robert, minister of Kirkcud-bright 99, 100–1

New Langholm 90
Nisbet, Rev. Charles, minister of Montrose 124
North, Lord 129
Northcote, Thomas 115
Norwich 22, 28
    radical societies 174, 182

opposition Whigs 121–2, 130, 133, 175–7, 200
Oxford, University of 201

Paine, Thomas 1, 7, 71–2, 142–3, 153, 158, 175, 178, 179
    Rights of Man 74, 142, 159, 168, 173, 175, 183, 186
Paisley 112
    radicals in 188–9, 199
Palgrave academy 4, 18–27, 30
Palmer, Thomas Fyshe 194–5
Passenger Act (1803) 87
patriotism 7, 17, 18, 23, 26, 125–6, 133, 209
    and improvement 86–9
Paris 4, 11
    ferment in summer of 1791 155–9
    Jacobin Club 151–2, 154, 155, 157, 161, 163, 165, 167, 181
    Palais Royal 151, 152
    Société des Amis de Noirs 160
Patronage, in Church of Scotland 54, 113, 124
Peebles Shooting Club 92
Pelham, Thomas, Lord, Home Secretary 1801–3 16
Percival, Thomas 202
Perry, James 177
Perth 42, 43, 100, 103, 121, 184, 199
    Academy 21
    grammar school 21
Pétion, Jérôme 154, 160, 163, 175
Phillipson, Nicholas 59
Pitt, William, the Younger 4, 114, 119
Playfair, John, professor of mathematics 62, 63, 150
    Illustrations of the Huttonian Theory of the Earth 81
Plymley, Katherine 166–7
Politeness 20, 24–5, 27, 50
Political Reform in Scotland, 54
    burgh reform 113, 116–7, 119, 121, 123–4, 126, 131, 183–4
    county reform 122–3
    parliamentary reform 182–99
    role of newspapers 118–9
Porter, Roy 201
Portpatrick 44
Price, Richard 10, 68, 69, 115, 117, 141, 154, 209

Priestley, Joseph 18, 23, 24, 25, 26, 29, 146
Pringle, Sir John 146, 147
Protestant Association 172

Queensberry, Charles, 3rd duke of 106, 111

Rathbone, William 165
Rational Dissent 22–3, 30
Reid, Thomas 71, 77, 78
Reid, Thomas 99, 104
Revolution Society 168, 174–5, 177, 181–2
Reynolds, William 204
Richter, John 174
road development 91–2, 95–8
Robbins, Keith 128
Robertson, William 32, 33, 44, 45, 52, 54, 59, 60, 113
  'View of the Progress of Europe' 73
Robespierre, Maximilien 154
Robison, John, professor of natural philosophy 60, 62, 66, 79, 81
Rochfoucauld–Liancourt, duc de la 142, 151
Roederer, Pierre Louis 165, 168, 211
Roscoe, William 13, 29, 210
Rous, George 165, 175
Rousseau, Jean-Jacques, 6
Rudé, George 151
Rush, Benjamin, 10
Russell, Lord John 56, 178
Rutherford, Daniel, professor of botany 60
Ryan, Alan 141

Saltoun, Lord 130, 134–6
Sands, Robert 195
Sayers, Frank, 19, 29
Scott, Alexander 198
Scott, William 47
Scottish political culture 110–28
  convergence with England 126–8, 214–15
  impact of newspapers and reading rooms 119–20
  role of Westminster parliament 120–2, 127–8
  and the Treaty of Union 126, 134–6

Scottish Enlightenment, 4–10, 82
  end of 64
  and liberty, 8–9; *see also* Stewart, Dugald, political views
  and science, 10
Scottish Friends of the People 3, 186–90, 194–99
Scottish peerage elections, 55, 128–32
Selkirk 100, 107
Semphill, Hugh, Lord 121, 130–1, 132, 189
Shaw, John 111
Sheffield, 22, 214
Sheffield Constitutional Society 173–4, 189, 194
Shelburne, earl of 117–8, 125, 131
Sheridan, Richard Brinsley, MP 175, 176
Short, William, American chargé d'affairs in Paris 155, 157
Siddons, Sarah 47, 53
Sieyès, Abbé 155, 160
Sinclair, Charles 197
Sinclair, Sir John 88, 134, 151, 212
  Board of Agriculture 98
Skelton, Lorna 40
Skirving, William 190, 194, 195, 200
Small, Rev. Robert, minister of Dundee 70
Smith, Adam 5–7, 53, 54, 62, 72, 104
Smith, Samuel 93, 96, 97–8
Smollett, Tobias 191
Smout, T. C. 7, 94
Society for Constitutional Information 118, 131, 168, 173–81, 182, 189, 194
Society for the Encouragement of Agriculture within the Counties of Dumfries, Wigtown and Kirkcudbright 90
Southwark Friends of the People 174, 179–81
Stair, John Dalrymple, 5th earl of 129
Stanhope, Charles, 3rd earl of 132, 153, 161
Stansfield, Dorothy 201
Stewart, Dugald 9, 11, 14, 17, 29, 32, 33, 35, 39, 53, 54, 56, 57, 62, 63, 83, 85, 211
  Elements of Moral Philosophy 66, 74

and the French Revolution 65–72, 139
lecturing style 64–5
on marriage 77
political views 56, 63–79
on progress 72–4, 78–9, 210
on providential order of the world 77
as tutor 61–3
Stewart, Helen D'Arcy, 35–6, 63
Stewart, Larry 202
Stewart, Matthew 62, 69
Stirling 116, 123
St Clair, James 184
Stock, John Edmonds 198
Stormont, David Murray, Viscount 130, 131
Stranraer 100
Stuart, Gilbert 116
Stuart-Mackenzie, James 129
Suffolk, Henry Howard, earl of, secretary of
     state for the Northern Department
     124–5

Tackett, Timothy 155, 159
Taylor, William, 19, 20, 24, 25, 27, 28,
     29–30
Telford, Thomas, 16, 107
Temple, Henry, 2nd Viscount Palmerston,
     61
Temple, Henry John, Lord Palmerston 61–3
Temple, Mary, neé Mee, 2nd Viscountess
     Palmerston 62–3
Thelwall, John 4, 179, 198
Thom, Rev. William, minister of Govan 124
Thomas, P. D. G. 170
Thompson, Edward 3
Thornton, Robert John 203
Tooke, John Horne 173, 179
tree planting 94–5
Trotter, William, 49

Tytler, James 5, 34, 48, 49
Tytler, William 50

United States of America 34

Vaughan, Felix 174

Walker, Bruce 93
Walker, John, professor of natural philoso-
     phy 33, 53, 54, 56, 59, 60, 79, 80–1,
     82
Walker, Richard 162–3
Walker, Thomas 162–3, 164, 175
War of American Independence, domestic
     political impact of 114–5, 124–6
Warrington Academy, 18, 19, 21, 23, 78
Watson, Richard, Bishop of Llandaff 147
Watson, Robert, secretary to Lord George
     Gordon 172
Watt, James 34, 147, 202, 204, 206, 207
Watt, James jnr 147, 163, 164, 181, 205
Watt, Janet ('Jessie') 205–6
Watt, Robert 198
     Watt Plot (1794) 198–9
Webster, James 94
Wedgwood, Thomas, 30, 163
Whig Association of the Friends of the
     People 176–7, 178, 188, 190, 194
Wigtown 98–9, 102, 195
     subscription library 101
Wilde, John, professor of civil law 58, 84
Wilkes, John 170–1
Wilson, James 195
Wodrow, Rev. James, minister of Stevenston
     125, 183
Wyvill, Rev. Christopher 114, 115, 116–17

Young, Arthur 140